SECOND EDITION

FUNDAMENTALS OF
SPORTS ETHICS

GREGG TWIETMEYER

Kendall Hunt
publishing company

Cover image by David Ammon

www.kendallhunt.com
Send all inquiries to:
4050 Westmark Drive
Dubuque, IA 52004-1840

Published in the United States of America

BRIEF CONTENTS

CONTENTS

CONTENTS

ACKNOWLEDGEMENTS

As with any such project, many hands made the text of this book possible. It seems to me that those in need of acknowledgement fall into three groups. First, I need to thank the folks at Kendall Hunt who have supported this project over the last several years. Second, I need to thank those teachers, coaches, classmates, and co-workers from whose example and knowledge I have learned and been inspired. Finally, I need to thank my family without whose support and love I could never have written this book. It is impossible to thank everyone who deserves it by name. Here are but a few of the most deserving.

Regarding the first group, I would like to specifically thank three people. First, is Paul Carty, the Director of Publishing Partnerships at Kendall Hunt, without whose encouragement I would not have dreamed of writing this book. It was his unsolicited call to my office in late 2014 which first got me considering taking on the challenge of writing this text. Second, I would like to thank Lynne Rodgers, the Development/Production Supervisor at Kendall Hunt, whose editorial expertise (and patience) made writing the first edition of this book a pleasure. Finally, I would like to thank Brenda Rolwes, the Senior Production Manager at Kendall Hunt who shepherded me through the editing of the second edition.

Regarding the second group, I would like to thank my German teacher, Herr Piekarek, who made high school tolerable, if only for one period a day. I would like to thank Dr. David Carlson and Rev./Dr. Paul Marschke, both of whom taught me at Concordia University. Dr. Carlson first introduced me to the work of Peter Berger, which convinced me of many things, most importantly, that not all academic writing was pedantic and self-absorbed. Instead, in Berger, I saw academic writing which was engaging and that could produce real insight. Obviously, Berger is not alone in that regard, but to my undergraduate self, he was the first to break through my skepticism. Dr. Marschke, in turn, first encouraged my academic career, by innocuously commenting in the margin of a paper which I had written for him, that if "I ever hoped to get published, I would have to write more seriously" (by which he meant avoiding an irreverent, flippant or sarcastic tone). That note, made in passing, first convinced me that I might write well enough to be published. In one sense, then, this book is the result of that encouragement. Thank you Dr. Marschke. I would also like to thank Dr.'s Doug Anderson, Chris Long, Mark Dyreson, and Scott Kretchmar at Penn State. Dr. Anderson's erudition and patience was invaluable as I first engaged academic philosophy. Dr. Long introduced me to Aristotle in such a way that I really began to understand him. If you know Aristotle, what else needs to be said? Dr. Dyreson taught me that good writers write and re-write, a point I don't think I fully appreciated until I was a Ph.D. student with him. Writing skills should not simply be rested upon, but rather cultivated. Dr. Kretchmar was my Ph.D. advisor. He too furthered and polished my writing ability. Furthermore, he taught me how to teach, he challenged me intellectually, and he offered me his excellent professional example. Finally, Dr. Kretchmar introduced me to Polanyi! Again, if you know Polanyi, what else needs to be said? For all of this, and many other things, I am extremely grateful.

Finally, I need to thank my family. First, by thanking my parents and siblings for their love and support. I have learned much from my mother's intellectual curiosity and willingness to fight for an idea she thinks is important, as well as from her willingness to simply serve others. I have also learned much from my father's unapologetic love of play and his willingness to put honesty, learning and skill development in kinesiology above accolades, prestige, or money. I try every day to live up to my father's legacy of professional integrity.

Of course, I must close by thanking my beautiful wife Sarah and our five wonderful children; Aaron, Luke, Elsa, Emily Rose, and Isaiah. To them, what more can be said than I love you very much. Thank you for your love, patience and support. In each of you, God has blessed me far more than I deserve.

PREFACE

Fundamentals of Sport Ethics is a book about initiation. Its purpose is to recruit you into the world of philosophy and convince you that philosophy is a fundamentally human enterprise. Ethics is not simply a requirement on your way to a degree, but a practical reality, at the very heart of how we live and how we treat one another. In attempting to initiate you into the importance, relevance and wonder of philosophy, I have endeavored to be fair but not neutral. On each of the given issues in this text whether it is "realism vs. relativism" or "virtue ethics," even as I give the strengths and weaknesses of each position, idea or argument, I do not hide my convictions.

Feigning neutrality is dangerous for several reasons. First, it suggests that answers do not matter. But if one philosophic position is as good as any other, why bother with philosophy at all? Rather it is clear that our ideas, values and convictions make a great deal of difference in how we lead our lives. Second, neutrality is dishonest. A philosopher is by disposition open to discussion and counter argument, but he is open to such because of a *passionate conviction* that the truth matters. Argument for argument's sake is at best merely a hypothetical academic exercise and at worst pedantic navel gazing. We should argue about ethics to arrive at truth and thereby lead better lives. We should pursue ethics not to simply know the good *but to be good!* Moreover, given a disposition of openness, convictions are not a threat, but are the ground upon which we reach out towards the truth. Finally, neutrality is sterile and dead. Yet, philosophy is engaged in by living human beings! Ethics regards inquiry into the nature of the *good* life! As was just emphasized, we engage ethics not to prove how smart we are, nor simply to understand, but to lead *better* lives. We want to do the *right* thing. Answering questions in this regard is anything but antiseptic! *Good* and *bad*, *better* and *worse*, *right* and *wrong*, are words of distinction not neutrality. Therefore, to be a philosopher is not about neutrality. Instead, philosophers must commit themselves to fairness, to argument, to tolerance, to discussion and to truth.

Given such a commitment to truth, it is worth mentioning the limits of the text. The text is limited by its introductory nature. I cannot cover every idea in absolute detail. The most I can do in many cases is initiate enough of a discussion to hopefully whet your philosophic appetites. If you are intrigued by the ideas in the text, don't stop when the chapter ends, but pursue further reading by using the "suggested readings" or the chapter bibliography to learn more about the topic.

The text is also limited by the frailties of its author. Though I have endeavored to be fair and though I have endeavored to be articulate and though I have endeavored to understand the material I am presenting, I will have no doubt failed in this regard from time to time. Critics may find places where I wasn't entirely fair to a person or idea. Students may find places where I didn't clearly communicate in a way that helped them learn. Scholars may find places where they object to my ideas or where I was simply ignorant or mistaken. Finally, many ideas in this text are, by nature, controversial. As you will see, there is more than one plausible set of philosophic convictions. Similarly, there is more than one plausible answer to many of the ethical questions and dilemmas in sport. Therefore, even when you agree with me or with an idea or philosopher presented in the text, you should treat it (and the text) *as the first word not the last.*

Again, the point of this book is to initiate you into the world of philosophy and ethics. Philosophy is not (or at least ought not be) an esoteric discipline. It is meant for human beings. It is not meant for specialists! Philosophy is at the heart of human life. Our philosophy shapes our convictions and values and our convictions and values determine our choices and behavior, which in turn shape our lives. This is as true in our general day to day lives as it is in sport. Is winning or integrity more important? Is cheating ever justified? Should college athletes be paid a salary? Only philosophy can answer these questions.

Once we develop our philosophic awareness, we see that in both word and deed philosophy guides people and institutions to answer these questions the way they do. This insight naturally leads to the question: which philosophic or ethical views are correct? Consider but one example. Right or wrong the National Collegiate Athletic Association (NCAA) has decided that college athletes should not be paid. Is that correct? Is it incorrect? No matter how you answer this question, it is clear that the NCAA's position is an expression of the NCAA's ethical stance on the issue. They believe (whether genuinely or cynically) that intercollegiate sport should be amateur. The love of the game and the educational value of sport are the most important things, therefore these goals should not be sullied by paying athletes like professionals. Yet, even if you believe that the NCAA is actually acting out of a pecuniary (monetary) motive, where amateurism is a cover for "free labor," such a cynical motive would still be a *reflection of their philosophy!* The same point holds in every other case as well. Philosophy and ethics are inescapable! Our decisions and behavior result from our values and our values are born of our philosophy. Philosophy is everywhere! Therefore, interest and skill in philosophic inquiry is one of the most important things one can acquire if one wants to lead a good life.

As a result, this text is designed with two practical goals in mind. The first goal is to convince you that philosophy matters. The second goal is to build your basic philosophic skills to the point that you can proceed from the foundation this text provides into the larger world of sport philosophy and ethics.

Each of these goals is accomplished through the chapter structure. At the beginning of each chapter you are introduced to the key philosophic ideas and theory of the topic at hand. In each case the strengths and weaknesses of the ideas proposed are examined. You will notice that although I tend to endorse certain ideas as true, I also acknowledge the plausibility of alternative positions. This is done to allow you to weigh the alternatives yourself. After reviewing strengths and weaknesses, each chapter's text then ends with the implications of the chapter's topic for the practice and administration of sport.

Following each chapter is a set of primary source readings. These readings are both theoretical and applied. For instance, you might read a selection from Aristotle's *Ethics*, followed by a newspaper account of a coach resigning to spend more time with his family, followed by a journal article about the place of "virtue in sport." In doing so, you will develop your ability to read and understand primary source philosophic texts. You will also see how philosophic ideas and commitments play out in the "real world."

The purpose of this text is not to get you to "agree with Twietmeyer" but *to get you to think!* Do not accept an argument in the text simply because it is in print, or because I or any other philosopher said so, but because you are convinced it is the truth. Truth, even in the high stakes world of sport, should always be your goal. I have joked in the past that half of the philosophy I've read I didn't understand, while the other half I don't remember . . . to paraphrase one of my great intellectual heroes, I hope that by the end of this text you can say that "you're a friend to Twietmeyer but a greater friend to truth."

ABOUT THE AUTHOR

©Sunyoung Kwon.

Dr. Twietmeyer has taught sport philosophy and sports ethics for over 10 years. He received his bachelor's degree in Art from Concordia University, Ann Arbor in 1997 where he also played soccer and worked in the athletics department. Between 1997 and 2003 Dr. Twietmeyer worked in graphic arts, marketing and coaching. In August 2003 he received his Master's Degree in Sport Management from the University of Michigan. Dr. Twietmeyer then spent a year working at Albion College, in Albion, MI as the Assistant Sports Information Director, where he was involved in media production, web design and game management. After working for a year at Albion, Dr. Twietmeyer decided to pursue a Ph.D. in sport philosophy at the Pennsylvania State University. He first taught sports ethics while at Penn State University as a graduate student. Since graduating from Penn State in 2008, he has continued to teach sports ethics, first at Marshall University (2008–2015) and now at Mississippi State University (2015–present). Dr. Twietmeyer has published widely and presented his research around the world. He has coached high school and YMCA soccer and currently volunteers as a U8 and U10 recreational soccer coach for the Starkville Soccer Association. Dr. Twietmeyer also continues to play soccer whenever possible. For the past 7 years he has run a summer camp, through a partnership with the nonprofit charity iCanShine, which helps special needs children and adults learn how to ride a two wheel bike independently (www.bulldogbike.msstate.edu). In each of the 7 years the camp has been offered, the students in Dr. Twietmeyer's summer section of sports ethics and the Department of Kinesiology have volunteered at the camp. Dr. Twietmeyer resides in Starkville, MS with his wife Sarah and their five children.

Chapter 1

What is Ethics? Why Bother Studying Sports Ethics?

"After many years during which I saw many things, what I know most surely about morality and the duty of man I owe to sport . . ."

—Albert Camus[1]

Students will be able to:

1. Recognize the difference between normative and descriptive ethical claims.
2. Recognize the difference between intrinsic and extrinsic goods.
3. Define the nature of ethics and explain its relationship to metaphysics and aesthetics.
4. Evaluate the arguments for why sports ethics matter.
5. Explain the limitations of a "just win" philosophy.

One of the unwritten rules for undergraduates—and perhaps eighteen to twenty-one year olds in general—is "why bother?" One might put the same question more clearly in this context by asking: "What value, import or truth can be found in engaging the material of this course?" While defending the importance of higher education *per se* would take us far afield, it is a certainly a fair question to ask about this text and the course(s) it is meant to serve. What value, import or truth will be found in studying the "fundamentals of sports ethics"?

To answer this question this chapter will address two main questions. First, what is ethics? How does ethical reflection and practice fit into the larger discipline of philosophy? More importantly, how does ethical reflection and practice shape one's life? Second, assuming ethics matters, why does *sports* ethics matter? Is it not the case that ethics in sport is simple? As former New York Jets coach Herm Edwards (Battista, 2002) famously said "you play to win the game!" If this is right, then one might argue that sport ethics can therefore be summarized simply: "Those actions that promote winning are to be

---

[1] There are many alleged variations of this quote. This seemed the most accurate and comes from a reliable but secondary source, The Albert Camus Society, which claims that the original source is from a piece Camus wrote for an alumni sports magazine in the 1950s (Lea, 2006).

Is there anything more to sport than winning?
Simon Bruty/Getty Images Sport/Getty Images.

applauded. Those actions that hinder one's likelihood of winning ought to be condemned." What, if anything, is wrong with such an ethic?

Foundational Concepts

Descriptive Claim: An ethical claim which focuses on describing rather than evaluating actions or beliefs (e.g., "Many baseball players lie to the referee"; "Most Americans believe lying to the referee is wrong").

Before turning to our first question, the nature of ethics, there are a couple of key concepts that must be examined. These ideas appear again and again and again in ethics. Hence their foundational importance. The first idea is a distinction between two types of claims. The second idea is a distinction between two types of goods.

Normative & Descriptive Ethical Claims

Descriptive ethical claims catalog people's moral actions as well as their attitudes and beliefs regarding ethical behavior. One making a descriptive claim simply wants to point out how people act or what they think. For example, one might say that "Most Americans think lying to the referee is acceptable if it leads to victory," or one might say "Most Americans who play sports lie to the referee." Each claim, whether about attitudes or actions, is *describing* people's ethical behaviors and ideas.

Normative Claim: An ethical claim which focuses on the in principle goodness or badness, rightness or wrongness of an action or belief. Normative claims are about "what *ought* to be done" (e.g., "one should never lie to the referee").

Normative ethical claims are claims about what is right or wrong in principle; what is good or evil, what is just or unjust, what is moral or immoral. They revolve around assessing how people *ought* to behave. For instance, one might say; "Taking a dive (faking a foul) in soccer is always wrong." This claim would be normative because it sets a standard, *a norm*, for how soccer player *ought* to behave.

That many soccer players do in fact take dives is beside the point. One making a normative claim is interested in what *should be done*. The normative claim is the ideal to which we should aspire. The fact that soccer players often *do* take dives does not indicate that they *should* take dives. After all, many wrong practices throughout human history have had popular support. Consider, for instance that slavery still survives today, throughout the world, including an estimated 60,000 slaves who "exist in the shadows of American society" (Noack, 2014). Surely one would not say that the mere existence of slavery proves its goodness. Similarly, to defend the legitimacy of diving in soccer, would take far more than an assertion of its prevalence.

The mere fact that something occurs, is no evidence of its goodness.
©Patrick Tuohy/Shutterstock.com

The reason this distinction between normative and descriptive claims is so important is because ethics is primarily normative. Ethicists are concerned about what is right and wrong in principle. The fact that practice sometimes deviates from principle is of limited interest. For an ethicist, how people should behave is far more important that how they do behave.[2] Nevertheless, you will find that people, in both academic as well as polite conversation, often rely on the "everybody is doing it" argument as a way to justify a particular action, behavior, tradition or practice. In fact, many students initially often have trouble distinguishing the two types of claims from each other (see next page). Although in the course of ethical argument, normative and descriptive claims are often conflated, as a budding sport philosopher you now have the tools to see the inherent weakness of such a claim and ask in reply, "Even if everyone does it, the question still remains, is it good?"

---

[2] This is not so say that actual human behavior has no value for determining normative standards. It is simply a matter of pointing out that the persistence of a behavior—by itself—does not indicate the goodness of the behavior.

Normative or Descriptive?

a. The majority of Americans think sexism in sport is wrong.

b. Often, coaches will argue that you have to lie to the referee if you want to win.

c. Lance Armstrong felt his blood doping and steroid use was justified.

d. Despite its popularity, trashtalking is immoral.

e. Though most hockey players argue for it, fighting in hockey is wrong.

f. Most people, in a high pressure situation, will lie to the umpire.

g. Children should never be forced to participate in sport just to please their parents.

h. There is nothing wrong with taking a dive in soccer.

Intrinsic and Extrinsic Goods

Broadly speaking, there are two types of goods in the world. The first type of goods are those goods which we pursue for their own sake. These are goods that we value in and of themselves. Love, for example, is pursued for its own sake. We pursue love for the sake of love. That is, *the end* (the purpose) of the good (love) is not to be found in using love to procure some other good. Love, as such, is that which we desire. In fact, to pursue "love" to some other end—such as using a friend or relative to procure some sort of fame or fortune—is not really love! Therefore, we call such goods **intrinsic goods**, because the good is inherent to itself. Philosophers often put the idea this way: intrinsic good are "ends in themselves."

Intrinsic Good: Any good which humans value for its own sake (e.g., playing baseball because we love baseball).

Love is an intrinsic good.
©Gregg Twietmeyer

Extrinsic Good: Any good which humans value for the sake of something else (e.g., playing baseball for the money).

In contrast to intrinsic goods are those good which we pursue for the sake of something else. These goods are called **extrinsic goods**. We value these goods, and they really are goods, but they are valued as tools (that is, as *means* to some other end) rather than as ends in themselves. In fact, that is exactly how philosophers talk about extrinsic goods, they are "means to an end." For example, one might say that going to the dentist is good. Or a soccer player might say that fitness (being in shape to run for 90 minutes) is good. However, it is likely in both cases that what is valued is not going to the dentist *per se* or being fit *per se*. Rather what is valued is what each extrinsic good procures. That is, some further end. In the case of the dentist, healthy teeth. In the case of the soccer player, the ability to play the game without tiring. The dentist and the fitness are the *means* by which other goods, namely healthy teeth and the ability to play are procured.[3]

Going to the dentist is an extrinsic good. We value it for what it procures.
©Glayan/Shutterstock.com

The reason this distinction is so important is because ethics is about the good life. Which means one is constantly relying on commitments and assumptions regarding the good, including distinctions about which means and ends are the most important. In other words, any examination of the good will rely upon the distinction between intrinsic and extrinsic goods. Although most everyone agrees in principle that intrinsic goods are more important than extrinsic goods—on the grounds that intrinsic good are ends while extrinsic goods are merely means to those ends—people often disagree in practice when discussing or evaluating goods.

One might say, for instance, that the current model of National Collegiate Athletic Association (NCAA) Division I athletics is good because "college athletics is entertaining and generates a lot of revenue and publicity for schools." This is undoubtedly true. But many critics of the current model of intercollegiate sport would willingly concede the point without being impressed by it. This is because these critics do not view entertainment or revenue generation as the *end* of college athletics but, at best, as merely a *means to the end* of "education." In fact, these critics would likely contend that the elevation of revenue from *means* to *end* is exactly what is wrong with college sport. They would likely make this assertion on the grounds that treating revenue as an end

---

[3] Of course the distinction isn't always so clean. In sport for example, there may be mixed motives where one values "soccer" both because of the "joy of the game" (intrinsic) as well as the fact that it "draws the attention of the opposite sex" (extrinsic).

encourages administrators and coaches to compromise academic integrity in pursuit of more money, victories and publicity.[4]

Of course, this argument depends upon a premise which itself may be questioned: That colleges are solely about "education." Is that true? Perhaps universities have "multiple missions" (French, 2004, p. 116) which go beyond mere academics to things such as community service. In essence, such a defender of the current model of college athletics would be saying college is about multiple *ends*. If so, then perhaps the current model of intercollegiate athletics can be defended.

The key point is this. However one evaluates such controversies will necessarily entail an evaluation of the intrinsic and extrinsic goods of the issue at hand, whether the issue is college athletics or anything else. The determination and valuation of goods, as either means (extrinsic) or ends (intrinsic), is vitally important in ethics and is often a matter of dispute. Good sport philosophers will always keep such distinctions in mind.

What is Ethics?

Ethics: The branch of philosophy which focuses on the nature of the good life as well as on how we should treat other people.

Ethics is a branch of philosophy which focuses primarily on two issues. First, as just suggested, ethics focuses on the question "what is a *good* life?" Second, ethics examines the question "how should we treat each other?" The first question deals with evaluations of the place of human beings in the world; what meaning, if any, does life have? How should one define success? What actions are praiseworthy? How should I conduct my life? Why? The second question deals with our relationships, obligations, and behavior toward one another; what obligations—if any—do I have to the people around me? Why?

The great Greek philosopher Aristotle (whom we will encounter in detail in Chapter 6) argued in the *Politics,* over two thousand years ago that, "man is by nature a political animal" (1253a1), by which he meant human beings are *by nature* communal and deliberative. That is, we are social and rational creatures. As social creatures we live in communities and rely on each other to achieve a full human existence. As rational creatures, unlike other animals, we debate the form, content and justice of our social organizations. According to Aristotle, human beings associate with each other *by nature* and human beings *by nature*, debate how they should organize such associations (e.g., governments, teams, leagues, families, etc.). Philosopher Alasdair MacIntyre (1999) put Aristotle's point in modern terms when he said that human beings are "dependent, rational animals." What MacIntyre was insisting on was that human beings *need* each other. Human community is a not an arbitrary convenience but rather a necessity![5]

A simple but crucial insight is now in view. Claims about human nature, that is, what it means to be a human being, affect ethics. A moment's reflection on human life, whether by considering the natural helplessness of infants, or the desire to alleviate a toothache, or to learn to play an instrument, or to throw a curveball, quickly demonstrates that human beings need each other. Aristotle's claim to the social nature of human beings, is incontestable. Playing (much less learning) baseball by oneself, for instance, would not work at all.

This general point has important implications. Once the social nature of human beings is acknowledged, ethical questions, requiring the use of human reason, quickly follow. For to acknowledge that we are naturally dependent on other human beings leads to questions regarding how we should relate to each other; How should families be

---

[4] See, for example, the Big Ten Conference's recent decision to add Friday night football games, staring in 2017, as part of their new TV contract (Olson, 2016).

[5] Consider the case of feral children who through tragedy or accident are raised in the wild. These children, even after rejoining human society, continue to act like the animals which raised them.

formed? What laws should there be? What does good coaching look like? What rules should there be in sport? What is a just society?

Similar questions appear in sport all the time, from relatively trivial concerns such as "Should the designated hitter be allowed in baseball?", to more profound questions related to issues of access, cheating, or violence. For example, recent evidence on the dangers of American football to brain health (Fainaru-Wada & Fainaru, 2013), have raised serious questions about whether or not the game is safe. This evidence, in turn, raises questions about the morality of participating in a sport where the risk of causing permanent brain damage to oneself or to others is significant.

Can the morality of football be defended?
Fred Vuich/Sports Illustrated/Getty Images

However one feels about the morality of football, if one sees the connection between our social nature and our ability to reason about how we should associate with each other, then one has seen Aristotle's point. Our social and rational nature means that all human beings, through their words and their actions, are constantly answering the two key questions of ethics; "What is a good life?" and "How should we treat each other?" The next time you see an ethical debate or scandal in sport ask yourself this question; "What does the behavior of the actors involved imply about their answers to these two foundational ethical questions?"

Ethics and Other Branches of Philosophy

Ethics also has much to do with two other branches of philosophy which are usually looming in the background of any ethical discussion; **metaphysics**, the study of the nature of things, as well as **aesthetics**, the study of beauty.

We will not focus directly on metaphysics or aesthetics here. But it important to keep the interpenetration of these branches of philosophy in mind, for the pursuit of philosophy, the "love of wisdom," will often lead from one branch to another. Consider, for example, that the first question of ethics, "what is a good life?" depends upon some vigorous definition of *the good*, which in turn will likely be dependent on some declarations

Metaphysics: The branch of philosophy which focuses on the nature of things (e.g., "does God exist?"; "what is a human being?"; "Is chess a sport," etc.).

Aesthetics: The branch of philosophy which focuses on the beautiful (e.g., "Is beauty objective or subjective?"; "Can beauty be measured?"; "Is sport a form of art?," etc.).

or assumptions or commitments about what a human being *is*. In fact, we have already seen one such claim in Aristotle's declaration that man is *by nature* a "political animal." To make claims about the nature of things (or of reality as such), *is metaphysics*. Each of us—even if only implicitly and unreflectively—has committed ourselves to certain metaphysical positions regarding the nature of goodness and regarding the nature of human beings.

For instance, there is a very popular school of philosophic thought among undergraduates called *hedonism*. Adherents to this school of thought live their lives for pleasure.[6] To be a hedonist is to live one's life in accord with the following claims; pleasure *is* good, pain *is* evil, because human *nature* is such that human beings enjoy pleasure and dislike pain, the *good* human life *is* the life of maximal pleasure. One crude example of this philosophic idea would be the "sex, drugs, and rock & roll" mentality of many undergraduates who see college as primarily about partying (McMurtrie, 2014).

We will examine hedonism in greater detail later (see chapter 2). For present purposes, it suffices to point out that there are two controversial *metaphysical* claims built into the hedonistic ethic.

1. **Definition of the good:** Pleasure is an intrinsic good. (Perhaps the only intrinsic good.)
2. **Definition of human nature:** Human beings are "always motived by the desire for pleasure" (Lee & George, 2008, p. 95).

Similarly, aesthetic ideas and commitments show up in ethical claims all the time. Consider, for example, how often (especially in sport) "good" and "beautiful" are used interchangeably: "That was a gorgeous catch!", "They really executed that play beautifully!", "That shot was a thing of beauty!" The precise relationship between goodness and beauty and truth has generated mountains of commentary and discussion between philosophers. We will not settle the question here. Again, for our present purposes we simply need to acknowledge that questions regarding metaphysics, aesthetics, and ethics will often implicate one another. To think well ethically, one must be aware of the fact that ethical claims often rely on premises initially built in other areas of philosophy.

Once one realizes this, one will have made two crucial philosophic insights which, though basic, are often forgotten or ignored. First, conclusions follow from premises. Second, all premises (even those we take for granted) can be questioned.[7] That is, a valid conclusion—one that correctly flows from its premises—is only as strong as the premises upon which it rests. Yet, if the premises can be doubted or even refuted, so can the conclusion.

To see how these points play out, consider the following example. What one finds beautiful about baseball, will invariably lead to (or be formed by) claims about the nature of baseball, which in turn will lead to (or be formed by) claims regarding what ought or ought not be done by baseball players. That is, *normative* ethical claims. To make this abstract point more tangible, consider the following humorous dialogue

---

[6] One practical outcome of an unreflective commitment to hedonism among undergraduates is the culture of partying, which is often spurred on by following the universities' sports teams. One scholar has called this toxic mix "beer and circus" (Sperber, 2000).

[7] "Philosophers disagree with each other and have so disagreed from the beginning. And no matter how well developed their arguments in favor of some particular conclusion may be, there is never a point at which such a conclusion becomes invulnerable to further argument from some alternative and rival point of view" (MacIntyre, 2009, p. 11).

between two budding baseball philosophers sitting in the dugout during a game. You should notice as your read that although the conclusions follow from the premises the premises are nonetheless controversial.

> **Player 1 (pitcher):** "The most *beautiful* part of baseball is the confrontation between the hitter and pitcher. It is sublime to witness the battle between a good pitcher and a good hitter" *(spits sunflower seeds and looks wistfully out toward the pitcher's mound)*

> **Player 2 (bench-warmer):** "So the essence or *nature* of the game boils down to the pitcher trying to get three strikes on the hitter before he can safely reach base? Baseball is *primarily about* this confrontation?"

> **Player 1:** "Why, yes. I think you have put that quite well."

> **Player 2:** "So baseball's rule makers *should be* concerned about maximizing (or heightening) the quality of these confrontations?" *(Grabs bat)*

> **Player 1:** "Yes."

> **Player 2:** "And you would admit that since pitchers rightly focus on pitching, it is the case that when pitchers are asked to hit instead of pitch, they generally do not present much of a challenge to the pitcher on the mound and so do not advance the central *good* of baseball?" *(Moves to the top of the dugout steps)*

> **Player 1:** "Yes, I suppose that's true."

> **Player 2:** "Good. Then you won't mind that I am taking your spot in the lineup . . . in fact *I feel morally obligated to do so!* Long live the DH!" *(Smiles and moves into the on deck circle)*

To summarize then, ethics is the *necessary* deliberation human beings constantly have on how one can lead a good life and on the question of "how should we order our lives together?" (Neuhaus, 2009). Our answer(s) to these questions shape our actions; what we do, what we leave undone, what we pay attention to, and what we ignore. All of this flows out of our philosophic commitments regarding how human lives *ought* to be ordered.

As a result, you should see that philosophy is *necessarily human* (MacIntyre, 2009). The impact of philosophy is all around us. What is a good life? How should I treat other people? These two questions go to the very heart of our lives (both inside and outside of sport). If this is right, then the study of ethics is vitally important, not just to pass a class or a test or get a degree, nor even to simply understand the competing theories of ethics, but rather because we should earnestly want to lead better lives![8]

Why Bother with Sports Ethics?

You may remember that at the beginning of the chapter, we left a question in the air regarding *sports* ethics. The claim was put forth that sports ethics was a simple matter: "Those actions that promote winning are to be applauded. Those actions that hinder one's likelihood of winning ought to be condemned." What specifically is wrong with this viewpoint? More generally, why is sports ethics worth studying? To answer these questions, we will start by addressing the general question of *sports* ethics and then finish the chapter by addressing the specific claim that sports ethics is reducible to "maximizing your chance of winning."

There are two broad arguments for why sports ethics is worth studying. First, sport, games and play are an enduring and significant part of human culture. Men and women

---

[8] "For we are investigating [ethics] not in order that we might know what virtue is, but in order that we might become good . . ." (Aristotle, *Nicomachean ethics*, 1103b28).

have engaged in sport throughout all of human history. Sport is also universal in modern culture. It can be found everywhere (Simon, Torres, & Hager, 2015). Second, ethical dilemmas are ubiquitous in sport. Everywhere one turns in the world of sport one finds ethical controversy.

Sport and Human Culture

Sport has always played an important part in human culture. This is clear from both contemporary and historical evidence. Consider some historical evidence first. Sport, games and play are found around the globe, at all times and in all human cultures (Guttmann, 2004). In fact, Johan Huizinga (1955) went so far as to argue that "play is older than culture" (p. 1). Evidence to support these types of claims is not hard to find. Sport is found in ancient Egypt, Greece and Rome (Baker, 1982). It is found in ancient China (Guttmann, 2004). It is found among the Maya and Aztecs (Scarborough & Wilcox, 1993). It is found in the Middle East, the Middle Ages, and the early modern era (Guttmann, 2004). The historical record is unanimous in support the perennial fascination of human being with play, games and sport.

Now let us examine just a few contemporary examples. The 2019 Super Bowl between the Los Angeles Rams and New England Patriots was "was watched by about 98.2 million people" (Handley, 2019, para. 2). That means that at any given time approximately thirty percent of the American public was watching the game. Furthermore, compared to global events, the Super Bowl is an insignificant event. The 2018 Men's World Cup Final, for example, "attracted a combined global audience [on television and digital platforms] of 1.12 billion" (Reed, 2018, para. 5). Yet, spectating only tells part of the story. Participation rates also indicate the important place sport holds in modern culture. ESPN estimates that 21.5 million American children between the ages of 6 and 17 participate in youth sports (Kelley & Carchia, 2013). Finally, the amount of money spent

Sport is an enduring part of human culture: The Roman Colosseum.
©Belenos/Shutterstock.com

Sport is an enduring part of human culture: A Mayan ballgame court.
©Vadim Petrakov/Shutterstock.com

on sport and recreation is astounding. Whether one ponders the fact that in 2018 Major League Baseball had gross revenues of "$10.3 billion" (Brown, 2019, para. 2) or that Texas A&M University spent $485 million to renovate their football stadium for the 2015 season (Muret, 2014), it is clear that spending on sport further buttresses the claim that sport is a significant part of modern culture.

What then does this evidence imply for our philosophic question: "Why bother with sports ethics?" First, it implies that sport is an enduring part of culture. Second, it implies that the time, talent and treasure sunk into sport affects everyone, even its critics. As sport philosophers Simon, Torres and Hager (2015) point out, even critics "must admit sport plays a significant role in our lives" (p. 2).

Moreover, it is quite rare for critics to give merely economic or biological or procedural criticisms of sport. In fact, they almost always use the language of moral censure. It is not merely that sport is "inefficient" or "wasteful," but that this or that aspect of sport is "bad," "corrupt" or "wrong"! That is, critics of sport talk about how sport harms the pursuit of "the good life" and how the institutions of sport and actors within sport fail to "treat others as we ought." Now, whether the critics are right and need support, or whether the critics are wrong and deserve a response, one should see that when one is engaged in answering such questions one is engaged in *sports ethics*.

Finally, ethical issues and controversies found in sport are not uncommon. This is true on the conceptual level with questions such as; "Is competition ethical?" or "Is Title IX a just way to enforce sex equity in school sport?" This also true on the practical level with problems and dilemmas such as the Penn State child sexual abuse scandal, the University of North Carolina academic fraud scandal, or FIFA bribery scandals. The bottom line is this: The ethical attitudes we have and endorse, as well as the decisions we make or fail to make will have a profound effect on how sport is practiced (as examples such as Penn State indicate). Sports ethics is anything but trivial.

Just Win?

You should already have noticed some preliminary reasons to be suspicious of the claim that sport ethics can be reduced to a "just win!" mentality. It should be clear, for example, that the ethical issues arising in sport concern far more than the mere conduct or results on the field. However, let us set such initial intuitions aside, and attack the claim directly. As you recall the philosophic position on offer goes something like this: "Those actions that promote winning are to be applauded. Those actions that hinder one's likelihood of winning ought to be condemned." What, specifically, is wrong with this claim?

There is a vast literature on the significance or insignificance or winning in sport (see suggested readings at the end of the chapter). Rather than review all of it, let us consider two pertinent objections to the "just win" philosophy and see how well they hold up. The first counter argument to the "just win" philosophy can be summed up like this: "focusing on winning is insufficient, because sport is about the process not merely the product." The second response is related: "There are many shared excellences in sport that are good and important independent of whether you have won or lost." In fact, an inordinate focus on winning may directly threaten those goods and thereby cheapen and flatten the game. Let us unpack each of these counter arguments in turn.

Sport is About the Process Not Merely the Product

If the result (winning) is all that matters, then it would logically follow that all means that promote the likelihood of winning should be endorsed. This would seem to necessarily include; bribing officials or opponents, stacking teams with talent (even in educational and recreational settings), and cheating. Of course defenders of the "just win" position may argue that such a counter argument is unfair. What proponents really mean is "do everything possible, *within the rules,* to win."

Does such a rejoinder succeed? It is quite unclear that it does. First, stacking isn't strictly against the rules and certainly isn't against the rules in most educational or recreational settings. Furthermore, if winning was the only thing that mattered then one could circumvent competition and still procure victory through forfeit or through scheduling of mismatched "cupcake" opponents. Neither strategy is against the rules. In fact, one extreme interpretation of the "just win" philosophy would seem to suggest that forfeit is the best possible outcome in sport and should therefore be pursued as often as possible. For in forfeit one gains victory with no possible chance of losing. Nevertheless, most will find such a position logically and experientially dissatisfying. Why?

The reason is because sport is about the process and not just the product. That is, although the goal of sport is victory, it matters how victory is procured. The competitive pursuit of victory is as important as whether or not one ends up procuring victory. Consider, for example, baseball connoisseurs. That is, those players, fans, and administrators who really love the game of baseball. They will (or at least should) want no part of any of the strategies (e.g., bribery, pursuing forfeit, stacking, etc.) discussed above, for they *want to play baseball* not merely procure a result.

The excellences and skills of baseball, such as running, hitting, catching and throwing are debased by a "just win" philosophy. How so? Let us look at each of three options in turn:

1. Scheduling "cupcakes" and "stacking" teams mismatches talent to the point of cheapening the competitive test.
2. Bribery and cheating eliminate the integrity of the competitive test.
3. Forfeit eliminates the test altogether.

In the first case the skill based challenges of baseball are deliberately weakened. In the second case the skills based challenges of baseball are invalidated by the corruption of one's opponents' motives or corruption of one's own. In the third case, the intentional pursuit of forfeit would be a deliberate attempt to eliminate the opportunity to exercise and test one's skills in the game.

If one loves "strike outs" and "diving catches" and "home runs" then it should be clear that all three strategies are necessarily unsatisfactory, for each impedes (or removes) the integrity of the contest of baseball which makes the experience of "strike outs" and "home runs" worthwhile. Although winning matters, sport is about far more than mere victory. The process and product are both important. This insight can also be expressed thusly: winning only matters when you really risk losing.

It is the process (the experience) of sport the we want, not merely the product (victory).
©Maxisport/Shutterstock.com

There are Many Shared Excellences in Sport

As we have just seen, the central excellences and skills of sport may be threatened—or at least cheapened by an inordinate pursuit of victory. What do sport philosophers mean by "the central excellences of sport"? Proponents of this "central excellences" view are known as "broad internalists" (For more on broad internalism, see the suggested readings as the end of this chapter as well as Chapter 5). For our present purposes, suffice it to say that in advancing the theory that there are "shared excellences" in sport, broad internalists are following the work of Alasdair MacIntyre (1984). MacIntyre argues in a text on moral theory, *After Virtue*, that these central excellences, or **internal goods**, as MacIntyre calls them, are made possible through "practices," which are forms and institutions of "cooperative human activity" (p. 187). MacIntyre believes that this cooperative human activity make the internal goods of any given practice possible.

Applied to a sport—such as baseball—this means that the central excellences of baseball can be understood as the "internal goods" of the game. Furthermore, these goods are made possible and are cultivated and defended by the institution (the practice) of baseball. Internal goods are "internal" because they are only achievable in the context of the

Internal Goods: The "central excellences" of the game or "practice" which are made possible by and can only be found in the game or practice itself (e.g., the "stolen base" is an internal good of baseball because it can only be procured in baseball, the "diving header" can only be found in soccer, etc.).

External Good: Any good or excellence which, though a real good, is not internal to the game or "practice" itself (e.g., "winning," "health," "fame," and "money" are real goods, which often come from sport, but which can also be procured many other ways such as "medicine," "politics," "employment," etc.).

practice in which they are created and cultivated. Just as the "diving header" is an internal excellence of soccer, so too the "stolen base" is an internal excellence of baseball. You cannot get the "diving header" in baseball. Nor can you get the "stolen base" in soccer.

This has important implications for the "just win" philosophy. This is because the internal goods of baseball—be they the "stolen base" or the "home run," etc.—are more fundamental to the practice of baseball than is mere victory. Why? First, because victory is not an internal good. That is, it is not an excellence internal to the practice of baseball. Victory is an "**external good**," because, although it is a real good, it can be achieved in many ways apart from the practice of baseball. Second, the "just win" philosophy is lacking because victory is meant to be the test and measure of how well one succeeded at procuring, exercising, performing or facilitating the internal goods of baseball. Yet, logically, we all know that one can play poorly, while having a no fun, miserable afternoon, and still win. Just as we all know that one can play excellently, in a tight fought and dramatic contest, and still end up the loser. Therefore, victory, absent the actual procurement of at least some of these internal goods will—for the lover of baseball—ring hollow. This is because the lover of baseball wants victory within the context of demonstrating the "excellences of the game." They want to have hit, run, pitched and fielded well, and they want the experience of executing and performing those excellences. They want to *play the game*, not merely acquire victory. What they love about baseball is participating in the game, growing in skill, and sharing these excellences with other connoisseurs of the game. Put succinctly, winning is *a* measure of success, not *the* measure of success.

It is important to emphasize then, that these internal goods are shared goods. That is, internal goods are shared among the community of baseball players (the practice), independent of the result of any particular contest. The same is true of any other sporting practice. A beautiful relay to gun a runner out at the plate, a diving catch in the corner of the end zone, a give-and-go slam dunk; each is shared by all participants (and fans) present whether they end up on the winning or losing side.

Therefore—although there is nothing wrong with trying to win—the cultivation of the internal goods of any sporting practice *always trump* mere victory. This is especially true in educational contexts. MacIntyre, for instance, famously argues that in teaching a seven year old the game of chess, he would "play in such a way that it will be difficult but not impossible, for the child to win" (p. 188). He says this because from the point of view of his theory of practices, the purpose of chess is larger than procuring victory. For the institution of chess will only thrive to the degree that the game (and its excellences) are taught and passed on. To pass on chess successfully one must carefully and consistently cultivate the skills necessary to develop a love for the game. Such cultivation is deeply hindered by a "no quarter" philosophy. To take advantage of the initiate is mere selfishness. Yet, what is true of this particular example is applicable to all such sporting practices. Baseball, soccer, hockey, volleyball, etc., are all necessarily about more than winning. If this is right, then sports ethics matters a great deal, for our behavior—our action and inaction—will have a direct and enduring impact on the health and vitality of the practices which sustain and make possible the sports that we love.

PHILOSOPHIC SELECTIONS

Selection #1: Aristotle, *Politics*. (1252b27-1253b1)

Introduction: Aristotle begins the section of the *Politics* by arguing that marriage, the family, the village, and the state exist by nature. These institutions are not mere conventions nor are they simply conveniences but are necessary for the true flourishing of human beings, "for man is by nature a political animal" (1253a1). As such, politics relies upon each of these lower and smaller human institutions. It is worth noting here that politics comes from the Greek word *polis* meaning "city." Man is meant to live in a deliberative community and this community relies on these other types and levels of human organization. Aristotle then examines the purpose and value of the state, man's role in the state, and the state's role in promoting justice. Ethics is therefore not merely theoretical but institutional and practical as well.

"When several villages are united in a single complete community, large enough to be nearly or quite self-suffing, the state comes into existence, originating in the bare needs of life, and continuing in existence for the sake of a good life. And therefore, if the earlier forms of society are natural, so is the state, for it is the end of them, and the nature of a thing is its end. For what each thing is when fully developed, we call its nature, whether we are speaking of a man, a horse, or a family. Besides, the final cause and end of a thing is the best, and to be self-suffing is the end and the best.

Hence it is evident that the state is a creation of nature, and that man is by nature a political animal. And he who by nature and not by mere accident is without a state, is either a bad man or above humanity; he is like the

"Tribeless, lawless, heartless one"

Whom Homer denounces—the natural outcast is forthwith a lover of war; he may be compared to an isolated piece at draughts.

Now, that man is more of a political animal than bees or any other gregarious animals is evident. Nature, as we often say, makes nothing in vain, and man is the only animal whom she has endowed with the gift of speech. And whereas mere voice is but an indication of pleasure or pain, and is therefore found in other animals (for their nature attains to the perception of pleasure and pain and the intimation of them to one another, and no further), the power of speech is intended to set forth the expedient and inexpedient, and therefore likewise the just and the unjust. And it is a characteristic of man that he alone has any sense of good and evil, of just and unjust, and the like, and the association of living beings who have this sense makes a family and a state.

Further, the state is by nature clearly prior to the family and to the individual, since the whole is of necessity prior to the part; for example, if the whole body be destroyed, there will be no foot or hand, except in an equivocal sense, as we might speak of a stone hand; for when destroyed the hand will be no better than that. But things are defined by their working and power; and we ought not to say that they are the same when they no longer have their proper quality, but only that they have the same name. The proof that the state is a creation of nature and prior to the individual is that the individual, when isolated, is not self-suffing; and therefore he is like a part in relation to the whole. But he who is unable to live in society, or who has no need because he is sufficient for himself, must be either a beast or a god: he is no part of a state. A social instinct is implanted in all men by nature, and yet he who first founded the state was the greatest of benefactors. For man, when perfected, is the best of animals, but, when separated from law and justice, he is the worst of all; since armed injustice is the more dangerous, and he is equipped at birth with arms, meant to be used by intelligence and virtue, which he may use for the worst ends. Wherefore, if he have not virtue, he is the most unholy and the most savage of animals, and the most full of lust and gluttony. But justice is the bond of men in states, for the administration of justice, which is the determination of what is just, is the principle of order in political society.

Aristotle, *Politics*. Public Domain.

Discussion Question(s)

1. What do you make of Aristotle's ideas regarding the political nature of human beings? Although the institutions of sport are not natural in the fundamental sense in which Aristotle suggests the family or state are, would it nevertheless be fair to say that sport is part the web of institutions necessary for human flourishing? Why? Why not?

2. Aristotle claims that "For man, when perfected, is the best of animals, but, when separated from law and justice, he is the worst of all." What, if anything does this imply for the understanding and cultivation of sportsmanship?

3. What does Aristotle's conception of the political nature of human beings (that we are necessarily social, communal, and deliberative) imply for one's understanding of the nature and purpose of competition in sport?

Selection #2: Gordon Brunskill, *Centre Daily Times*, "Penn State assistant taking different road," May 2nd, 2006, page 1.

Introduction: "What counts as success?" is a vitally important but neglected question in sport. Too often, as we have seen in this chapter, sports ethics is reduced to a "just win" philosophy. In this reading we see a coach, Mike Schall, who thought more broadly about what it means to succeed. After careful consideration he came to the conclusion that his job and his family life were coming into conflict. Because he thought fathering his young children was more important than his job, he gave up coaching at the premier college women's volleyball program in the United States.

Taking different road.

Coaching, especially in college, can be really trying on family life.

Just ask Mike Schall, who has 2- and 4-year-old children at home but he has not seen them as much as he wants.

It is one of the unglamorous sides of being a coach, head or assistant, of a big-time college program.

It is for that reason Schall is leaving the Penn State women's volleyball team, heading to a non-coaching job in Chambersburg.

"I knew that my schedule wasn't going to slow down in the foreseeable future," he said. "With our kids the ages they are, it kept getting harder and harder for us to have the type of family life that we wanted to have at home. It's nobody's fault. It's the nature of what we do."

It is true for every sport. Fans see the coaches on the sidelines, and that is certainly a big part of what they do, but it does not end after the final horn blows on the season. That is when the recruiting gets heavy, whether it is volleyball, soccer, basketball, baseball or anything else.

"If you want a program competing at the highest level," head coach Russ Rose said, "then you need to compete in the gym and compete in recruiting as well."

Rose knows plenty about success. He has 859 career wins, one of only a handful of coaches with more than 800, and a national title in his 27 seasons. He also has had scores of All Americans who have graced the campus from all corners of the country. The incoming recruiting class for the fall is the best in the nation, with state players of the year from North Carolina, Virginia, Illinois and Michigan.

To get those athletes, however, Rose and his assistants, Schall and Kevin Starns, had to cover the nation. Just in the last few weeks either he or his assistants have been to Dallas, Phoenix, Reno, Ohio, Minnesota and Baltimore, among other places. For one stretch this spring Rose figured he was gone for 10 straight weekends.

"I can't list all the things that I have missed that were significant," said Rose, who has four sons. "My youngest son a week or so ago hit his first home run. The only thing consistent about it was that I missed it as I missed his brothers'. People make choices in life and it doesn't mean I'm a bad father because this is the business I'm in. This is my way of contributing to the family. My work takes me out of town."

Schall knew he could not keep living that way.

Volleyball is in his blood. His father coached at Derry Area High School and he played four seasons as a defensive specialist in the 1990s with the Nittany Lions. His two brothers also played for the Nittany Lions and are coaches in high school and his wife, Sarah, has been the coach the last three seasons at State College.

In that short amount of time she has raised the Lady Little Lions to a level among the state's elite, reaching the PIAA semifinals last fall. However, she, too, is leaving her post, which was a tough thing to break to the team with a return visit to the state tournament at Central York High School appearing likely.

"I do have a deep connection to these girls now, we have been very successful and they'll be very successful next year as well," Sarah Schall said. "I told them I'm rooting them on, they're my favorite team in the state and I'll come to a couple tournaments and I'll be at states in York rooting them on."

In Chambersburg, Mike will be taking a job with a company run by Sarah's parents which sells Tee Time Golf Passes. It is a discount program for hundreds of courses around the mid-Atlantic region, and Mike will be a representative of the company, building relationships with the courses. He will still be on the road some, but nowhere near as much or as far-flung.

"For me, it's the opportunity to see my kids grow up," Mike Schall said. "I knew that was going to be very difficult with any type of coaching job."

He told his former team members he would never coach any college program again. Sarah also said she would not be coaching again, at least for a while. They both may get into club or youth programs, but the high-pressure life as a coach for both has been put on a shelf, maybe for a while, maybe forever.

State College is already advertising for its coaching position, and Schall thinks there will be plenty of interest.

Rose is also looking, but his search criteria are a little different.

"I always felt that Mike was going to replace me as the head coach at Penn State," Rose said. "The question is, am I replacing my opening or am I trying to select my replacement?"

And, it has to be someone willing to cover the country to keep the Nittany Lions among the best programs in the nation.

"The job is what the job entails," Rose said. "If you want to be successful, then you need to put the time into it."

Discussion Question(s)

1. Did Coach Schall make the right decision? Why? Why not? What would you have done in his situation? How would considering the distinction between *intrinsic* and *extrinsic* goods help inform your decision?
2. Is there an inherent conflict between coaching and family life? Is that conflict any greater than myriad other jobs which require long hours or travel? If there is, what should be done to allow coaches more time with their families?
3. Does the fact that Penn State went on to win four consecutive national titles from 2007 to 2010 (with players that Coach Schall recruited) have any bearing on whether or not Coach Schall made the right decision? Why? Why not?

From *Centre Daily Times*. © 2006 McClatchy. All rights reserved. Used under license.

Selection #3: Jim Caple, *At Play in a Land of Death*, ESPN.com

Please read article here: http://www.espn.com/espn/eticket/print?page=zambia_story

Introduction: This selection recounts one trip Olympic athletes made in service to the charity *Right to Play*. The athletes spent several weeks in the poverty- and AIDS-stricken country of Zambia. Their goal was to use games, play, and sport to inspire and to educate. As you read this article, think about what is really worthy of our attention, and how philosophic commitments impact how we answer that question. As Joey Cheek (an Olympic speedskater on the trip) put it in the article:

> "Ultimately, winning a medal doesn't really matter. But if you can do something that has some sort of impact on someone else, and that person can go on and have a better life, even if you never get any public recognition for it, that's something that is much more lasting. That's something that can trickle on throughout history."

Is it possible that the importance and power of play has been lost in the noise of our overly commercialized and hype-driven Western sporting culture?

Discussion Question(s)

1. In what ways does this account of Right to Play's work in Zambia support the claim made in Chapter 1 that there must be more to sports ethics than a "just win" philosophy?
2. What is the proper relationship between "sport as play" and using sport as a "vehicle for social change/education"? Is it natural to teach lessons about AIDS through sport or is there something dangerous about turning sport into a primarily extrinsic good? If we *use sport*, are we still "at play"?
3. Are we spoiled in the United States? If so, how might we cultivate a greater sense of gratitude for our access to sporting equipment, facilities, etc., as well our access to the basic necessities of life such as food, clothing, shelter, medicine, etc.?

Suggested Readings

Dixon, N. (1999). On winning and athletic superiority. *Journal of the Philosophy of Sport, 26,* 10–26.

Kretchmar, S., & Elcombe, T. (2007). In defense of competition and winning. In W. J. Morgan (Ed.), *Ethics in Sport* (2nd ed., pp. 181–194). Champaign, IL: Human Kinetics.

Scruton, R. (2011). *Beauty: A very short introduction.* New York, NY: Oxford University Press.

Simon, R. L. (2000). Internalism and internal values in sport. *Journal of the Philosophy of Sport,* 27, 1–16.

Bibliography

Aristotle. (1981). *Politics.* (T. Sinclair, & T. J. Saunders, Trans.) New York, NY: Penguin Books.

Aristotle. (2002). *Nicomachean ethics.* (J. Sachs, Trans.) Newburyport, MA: Focus Publishing.

Baker, W. J. (1982). *Sports in the Western world* (Revised ed.). Urbana and Chicago, IL: University of Illinois Press.

Battista, J. (2002, October 31). Edwards's take on Jets: Quitting is never an option. *The New York Times,* p. D5.

Brown, M. (2019, January 7). *MLB sees record revenues of $10.3 billion for 2018.* Retrieved May 22, 2019, from forbes.com: https://www.forbes.com/sites/maurybrown/2019/01/07/mlb-sees-record-revenues-of-10-3-billion-for-2018/#6515b3db5bea

Dixon, N. (1999). On winning and athletic superiority. *Journal of the Philosophy of Sport, 26,* 10–26.

Fainaru-Wada, M., & Fainaru, S. (2013). *League of denial: The NFL, concussions, and the battle for the truth.* New York, NY: Crown Archetype.

French, P. (2004). *Ethics and college sports: Ethics, sports and the university.* Lanham, MD: Rowman and Littlefield.

Guttmann, A. (2004). *Sports: The first five millennia.* Amherst and Boston, MA: University of Massachusetts Press.

Handley, L. (2019, February 5). *Super Bowl draws lowest TV audience in more than a decade, early data show.* Retrieved May 22, 2019, from cnbc.com: https://www.cnbc.com/2019/02/05/super-bowl-draws-lowest-tv-audience-in-more-than-a-decade-nielsen.html

Huizinga, J. (1955). *Homo ludens: A study of the play element in culture.* Boston, MA: Beacon Press.

Kelley, B., & Carchia, C. (2013, July 16). *Hey, data data—swing!* Retrieved June 29, 2015, from ESPN.com: http://espn.go.com/espn/story/_/id/9469252/hidden-demographics-youth-sports-espn-magazine

Kretchmar, S., & Elcombe, T. (2007). In defense of competition and winning. In W. J. Morgan (Ed.), *Ethics in sport* (2nd ed., pp. 181–194). Champaign, IL: Human Kinetics.

Lea, S. (2006). *Albert Camus and football.* Retrieved August 28, 2015, from camus-society.com: http://www.camus-society.com/camus-football.html

Lee, P., & George, R. P. (2008). *Body-self dualism in contemporary ethics and politics.* New York, NY: Cambridge University Press.

MacIntyre, A. (1984). *After virtue* (2nd ed.). Notre Dame, IN: University of Notre Dame Press.

MacIntyre, A. (1999). *Dependent rational animals: Why human beings need the virtues.* Chicago and LaSalle, IL: Open Court.

MacIntyre, A. (2009). *God, philosophy, universities: A selective history of the Catholic philosophical tradition.* Lanham, MD: Rowman & Littlefield Publishers Inc.

McMurtrie, B. (2014). Why colleges haven't stopped students from binge drinking. *The Chronicle of Higher Education,* pp. 10–14.

Muret, D. (2014, December 26). *Kyle Field renovation jumps to $485 million.* Retrieved June 29, 2015, from www.sportingnews.com: http://www.sportingnews.com/ncaa-football/story/2014-12-26/texas-am-kyle-field-demolition-video-stadium-renovation-populous-sec

Neuhaus, R. J. (2009). *American babylon: Notes of a Christian exile.* New York, NY: Basic Books.

Noack, R. (2014, November 18). *Map: The world's 36 million slaves.* Retrieved June 9, 2015, from www.washingtonpost.com: http://www.washingtonpost.com/blogs/worldviews/wp/2014/11/18/map-the-worlds-36-million-slaves/

Olson, E. (2016, November 2). *Big Ten to play 6 Friday night games a year starting in 2017.* Retrieved November 4, 2016, from espn.com: http://abcnews.go.com/Sports/wireStory/big-ten-play-friday-night-games-year-starting-43256010

Reed, A. (2018, December 21). *Half the world's population tuned in to this year's soccer World Cup.* Retrieved May 22, 2019, from cnbc.com: https://www.cnbc.com/2018/12/21/world-cup-2018-half-the-worlds-population-tuned-in-to-this-years-soccer-tournament.html

Russell, J. (1999). Are rules all an umpire has to work with? *Journal of the Philosophy of Sport, 26,* 27–49.

Scarborough, V. L., & Wilcox, D. R. (Eds.). (1993). *The Mesoamerican ball game.* Tuscon, AZ: University of Arizona Press.

Simon, R. L. (2000). Internalism and internal values in sport. *Journal of the Philosophy of Sport,* 1–16.

Simon, R., Torres, C., & Hager, P. (2015). *Fair play: The ethics of sport* (4th Ed.). Boulder, CO: Westview Press.

Sperber, M. (2000). *Beer and circus: How big-time college sports is crippling undergraduate education.* New York, NY: Henry Holt and Company.

Chapter 2

Good and Evil in Sport

"But, whether true or false, my opinion is that in the world of knowledge the idea of good appears last of all, and is seen only with an effort; and, when seen, is also inferred to be the universal author of all things beautiful and right . . . this is the power upon which he who would act rationally, either in public or private life must have his eye fixed."

—Plato[1]

Students will be able to:

1. Identify and explain the reasons offered for why "good and evil" necessarily impact sports ethics.
2. Summarize the different schools of thought regarding good and evil in sport (i.e., transcendence, hedonism, illusion/useful fiction).
3. Evaluate and critique the truth of the different schools of thought regarding good and evil, so as to begin planning one's professional philosophy.
4. Explain the difference between "subtle" and "explicit" goods and evils in sport.
5. Explain how one's philosophic position on the good impacts practical day-to-day behavior.

You may recall that a major element of Chapter 1 was justifying the importance of sports ethics. At the risk of sounding redundant we must begin this chapter in a similar manner. For over the years, I have heard a common objection from students to the effect that good and evil "are abstract philosophical concepts that don't have any bearing in the daily life of sport managers." In essence, these students are arguing that an examination of the nature of good and evil, even in the context of a sports ethics course, is not practical. What responses can be offered to this position?

---

[1] The Republic, Book VII, p. 179.

What, if anything, does "good and evil" have to do with sport management?
©dotshock/Shutterstock.com

First, one might point out that although our hyper-regimented modern culture sometimes convinces us otherwise, we do not, in fact, live compartmentalized lives. The integrated nature of human existence means philosophic reflection on the nature and meaning of life will spill into the workaday world just as life events outside of work necessarily spill into the workaday world. Second, all of us are concerned about more than the practicalities of life. Those who have reduced the good to the procurement of things, or to a technical or tactical success are unhappy. Finally, as we saw in Chapter 1, moral questions abound in sport. Yet evaluating such moral claims and choices; deciding which is right or wrong, will necessarily rely on an understanding on the nature of good and evil. Therefore, if we want to think well regarding sports ethics, we will have to think hard about good and evil.

We Don't Live Compartmentalized Lives

Life and death, right and wrong, good and evil all permeate our lives. That is, just as we don't stop being a son or daughter, a husband or wife, a friend or neighbor simply because we have gone to work, so too the joys, pains, triumphs and tragedies of life are unavoidable, even at work. Sport managers, athletes, coaches and fans do not stop being human beings simply because they are "on the job" or "at the game."

Consider, for example, the tragic death of 21-year-old Michael Philbin in January of 2012. Michael was the son of Green Bay Packers offensive coordinator Joe Philbin. Michael drowned in an icy river just days before the Packers were to play the New York Giants in an NFL Playoff Game (Klemko, 2012). It is surely the case that Philbin's grief, as well as his desire to care for and mourn with his family held (and should have held) his attention that weekend and beyond. A job is merely a *part* of our lives.

Nor is Philbin unique. All of us have and will have our work lives "interrupted" by the experiences, triumphs, joys, disappointments and tragedies of our larger lives. We may, as the saying goes, "wear different hats" in the modern world, but they all go on the same head. The basic point is this: Our lives are permeated with events, ideas, and decisions which naturally call forth questions regarding the meaning and reality of good and evil.

To say that sport is "an escape from such things" is a misnomer. To put it more accurately, sport can be (and often has been) an affirmation of life in the face of evil, tragedy, and misfortune (be it physical, natural, or moral). Of course, sport has also been a vehicle for evil. Consider, for example, how Adolph Hitler used the 1936 Olympic Games to spread Nazi propaganda (Guttmann, 2002). Yet, sport, at its best, allows us to transcend evil. How and why is this possible? The only way to answer such a question involves defining the nature of good and evil.

This experience of transcending evil through sport was also seen in the *Right to Play* "philosophic selection" article in Chapter 1. Additional examples are not hard to identify. Consider the Woldenburg Olympic Games, held by prisoners of war in a Nazi prison camp in 1944 (Grys, 1996). One POW put the idea this way: "It seemed to us, who were removed from the war game that was being waged for life and death that it would be good if somebody, somewhere—even in the prison camp—remembered this [Olympic] banner, which has always been a symbol of struggle, though never stained with blood" (p. 69). Using sport to reaffirm life in the face of death also plays a role in the Western world's earliest literature. In the *Illiad* Achilles mourns Patrokles by providing the prizes necessary to hold funerary games in honor of his dead friend.

There is More To Life than Practicalities

What each of these examples indicates is that human life is greater than the mere satisfaction of desires. Or, if one wanted to keep the language of desire, that human desires are deeper than food, shelter and clothing. Similarly, those who have centered their lives on the procurement of things (even victory) find it void of meaning. Normatively speaking, sport is good, but sport is *only one good* among others. As educator George B. Leonard (1973) opined in regard to former Dallas Cowboys coach Tom Landry's obsession with winning:

> ". . . even after you've just won the Super Bowl – *especially* after you've just won the Super Bowl—*there's always next year.* If 'Winning isn't everything. It's the only thing' then 'the only thing' is nothing—emptiness, the nightmare of life without ultimate meaning" (p. 46).

This insight clarifies an important truth; when one centers their life on sport and only sport, one will be miserable. *It is only a matter of time.* This was put bluntly by Andre Agassi (2009) in his autobiography when he stated "I hate tennis" (p. 3).[2]

---

[2] "'But it becomes more than a job, it takes over your life,' says former British tennis professional Barry Cowan, perhaps best known for taking Agassi's nemesis, Pete Sampras, to five sets in Wimbledon in 2001. 'If you're at the top of tennis, you're on tour 30-plus weeks of the year—and when you're doing that, everything revolves around tennis. Every decision you make, tennis is at the back of your mind. That's the main reason for burnout among tennis players in their 20s'" (Jeffries, 2009, para. 3).

"I play tennis for a living, even though I hate tennis, hate it with a dark and secret passion, and always have."

©Photo Works/Shutterstock.com

Moral Questions Abound in Sport

The key point here is the gravity of many of the moral questions in sport. Sports ethics deals in genuine goods and in some cases confronts genuine evil. Two profound examples of this can be found in the readings as the end of this chapter. The first deals the question of altruism: Is it possible to think of others before ourselves? The article recounts the story of Dave Hartsock, a regular guy who did an extraordinary thing. It relates the tale of how Dave sacrificed his own safety to save the life of a total stranger. When you read this article you will *see the good*. This does not mean Dave has been a perfect person. By his own admission he is no saint, but that doesn't change the fact that he did a *saintly thing*. In contrast, consider the actions of Jerry Sandusky, as well as the alleged complicity of members of the Penn State University administration in his sexual crimes against children. There is no other way to describe the crimes Sandusky committed than as evil. Yet, why? What is the nature, if any, of good and evil?

Accounts of Good and Evil

We must give some account of good and evil. What account should we give? There are at least three broad schools of thought regarding good and evil which are worth considering, even if our analysis will be necessarily cursory. The first school of thought is what might be called the transcendent school (Pojman & Vaughn, 2011). Those who subscribe to **transcendence** see good and evil as something above and beyond human volition. Good and evil are not categories we create, but rather a reality to which we are beholden. In this sense good and evil are mysterious. The second school of thought is hedonism, which we discussed briefly in Chapter 1. **Hedonism**, you may recall, is the idea that life is about the procurement of pleasure and the avoidance of pain. As such, hedonists find no mystery in good and evil. Things, in contrast to the transcendent school, are quite simple. Pleasure is good. Pain is evil. The third and final school of thought is the **illusion/"useful fiction"** school. According to proponents of this position the examination of good and evil is itself problematic. Distinctions between good and evil are not timeless truths but are born of antiquated cultural baggage. Therefore, metaphysical distinctions between good and evil should be abandoned.

Transcendence

According to the transcendent view, good and evil are objective realities above and beyond both the natural world and man's will. Truth itself is real and must be served. As Plato says in *The Republic*: the good, once recognized "is the power upon which he who would act rationally, either in public or private life must have his eye fixed" (p. 179). The good is not created by human beings nor is it reducible to the laws of the material world.

Yet, such an assertion begs for explanation. How and why does the good exist? Thus, the transcendent view of good and evil often leads to (but does not require) a religious or mystical interpretation of life, for religion seems to provide a source for the good. That being said, proponents of the transcendent view can and have endorsed a wide range of specific beliefs justifying their commitment to a transcendent good; from Plato's "forms" to the Eastern "Tao" to the "deism" of the Enlightenment. Even atheism is compatible with the transcendent view as long as an atheist is committed to the good as an *objective* and *universal* reality.

Among the various religious explanations for the existence of a transcendent good, the most common explanation in the Western tradition is that the truth *is* God, whom is understood as the source of all things. As such there is a nature and purpose to life and to human beings.[3] Within this tradition, God is what the classical philosophers called the **summum bonum**, the highest good.[4] This is not because God is a divine despot who demands our acquiescence, but because God created and *maintains* our existence. He is, so the theory goes, the source of our existence (and all reality) *here and now,* even as you read this sentence. To oppose him is to oppose reality itself, for God is the beginning and the end of all things.[5]

St. Augustine (1997) makes the point this way:

> "We exist because he is good, and we are good to the extent that we exist. Moreover, because he is also just, we are evil with impunity; if we are evil, to that extent we exist less. God exists in the supreme sense, and the original sense of the word. He is altogether unchangeable, and it is he who could say with full authority 'I am who I am' . . . so it is true of other things which exist that they could not exist except by him, and that they are good to the extent that they have received their existence from him" (p. 24).

Transcendence: A school of thought which argues that good and evil are based in reality. That is, good and evil transcend human will or desire. As such human beings are obligated—by reality—to pursue the good and avoid evil. The source of this transcendent reality is usually understood, but does not have to be, God.

Hedonism: A pleasure-based philosophy which sees the good as pleasure and evil as pain.

Illusion/"Useful Fiction": A philosophy which argues that standards of good and evil are manmade. As such, good and evil either don't really exist or are convenient bureaucratic fictions which have practical value, but which are not actually true.

Summum Bonum: The highest good, often equated with God or one's right relationship with God.

---

[3] As the philosopher Josef Pieper (2011) puts it, "One who does not know how things really are cannot do good; for the good accords with reality" (p. 13).

[4] "There is, accordingly, a good which alone is simple and, therefore, which alone is unchangeable—and this is God" (Augustine, *City of God*, 11.10).

[5] There are, of course, even within the theistic traditions, profound disagreements upon what this realization implies or requires for human action and behavior.

If this is right, then all the other goods of the world and of life will necessarily flow out of a recognition of this highest good. Furthermore, the goods of the world as well as the nature of right and wrong action are objective realities. There are right and wrong, better and worse answers to the two basic questions of ethics; "What is a good life?" and "How should we treat each other?"

What then is the nature of evil according to the transcendent view? There are essentially two answers. The first view is that evil is a corruption, lack or misuse of some good. In philosophic terms evil is a **privation**. Evil is parasitic on the good. Again Augustine (1958) is instructive. "For, evil has no positive nature; what we call evil is merely the lack of something that is good" (p. 217). Within the Christian tradition the implications are as follows: (1) The world is not fundamentally evil, but fundamentally corrupted by sin, that is, rebellion against God. (2) Evil is born from a misuse of a good—our free will. (3) Redemption from evil is possible, for evil always relies upon (is parasitic upon) a more fundamental good. If the corruption is cut out, then only good remains.

Privation: A lack of some good that something ought to have. Evil is often defined as a privation (a lack, misuse, or corruption of some real good).

Is evil best understood as corruption?
©Smit/Shutterstock.com.

The second view is that evil is opposite of the good. It is an equal, necessary and antagonizing force to the good. Good and evil define each other. Just as the night needs the day, and male needs female, good needs evil. Such dichotomies have led to this view being labeled dualistic. There have been many ancient and modern adherents to such thinking. Before converting to Christianity, Augustine himself belonged to an ancient religion called Manicheism which espoused this view. The Manicheans also believed that the good was spiritual while the material world was evil. Although Manicheism has died out, the general view of good and evil as equal and necessary forces can still be found in American pop culture, as well as in some versions of contemporary religion. For instance, there are echoes of the idea in the dualism of the yin/yang principle in Chinese philosophy (Wang, n.d.).

One could also arguably find a dualistic conception of good and evil in the contemporary philosophic and scientific movement called trans-humanism which seeks to transform and surpass human physical and intellectual limitations through the direct application of technology to the human person. This dualistic opposition between good (immateriality) and evil (materiality) can be seen in, for instance, the dream of "uploading" the mind to a computer, which will allegedly create a "digital consciousness" free from the frailties, fatigue and death of our physical bodies (Woollaston, 2013).[6] Suffice it to say that both the privation and the dualistic theories of evil are alive and well.

One way to see the importance of the transcendent school for sports ethics is to consider our moral imperatives in the context of sportsmanship. For instance, in a famous paper on the ethics of "running up the score," sport philosopher Nicholas Dixon (1993) examines the work of Peter J. Arnold (1983) who espoused a view of sportsmanship "as a form of altruistically motivated conduct that is concerned with the good or welfare of another" (p. 66). Importantly, Dixon then goes on to point out that Arnold's view suggests that altruistic acts in sport are **supererogatory**.[7] These acts are good, perhaps even desirable, but are nonetheless above and beyond the call of duty. The paradigm example here is the scenario where one long distance runner stops running the course to help a seriously injured competitor. Is stopping a moral obligation? Dixon (and Arnold) argue no. To do so may be noble but no one is obliged to do it. As Dixon puts it, "the competitor who does not perform [such acts] is guilty of no moral failing" (p. 10). Is that right?

Supererogatory Act: An action which is above and beyond the call of duty.

If your gut instinct is no, the transcendent school offers you a framework from which to respond. For the conviction that the good is objective has a way of stiffening our moral spines. For example, consider the Christian tradition again. In the Gospel of John (13:34, NIV), Jesus says the following; "A new command I give you: Love one another. As I have loved you, so you must love one another." Now, from a philosophical perspective what you should notice is this: It has some very serious implications for action for anyone who believes that this claim is true and comes from the Word of God (who is the source of all existence). What do I mean? First, it is a *commandment*. Jesus did not offer general caveats, or specific exceptions for marathon runners, it is a constant obligation in all areas of life. Second, he set the bar incredibly high, we are to *love* one another. Not concern, not even sympathy is sufficient, but only love, which one theologian has defined as "willing the good of the other and then doing something concrete about it" (Barron, 2013).[8]

---

[6] Futurist Ray Kurzweil put it this way, "'We're going to become increasingly non-biological to the point where the non-biological part dominates and the biological part is not important any more" (Woollaston, 2013, para. 14).

[7] Arnold and Dixon both are uncomfortable with the term supererogatory. This is because Arnold (1983) argues that "emotions of concern and care" (p. 68) better explain and promote moral action than does duty. Whether Arnold's "altruism" or duty-based "supererogatory actions" are the best term, the point holds, for whether one allies themselves with one verbiage or the other, each considers the act *optional*.

[8] "Love is willing the good of the other . . . and then doing something concrete about it. It's not an emotion, it's not an attitude. It's a move of the will. To want the good of the other, and do something about it. That's love." (Barron, 2013). Or one might point out this famous description of love from St. Paul "Love is patient, love is kind. It does not envy, it does not boast, it is not proud. [5] It does not dishonor others, it is not self-seeking, it is not easily angered, it keeps no record of wrongs. [6] Love does not delight in evil but rejoices with the truth. It always protects, always trusts, always hopes, always perseveres" (1st Corinthians 13:4–7).

What obligations do we have to each other?
Ian Walton/Getty Images Sport/Getty Images

Therefore, one could argue that stopping to help the runner is obligatory because the loving action is *always* called for and the loving action *always* puts the safety of a fellow competitor above such lesser goods as fame, success or victory. On this account, to refuse to stop *is* a moral failing. As such, proponents of this argument would insist that such an understanding helps us avoid rationalization, equivocation and moral mediocrity.

It goes without saying that this analysis is controversial for many reasons, not the least of which is that not everyone accepts the claims of Christianity.[9] The point here however is not theological. The point is, (as we discussed in Chapter 1), that our conclusions follow from our premises. Which means the premises we endorse are not trivial. What we believe, what our convictions are, have a direct impact on our actions. One person following the logic of the supererogatory premises discussed above will say stopping to help the runner is "nice but not necessary," while another, following the alternative logic of the commandment to love, will say one *must* aim for the moral excellence of stopping to help the fallen competitor; it isn't a nice *choice*, it is a moral *truth*.[10]

Hedonism

Hedonists claim that good and evil can be reduced to pleasure and pain. There is nothing mysterious going on. Human beings enjoy and therefore seek pleasure. Human beings do not enjoy and therefore seek to avoid pain. Even if one is not a hedonist, one must admit that there is intuitive force to this claim. They key question when one evaluates hedonism is this: can *everything* about good and evil be reduced to a simple pleasure/

---

[9] There is also room for legitimate prudential disagreements regarding in what situations (e.g., how injured one's competitor would really have to be) to oblige one to stop and help.
[10] "Moralism says: good is what obligation requires, and because obligation requires it. The doctrine of prudence says: good is what accords with reality; it is obligatory because it corresponds to reality" (Pieper, 2011, p. 16).

pain calculus? That is, when evaluating good and evil, are pleasure and pain *the only* things that matter? Is pleasure the only intrinsic good? The hedonist will say yes. The critic of hedonism, even in conceding the importance of pleasure and pain, will say no.

Philosophers like to make a distinction between two types of hedonism. The first type, called folk or **"crude" hedonism**, endorses the pursuit of sensual pleasure; the pursuit of "sex, drugs, and rock & roll."[11] The second type of hedonism, which we will call **philosophical hedonism**, broadens and deepens the meaning of pleasure beyond the sensual (Weijers, n.d.). Friendship, fond memories, and skillful performance would, on this account, all derive their value from the pleasure they induce. The most popular form of philosophical hedonism today is an ethical philosophy known as *utilitarianism* which seeks to evaluate ethical claims based upon which rule or action will produce the greatest good for the greatest number, that is, "maximize pleasure" for the most people. (We will be examining utilitarianism in detail in Chapter 4).

Given the descriptive reality that human beings *do* prefer pleasure to pain, as well as the reality that many people *are* motivated by the pursuit of pleasure (be it, philosophical or crude), what criticisms of hedonism can be offered? Furthermore, given the sensual nature of sport, does not a hedonistic account of sport make sense?

I have argued elsewhere there are at least three serious criticisms of hedonism in sport and physical activity (Twietmeyer, 2012). Here I will only review one: pleasure is a byproduct of, rather than the end of sport. For example, "When one plays baseball, it is not the experience of pleasure per se that is desired, but rather the actual activity of baseball" (p. 180). We want to *play baseball*, not merely *feel* the pleasures involved. In other words, pleasure is not primary in sport but rather derivative. Because we love *baseball*, baseball is able to produce pleasure in us. If true, then it is *baseball* that we ought to pursue rather than mere pleasure. This in turn means that the good consists of more than pleasure, for *good* baseball—baseball played well (skillfully) and played rightly (ethically)—consists of and relies on far more than the pleasures produced.

Good & Evil as an Illusion

According to the third account of good and evil, good and evil are social constructs (man-made categories) and are therefore either totally illusory or are "useful fictions," which allow society to function. By "allow society to function" proponents of this theory mean that there is no inherent truth to our laws; murder, for instance, is only wrong because we say so. Nevertheless, it is *useful* to have laws against murder and so forth because it prevents chaos. As with the hedonists, there is no mystery to good and evil. Nor is there any "cosmic truth" or God behind it. Contrary to the transcendence school, morality is a tool that serves man. We are its master. It follows that morality is made, and can be re-made. As a result, some proponents of this theory worry that those in power make and enforce laws which abuse the powerless. This is because laws are not and cannot be based on truth, but are rather designed to suit the needs of those in power.[12] In essence, this is a critique of the philosophy that "might makes right."

Crude Hedonism: A hedonistic philosophy centered on pursuing immediate sensual pleasure.

Philosophical Hedonism: A hedonistic philosophy centered on deeper, more enduring pleasures such as friendship or skilled performance.

---

[11] Another term often used in everyday speech is "epicurean." Interestingly enough the ancient Greek philosopher Epicurus (though he affirmed the reality of hedonism) was not a crude hedonist. In fact, he was essentially ascetic. For to indulge pleasure now was to set oneself up for even greater pain later (e.g., hangovers, addiction, etc.).

[12] Critics of the position like to point out that such a concern is self-contradictory. If morality is a fiction, there is no such thing as *abuse*.

It is worth noting that such concerns are not new. Doubts regarding "good and evil" reach back to at least ancient Greece. This can be seen in *The Republic* when a skeptical Thrasymachus challenges Socrates to prove to him that justice is anything more "than the interest of the stronger" (Plato, 2000, p. 12). Yet, the most influential modern proponent of this theory is the 19th Century German philosopher Friedrich Nietzsche. As you will see in one of this chapter's readings, Nietzsche argues that obsessive concerns over good and evil are a vestige of a now bankrupt Christian cultural inheritance. Why is this the case? At root, Nietzsche believes this because "**God is dead**," by which Nietzsche means that God is a man-made idea. Since we created God, we can kill him off (by realizing that he was and is nothing more than a fiction).

What are the consequences of this alleged insight? Here is what Nietzsche argues. True morality is not the traditional Christian ethic of human dignity and equality before God. Nor do the Christian virtues of humility, kindness and forgiveness make sense. This is a "slave morality" espoused by the weak, under the guise of Christianity, to restrain the powerful. The strong must reject these false claims and accept the "master morality" of the **"Will to Power."** The "slave morality" celebrates the mediocrity of the "herd" at the expense of individual excellence. The "Übermensch" (Overman; Superman) will rise above, embrace the "master morality" and be willing to dominate the weak in pursuit of excellence.

"God is Dead":
Nietzsche's famous claim which is meant to show that the foundations of Christian morality cannot survive the fact that we now know that God is not real, but rather an idea that we created. As a fiction, we can kill him off.

"The Will to Power":
Nietzsche's account of morality which defines moral excellence as domination (i.e., exercising one's powers, free from the constraints of traditional morality).

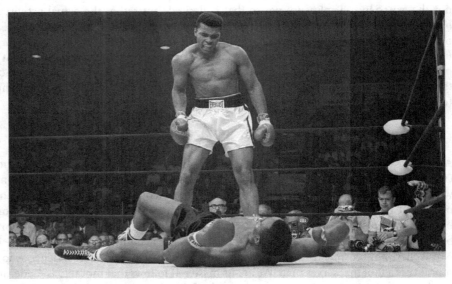

Is Nietzsche right? Is the Will to Power the most fundamental fact of life? If not life, then sport?
Bettmann/Getty Images

Why is this justifiable? Because in a godless world there cannot be equality before God, which means that some human beings are *necessarily* better (and more valuable) than others. Therefore Nietzsche's (1997) Übermensch must unapologetically seize power and dominate those around him.

> "Here one must think profoundly to the very basis and resist all sentimental weakness: life itself is *essentially* appropriation, injury, conquest of the strange and weak, suppression, severity, obtrusion of peculiar forms, incorporation, and at the least, putting it mildest, exploitation . . . 'Exploitation' does not

belong to a depraved, or imperfect and primitive society: it belongs to the nature of the living being as a primary organic function; it is a consequence of the intrinsic Will to Power, which is precisely the Will to Life" (pp. 125–126).

What should be made of such thinking? One thing that must be mentioned—whether one finds Nietzsche's argument compelling or vile—is that it has been influential. Nietzsche's thought has permeated our academic culture, as well as our popular culture (Ratner-Rosenhagen, 2012). We even see echoes of it in sport in attitudes that "might makes right,"[13] that "losing is a character flaw,"[14] and in the general suspicion of truth. Instead of honesty and truth being paramount, modern sport is too often about procedural maneuvering and power. Consider, for instance, how French soccer star Thierry Henry rationalized his blatant handball in a 2009 World Cup qualifying match against Ireland, "I will be honest, it was a handball. But I'm not the ref. I played it, the ref allowed it. That's a question you should ask him" (Ogden, 2009, para. 1).

Are good and evil in sport reducible to what the referees can detect?
Dan Mullan/Getty Images Sport/Getty Images

Here, in a nutshell is Henry's argument; "I cheated. It is the referee's fault." Astounding. Both for its brashness and for how commonplace such thinking has become. It would be unfair to Nietzsche to say that he has *caused* these things in sport, but it is fair to say that his thinking and his influence contributed significantly to the intellectual and cultural climate that buttresses these attitudes and behaviors in sport.

---

[13] In other words, winning absolves one of all sins. This is closely related to a "my team right or wrong" mentality that worries only about one's immediate partisan interests rather than the truth or the goods of the game.
[14] Consider these two quotes. The first is from Nick Saban after losing the 2005 Capital One Bowl on a last second Hail Mary: "The last 14 or 20 seconds of this game somewhat tarnish the things this team has accomplished in its four years" (Wine, 2005). How can losing one game tarnish the accomplishments of a separate season? The second quote comes from an *Ann Arbor News* sportswriter's lament following Michigan's 2005 Rose Bowl loss to Texas "Some will take solace in the Big Ten title and second straight trip to Pasadena. Other will see it as a *totally empty accomplishment* given those three losses" (Carty, 2005) [Emphasis added].

Both Good and Evil Occur in Sport

It should be clear that although I have attempted to be fair to each of these schools of thought regarding good and evil, my own sympathies lie with the transcendent school. I do not find either the hedonistic or illusion school compelling. That being said, there are intelligent proponents of each of these positions and you should seek to understand each one. That doesn't mean there is no right answer. I am fully convinced that there is. It simply means that as philosophers you must learn to see that even mistaken positions can and should be treated and discussed seriously. This is especially true considering the fact that many may think that it is the position which *you* endorse that is mistaken.

As noted above, our conclusions follow from our premises. If we endorse hedonism, we will end up in a very different place regarding good and evil in sport—both in theory and in practice—than if we endorse either of the other two schools. Moreover, real goods and real harms are at stake. These goods and evils occur in both subtle and explicit forms. **Subtle goods** are those we take for granted, but they are not given and should not be discounted. Think, for example, of the tradition in soccer to kick the ball out when an opposing player in injured, or of the tradition in hockey to shake hands after every game (no matter how hard fought). Sport depends on such behavior. Yet, sport can also be threatened by subtle evils such as; cheap shots, recruiting violations, and the disdain for one's opponents implied by taunting and trash-talking. Subtle evils are those evils we ignore, tolerate, and justify. This much is clear: Sportsmanship is not trivial.

Our culture encourages and discourages, tolerates and condemns certain behaviors. This evaluation is based in part upon (often unexamined) commitments regarding good and evil. As I (2012) have said elsewhere:

> "A post-game handshake in soccer or hockey is good, but the sportsmanship these handshakes embody are not the product of spontaneous generation. Sharing, taking turns, playing fair are all genuine goods, but they depend for their existence upon culture. The fact that these truths are taught, *does not make them any less true.* In other words, virtue is the product of tradition. Tradition can exist only insofar as those in positions of authority are willing to exercise their authority in pursuit of virtue" (p. 185).

If this is right then you should see how important it is to identify which understanding of good and evil is most likely to cultivate a society that promotes such goods. Which school will develop and sustain the traditions and institutions in sport necessary to cultivate the good?

This question takes on an even greater urgency when one considers the **explicit goods** and evils in sport. That is, those goods or evils that delight, surprise, shock or abhor us. These are not hard to identify. Consider the courage of Jackie Robinson in the face of racism, or the honesty of golfing great Bobby Jones, which compelled him to report a stroke no one even saw (and which ended up costing him the 1925 U.S. Open Championship). Unfortunately explicit evils, both old and new, easily come to mind as well. Here are a few examples. Think of the murder of Israeli athletes at the 1972 Munich Olympics, or of former Baltimore Ravens running back Ray Rice beating his fiancée unconscious in 2014, or of the more recent case of Cleveland Browns defensive end Myles Garrett using his helmet as a weapon to attack an opposing player during an on-field fight in 2019.

Both good and evil are possible, but we want (or at least, we should want) to promote the good. Our understanding of the good shapes; our priorities, our goals,

Subtle Goods/Evils: Those goods we take for granted (e.g., shaking hands) and those evils which we justify and rationalize (e.g., "cheap shots").

Explicit Goods/Evils: Those goods which delight or surprise us (e.g., acts of moral courage). Those evils which shock or abhor us (e.g., the 1972 Olympic massacre).

our evaluations, our relationships, our vision, and our convictions. What does it really mean to be a *good* coach, athlete, sport manager, or person? Answering such questions is at the very root of human life. Some, like Plato, actively and deliberatively seek the good, so that they may fix their eyes upon it. Others doubt that real goods or evils can be found. Many more stagger through life, flitting from one pleasure to another, never stopping to reflect on or seek a foundation for their actions beyond mere desire. What you should see is that each approach is, whether reflective or not, *a philosophy*; a claim to wisdom applied to life. No one can avoid answering the questions of good and evil. Therefore, every man, every woman, and every child's task, whether at home or school, whether at work or play, is to answer these questions well.

Good and evil exist in sport in both explicit and subtle forms. Here we see a subtle good (consolation) as well as—arguably—a subtle evil (indifference by MLB to fan safety). The picture, from May 2019, is of the Chicago Cubs' distraught outfielder Albert Almora Jr. He is being consoled by his teammate Jayson Heyward, after a foul ball Almora hit into the stands accidentally fractured the skull of a two year old girl.
Bob Levey/Stringer/Getty Images Sport/Getty Images

PHILOSOPHIC SELECTIONS

Selection #1: Fyodor Dostoevsky, *The Brothers Karamazov*, Book V Chapters III and IV.

Introduction: As was discussed in the chapter, religious explanations of the transcendent nature of good and evil are common. However, one of the perennial problems in any theistic account of the good is the "problem of evil." The problem of evil can be stated succinctly: If God is good and if God is all-powerful, why is there evil? For if God is good he should prevent evil. Therefore, we must assume he's not all powerful. In contrast, if God is all-powerful and does not do anything about evil, he cannot be called good.

In this selection from *The Brothers Karamazov*, which is believed by many to be greatest novel ever written, we have one of the most famous and compelling retellings of the problem of evil in all of literature. In this scene Ivan (an intellectual) is telling his younger brother Alyosha (a novice monk) why he rejects God. Ivan begins by insisting that even if God is going to justify all things in the end, he rejects it. For justice demands that evil (particular evil to children) is reprehensible. Therefore, if God requires the suffering of the innocent, Ivan wants no part of God. The cost is too high.

"Well, tell me where to begin, give your orders. The existence of God, eh?"

"Begin where you like. You declared yesterday at father's that there was no God." Alyosha looked searchingly at his brother.

"I said that yesterday at dinner on purpose to tease you and I saw your eyes glow. But now I've no objection to discussing with you, and I say so very seriously. I want to be friends with you, Alyosha, for I have no friends and want to try it. Well, only fancy, perhaps I too accept God," laughed Ivan; "that's a surprise for you, isn't it?"

"Yes, of course, if you are not joking now."

"Joking? I was told at the elder's yesterday that I was joking. You know, dear boy, there was an old sinner in the eighteenth century who declared that, if there were no God, he would have to be invented. *S'il n'existait pas Dieu, il faudrait l'inventer.* And man has actually invented God. And what's strange, what would be marvelous, is not that God should really exist; the marvel is that such an idea, the idea of the necessity of God, could enter the head of such a savage, vicious beast as man. So holy it is, so touching, so wise and so great a credit it does to man. As for me, I've long resolved not to think whether man created God or God man. And I won't go through all the axioms laid down by Russian boys on that subject, all derived from European hypotheses; for what's a hypothesis there, is an axiom with the Russian boy, and not only with the boys but with their teachers too, for our Russian professors are often just the same boys themselves. And so I omit all the hypotheses. For what are we aiming at now? I am trying to explain as quickly as possible my essential nature, that is what manner of man I am, what I believe in, and for what I hope, that's it, isn't it? And therefore I tell you that I accept God simply. But you must note this: if God exists and if He really did create the world, then, as we all know, He created it according to the geometry of Euclid and the human mind with the conception of only three dimensions in space. Yet there have been and still are geometricians and philosophers, and even some of the most distinguished, who doubt whether the whole universe, or to speak more widely the whole of being, was only created in Euclid's geometry; they even dare to dream that two parallel lines, which according to Euclid can never meet on earth, may meet somewhere in infinity. I have come to the conclusion that, since I can't understand even that, I can't expect to understand about God. I acknowledge humbly that I have no faculty for settling such questions, I have a Euclidian earthly mind, and how could I solve problems that are not of this world? And I advise you never to think about it either, my dear Alyosha, especially about God, whether He exists or not. All such questions are utterly inappropriate for a mind created with an idea of only three dimensions. And so I accept God and am glad to, and what's more, I accept His wisdom, His purpose—which are utterly beyond our ken; I believe in the underlying order and the meaning of life; I believe in the eternal harmony in which they say we shall one day be blended. I believe in the Word to Which the universe is striving, and Which Itself was 'with God,' and Which Itself is God and so on, and so on, to infinity. There are all sorts of phrases for it. I seem to be on the right path, don't I? Yet would you believe it, in the final result I don't accept this world of God's, and, although I know it exists, I don't accept it at all. It's not that I don't accept God, you must understand, it's the world created by Him I don't and cannot accept. Let me make it plain. I believe like a child that suffering will be healed and made up for, that all the humiliating absurdity of human contradictions will vanish like a pitiful mirage, like the despicable fabrication of the impotent and infinitely small Euclidian mind of man, that in the world's finale, at the moment of eternal harmony, something so precious will come to pass that it will suffice for all hearts, for the comforting of all resentments, for the atonement of all the crimes of humanity, of all the blood they've shed; that it will make it not only possible to forgive but to justify all that has happened with men—but though all that may come to pass, I don't accept it. I won't accept it. Even if parallel lines do meet and I see it myself, I shall see it and say that they've met, but still I won't accept it. That's what's at the root of me, Alyosha; that's my creed. I am in earnest in what I say. I began our talk as stupidly as I could on purpose, but I've led up to my confession, for that's all you want. You didn't want to hear about God, but only to know what the brother you love lives by. And so I've told you" . . . .

"I must make you one confession," Ivan began. "I could never understand how one can love one's neighbors. It's just one's neighbors, to my mind, that one can't love, though one might love those at a distance. I once read somewhere of John the Merciful, a saint, that when a hungry, frozen beggar came to him, he took him into his bed, held him in his arms, and began breathing into his mouth, which was putrid and loathsome from some awful disease. I am convinced that he did that from 'self laceration,' from the self-laceration of falsity, for the sake of the charity imposed by duty, as a penance laid on him. For any one to love a man, he must be hidden, for as soon as he shows his face, love is gone."

"Father Zossima has talked of that more than once," observed Alyosha; "he, too, said that the face of a man often hinders many people not practiced in love, from loving him. But yet there's a great deal of love in mankind, and almost Christ-like love. I know that myself, Ivan."

"Well, I know nothing of it so far, and can't understand it, and the innumerable mass of mankind are with me there. The question is, whether that's due to men's bad qualities or whether it's inherent in their nature. To my thinking, Christ-like love for men is a miracle impossible on earth. He was God. But we are not gods. Suppose I, for instance, suffer intensely. Another can never know how much I suffer, because he is another and not I. And what's more, a man is rarely ready to admit another's suffering (as though it were a distinction). Why won't he admit it, do you think? Because I smell unpleasant, because I have a stupid face, because I once trod on his foot. Besides, there is suffering and suffering; degrading, humiliating suffering such as humbles me—hunger, for instance—my benefactor will perhaps allow me; but when you come to higher suffering—for an idea, for instance—he will very rarely admit that, perhaps because my face strikes him as not at all what he fancies a man should have who suffers for an idea. And so he deprives me instantly of his favor, and not at all from badness of heart.

Beggars, especially genteel beggars, ought never to show themselves, but to ask for charity through the newspapers. One can love one's neighbors in the abstract, or even at a distance, but at close quarters it's almost impossible. If it were as on the stage, in the ballet, where if beggars come in, they wear silken rags and tattered lace and beg for alms dancing gracefully, then one might like looking at them. But even then we should not love them. But enough of that. I simply wanted to show you my point of view. I meant to speak of the suffering of mankind generally, but we had better confine ourselves to the sufferings of the children. That reduces the scope of my argument to a tenth of what it would be. Still we'd better keep to the children, though it does weaken my case. But, in the first place, children can be loved even at close quarters, even when they are dirty, even when they are ugly (I fancy, though, children never are ugly). The second reason why I won't speak of grown-up people is that, besides being disgusting and unworthy of love, they have a compensation—they've eaten the apple and know good and evil, and they have become 'like gods.' They go on eating it still. But the children haven't eaten anything, and are so far innocent. Are you fond of children, Alyosha? I know you are, and you will understand why I prefer to speak of them. If they, too, suffer horribly on earth, they must suffer for their fathers' sins, they must be punished for their fathers, who have eaten the apple; but that reasoning is of the other world and is incomprehensible for the heart of man here on earth. The innocent must not suffer for another's sins, and especially such innocents! You may be surprised at me, Alyosha, but I am awfully fond of children, too. And observe, cruel people, the violent, the rapacious, the Karamazovs are sometimes very fond of children. Children while they are quite little—up to seven, for instance—are so remote from grown-up people; they are different creatures, as it were, of a different species. I knew a criminal in prison who had, in the course of his career as a burglar, murdered whole families, including several children. But when he was in prison, he had a strange affection for them. He spent all his time at his window, watching the children playing in the prison yard. He trained one little boy to come up to his window and made great friends with him . . . . You don't know why I am telling you all this, Alyosha? My head aches and I am sad."

"You speak with a strange air," observed Alyosha uneasily, "as though you were not quite yourself."

"By the way, a Bulgarian I met lately in Moscow," Ivan went on, seeming not to hear his brother's words, "told me about the crimes committed by Turks and Circassians in all parts of Bulgaria through fear of a general rising of the Slavs. They burn villages, murder, outrage women and children, they nail their prisoners by the ears to the fences, leave them so till morning, and in the morning they hang them—all sorts of things you can't imagine. People talk sometimes of bestial cruelty, but that's a great injustice and insult to the beasts; a beast can never be so cruel as a man, so artistically cruel. The tiger only tears and gnaws, that's all he can do. He would never think of nailing people by the ears, even if he were able to do it. These Turks took a pleasure in torturing children, too; cutting the unborn child from the mother's womb, and tossing babies up in the air and catching them on the points of their bayonets before their mothers' eyes. Doing it before the mothers' eyes was what gave zest to the amusement. Here is another scene that I thought very interesting. Imagine a trembling mother with her baby in her arms, a circle of invading Turks around her. They've planned a diversion: they pet the baby, laugh to make it laugh. They succeed, the baby laughs. At that moment a Turk points a pistol four inches from the baby's face. The baby laughs with glee, holds out its little hands to the pistol, and he pulls the trigger in the baby's face and blows out its brains. Artistic, wasn't it? By the way, Turks are particularly fond of sweet things, they say."

"Brother, what are you driving at?" asked Alyosha.

"I think if the devil doesn't exist, but man has created him, he has created him in his own image and likeness."

"Just as he did God, then?" observed Alyosha.

" 'It's wonderful how you can turn words,' as Polonius says in Hamlet," laughed Ivan. "You turn my words against me. Well, I am glad. Yours must be a fine God, if man created Him in his image and likeness. You asked just now what I was driving at. You see, I am fond of collecting certain facts, and, would you believe, I even copy anecdotes of a certain sort from newspapers and books, and I've already got a fine collection. The Turks, of course, have gone into it, but they are foreigners. I have specimens from home that are even better than the Turks. You know we prefer beating—rods and scourges— that's our national institution. Nailing ears is unthinkable for us, for we are, after all, Europeans. But the rod and the scourge we have always with us and they cannot be taken from us. Abroad now they scarcely do any beating. Manners are more humane, or laws have been passed, so that they don't dare to flog men now. But they make up for it in another way just as national as ours. And so national that it would be practically impossible among us, though I believe we are being inoculated with it, since the religious movement began in our aristocracy. I have a charming pamphlet, translated from the French, describing how, quite recently, five years ago, a murderer, Richard, was executed—a young man, I believe, of three and twenty, who repented and was converted to the Christian faith at the very scaffold. This Richard was an illegitimate child who was given as a child of six by his parents to some shepherds on the Swiss mountains. They brought him up to work for them. He grew up like a little wild beast among them. The shepherds taught him nothing, and scarcely fed or clothed him, but sent him out at seven to herd the flock in cold and wet, and no one hesitated or scrupled to treat him so. Quite the contrary, they thought they had every right, for Richard had been given to them as a chattel, and they did not even see the necessity of feeding him. Richard himself describes how in those years, like the Prodigal Son in the Gospel, he longed to eat of the mash given to the pigs, which were fattened for sale. But they wouldn't even give him that, and beat him when he stole from the pigs. And that was how he spent all his childhood and his youth, till he grew up and was strong enough to go away and be a thief. The savage began to earn his living as a day laborer in Geneva. He drank what he earned, he lived like a brute, and finished by killing and robbing an old man. He was caught, tried, and condemned to death. They are not sentimentalists there. And in prison he was immediately surrounded by pastors, members of Christian brotherhoods, philanthropic ladies, and the like. They taught him to read and write in prison, and expounded the Gospel to him. They exhorted him, worked upon him, drummed at him incessantly, till at last he solemnly confessed his crime. He was converted. He wrote to the court himself that he was a monster, but that in the end God had vouchsafed him light and shown grace. All Geneva was in excitement about him—all philanthropic and religious Geneva. All the aristocratic and well-bred society of the town rushed to the prison, kissed Richard and embraced him; 'You are our brother, you have found grace.' And Richard does nothing but weep with emotion, 'Yes, I've found grace! All my youth and childhood I was glad of pigs' food, but now even I have found grace. I am dying in the Lord.' 'Yes, Richard, die in the Lord; you have shed blood and must die. Though it's not your fault that you knew not the Lord, when you coveted the pigs' food and were beaten for stealing it (which was very wrong of you, for stealing is forbidden); but you've shed blood and you must die.' And on the last day, Richard, perfectly limp, did nothing but cry and repeat every minute: 'This is my happiest day. I am going to the Lord.' 'Yes,' cry the pastors and the judges and philanthropic ladies. 'This is the happiest day of your life, for you are going to the Lord!' They all walk or drive to the scaffold in procession behind the prison van. At the scaffold they call to Richard: 'Die, brother, die in the Lord, for even thou hast found grace!' And so, covered with his brothers' kisses, Richard is dragged on to the scaffold, and led to the guillotine. And they chopped off his head in brotherly fashion, because he had found grace. Yes, that's characteristic. That pamphlet is translated into Russian by some Russian philanthropists of aristocratic rank and evangelical aspirations, and has been distributed gratis for the enlightenment of the people. The case of Richard is interesting because it's national. Though to us it's absurd to cut off a man's head, because he has become our brother and has found grace, yet we have our own speciality, which is all but worse. Our historical pastime is the direct satisfaction of inflicting pain. There are lines in Nekrassov describing how a peasant lashes a horse on the eyes, 'on its meek eyes,' every one must have seen it. It's peculiarly Russian. He describes how a feeble little nag has foundered under too heavy a load and cannot move. The peasant beats it, beats it savagely, beats it at last not knowing what he is doing in the intoxication of cruelty, thrashes it mercilessly over and over again. 'However weak you are, you must pull, if you die for it.' The nag strains, and then he begins lashing the poor defenseless creature on its weeping, on its 'meek eyes.' The frantic beast tugs and draws the load, trembling all over, gasping for breath, moving sideways, with a sort of unnatural spasmodic action—it's awful in Nekrassov. But that's only a horse, and God has given horses to be beaten. So the Tatars have taught us, and they left us the knout as a remembrance of it. But men, too, can be beaten. A well-educated, cultured gentleman and his wife beat their own child with a birch-rod, a girl of seven. I have an exact account of it. The papa was glad that the birch was covered with twigs. 'It stings more,' said he, and so he began stinging his daughter. I know for a fact there are people who at every blow are worked up to sensuality, to literal sensuality, which increases progressively at every blow they inflict. They beat for a minute, for five minutes, for ten minutes, more often and more savagely. The child screams. At last the child cannot scream, it gasps, 'Daddy! daddy!' By some diabolical unseemly chance the case was brought into court. A counsel is engaged. The Russian people have long called a barrister 'a conscience for hire.' The counsel protests in his client's defense. 'It's such a simple thing,' he says, 'an everyday domestic event. A father corrects his child. To our shame be it said, it is brought into court.' The jury, convinced by him, give a favorable verdict. The public roars with delight that the torturer is acquitted. Ah, pity I wasn't there! I would have proposed to raise a subscription in his honor! Charming pictures.

"But I've still better things about children. I've collected a great, great deal about Russian children, Alyosha. There was a little girl of five who was hated by her father and mother, 'most worthy and respectable people, of good education and breeding.' You see, I must repeat again, it is a peculiar characteristic of many people, this love of torturing children, and children only. To all other types of humanity these torturers behave mildly and benevolently, like cultivated and humane Europeans; but they are very fond of tormenting children, even fond of children themselves in that sense. It's just their defenselessness that tempts the tormentor, just the angelic confidence of the child who has no refuge and no appeal, that sets his vile blood on fire. In every man, of course, a demon lies hidden—the demon of rage, the demon of lustful heat at the screams of the tortured victim, the demon of lawlessness let off the chain, the demon of diseases that follow on vice, gout, kidney disease, and so on.

"This poor child of five was subjected to every possible torture by those cultivated parents. They beat her, thrashed her, kicked her for no reason till her body was one bruise. Then, they went to greater refinements of cruelty—shut her up all night in the cold and frost in a privy, and because she didn't ask to be taken up at night (as though a child of five sleeping its angelic, sound sleep could be trained to wake and ask), they smeared her face and filled her mouth with excrement, and it was her mother, her mother did this. And that mother could sleep, hearing the poor child's groans! Can you understand why a little creature, who can't even understand what's done to her, should beat her little aching heart with her tiny fist in the dark and the cold, and weep her meek unresentful tears to dear, kind God to protect her? Do you understand that, friend and brother, you pious and humble novice? Do you understand why this infamy must be and is permitted? Without it, I am told, man could not have existed on earth, for he could not have known good and evil. Why should he know that diabolical good and evil when it costs so much? Why, the whole world of knowledge is not worth that child's prayer to 'dear, kind God'! I say nothing of the sufferings of grown-up people, they have eaten the apple, damn them, and the devil take them all! But these little ones! I am making you suffer, Alyosha, you are not yourself. I'll leave off if you like."

"Never mind. I want to suffer too," muttered Alyosha.

"One picture, only one more, because it's so curious, so characteristic, and I have only just read it in some collection of Russian antiquities. I've forgotten the name. I must look it up. It was in the darkest days of serfdom at the beginning of the century, and long live the Liberator of the People! There was in those days a general of aristocratic connections, the owner of great estates, one of those men—somewhat exceptional, I believe, even then—who, retiring from the service into a life of leisure, are convinced that they've earned absolute power over the lives of their subjects. There were such men then. So our general, settled on his property of two thousand souls, lives in pomp, and domineers over his poor neighbors as though they were dependents and buffoons. He has kennels of hundreds of hounds and nearly a hundred dog-boys—all mounted, and in uniform. One day a serf-boy, a little child of eight, threw a stone in play and hurt the paw of the general's favorite hound. 'Why is my favorite dog lame?' He is told that the boy threw a stone that hurt the dog's paw. 'So you did it.' The general looked the child up and down. 'Take him.' He was taken—taken from his mother and kept shut up all night. Early that morning the general comes out on horseback, with the hounds, his dependents, dog-boys, and huntsmen, all mounted around him in full hunting parade. The servants are summoned for their edification, and in front of them all stands the mother of the child. The child is brought from the lock-up. It's a gloomy, cold, foggy autumn day, a capital day for hunting. The general orders the child to be undressed; the child is stripped naked. He shivers, numb with terror, not daring to cry . . . . 'Make him run,' commands the general. 'Run! run!' shout the dog-boys. The boy runs . . . . 'At him!' yells the general, and he sets the whole pack of hounds on the child. The hounds catch him, and tear him to pieces before his mother's eyes! . . . I believe the general was afterwards declared incapable of administering his estates. Well—what did he deserve? To be shot? To be shot for the satisfaction of our moral feelings? Speak, Alyosha!"

"To be shot," murmured Alyosha, lifting his eyes to Ivan with a pale, twisted smile.

"Bravo!" cried Ivan, delighted. "If even you say so . . . . You're a pretty monk! So there is a little devil sitting in your heart, Alyosha Karamazov!"

"What I said was absurd, but—"

"That's just the point, that 'but'!" cried Ivan. "Let me tell you, novice, that the absurd is only too necessary on earth. The world stands on absurdities, and perhaps nothing would have come to pass in it without them. We know what we know!"

"What do you know?"

"I understand nothing," Ivan went on, as though in delirium. "I don't want to understand anything now. I want to stick to the fact. I made up my mind long ago not to understand. If I try to understand anything, I shall be false to the fact, and I have determined to stick to the fact."

"Why are you trying me?" Alyosha cried, with sudden distress. "Will you say what you mean at last?"

"Of course, I will; that's what I've been leading up to. You are dear to me, I don't want to let you go, and I won't give you up to your Zossima."

Ivan for a minute was silent, his face became all at once very sad.

"Listen! I took the case of children only to make my case clearer. Of the other tears of humanity with which the earth is soaked from its crust to its center, I will say nothing. I have narrowed my subject on purpose. I am a bug, and I recognize in all humility that I cannot understand why the world is arranged as it is. Men are themselves to blame, I suppose; they were given paradise, they wanted freedom, and stole fire from heaven, though they knew they would become unhappy, so there is no need to pity them. With my pitiful, earthly, Euclidian understanding, all I know is that there is suffering and that there are none guilty; that cause follows effect, simply and directly; that everything flows and finds its level—but that's only Euclidian nonsense, I know that, and I can't consent to live by it! What comfort is it to me that there are none guilty and that cause follows effect simply and directly, and that I know it?—I must have justice, or I will destroy myself. And not justice in some remote infinite time and space, but here on earth, and that I could see myself. I have believed in it. I want to see it, and if I am dead by then, let me rise again, for if it all happens without me, it will be too unfair. Surely I haven't suffered, simply that I, my crimes and my sufferings, may manure the soil of the future harmony for somebody else. I want to see with my own eyes the hind lie down with the lion and the victim rise up and embrace his murderer. I want to be there when every one suddenly understands what it has all been for. All the religions of the world are built on this longing, and I am a believer. But then there are the children, and what am I to do about them? That's a question I can't answer. For the hundredth time I repeat, there are numbers of questions, but I've only taken the children, because in their case what I mean is so unanswerably clear. Listen! If all must suffer to pay for the eternal harmony, what have children to do with it, tell me, please? It's beyond all comprehension why they should suffer, and why they should pay for the harmony. Why should they, too, furnish material to enrich the soil for the harmony of the future? I understand solidarity in sin among men. I understand solidarity in retribution, too; but there can be no such solidarity with children. And if it is really true that they must share responsibility for all their fathers' crimes, such a truth is not of this world and is beyond my comprehension. Some jester will say, perhaps, that the child would have grown up and have sinned, but you see he didn't grow up, he was torn to pieces by the dogs, at eight years old. Oh, Alyosha, I am not blaspheming! I understand, of course, what an upheaval of the universe it will be, when everything in heaven and earth blends in one hymn of praise and everything that lives and has lived cries aloud: 'Thou art just, O Lord, for Thy ways are revealed.' When the mother embraces the fiend who threw her child to the dogs, and all three cry aloud with tears, 'Thou art just, O Lord!' then, of course, the crown of knowledge will be reached and all will be made clear. But what pulls me up here is that I can't accept that harmony. And while I am on earth, I make haste to take my own measures. You see, Alyosha, perhaps it really may happen that if I live to that moment, or rise again to see it, I, too, perhaps, may cry aloud with the rest, looking at the mother embracing the child's torturer, 'Thou art just, O Lord!' but I don't want to cry aloud then. While there is still time, I hasten to protect myself, and so I renounce the higher harmony altogether. It's not worth the tears of that one tortured child who beat itself on the breast with its little fist and prayed in its stinking outhouse, with its unexpiated tears to 'dear, kind God'! It's not worth it, because those tears are unatoned for. They must be atoned for, or there can be no harmony. But how? How are you going to atone for them? Is it possible? By their being avenged? But what do I care for avenging them? What do I care for a hell for oppressors? What good can hell do, since those children have already been tortured? And what becomes of harmony, if there is hell? I want to forgive. I want to embrace. I don't want more suffering. And if the sufferings of children go to swell the sum of sufferings which was necessary to pay for truth, then I protest that the truth is not worth such a price. I don't want the mother to embrace the oppressor who threw her son to the dogs! She dare not forgive him! Let her forgive him for herself, if she will, let her forgive the torturer for the immeasurable suffering of her mother's heart. But the sufferings of her tortured child she has no right to forgive; she dare not forgive the torturer, even if the child were to forgive him! And if that is so, if they dare not forgive, what becomes of harmony? Is there in the whole world a being who would have the right to forgive and could forgive? I don't want harmony. From love for humanity I don't want it. I would rather be left with the unavenged suffering. I would rather remain with my unavenged suffering and unsatisfied indignation, even if I were wrong. Besides, too high a price is asked for harmony; it's beyond our means to pay so much to enter on it. And so I hasten to give back my entrance ticket, and if I am an honest man I am bound to give it back as soon as possible. And that I am doing. It's not God that I don't accept, Alyosha, only I most respectfully return Him the ticket."

"That's rebellion," murmured Alyosha, looking down.

"Rebellion? I am sorry you call it that," said Ivan earnestly. "One can hardly live in rebellion, and I want to live. Tell me yourself, I challenge you—answer. Imagine that you are creating a fabric of human destiny with the object of making men happy in the end, giving them peace and rest at last, but that it was essential and inevitable to torture to death only one tiny creature—that baby beating its breast with its fist, for instance—and to found that edifice on its unavenged tears, would you consent to be the architect on those conditions? Tell me, and tell the truth."

"No, I wouldn't consent," said Alyosha softly.

Dostoevsky, *The Brothers Karamoazov*, Book V. Public Domain.

Discussion Question(s)

1. Ivan's critique is powerful because there are no easy answers to human suffering, in particular to the profound suffering human beings cause each other. Ivan is right to point out the repugnance of the simplistic, saccharine optimism of many answers to the problem of evil. What the sufferer needs most is sympathy, not justification, even if justification can be found. However, even if clean answers cannot be offered, can legitimate responses be made to Ivan's critique? Here are two responses. Are either compelling?

   a. **Transcendent Response:** God is not the author of evil. Evil is part of a *corrupt* world. Evil is a result of rebellion against God. Evil is not something that is required, but something that we are redeemed from. We should not try to justify the necessity of earthquakes, disease, inhumanity . . . our position should be one of hope, rather than the justification of evil.

   b. **Logical Response:** Evil can and should make us sick to our stomachs. But rather than being a testimony against God it is testimony in his favor. For in a godless world there is no good nor evil. Why? It is hard to say children *should not* die of malnourishment if everything that is, is here by random chance and accident. Then there literally is no way things *should be*.

Selection #2: a. Friedrich Nietzsche, *The Gay Science*, Section 125 "The Madman and the Death of God"; b. Friedrich Nietzsche, *Beyond Good and Evil*, Sections 257–259, "What is Noble?"; c. Friedrich Nietzsche, *The Antichrist*, Section 2, "Goodness and the Will to Power."

Introduction: In these three brief selections from Nietzsche we see his desire to turn the traditional conception of "good and evil" on its head. First, he argues that "God is dead." The "death of God" has implications for theory and practice, all of which Nietzsche is willing to follow through on. Next, Nietzsche argues that the "Will to Power" is the fundamental feature of life. To deny this is mere confusion. Finally, Nietzsche identifies the alleged source of this confusion, the embrace of weakness engendered by Christianity.

2a. *The Gay Science*, Section 125

"The Madman.—Have you ever heard of the madman who on a bright morning lighted a lantern and ran to the market-place calling out unceasingly: "I seek God! I seek God!"—As there were many people standing about who did not believe in God, he caused a great deal of amusement. Why! is he lost? said one. Has he strayed away like a child? said another. Or does he keep himself hidden? Is he afraid of us? Has he taken a sea-voyage? Has he emigrated?—the people cried out laughingly, all in a hubbub. The insane man jumped into their midst and transfixed them with his glances. "Where is God gone?" he called out. "I mean to tell you! *We have killed him,*—you and I! We are all his murderers! But how have we done it? How were we able to drink up the sea? Who gave us the sponge to wipe away the whole horizon? What did we do when we loosened this earth from its sun? Whither does it now move? Whither do we move? Away from all suns? Do we not dash on unceasingly? Back-wards, sideways, forewards, in all directions? Is there still an above and below? Do we not stray, as through infinite nothingness? Does not empty space breathe upon us? Has it not become colder? Does not night come on continually, darker and darker? Shall we not have to light lanterns in the morning? Do we not hear the noise of the grave-diggers who are burying God? Do we not smell the divine putrefaction?—for even Gods putrefy! God is dead! God remains dead! And we have killed him! How shall we console ourselves, the most murderous of all murderers? The holiest and the mightiest that the world has hitherto possessed, has bled to death under our knife,—who will wipe the blood from us? With what water could we cleanse ourselves? What lustrums, what sacred games shall we have to devise? Is not the magnitude of this deed too great for us? Shall we not ourselves have to become Gods, merely to seem worthy of it? There never was a greater event,—and on account of it, all who are born after us belong to a higher history than any history hitherto!"—Here the madman was silent and looked again at his hearers; they also were silent and looked at him in surprise. At last he threw his lantern on the ground, so that it broke in pieces and was extinguished. "I come too early," he then said, "I am not yet at the right time. This prodigious event is still on its way, and is travelling,—it has not yet reached men's ears. Lightning and thunder need time, the light of the stars needs time, deeds need time, even after they are done, to be seen and heard. This deed is as yet further from them than the furthest star,—*and yet they have done it!*"—*It* is further stated that the madman made his way into different churches on the same day, and there intoned his *Requiem æternam*

deo. When led out and called to account, he always gave the reply: "What are these churches now, if they are not the tombs and monuments of God?"—

Nietzsche, *The Gay Science.* Public Domain.

2b. *Beyond Good and Evil,* Sections 257–259

EVERY elevation of the type "man," has hitherto been the work of an aristocratic society and so it will always be—a society believing in a long scale of gradations of rank and differences of worth among human beings, and requiring slavery in some form or other. Without the PATHOS OF DISTANCE, such as grows out of the incarnated difference of classes, out of the constant out-looking and down-looking of the ruling caste on subordinates and instruments, and out of their equally constant practice of obeying and commanding, of keeping down and keeping at a distance—that other more mysterious pathos could never have arisen, the longing for an ever new widening of distance within the soul itself, the formation of ever higher, rarer, further, more extended, more comprehensive states, in short, just the elevation of the type "man," the continued "self-surmounting of man," to use a moral formula in a supermoral sense. To be sure, one must not resign oneself to any humanitarian illusions about the history of the origin of an aristocratic society (that is to say, of the preliminary condition for the elevation of the type "man"): the truth is hard. Let us acknowledge unprejudicedly how every higher civilization hitherto has ORIGINATED! Men with a still natural nature, barbarians in every terrible sense of the word, men of prey, still in possession of unbroken strength of will and desire for power, threw themselves upon weaker, more moral, more peaceful races (perhaps trading or cattle-rearing communities), or upon old mellow civilizations in which the final vital force was flickering out in brilliant fireworks of wit and depravity. At the commencement, the noble caste was always the barbarian caste: their superiority did not consist first of all in their physical, but in their psychical power—they were more COMPLETE men (which at every point also implies the same as "more complete beasts").

Corruption—as the indication that anarchy threatens to break out among the instincts, and that the foundation of the emotions, called "life," is convulsed—is something radically different according to the organization in which it manifests itself. When, for instance, an aristocracy like that of France at the beginning of the Revolution, flung away its privileges with sublime disgust and sacrificed itself to an excess of its moral sentiments, it was corruption:—it was really only the closing act of the corruption which had existed for centuries, by virtue of which that aristocracy had abdicated step by step its lordly prerogatives and lowered itself to a FUNCTION of royalty (in the end even to its decoration and parade-dress). The essential thing, however, in a good and healthy aristocracy is that it should not regard itself as a function either of the kingship or the commonwealth, but as the SIGNIFICANCE and highest justification thereof—that it should therefore accept with a good conscience the sacrifice of a legion of individuals, who, FOR ITS SAKE, must be suppressed and reduced to imperfect men, to slaves and instruments. Its fundamental belief must be precisely that society is NOT allowed to exist for its own sake, but only as a foundation and scaffolding, by means of which a select class of beings may be able to elevate themselves to their higher duties, and in general to a higher EXISTENCE: like those sun-seeking climbing plants in Java—they are called Sipo Matador,—which encircle an oak so long and so often with their arms, until at last, high above it, but supported by it, they can unfold their tops in the open light, and exhibit their happiness.

To refrain mutually from injury, from violence, from exploitation, and put one's will on a par with that of others: this may result in a certain rough sense in good conduct among individuals when the necessary conditions are given (namely, the actual similarity of the individuals in amount of force and degree of worth, and their co-relation within one organization). As soon, however, as one wished to take this principle more generally, and if possible even as the FUNDAMENTAL PRINCIPLE OF SOCIETY, it would immediately disclose what it really is—namely, a Will to the DENIAL of life, a principle of dissolution and decay. Here one must think profoundly to the very basis and resist all sentimental weakness: life itself is ESSENTIALLY appropriation, injury, conquest of the strange and weak, suppression, severity, obtrusion of peculiar forms, incorporation, and at the least, putting it mildest, exploitation;—but why should one for ever use precisely these words on which for ages a disparaging purpose has been stamped? Even the organization within which, as was previously supposed, the individuals treat each other as equal—it takes place in every healthy aristocracy—must itself, if it be a living and not a dying organization, do all that towards other bodies, which the individuals within it refrain from doing to each other it will have to be the incarnated Will to Power, it will endeavour to grow, to gain ground, attract to itself and acquire ascendancy—not owing to any morality or immorality, but because it LIVES, and because life IS precisely Will to Power. On no point, however, is the ordinary consciousness of Europeans more unwilling to be corrected than on this matter, people now rave everywhere, even under the guise of science, about coming conditions of society in which "the exploiting character" is to be absent—that sounds to my ears as if they promised to invent a mode of life which should refrain from all organic functions. "Exploitation" does not belong to a depraved, or imperfect and primitive society it belongs to the nature of the living being as a primary organic function, it is a consequence of the intrinsic Will to Power, which is precisely the Will to Life—Granting that as a theory this is a novelty—as a reality it is the FUNDAMENTAL FACT of all history let us be so far honest towards ourselves!

Nietzsche, *Beyond Good and Evil*. Public Domain.

2c. *The Antichrist*, Section 2

"What is good?—Whatever augments the feeling of power, the will to power, power itself, in man. What is evil?—Whatever springs from weakness. What is happiness?—The feeling that power *increases*—that resistance is overcome.

Not contentment, but more power; *not* peace at any price, but war; *not* virtue, but efficiency (virtue in the Renaissance sense, *virtu*, virtue free of moral acid). The weak and the botched shall perish: first principle of *our* charity. And one should help them to it. What is more harmful than any vice?—Practical sympathy for the botched and the weak—Christianity . . . "

Nietzsche, *The AntiChrist*. Public Domain.

Discussion Question(s)

1. How would Nietzsche's philosophy manifest itself in sport? That is, what implications do Nietzsche's ideas (if taken seriously) have for sporting practice (e.g. winning and losing, cuts, "mercy rules", etc.)?
2. What do you make of Nietzsche's claim that "God is dead"? If true, can good and evil have a grounding in something other than the "will to power"? In other words, is Nietzsche right to assume that without God, traditional morality cannot survive?

3. Can the competitive desire for victory be defended if Nietzsche's "will to power" is denied? Could the concept of sportsmanship be used to make a distinction between the two? If so, what does good sportsmanship look like and how might it reign in competitive excess?

Selection #3: Chris Ballard, *Sports Illustrated*, "A First-time Skydiving Experience, a Fall to Earth and a Terrible Accident," July 28, 2014.

Please read article here: http://www.si.com/edge/2014/07/28/skydiving-accident-unifies-pair-forever.

> **Introduction:** This selection recounts the extraordinary actions of an ordinary man. One of the great benefits of philosophy is that it allows us to settle our principles, so that in moments of crisis, there is a glimmer of hope that we will act as we ought. Our scruples are often tested at the times (and in the ways) we least expect. In an emergency situation, skydiving instructor Dave Hartsock sacrificed himself for a complete stranger. Such dramatic actions bring the importance of good and evil into stark relief. As you read this selection, ask yourself honestly if you would have the courage to do the same thing.

Discussion Question(s)

1. It seems that Dave Hartsock proves that altruism is possible (thinking of others before yourself). Were his actions supererogatory or does goodness demand that his selfless actions were obligatory? That is, they weren't just a choice, but the *right* thing to do?
2. Which of the three schools of thought regarding good and evil would be most likely to encourage people—in situations similar to Dave Hartsock's—to do the right thing? Why?
3. Who or what would you be willing to risk your life for? Why?

Selection #4: Brad Wolverton, *The Chronicle of Higher Education*, "Penn State's Culture of Reverence Led to 'Total Disregard' for Children's Safety," July 12, 2012.

http://www.chronicle.com/article/Penn-States-Culture-of/132853/; *Timothy Sandoval contributed to this article from Philadelphia, Jack Stripling from Washington.*

> **Introduction:** This article recounts several disturbing details regarding the sexual abuse scandal at Penn State University. The scandal centered around former Penn State football defensive coordinator Jerry Sandusky who sexually abused boys both on and off of Penn State's campus. However, the scandal also involved a culture of cover-up and negligence by many other leaders of the university. How did this happen? How was such evil ignored? To what degree is Sandusky responsible? To what degree are university leaders morally (and criminally) culpable for enabling his behavior? Perhaps the article itself reveals an answer to the first question when it recounts that the evidence investigators found suggested that at Penn State, "the corporate brand—and a blind faith in big-time athletics—is often seen as more important than the educational mission." What a strange, but disturbingly common, definition of the good.

A reverence for football was largely to blame for a series of missteps by top Pennsylvania State University administrators in failing to report repeated allegations of child sex abuse by Jerry Sandusky, according to an independent report released on Thursday.

Two Penn State officials—Graham B. Spanier, the university's former president, and Joe Paterno, the revered coach—took the brunt of criticism in the report. They and other top leaders displayed a "total disregard for the safety and welfare" of children, the report says, and hid critical facts from authorities about the alleged abuses.

The report, the culmination of an eight-month investigation by Louis J. Freeh, the former FBI director commissioned by the university's Board of Trustees, also describes repeated breakdowns in board governance and a failure of university officials to carry out provisions of the Clery Act, the federal law requiring the reporting of crimes like the ones Mr. Sandusky committed. He was convicted last month on 45 counts of molesting children.

In a televised news conference in Philadelphia, Mr. Freeh stopped short of describing a cover-up by university officials, instead saying that senior leaders had "repeatedly concealed facts." But various e-mails and documents suggest that Mr. Spanier and Mr. Paterno, along with Gary C. Schultz, the former senior vice president for finance and business, and Timothy M. Curley, the athletic director now on administrative leave, knew for years about the sexual nature of accusations against Mr. Sandusky and kept them under wraps.

"The most powerful men at Penn State failed to take any steps for 14 years to protect the children who Sandusky victimized," Mr. Freeh said. Those four administrators "never demonstrated, through actions or words, any concern for the safety and well-being of Sandusky's victims until after Sandusky's arrest."

The findings of the 267-page report could be seen as evidence of a changing university climate in which the corporate brand—and a blind faith in big-time athletics—is often seen as more important than the educational mission.

"The university completely abdicated its role as an educational institution committed to the public good in order to protect its corporate brand, image, and market value," said Michael D. Giardina, an assistant professor of sport management and associate director of the Center for Physical Cultural Studies at Florida State University. "The outrage over this case is certainly justified, and we should encourage greater degrees of transparency and accountability in our institutions.

"At the same time," he continued, "we shouldn't overlook or forget that the corporate university of today makes ethically suspect decisions all the time."

Bad Decisions

Top university officials first had concerns about Mr. Sandusky's behavior around children in May 1998, according to the report, after the mother of an 11-year-old boy reported that the coach had showered with her son in the Lasch football building. The campus police began an investigation, which Mr. Schultz was immediately informed of.

In a confidential note, Mr. Schultz wrote, "Behavior—at best inappropriate @ worst sexual improprieties." He also noted, "Is this the opening of Pandora's box?" and "Other children?"

The head of the police decided against pressing charges against the coach, saying, "I can justify that decision because of the lack of clear evidence of a crime." Mr. Curley then notified Mr. Spanier and Mr. Schultz that he had "touched base with" Mr. Paterno about the incident, and Mr. Sandusky continued to coach.

Days later, when the university's trustees met, Mr. Spanier did not notify them of the continuing investigation, a disturbing pattern he repeated during a 2001 investigation into the coach, the report says.

"By not promptly and fully advising the Board of Trustees about the 1998 and 2001 child-sexual-abuse allegations against Sandusky and the subsequent grand-jury investigation of him, Spanier failed in his duties as president," the report concludes. "The board also failed in its duties to oversee the president and senior university officials in 1998 and 2001 by not inquiring about important university matters and by not creating an environment where senior university officials felt accountable."

Reporting problems were not contained to corner offices. Several staff members and coaches regularly observed Mr. Sandusky showering with young boys in the university's Lasch building before 1998, but none of them reported the behavior to their superiors. In 2000 a temporary janitor observed Mr. Sandusky pinning a boy against a wall in the Lasch building and performing oral sex on him. The janitor told a fellow worker what he had seen, stating that he had "fought in the [Korean] War, . . . seen people with their guts blowed out, arms dismembered. . . . I just witnessed something in there I'll never forget."

When one of the janitors suggested reporting the problem, the other said, "No, they'll get rid of all of us."

That fear of taking on football was pervasive at the university, Mr. Freeh said at the news conference. "They knew who Sandusky was," he said of the janitors. "They said the university would circle around it. It was like going against the president of the United States. If that's the culture on the bottom, God help the culture at the top."

A Change of Mind

During the 2001 investigation, Mr. Schultz consulted with Wendell V. Courtney, the university's outside counsel, "re reporting of suspected child abuse," according to documents Mr. Freeh's investigators found.

Mr. Spanier, Mr. Schultz, and Mr. Curley then met to discuss the situation. Mr. Schultz's confidential notes indicated that he spoke with Mr. Curley, reviewed the history of the 1998 incident, and agreed that Mr. Curley would discuss the matter with Mr. Paterno.

Mr. Schultz made notes suggesting that the university should report Mr. Sandusky to the state's Department of Public Welfare, saying: "Unless he confesses to having a problem, [Curley] will indicate we need to have DPW review the matter as an independent agency concerned w child welfare."

The three administrators devised a plan, reflected in Mr. Schultz's notes, that would include telling the chair of the board of the Second Mile, the charity Mr. Sandusky started and where he preyed on children, and asking the coach to avoid bringing children alone into the Lasch building.

But after Mr. Curley later spoke with Mr. Paterno, the athletic director e-mailed Mr. Spanier and Mr. Schultz, saying he had changed his mind about the plan. Instead, Mr. Curley proposed telling Mr. Sandusky that "we feel there is a problem" and offering him "professional help."

"This approach is acceptable to me," Mr. Spanier wrote in an e-mail to Mr. Schultz and Mr. Curley. "The only downside for us is if the message isn't 'heard' and acted upon, and we then become vulnerable for not having reported it.

"But that can be assessed down the road," he continued. "The approach you outline is humane and a reasonable way to proceed."

Those decisions, the report says, illustrate a "striking lack of empathy for child-abuse victims by the most senior leaders of the university."

Mr. Spanier, who was interviewed by Mr. Freeh's staff in early July, told the investigators that he had never heard a report from anyone that Mr. Sandusky was engaged in any sexual abuse of children. Both Mr. Schultz and Mr. Curley, who face charges of lying to a grand jury and failing to report child abuse, have also denied knowing that Mr. Sandusky's behavior was of a sexual nature.

The report paints a different picture, stating that top officials abdicated their responsibilities in the interest of avoiding bad publicity.

"It is more reasonable to conclude that, in order to avoid the consequences of bad publicity, the most powerful leaders at Penn State University," including Mr. Spanier, Mr. Schultz, Mr. Paterno, and Mr. Curley, "repeatedly concealed critical facts relating to Sandusky's child abuse from the authorities, the Board of Trustees, the Penn State community, and the public at large," the report says. "Although concern to treat the child abuser humanely was expressly stated, no such sentiments were ever expressed by them for Sandusky's victims."

The revelations could lead to an indictment of Mr. Spanier, one legal expert told The Chronicle.

"The Freeh report is a scathing indictment of Graham Spanier and others who fostered a culture at Penn State that valued football over possible child sexual-assault victims," said John M. Burkoff, a University of Pittsburgh law professor and expert on criminal law in Pennsylvania. "It certainly appears to me that an actual indictment of Spanier would appear now to be all but inevitable."

Sense of Relief

The report, which was released three weeks after Mr. Sandusky's conviction, left some members of the Penn State community feeling bruised.

"This is very painful for those who love Penn State, and this is personally embarrassing for me," said Scott Kretchmar, a professor of exercise and sport science who was the university's faculty athletics representative from 2000 to 2010. "But it also brings a sense of relief. Waiting and not knowing is, in some ways, harder than getting the story—as difficult as it may be."

People with strong connections to Mr. Paterno felt let down—not so much by the late coach, but by an investigative process that they feel treated him unfairly. Brian Masella, a member of the group Penn Staters for Responsible Stewardship, who played for Mr. Paterno in the 1970s, generally defended the coach and said he did not believe that all the facts had come out.

"When you're a second or third party to information and you did not have that first-hand knowledge, how are you going to accuse and report somebody?" he said.

Matthew Casey, a lawyer for several of the boys who were molested by Mr. Sandusky, said the document gives clues about how liable the university might be for the criminal activity that took place there.

"It was even worse than the leaked information might have suggested," Mr. Casey said. "Words like 'concealment,' words like 'shocking,' used by a former federal judge who was hired by Penn State—those are bad words for any institution that now has to assess their own liability."

Jeffrey P. Fritz, who represents another victim of Mr. Sandusky, said he and his client would look at the report and consider their options, including the possibility of pursuing civil action against "anyone who's responsible for what happened."

"There is no question that these weren't mistakes," Mr. Fritz said. "These were crimes which occurred, and I would anticipate that the attorney general's office would be bringing further charges."

Fallout from the scandal has affected Chad Seifried at a personal and professional level. He grew up in State College, Pa., and played high-school basketball in the early 1990s with some of Mr. Sandusky's sons, even spending time in the coach's house. He later played basketball for the Nittany Lions while Mr. Curley was the athletic director, and got to know Mr. Spanier.

Now an assistant professor and the graduate coordinator for sport management at Louisiana State University at Baton Rouge, Mr. Seifried is co-editing a special issue of the Journal of Issues in Intercollegiate Athletics, due out early next year, that is focused on the problems at Penn State.

Following the release of the Freeh report, his first concern was to take stock of what the people at Penn State think about themselves. "We need to keep reminding ourselves as Penn Staters of all the good things we've done in light of all the things that have come out," he said. "But if we had things wrong, we need to look at how to fix those things."

"When you don't have oversight on people either because they created a long legacy of making decisions at the university, or you relax because you think they'll continue to do the right thing," he said, "there's some danger in that."

A Turning Point?

Ellen Staurowsky, a professor of sport management at Drexel University, sat in the courtroom during the Sandusky trial and is considering writing a book on the news media's role in the scandal.

She is concerned that the university will try to distance itself from the report's negative news before adequately responding to the problems it details.

"There's a natural tendency to want to separate away and say, 'Well, Sandusky was a pedophile, and that didn't have anything to do with us.' Or, 'We had a couple of leaders who were bad leaders but who didn't have anything to do with us,'" she said. "But until people there admit that these events are actually saying something about who they are, there will be no closure on this."

Two days before the report was released, Penn State trustees met privately to discuss how they might respond to Mr. Freeh's findings. Among their considerations were protecting the confidentiality of sensitive documents that the university had turned over to Mr. Freeh's investigators, ESPN reported. The Freeh report quoted extensively from those documents, and civil litigants and criminal defendants will very likely seek their disclosure from the university.

But if that's one of the takeaways for trustees, it worries Ms. Staurowsky. "If this is all just a matter of avoiding liability, then I don't think the real lessons from this case have been learned," she said.

It is unclear what changes Penn State might make in response to the report's recommendations. The university approved a new policy this week limiting access to its athletics facilities to players and athletics personnel during normal operating hours. The move is part of a plan to provide the "safest environment possible to our constituents," according to a university statement.

But as long as its leadership has a reputation for showing a "total and consistent disregard" for the welfare of children, the university will continue to face fallout, said Teresa Valerio Parrot, a crisis-communications expert at TVP Communications.

Other observers, however, said the way the university has handled the crisis in recent months may help it put the story to rest sooner than if it had made different choices.

"They wouldn't have been able to put this behind them for the next several years if they hadn't gone about doing this the way they've done it—getting someone like Judge Freeh, whose character is pretty unassailable and who was given carte blanche to see what he found and report it without fear or favor," said John F. Burness, a visiting professor of public policy at Duke University and the university's spokesman during the 2007 lacrosse scandal.

"There is some very bad news in here for Penn State and Coach Paterno and a lot of the leadership of Penn State," he said. "But this is a really critical inflection point for the institution because it is one of the thresholds they had to get through. As difficult as it will be, it was necessary to restore confidence in the integrity of the institution."

Discussion Question(s)

1. In what ways were the evils committed at Penn State subtle (those evils we ignore, tolerate and justify)? In what ways were the evils committed at Penn State explicit (evils that shock or abhor us)?
2. What good can come from shedding light on the Sandusky Scandal? What good can come at Penn State? What good can come to our larger athletics culture?
3. Is the Penn State situation an outlier? Or, should the lesson be one of sobriety? That is, if it can happen at Penn State, it can happen anywhere?

Suggested Readings

Athletes often forced into heartbreaking decisions. (2007, May 13). Retrieved September 29, 2015, from www.ESPN.com: http://sports.espn.go.com/ncaa/news/story?id=2865230

Skillen, A. (1998). Sport is for losers. In M. McNamee, & S. Parry, *Ethics and Sport* (pp. 169–181). New York, NY: Routledge.

Stripling, J. (2014, October 23). Widespread nature of Chapel Hill's academic fraud is laid bare. Retrieved September 29, 2015, from www.chronicle.com: http://chronicle.com/article/Widespread-Nature-of-Chapel/149603/

Ungerleider, S. (2001). *Faust's gold: Inside the East German doping machine.* New York, NY: St. Martin's Press.

Bibliography

Aggasi, A. (2009). *Open.* New York, NY: Vintage Books.

Arnold, P. J. (1983). Three approaches towards and understanding of sportsmanship. *Journal of the Philosophy of Sport, X,* 61–70.

Augustine, St. (1958). *The city of God.* (G. G. Walsh, D. B. Zema, G. Monahan, & D. J. Honan, Trans.) New York, NY: Bantam Doubleday.

Augustine, St. (1997). *On Christian teaching.* (R. Green, Trans.) New York, NY: Oxford University Press.

Barron, F. R. (2013, January 31). *Fr. Robert Barron on faith, hope, and love.* Retrieved from www.wordonfire.org: http://www.wordonfire.org/resources/video/faith-hope-and-love/264/

Carty, J. (2005, January 2). With game on the line, defense fails. *Ann Arbor News,* D1.

Dixon, N. (1993). On sportsmanship and "running up the score". *Journal of the Philosophy of Sport, XIX,* 1–13.

Grys. (1996). The Olympic idea transcending war. *Olympic Review, 8,* 68–69.

Guttmann, A. (2002). *The Olympics* (2nd ed.). Champaign, IL: University of Illinois Press.

Jeffries, S. (2009, October 28). *Why did Andre Agassi hate tennis?* Retrieved September 25, 2015, from www.theguardian.com: http://www.theguardian.com/sport/2009/oct/29/andre-agassi-hate-tennis.

Klemko, R. (2012, January 10). *Packers coach Joe Philbin's son found dead in river.* Retrieved September 28, 2015, from www.USAtoday.com: http://usatoday30.usatoday.com/sports/football/nfl/packers/story/2012-01-10/joe-philbin-son-dead/52479770/1

Leonard, G. B. (1973). Winning isn't everything. It is nothing. *Intellectual Digest, 4,* 45–47.

Nietzsche, F. (1997). *Beyond good and evil: Prelude to a philosophy of the future* (H. Zimmern, Trans.). Mineola, NY: Dover Publications.

Ogden, M. (2009, 19 November). *Thierry Henry admits to handball that defeated Ireland in World Cup play-off.* Retrieved September 23, 2015, from telegraph.co.uk: http://www.telegraph.co.uk/sport/football/teams/republic-of-ireland/6599687/Thierry-Henry-admits-to-handball-that-defeated-Ireland-in-World-Cup-play-off.html

Pieper, J. (2011). *The Christian idea of man.* South Bend, IN: St. Augustine's Press.

Plato. (2000). *The Republic.* (B. Jowett, Trans.) Mineola, NY: Dover.

Pojman, L. P., & Vaughn, L. (2011). *The moral life: An introductory reading in ethics and literature* (4th ed.). New York, NY: Oxford University Press.

Ratner-Rosenhagen, J. (2012). *American Nietzsche.* Chicago, IL: The University of Chicago Press.

Twietmeyer, G. (2012). The merits and demerits of pleasure in kinesiology. *Quest, 64*(3), 177–186.

Wang, R. R. (n.d.). *Yinyang (Yin-yang).* Retrieved September 18, 2015, from Internet encyclopedia of philosophy: http://www.iep.utm.edu/yinyang/

Weijers, D. (n.d.). *Hedonism.* Retrieved September 21, 2015, from Internet encyclopedia of philosophy: http://www.iep.utm.edu/hedonism/

Wine, S. (2005, January 2). An improbable finish. *AP report in the Ann Arbor News.*

Woollaston, V. (2013, June 19). *We'll be uploading our entire MINDS to computers by 2045 and our bodies will be replaced by machines within 90 years, Google expert claims.* Retrieved September 25, 2015, from www.dailymail.co.uk: http://www.dailymail.co.uk/sciencetech/article-2344398/Google-futurist-claims-uploading-entire-MINDS-computers-2045-bodies-replaced-machines-90-years.html

Chapter 3

Realism and Relativism in Sport

"Man is the measure of all things."   —Protagoras[1]

Learning Objectives & Outcomes

Students will be able to:

1. Define moral realism and moral relativism.
2. Explain how assenting to moral realism or moral relativism will necessarily lead to very different places, priorities, outcomes, and choices when applied to sports ethics.
3. Summarize the strengths and weaknesses of moral realism and moral relativism.
4. Evaluate Twietmeyer's claim that "moral realism is the only tenable position."
5. Apply the philosophic claims made by realists and relativists to concrete moral dilemmas in sport (such as the 2008 Olympic boycott controversy).

Moral Realism: The claim that *real* and objective answers to moral questions exist and can (at least sometimes) be found.

Moral Relativism: The claim that morality is merely the result of cultural forces. That is, morality is *relative* to race, religion, language, etc.

This chapter deals with one simple question: Are objective moral claims possible? Is ethics about finding real answers to moral questions or is ethics merely about stating one's opinions regarding this or that ethical controversy? The belief that ethics allows for finding, at least on occasion, objective answers that are true and binding on all peoples at all times and in all cultures is called **moral realism** (or just *realism* for short). It is so called because the truth of moral claims is considered to be real, that is, existing beyond the vagaries of time, space and human culture or history. There are, according to realists, right and wrong answers to moral questions because true moral claims reflect *reality*. Moreover, these answers can be found with careful reflection and reasoning. Moral truth exists.

In contrast, the belief that ethics is merely the expression of the language, history, and prejudices of this or that particular culture is called **moral relativism** (or just *relativism* for short).[2] This position is so called because moral claims are relative to different aspects of culture. There is not moral truth, but "moral truths," that is, *claims* to truth that are held by their claimants not because of the claims' actual veracity but because of the claimant's sex or religion or race or language or nationality, etc. This is what the pre-Socratic philosopher Protagoras meant when he argued that "Man is the measure of all

---

[1] Plato, *Theaetetus*, 152a.

[2] The related position of emotivism is worth brief mention. Emotivism is the claim that "all evaluative judgments and more specifically all moral judgments are *nothing but* expressions of preference, expressions of attitude or feeling, insofar as they are moral or evaluative in character" (MacIntyre, 1984, p. 12). Ethics is about expressing our feelings not truth.

things." Given this position, there can be no morally binding claims that transcend individual preference or cultural bias. This is because, "normality, in short, within a very wide range, is culturally defined" (Benedict, 1934, p. 73). Morality is no more than competing preferences. Crude contemporary expressions of this position often sound something like this, "Sure I don't like X (this or that moral behavior or position), but who am I to say that X is wrong?" Moral "truth" is relative.

If you reflect on the previous two chapters of this book in reference to the discussion of realism and relativism, you should notice two things. First, you should notice that we have already indirectly addressed this topic. In Chapter 1, we examined the question of "why bother with sports ethics?" and you may recall that it was argued there that "the ethical attitudes we have and endorse, as well as the decisions we make or fail to make will have a profound effect on how sport is practiced" (p. 11). Yet, if moral relativism is true, then there isn't *really* a right or wrong answer to any moral problem. There are only preferences and biases which express themselves relative to our culture, race, religion, etc. But if that is true, then how can one say that the impact of decisions could be evaluated? In fact, how could one even say that the impact is "profound"!?! After all, according to a consistent moral relativism even the claim to profundity is culturally conditioned.[3]

Can we say with confidence that some things are right and other things are wrong?
Xinhua News Agency/Getty Images

---

[3] "Now, to return to my subject, I think there is nothing barbarous and savage in that nation, from what I have been told, except that each man calls barbarism whatever is not his own practice; for indeed it seems we have no other test of truth and reason than the example and pattern of the opinions of the country we live in. *There* is always the perfect religion, the perfect government, the perfect and accomplished manners in all things" (Montaigne, 1948, p. 152).

In Chapter 2, the question of the truth status of moral claims was implicated in all three schools of thought which we examined. However, it was perhaps most obvious in the position of Nietzsche, who claimed that "traditional morality" was a (Christian) fiction that should recede in the face of the "will to power." Though not precisely congruent, the claims that "good and evil are an illusion" and that "truth is relative" have much in common. At the very least, each seeks to shake the confidence contemporary people have in traditional moral norms. Can convincing reasons be given to reject such doubts regarding moral truth?

The second thing you should notice is that the truth status of moral claims is a vitally important question. If we endorse and cultivate realism we'll end up with very different normative understandings of the goods of our culture, our sports and ourselves, than if we endorse and cultivate relativism. In fact, it can be plausibly argued that the only "objective" value that can withstand the acid of moral relativism is hedonism. This is because everyone values pleasure, even if they do not all find pleasure in the same things. More will be said on this in Chapter 4. For now, it suffices to simply reinforce our recurring point that philosophy makes a difference. If we believe that moral questions can have objective answers *that matters!* If we believe that moral questions are merely the result of upbringing, culture and "taste" *that matters as well!* Endorsing one or the other will have a direct impact on how we lead our lives.[4]

Consider the idea this way. If we look for moral truth in a world that has none, we're not only mistaken, we're wasting precious time. If, on the other hand, due to an erroneous commitment to relativism, we are oblivious to the reality of moral truth, we're not only missing out on truth, we're likely going to encounter more confusion, pain, and

Our choices make a real difference.
Fuse/Getty Images

---

[4] Or perhaps better put, how we lead our lives indicates what we believe. See for example (James, 1896/1956).

foolishness in the course of our lives and the lives of those we love. For we will have failed to recognize or follow through on important moral realities. Furthermore, these two positions (realism and relativism) are irreconcilable. If moral truth exists, relativism is wrong. If moral claims are nothing more than the expression of our cultural heritage and personal attributes (language, sex, religion, etc.) then realism is wrong. In this instance at least, there is no middle ground.

Therefore we will proceed in the following manner. First, we will examine the strengths and weaknesses of moral relativism. This will be followed by a brief examination of realism. It will be my contention in this chapter that any intellectually consistent philosophy will necessarily endorse some form of moral realism. The chapter will then close with the application of realism and relativism to the world of sport. Why and how does the status of moral truth matter to athletes, coaches, administrators or fans?

The Strengths of Relativism

There are three common arguments in favor of moral relativism which we will consider in turn. First, is the claim that moral relativism is epistemologically modest. **Epistemology**, from the Greek word for knowledge, is the philosophical study of what can be known. The point that the defenders of relativism are making is that relativism does not make unsupportable claims to moral truth. It modestly allows each culture to define "truth" for itself rather than imposing one set of moral claims upon all cultures. Second, is the claim that relativism is tolerant. Because relativists are modest regarding what can be known about right and wrong, they are tolerant of those individuals and cultures which deviate from their own cultural norms. Third, is the claim that relativism is empirically verifiable. The point the relativists are making here is a simple one; if you look around the world it seems quite clear that ethics differs in China and the USA, or between young and old, or between Christians and Buddhists, etc. Therefore, it would seem clear that relativism is true because different cultures, peoples and religious communities believe different things regarding ethics.

Epistemology: The branch of philosophy which studies the nature of knowledge. That is, what do we know and how do we know it? What does it mean to know? What forms of knowledge claims deserve intellectual assent? What forms of knowledge claims deserve to be treated with skepticism, etc.?

Modesty, Tolerance, and Empiricism, Oh My!

One of the elements of relativism that is attractive to many people today is its apparent resistance to "dogmatism," by which most people mean an over-confidence regarding the truth of moral claims. Dogmatism leads to the imposition of one culture's values upon the values of another culture. In contrast, relativism modestly allows for a plurality of moral systems and moral claims. This is because the moral claims one endorses are said to be *merely* the result of one's individual characteristics and cultural inheritance. Moral claims are not really true. Instead, moral claims are the expression of what are ultimately idiosyncratic desires.

Although moral claims might be useful—in that they order our societies and make our day to day lives go better—they have no truth value beyond such utility.[5] They are conventions based not in reality but rather convenience and custom. To claim otherwise, is to immodestly impose one's own values upon others by mistaking custom for truth. It is to claim moral knowledge that simply is not there.

As such the one great sin most relativists are willing to condemn is the sin of intolerance. By which they mean the public expression of objective moral claims. One is free to hold to the truth of their own moral code in private. However one should not bind others to one's

---

[5] One should see here an echo of the "useful fiction" idea discussed during our examination of Nietzsche in Chapter 2.

own moral claims. Again, this is because one's own code is not based in reality but in one's own culture or personal characteristics. It is OK for a "Catholic" to think "Catholic" things. However, it is intolerant for a "Catholic" to suggest that others should recognize the truth of "Catholic" claims. "Catholic" is, of course in scare quotes here, because it is simply one type of cultural category to which the relativistic claim would hold (such as "male," "American," "Buddhist," etc.). This type of tolerance is important, so it is argued, because it allows for a broad range of moral claims to stand on equal footing in the public sphere. Given the all too common reality of moral bullying, it only makes sense in a pluralistic society to mute the "moral confidence" of those who would impose their values on others.[6]

Descriptive Relativism:
The claim that any careful survey of human customs, cultures, moral codes, and behaviors will reveal that human beings disagree in a multitude of ways regarding what is morally right or wrong.

The relativist's call for modestly and tolerance is then buttressed by the claim that relativism is empirically true. When we look around the world we see countless moral beliefs and practices. This position is also sometimes called **descriptive relativism**, because it describes the myriad ways people behave. What moral relativists mean when they make the descriptive relativism argument is that any careful survey of human customs, cultures, moral codes and behaviors will reveal that human beings disagree in a multitude of ways regarding what is morally right or wrong. The reason such disagreement persists is because *culture* (rather than truth) is the foundation of moral claims. Descriptive relativism proves moral relativism. A famous story told by the ancient Greek historian Herodotus (1952) will illustrate the point well:

> "Darius [the king of Persia], after he had got the kingdom, called into his presence certain Greeks who were at hand, and asked—'What he should pay them to eat the bodies of their fathers when they died?' To which they answered, that there was no sum that would tempt them to such a thing. He then sent for certain Indians, of the race called Callatians, men who eat their fathers, and asked them, while the Greeks stood by, and knew by the help of an interpreter all that was said—'What he should give them to burn the bodies of their fathers at their decease?' The Indians exclaimed aloud, and bade him forbear such language. Such is men's wont herein; and Pindar was right, in my judgment, when he said, 'Law [Custom] is king o'er all'" (pp. 97–98).

Ben Radford/Corbis Sport/Getty Images

Was Herodotus right: Is custom king o'er all?
Bettmann/Getty Images

---

[6] In an ironic inversion, relativists seem oblivious to the possibility that they might be imposing their "moral doubt" on others and that such an imposition runs the same risk of moral bullying as does "moral confidence".

It follows from examples such as this, so relativists commonly argue, that moral relativism is the necessary outcome of any serious reflection on the truth status of moral claims.

The Weaknesses of Relativism

Although all of these arguments can initially seem quite compelling they each have serious —even fatal—flaws. Why, then, are the arguments compelling? Because they each contain partial truths. Modestly and tolerance are good things.[7] It is also quite clear that culture, language, and religion influence our moral beliefs and actions. "Americans" are likely to espouse "American" values, "English speakers" are inclined think within the forms and limitations of the "English language" and "Baptists" are inclined to believe "Baptist" doctrine.

The problem for the proponents of relativism is that admitting these partial truths does nothing to strengthen the arguments put forth in favor of moral relativism. To see why this is the case, let us again examine each in turn. The first argument was that relativism was epistemologically modest. This is so because the moral skepticism of the relativist is said to be cautious regarding the status of any specific moral claim. The realist, for example, might insist that "genetic engineering in sport is immoral." In contrast, the relativist could say something to the effect that "21st Century Americans find genetic engineering to be immoral." It seems clear that the latter is a more cautious assertion than the former. Does this not prove the general point that relativists are more modest than realists regarding moral claims?

The answer is no for two reasons. First, because each type of claim requires epistemic confidence; (in each instance, we have to claim *with confidence* that *we know* or claim *with confidence* that *we don't know*). Whether the claim regards genetic engineering or anything else, whether the claim is for or against any specific morally controversial practice, each type of claim boils down to either; 1. "x is/is not ethical" or 2. "the belief that x is/is not ethical is a function of x's culture." Again, each of these claims *requires* real knowledge. In fact, claim two requires more knowledge than claim one! Claim one needs to rehearse, evaluate and then endorse the reasons (to stick with the example) that genetic engineering is immoral, while claim two needs to do consider all that philosophical work *and* further claim that it is clear that those reasons are *only found to be compelling* because of the culture in which they have been made.[8] That may or may not be true, but in either case it is a bold rather than a modest claim.

Second, this lack of modesty is the case in all instances. Relativism is by definition a comprehensive claim. It is a brutish position *with no in principle room for nuance.* The realist, in contrast, can admit the influence of culture on our thinking, even to a great degree, as long as he holds out the smallest of room for the reality of truth. In other words, realists do not need to deny the importance and power of culture. They simply

---

[7] Notice what has been said. Modesty and tolerance are good things. To say that they are good would seem to be very close to saying that they are true. That is, their goodness is not mere preference or individual idiosyncrasy but rather an objective reality.

[8] This would require not only a mastery of philosophy and a basic understanding of the scientific details of genetic engineering, it would also require a comprehensive understanding of the anthropology, history, sociology and psychology of the culture, in which the claim was being made.

needs to deny that morality is *only* a matter of culture. The relativist, on the other hand, cannot admit the slightest influence of truth and remain a relativist![9]

What then of the second argument, that relativists are more tolerant than realists? This alleged strength of relativism actually points out its most glaring weakness; the fact that relativism is self-defeating. How so? This is the case because the claim that relativism is more tolerant than realism relies on an implicit commitment to *the truth (and goodness) of tolerance*. As the philosopher Mary Midgley (1981; 2003) puts it, "We are rightly angry with those who despise, oppress or steamroll other cultures. We think that doing these things is actually *wrong*" (p. 84).

Yet, according to a consistent relativism either the virtue of tolerance is not really true (or good) or tolerance is reducible to a cultural preference. In either case the relativist has no real grounds upon which to defend the importance of tolerance. For there is, according to their own philosophy, no reason (other than cultural whim) to judge that "tolerance" is better than "intolerance."

Unfortunately for the relativists this problem only compounds. For relativism is itself a *truth claim*. This means that for relativism to have any value, the relativist is bound by the logic that there is at least one truth (relativism). Yet, this admission would paradoxically falsify the truth of relativism by claiming the absurd; "the one truth is 'that there is no truth.'" Likewise, if we can suppose that there is one objective truth (relativism) why couldn't we suppose that there are others? It is in this sense that philosophers mean that relativism is self-defeating. The very assertion of relativism necessarily undermines the truth of relativism.

If the relativist answers such criticism by claiming that it is only *moral truth* that does not exist, they are still stuck in a self-defeating position. To claim that relativism is merely one more relativistic expression of any particular culture's fabricated moral code again means that relativism isn't really true. If the relativist were to try to respond to this problem by saying that in asserting relativism they are moving beyond "truth" and "falsity," they would only end up emasculating their position in the name of consistency. As Philosopher Edward Feser (2015) points out, any one claiming to move beyond truth and falsity,

> "cannot really claim to be asserting any proposition or statement at all, since a proposition or statement is susceptible of being either true or false. His utterance of 'There is no truth' will therefore have to be taken as a mere string of sounds lacking meaning or semantic content—like a grunt or a moan—rather than as a literal English sentence"(para. 16).

The bottom line is this: The relativist is not outside their own system. According to their own philosophy, their claim to relativism is itself merely the expression of the "faculty lounge" or "post-modernity" or what have you. Yet that means relativism is not really true. As a result, to say that "tolerance is a good thing" and actually mean it, is to be a realist. It is to stake a claim to the truth of a universal moral reality.

---

[9] Perhaps equally important in practice is that relativists cannot brook any moral dissent from their position. For their claim is a universal acid *dissolving all moral claims*. Which means anyone who disagrees with them by asserting this or that truth, must be acting out of one of two *intolerable* vices; ignorance or malice. That is, their opponents are either stupid people who can't understand the reality of relativism or they are bad people who malevolently suppress the recognition of relativism for their own selfish motives. To assume either motive does not encourage tolerance of one's opponents. Realists on the other hand can in principle (if not always in practice) allow for serious debate and discussion, for even deeply opposed sides within the realist camp would each admit that the truth exists. This means that realism at its best is about confession (declaring the reasons for one's beliefs) and persuasion rather than imposition or compulsion.

Let us conclude this section by examining more closely the argument that relativism is empirically true. Does the truth of descriptive relativism prove moral relativism? How much argumentative weight in favor of relativism should the reality of moral diversity carry? It is, after all, a demonstrable fact that different peoples and different cultures have different moral beliefs and behaviors. It is quite clear that ethics in both theory and practice differs around the globe and across time. How then can it be that relativism is false?

Two important responses to descriptive relativism can be offered. First, many have claimed that upon closer analysis, it may be that there is deeper moral agreement than a superficial examination allows for. This doesn't mean there aren't obvious and real moral disagreements across cultures.[10] The point is that these disagreements often hide more fundamental moral agreements. We may disagree, for example over what is the best way to promote sexual equality in sport, even as both parties agree that men and women should be treated equally in sport. One party might think **Title IX** is functioning well, while another party might think that Title IX needs to be reformed.[11] In each case the desire of each party is for a just and equitable treatment of both men and women in sport.

The point is not that these differences are trivial. Such disagreements have important practical implications. Such disagreement are real and often bitter. (In the case of Title IX they are definitely bitter). However, no matter how heated the arguments over Title IX get, that specific disagreement does not prove—by itself—that there is not an underlying agreement on the importance of sex equity.[12] The same point, so the critic of relativism holds, can be made about a host of moral claims; below the real disagreements we will often find—at a more generic level—a commitment to common human values. If this is right, if deeper universal or fundamental values can be found, then descriptive relativism may not be true after all.

What do these "universal values" look like? Here is how one author put it:

> "All human societies show a concern for the value of human life; in all, self-preservation is generally accepted as a proper motive for action, and in none is the killing of other human beings permitted without some fairly definite justification. All human societies regard the procreation of a new human life as itself a good thing unless there are special circumstances. No human

Title IX: A law passed by the U.S. Congress in 1972 which bars discrimination on the basis of sex in all federally funded educational programs (including athletics).

---

[10] A third criticism that calls this point into question deserves brief note: "The most serious obstacle to formulating contrastive judgments about moral practices of particular human groups, and to establishing the truth of descriptive relativism, reflect a difficulty peculiar to the study of cultures: that of deciding who—if anyone—has the 'authority' to represent the defining principles, especially the basic moral principles, of a given culture" (Moody-Adams, 1997, p. 43). The point Moody-Adams is making is that cultures are not monolithic or static things. Within any given culture one will find various and often opposing beliefs and practices (e.g. Americans opposed to PED use and Americans who support PED use). How then could we ever say with confidence what this or that culture really believes?

[11] Title IX was passed by the U.S. Congress in 1972. It states "No person in the United States shall, on the basis of sex, be excluded from participation in, be denied the benefits of, or be subjected to discrimination under any education program or activity receiving Federal financial assistance" (U.S. Dept. of Education, 2015, para 2.).

[12] Timmons (2013) makes a similar point regarding capital punishment. "You and I agree in our basic convictions about the morality of punishment [only employ methods that have beneficial consequences for society]; our disagreement about the morality of capital punishment is due to differences in nonmoral beliefs about this kind of punishment [you think it deters crime and thereby benefits society, while I do not]" (p. 52). The argument is that pointed and even bitter disagreement on any particular moral issue may hide a more fundamental moral agreement.

Is play just one of many universal human values?
©Joseph Sohm/Shutterstock.com

society fails to restrict sexual activity; in all societies there is some prohibition on incest, some opposition to boundless promiscuity and to rape . . . All human societies display a concern for truth, through education of the youth in matters not only practical (e.g. avoidance of dangers) but also speculative and theoretical (e.g. religion) . . . All value play, serious and formalized, or relaxed and recreational. All treat the bodies of dead members of the group in some traditional and ritual fashion different from their procedures for rubbish disposal. All display a concern for powers and principles which are to be respected as superhuman; in one form or another, religion is universal" (Finnis, 1980, pp. 83–84).

This is an intriguing but nevertheless limited argument. It is limited for two reasons. First, because it responds to an empirical claim ("different cultures believe different things") with another empirical claim ("actually they agree on a lot more than you think"). The problem with this strategy is that even if true, it always leaves room for the defender of relativism to wait on a counter example. The argument, for example, "that all cultures play" is an **inductive** claim based on experience. This means that we must always allow for the possibility that a future culture will not, or a yet undiscovered culture did not, value play. In other words, there is always room for new experience or new insight into past experience which would modify or contradict the claim that "all cultures play." Once such a counter example is established the value would no longer be universal. As a result, this type of inductive argument can *never* fully shut the door on the possibility of counter examples from relativists.

Inductive Argument:
A probabilistic argument based in experience. (e.g., "All NBA basketball players I've ever seen are tall, therefore all NBA basketball players are tall," or "this new NBA basketball player is likely to be tall").

The second criticism of this argument worth noting is that the level of specificity in the claims made to support "universal moral norms" may simply be so general as to be uninteresting. In other words, the claims are so generic ("All human societies show a concern for the value of human life") and so qualified ("unless there are special circumstances") that they don't really show universal assent to even basic human values. Moreover, the critic would argue that the evidence used to support "universal moral norms" is biased by the fact that every potential counter-example is subsumed under "special circumstances." (The basic strategy is this: Find an exception?!? Mark it under "special circumstance"!)[13] Such qualifications make it seem like relativism has been undermined, when in reality those claiming evidence of "universal values" are merely manipulating the language they use to find only what they want to find in human behavior. Because of these criticisms, one must conclude (even if one finds the argument persuasive, as I do) that it is not a determinative response to the descriptive relativism argument.

A second more powerful response to the argument that descriptive relativism proves moral relativism is **deductive** (logical) rather than inductive (based in experience). What this counter-argument shows in principle (as a logical necessity), is that moral relativism does not follow from descriptive relativism. Put simply: the existence of moral disagreement proves nothing beyond moral disagreement.

To show why this is the case, let us think through a couple of simple examples. Imagine you're with your friends at volleyball practice. While warming up, an argument gets started regarding which country won the 1984 Olympic gold medal in men's volleyball. You maintain (correctly) that it was the United States, while several of your friends insist it was Brazil and your coach says it was the Soviet Union. What logically follows from this state of affairs? It certainly is not the case that disagreement over who won indicates that there is no right answer to the question. Perhaps, even more significantly, no one would argue that disagreement shows each answer is equally correct for those who hold it. No one would say "Your truth is that Brazil won, while my truth is that it was the USA."

The facts regarding whether there is or is not a right answer to the question of who won the 1984 Olympic men's volleyball gold are logically independent of the existence of separate answers offered by the different members of your team. Unanimity or controversy on the issue, by themselves, *tell us nothing* about who won the medal or whether an objective answer to the question exists. The only thing that follows from the disagreement is that there is disagreement about what the right answer is.

Now, let us consider a similar example. You're sitting in practice the next day, when an argument gets started regarding the morality of correcting a referee's mistaken call (e.g. letting them know you were in the net or touched a ball that was called out, etc.). You argue that the referee's authority should not be challenged even when you know they're wrong, while several of your friends insist that integrity demands that you should always try to respectfully correct the referee, so that you will not receive unearned points. Finally, your coach, after hearing the argument, pipes in that "gamesmanship" demands that one should correct the referee's calls only when not doing so will hurt your own team. Referee mistakes in your favor, he insists, should be ignored.

Deductive Argument: A logic-based argument where, if your reasoning is valid, the conclusion *necessarily* follows from the premises (e.g., if all great basketball players deserve to be in the Hall of Fame, and if LeBron James is a great basketball player, then it follows (necessarily) that LeBron James deserves to be in the Hall of Fame).

---

[13] Abortion, for example, would seem to contradict the claim that "All human societies regard the procreation of a new human life as itself a good thing". Does subsuming abortion under "special circumstance" legitimately qualify the point or undermine it? (Is this an example of the "Moving the goalposts fallacy" found in Appendix II)?

What logically follows from this state of affairs? Today, many are tempted to say that this type disagreement proves that there are no right answers to moral questions. But, hopefully you see that this scenario is exactly the same logically as the one that preceded it. Disagreement proves nothing beyond disagreement.

Disagreement proves nothing beyond disagreement.
©ale_rizzo/Shutterstock.com

"Beg the Question" Fallacy: A form of circular reasoning where one assumes a conclusion rather than give arguments for it (e.g., "Paying college players a salary is wrong because intercollegiate sports are meant to be amateur"). This claim begs the question because it assumes as true what is under dispute (should college sport be amateur?).

To say that the second argument is different because moral questions are merely matters of opinion would be to **beg the question**. That is, to presume the conclusion which is at issue, rather than make an argument for it. Now, it is true that the second scenario is more complicated than merely looking up a historical fact (such as the Olympic victor in argument #1). Furthermore, any serious ethical analysis will likely need to take context, circumstance and situation into account. For example, perhaps the correct moral principle (e.g. the Golden Rule) can be prescribed for referee interaction, but the correct moral action depends on the situation (the precise foul, the level of competition, the implicit understanding of what is expected between players and coaches, etc.). In that case, then perhaps on this issue there is not really a right answer beyond the moral principle.

Yet, even if that reasoning is sound, it nevertheless remains true that moral disagreement did not establish that fact, argument(s) did. *Again, the existence of moral disagreement, like any other disagreement, proves nothing beyond disagreement!* To say that people disagree on the morality of taking dives in soccer, or paying college players a salary, or using performance enhancing drugs (PEDs), tells us nothing about whether dives are actually good, or players ought to be paid, or whether PEDs are immoral. As Simon, Torres and Hager (2015) rightly insist, "In disagreement or agreement, justification depends on the kinds of reasons that can be provided to support our moral views, not simply on whether [or not] others share our values" (p. 12).

Moral Realism is the Only Tenable Position

All three arguments which we have examined in favor of moral relativism fail. Relativism relies on confident knowledge claims regarding the truth of moral claims and therefore is no more "modest" than is realism. Relativism can only support tolerance by implicitly acknowledging, in a self-contradictory manner, that tolerance is an objective moral good. Finally, as we just saw, the reality of moral disagreement (descriptive relativism) cannot show that moral relativism is true.

In contrast, moral realism has several generally unacknowledged strengths. In positing moral truth, realism demands rational debate. That is, realists (even as they disagree) are intensely interested in the reasons and arguments that can be put forth for the truth of this or that moral position. MacIntyre (2009) explains the idea this way,

"Philosophy is in any case a social and not a solitary form of enquiry. It requires a setting in which different and rival answers to philosophical questions can be proposed and objections to each considered in detail, so that such answers may be revised or rejected and such objections [are] themselves subjected to critical scrutiny" (p. 17).

At the very least, this desire would be muted—if not eliminated—by a commitment to relativism. When moral arguments are nothing more than the expression of individual idiosyncrasy or cultural bias, they are all equally (un)sound. But in that case, why would one ever engage in the hard philosophic work of evaluating them?

Realism also stiffens our moral spines. Unfortunately, this is rarely recognized as a strength, because of the alleged link between realism and moral bullying, oppression, and brutish insensitivity. Yet, as Midgely (1981; 2003) points out, we can only condemn such behavior on the grounds of realism.

"We could not condemn oppression and insolence if we thought that all our condemnations were just a trivial quirk of our own culture . . . Real moral skepticism, in fact, could lead only to inaction, to our losing all interest in moral questions, most of all in those which concern other societies" (p. 84).

To say that tolerance is a good thing is to be a realist. This is no small matter. The world is moved by passionate men and women willing to stand up and defend their convictions. A commitment to truth may spur both good and bad ideas, but it certainly does not spur indifference. In contrast, it is hard to see how a consistent relativism can do otherwise. Why, for instance would Jackie Robinson and Branch Rickey have stood up to the institutional racism of Major League Baseball and America at large, if each was convinced that a commitment to racial equality was merely one culturally conditioned belief among many?

To conclude our defense of realism it is worth reiterating that the truth of descriptive relativism does not show that moral realism is mistaken. The existence of alternative answers and various moralities proves nothing beyond disagreement over what the truth is. As was shown in the examples above, moral relativism does not follow from moral disagreement.

The world is moved by passionate men and women willing to stand up and defend their convictions.
Bettmann/Getty Images

In fact, moral realism deals with pluralism better than does relativism. Relativism flattens out the world, by saying that nothing is true. This apparently flexible philosophy is at heart deeply rigid. A commitment to realism, on the other hand, is far more flexible. Realism demands that reasons, comparison and argument matter, for they can and often do lead to the truth. Moreover, tolerance grows out of the realist's recognition of *the truth* that culture deeply influences our thinking and beliefs. As such, we should tolerate—as much as possible—those beliefs we are convinced are mistaken. Perhaps the most important argument in favor of realism then is this: Realism can and should admit the influence of culture. Relativism cannot ever admit the influence of truth.

Why Does the Status of Moral Truth Matter to Athletes, Coaches, Administrators or Fans?

To explain the importance of the status of moral truth for sport, we will be focusing on one issue as a paradigm example. Many other examples could be given, but for our limited purposes it will suffice to focus on the moral debate that surrounded the call for a boycott of the 2008 Olympic Games in Beijing, China.[14] The point of this analysis will not be to prescribe what the proper action is regarding Olympic boycotts. There are good arguments on both sides of that debate.[15] Rather the point will be to show that

[14] A contemporary echo of this very same issue, at least as regards moral reticence due to relativism, is the 2019 "NBA/Hong Kong" controversy. For details, see (McCann, 2019).
[15] See for example (Applebaum, 2008) and (Walt, 2008).

moral evaluation is an inherent part of sport and that one's position as a realist or a relativist makes a difference as to whether one acknowledges or ignores these ubiquitous moral questions.

Moral questions are everywhere in sport, as the Olympic Boycott controversy (and Chapter 1) should make plain. Such moral questions must be addressed within the framework of one's commitments regarding the existence (or lack thereof) of moral truth. As we have seen, realism has the tendency to stiffen one's moral spine, while relativism encourages hesitation regarding definitive moral judgments. Such hesitation then leads to the quarantining of moral questions from the realm of significant or relevant administrative action in sport.

Realists, because they believe that moral truth exists are more likely to take the moral issue or question at hand seriously, while relativists (or those using relativism for cover) tend to short circuit such debate, by positing the indeterminacy of moral claims or reducing moral issues to technocratic problems to be "solved." Too often, a commitment to relativism encourages sports leaders to see sport as a technical rather than moral enterprise. That is, given the pretext of relativism, the administrator's job can be quickly rationalized as merely dealing with organizing and running competitions, marketing events, financing organizations, and so forth. Moral questions are not and should not be considered part of their job or their competence.[16]

Despite the popularity of this position, it is untenable. To see why let us return to the controversy over the 2008 Beijing Olympic Games. There were essentially three moral objections made to the suitability of Beijing as the host of the Games; (1). The prevalence of human rights abuses in China including; forced abortion, political imprisonment and religious persecution (Jacobs, 2008; Jian, 2013; Labott, 2008), (2). China's occupation of Tibet (Burns, 2008), (3). China's sale of weapons to rebels in Darfur, Sudan, where there was widespread documentation of war crimes occurring (Andersson, 2008).[17]

How should one react to the existence of such behavior by the Chinese government? Philosophically this is a live issue, especially considering that the Olympics are scheduled to return to Beijing in 2022 for the Winter Games.

Here is how Jacque Rogge the President of the International Olympic Committee (IOC) addressed concerns regarding China's human rights abuses. As you read his comments notice how reticent he is to judge, how he rationalizes his reticence by implying that our own shortcomings show we have no right to judge other cultures, and how he assumes time (and even the Games themselves)[18] will inevitably bring the Chinese around to the adoption of human rights.

---

[16] The same can be said for athletes, coaches and fans. One famous example of an athlete absolving himself of moral responsibility can be seen in baseball slugger Mark McGwire's response to a question asked during a congressional inquiry into steroid use in sport. Despite the grandstanding and moral posturing by his interrogators, McGwire's response is nonetheless pathetic. When "Asked whether use of steroids was cheating, McGwire said: 'That's not for me to determine'" (ESPN.com news services, 2005, para. 4).

[17] Some also raised questions about the morality of allowing an oppressive dictatorship the propaganda value of selling "Communism with a happy face" to the viewing public.

[18] "The Games we believe, over time, will have a good influence on social evolution in China, and the Chinese admit it themselves" (Blitz & McGregor, 2008, para. 11). This can only be characterized as hubris, duplicity, naiveté or willful ignorance. None of which reflect well on Rogge or the IOC.

How should we interpret Rogge's defense of China? Does relativism encourage moral indifference?
©Sam DCruz/Shutterstock.com

"'It took us 200 years to evolve from the French Revolution. China started in 1949,'[19] he said, a time when the UK and other European nations were also colonial powers, 'with all the abuse attached to colonial powers. It was only 40 years ago that we gave liberty to the colonies. Let's be a little bit more modest'" (Blitz & McGregor, 2008, para. 3–4).

Now let us evaluate Rogge's relativistic wavering in light of a concrete example of the horrors inflicted upon the Chinese people by their government.

"Almost every one of the pregnant women I spoke to had suffered a mandatory abortion. One woman told me how, when she was eight months pregnant with an illegal second child and was unable to pay the 20,000 yuan fine (about $3,200), family planning officers dragged her to the local clinic, bound her to a surgical table and injected a lethal drug into her abdomen.

For two days she writhed on the table, her hands and feet still bound with rope, waiting for her body to eject the murdered baby. In the final stage of labor, a male doctor yanked the dead fetus out by the foot, then dropped it into a garbage can. She had no money for a cab. She had to hobble home, blood dripping down her legs and staining her white sandals red" (Jian, 2013, para. 8–9).

---

[19] There is a great irony in the historical events he chooses to defend his position. Rogge fails to acknowledge the French Revolution's connection to the "reign of terror" as well as the fact that the 1949 Chinese Civil War is exactly what put the Communist Party in power. In no sense can either regime be considered progressive steps towards human rights. For evidence, see (Dikötter, 2015) and (Burleigh, 2005).

What Rogge said may placate journalists at a press conference, but his words do nothing to address China's brutal treatment of its own people. Nor do his words make sense of the IOC's decision to grant Beijing the right to host the Games. While keeping the evils just mentioned fresh in your mind, now consider the Olympic Charter (2013), which states as its first fundamental principle that:

> "Olympism is a philosophy of life, exalting and combining in a balanced whole the qualities of body, will and mind. Blending sport with culture and education, Olympism seeks to create a way of life based on the joy of effort, *the educational value of good example, social responsibility and respect for universal fundamental ethical principles*" (International Olympic Committee, 2013, p. 11).

There is a grave contradiction between the values of the Olympic Charter and the Communist government of China. How can this be reconciled? Should China be awarded the Games if they can't be reconciled? Can a boycott be justified? Would it be effective? What is the right thing to do?

All of these questions seem to have been ignored by Rogge. Why? One plausible explanation is that relativistic thinking encouraged him to believe these questions are not relevant or serious to the Olympic movement. From within this mindset, the boycott movement is just one more PR problem to be overcome, so that the IOC can get on with the "serious business" of hosting a "successful" Olympic Games.

Realism, on the other hand forces us to recognize the moral weight of our decisions, our actions as well as our inactions. To be a realist certainly does not commit one to the boycott movement in this instance or to any particular moral action in any other. What it does require is moral seriousness, for our decisions are accountable to the truth. Whereas relativism encourages us to move away from "intractable and irresolvable moral problems" so that we get on with the important business of addressing "practical problems," realism encourages us to carefully consider our decisions in light of the good, the true and the beautiful.

Again, we see the importance of philosophy. After all, realism is itself a philosophic commitment said to be true. Moreover, despite their commitment to truth, realists themselves can be wrong. Human beings are fallible, which means realists, even as they are right about the status of truth, can be otherwise deeply mistaken. They may misunderstand, ignore, or deny the good, even as they believe that it exists. The stakes are high, for ethics, even at its most abstract, always implies, supports and justifies concrete actions which are then *put into practice*. Consider, again, that the 2022 Games will return to Beijing, even as the vast majority of the human rights abuses from 2008 remain. What does that fact suggest about the IOC's philosophic commitments? That is, what philosophy have *they* put into practice?

To think well we will need sound moral reasoning which relies upon careful arguments. What counts in advancing or defending an ethical theory are the reasons we can offer regarding what is good and regarding how we should or should not lead our lives. What should be done? How should we treat each other? Our answers to these questions will rely upon our general philosophic commitments (such as we've examined in the first three chapters of this text) as well as the moral theory we endorse and live by. But which theory should we endorse and why? Divergent and irreconcilable answers are on offer. Is morality best understood in terms of maximizing pleasure, or in doing our duty, or in cultivating virtue?[20] It is to a direct examination of these theories that we now turn.

---

[20] There are, of course, more than three moral theories on offer in the discipline of philosophy. For the purposes of this text however we will be examining only Utilitarianism, Deontology and Virtue Ethics which are three of the most important and enduring theories on offer.

PHILOSOPHIC SELECTIONS

Selection #1: Jean Bethke Elshtain, *First Things*, "Judge not?," October 1994.

Introduction: In this selection, Elshtain argues that judgment is both necessary and unavoidable. In fact, when done well judgment is good. Sound judgment is not mere prejudice, but a careful, fair, and reasoned evaluation of the rightness or wrongness of some act or behavior. What, then, should be made of Jesus' famous admonition to "judge not, lest ye be judged"? Elshtain, following British philosopher Mary Midgley, argues that Jesus' admonition should be understood, not as a rejection of the necessity of judgment (moral evaluation of behavior), but rather as a grave warning against condemning people as such, rather than simply evaluating their actions. This is especially dangerous when done vindictively and with a standard we are not willing to apply to ourselves. Such comprehensive evaluations of others' lives are beyond our capabilities, and should therefore be left to God alone. However, judgment, in the proper sense, is a mark of moral seriousness. If we want to lead good lives and treat each other as we ought, judgment is indispensable. As such, it should be rehabilitated.

https://www.firstthings.com/article/1994/10/judge-not.

We are a society awash in exculpatory strategies. We've devised lots of fascinating ways to let ourselves or others off the hook: all one need do is think of recent, well-publicized trials to appreciate the truth of this. We Americans are at present being bombarded with sensationalistic tales of victimization and equally sensationalistic proclamations of immunity from responsibility. Alternately bemused and troubled by the Oprah Winfrey-ization of American life, I sometimes think of my grandmother.

Dear Grandma (may she rest in peace) knew how to judge. She was tough as nails on people she found despicable or merely wanting. She chewed them out in her low German dialect (being a Volga German, hochdeutsch was not her tongue), and we grandchildren could figure out a thing or two. We knew when she was describing someone as "swinish" or "dirty," these being ways to characterize those who stole from others, beat their wives or their livestock, or abused their children. (Women, of course, could be abusers, too.) We missed a good bit of her assessments, though, as it was the policy of my grandmother, my mother, and Aunts Mary and Martha not to teach us plattdeutsch. When Grandma was really on a roll and wanted nothing less than to condemn someone to perdition, her favorite judging word was "Russki." Hearing it sent a frisson through our tender flesh and bones. The last time I heard her say this I was forty-three or forty-four years old and it still frightened me, not quite out of my wits, but I remained convinced, as I had been since the age of five or six when I had acquired some inkling of what was at stake, that that person was doomed, no two ways about it.

"Russki" was her shorthand judgment on the garden-variety cheat, the ordinary bum, the farmer who shortchanged his hired hands, or the mother who kept her kids in dirty clothes, let their noses run, and never washed their hair. Why "Russki" as a term of judgment? That was historic overdetermination. It was the Russians who had begun to undermine the historic immunities of the Volga German communities. Under Tsar Nicholas, on the throne when my grandparents' families emigrated to the New Country from what my grandmother always called the Old Country, their sons were being drafted into the Russian Army; and they were so fearful that they hid their Bibles (Luther's German translation) in secret places.

I suppose my grandmother would be a good candidate for sensitivity training. She is beyond the reach of the enthusiasts of pop psychology with its quivering "non-judgmentalism," having died at the age of ninety-four two years ago, but it gives me a shiver of another sort (one of delight) to imagine a confrontation between Grandma and a "facilitator," eyes agleam with programmed goodness, saying things like, "Now, Mrs. Lind, why do you feel that way?" Or: "Don't you think that's a little harsh? Have you considered how hurtful such words can be?" Probably the facilitator would want to take a good look at my mother, and, in addition to Aunts Mary and Martha, Uncle Bill and Uncle Ted, too, no doubt damaged beyond repair, having been reared by such a no-nonsense judger. Good luck! I doubt they would have the slightest inkling of what she was going on about. There was no room in the family idiom for evasions of responsibility and you would find yourself the subject of an assessment of a rather decisive sort if you tried one.

No doubt from time to time my grandmother and her children rushed to judgment. I know my sisters and brothers and I sometimes wished Mom wouldn't embarrass us in public by being so, well, decisive in her assessment of things—more than once delivered up in front of those being assessed, too. I recall wanting to seek the nearest exit on more than once occasion. But then I thought, even at the time, better this than someone agree-able and eternally smiling, like my nemesis, the mother of Judy Belcher (not her real name), who was a "pal" to her daughter. They "talked about everything," especially "boy-friends" and "fashion," and they liked to "have fun together." I found this pretty disgust-ing. I still do. Judging seems to run in the family.

But to say this is not to say much. For what is at stake is the capacity to make judg-ments as an ethical issue of the gravest sort, and along with it, the discernment of what it means to judge well. In other words, we need a clear sense of why judging is important and what is involved in the activity of judging, and we need a way to distinguish between rash judging—not judging well—and the kind of judging that lies at the heart of what it means to be a self-respecting human subject in a community of other equally self-respecting subjects.

Judging has been in bad odor for quite some time in American culture. It is equated with being punitive, or with insensitivity, or with various "phobias" and "isms." It is the mark of antiquated ways of thinking, feeling, and willing. Better, no doubt, to be some-thing called "open-minded," a trait thought to be characteristic of sensitive and supportive persons. A young woman well known to me reports that she and her fellow teachers at one of the elite New York public high schools were enjoined not to make students "feel bad" by being too decisive in their assessments of student work and effort. I breathed a sigh of recognition when she told me this; it is the sort of thing one hears in the higher reaches of the academy, too. In fact, this attitude is everywhere, even on bumper stickers. At least some of the readers of this essay will have sighted a bumper sticker that reads: "A Mind is Like a Parachute. It Works Best When It Is Open." Yes, indeed, one wants to counter, the more open—meaning the more porous and thin—the better. A rather more convenient way of being in the world than being called upon to discriminate in the old—best—sense of the word. An open mind of the sort celebrated by the bumper sticker may signify an empty head, a person incapable of those acts of discernment we call "judging," one who is, in fact, driven to see in such acts mere prejudice.

But prejudice and judgment are two very different human possibilities; indeed, the more we proliferate prejudices, free from the scrutiny of that discernment we aim to evade, the less capable we are, over time, of making judgments. An example or two, in line with Kant's insistence that "Examples are the go-cart of judgments," may suffice. When I first began university teaching, in 1973, I taught a course called "Feminist Politics and Theory." I taught it for several years until I decided the tumult was too much to put up with semester after semester. One problem I encountered went like this. I had designed the course as a sustained exercise in assessing, and critically contrasting, competing feminist accounts of culture and politics. I asked my students to engage certain questions that presupposed their capacity for judgment: What sort of picture of the human condition is presented by this theorist? Could her prescription for change be implemented? How? What would the world look like if it were? And so on. But I ran into trouble straight-off for, in the eyes of many of my students, what I was supposed to be doing was condemning that big booming abstraction, Patriarchy, for fifty minutes three times a week. I was supposed to embrace, not criticize, feminist doctrines—all of them—even though the ideas of the radical separatist feminists scarcely comported with those of liberal feminists on many issues. Needless to say, the Marxist feminists and the eco-feminists didn't see eye-to-eye on lots of things either.

Students sometimes showed up in my office bereft and troubled. One told me she had been a feminist since she was fourteen and didn't need to hear feminism criticized. Another told me she was so "upset" by my criticism of the text of a feminist who proposed test-tube reproduction and a world run by beneficent cyber-engineers, and so "shocked" at my insistence that she respond to a series of questions asking her to sift, discriminate, and assess this text and others, that she had complained to, and sought refuge in, a support group at the women's center. Yet another refused to write a paper contrasting Freud's essays on female development with what the psychoanalytic feminists were doing with Freud because "Freud was a cancer-ridden, cigar-smoking misogynist." This expression of prejudice was not an authentic moment of judging, of course, not least because the student had refused to read the assigned texts. She was repeating a prejudice, not forming a judgment.

A teacher quickly wearies of this sort of thing because it undermines the presuppositions that guide and help to constitute the pedagogical enterprise, one of the most important of these suppositions being that students are capable of weighing alternatives with a generosity of spirit and quality of discernment that makes their subsequent judgments at least plausible if not unassailable. I have always been fond of a pithy sentence in a letter Freud wrote to his fiancee, Martha: "A human being must be able to pull himself together to form a judgment, otherwise he turns into what we Viennese call a guten Potschen [doormat]." Apart from being stepped on, what is the problem with persons as doormats? Precisely this: they have sloughed off that which is theirs to do—to enter a community of judging, meaning that one can see error and try to put it right, one can distinguish the more from the less important, one can appropriately name phenomena and act accordingly. As an example of the latter, think of the distinction to be marked between "misfortune" and an "injustice" and what we are enjoined to do whether we confront one or the other. Now Freud was not urging Martha to be cruel or incapable of compassion or forgiveness; rather, he was urging her to stiffen her spine a bit, to stand up for herself, and not to shrink from acts of assessment and discernment.

Judging involves calling things by their real names, embracing the difficult recognition that what Hannah Arendt called "an enormously enlarged empathy" does not in itself suffice to sustain the capacity for that critical thinking we call judging. Arendt had little use for those who treated adults as if they were children by spoon-feeding them palatable "truths" rather than the harder truths of life and politics. If we over-assimilate our situation to that of others, and pretend that we are "at one" with them, we may lose the point at which we leave off and they begin. We are then in danger of losing the faculty of judgment that, for Arendt, consists in "thinking the particular" and through this concrete act reaching for more general conclusions and truths.

Why is judging—what Arendt called the preeminent political faculty—at a nadir among us? Surely much of the explanation lies in the triumph of the ideology of victimization coupled with self-esteem mania. The two are, of course, closely linked. Examples are so numerous it is hard to pick and choose. Take one from the public schools. By now most discerning citizens are familiar with the study showing that American schoolchildren scored much lower on math accomplishment tests than did their counterparts from several other societies—even while these same Americans were the ones who "felt best" about their math ability. Here the emphasis on "feeling good" by contrast to concrete accomplishment results in students being incapable of an accurate discernment of where they really stand on their math ability. Here is a second story, this from the literary front. My son is an aspiring poet and he finds increasingly depressing the many moments, whether in class or out, when a poem that is weak in execution and flat in evocative power is embraced as something "real" and important because it speaks about the poet's own undigested experiences, which by definition can never be assessed and criticized. In other words, the self-referential prejudices of our time swamp a cooler set of criticisms and judgments, and wind up making a triumph of something rather petty. In the process, the work of those young men and women who really struggle with form and language and getting it right is trivialized, their accomplishments discounted. In some circles, if you carefully and precisely criticize a weak poem, you may face censure because the poem and its author's psyche or identity are at one; thus, you find yourself in the position of criticizing her (or his) life, given the utter collapse of one into the other, when what you really want to do is to explain why you think this isn't a very good poem.

The culture of victimization, then, and the triumph of pop-psych notions of "self-esteem," in contrast to a self capable of discernment and judging well, seems a pretty clear source of our discontents in this matter. Of course, any decent person is concerned about victims, and there are real victims in our less than perfect world. But that is not the issue. An ideology of victimization (of the feminist sort) casts women as victims of male oppression from the very beginning of time; indeed, female victimization has taken on foundational status. But this victim ideology diverts attention from concrete and specific instances of female victimization in favor of pushing a relentless worldview structured around such dichotomies as victim/victimizer, guilty/innocent, tainted/pure. The female victim, construed as innocent, remains somehow free from sin. Remember Arendt's insistence, following Kant, that judging "is the faculty of thinking the particular." An ideology of victimization—with its harsh and exaggerated polemicism—actually hurts the cause of women's rights, for it provides grounds for callous or sexist individuals to deprecate the claims of actual victims.

Victimization ideology is little more than a politics of resentment, given the growing body of evidence demonstrating that women, though they often have been victims of injustice, have played a variety of active roles throughout history and in every culture. Of course, who didn't know that? It is quite incredible that one must make this point against those who, in the name of feminism, promote the generic prejudice that women are victims simpliciter. Our world is filled with noisy forces urging us to refrain from judging precisely in the name of justice. This dangerous nonsense is in evidence in every issue of any daily newspaper anywhere. The jurors in the Reginald Denny beating case decided not to convict because the thugs who smashed a man's face to an unrecognizable pulp and exulted for the cameras as if they had just made the winning touchdown at a Superbowl Game were in the grip of a "mob psychology" and could not, therefore, be judged for their specific acts of wanton, and repeated, violence. The Menendez brothers were "victims" who, although they blasted their parents numerous times with a shotgun, were not to be held accountable. We cannot judge them given what they "went through," as one juror put it.

Take another case, one worth looking at in some detail. A woman in Nashville, Tennessee, starved her infant son to death. Turned into a robot, so it was claimed, she was unable to feed the infant even though the husband was away at work all day. Her defense was based on her having been abused by this husband even though when he got home from work, the two of them would dress up and go out on the town, frequenting sleazy bars, looking for men and women for three-way sex. Meanwhile, a baby is starving to death. Of this terrible story, victimization doctrine holds that as a victim of abuse herself, the woman, by definition, could not in turn be victimizing another. We cannot judge her actions because she is oppressed. According to her lawyers, who are now mounting an appeal, the jury that found her guilty has victimized her twice. But one who looks at victimization as a concrete and specific act would argue that, although it is terrible to be abused, for a twenty-three-year old woman with a range of options open to her (she might have given the infant to her mother to care for, as she had done with an older child) to starve an infant to death is more terrible yet. Surely, to make that assessment is not an act prompted by a harsh desire for revenge. It flows, rather, from a recognition that we are able to distinguish real victims from rhetorical ones, evil acts and crimes from less serious misdeeds.

As the lawyers for this woman said, the woman cannot be "held accountable," and to do so is a "male deal . . . or a society deal, but some people just don't get it." Now, we are told, the perpetrator is a victim twice or even thrice—of that amorphous entity, society, of her husband, and of the jury that found her guilty. The woman's mother has stepped in, proclaiming that she, too, is a "victim" for she "lost a grandson." Notice the language: she "lost" the grandson, as if he had been misplaced, not knowingly, over a six-week period, starved to death as he lay, immobile, listless, no longer able to cry, in his own waste in a filthy crib in a locked room as his parents played out their fantasies with male and female prostitutes. This is nigh unbelievable, but there it is. Even if this awful case gets turned back on appeal, we—all of us—are in danger of being worn down by arguments of this sort; hence, the more likely it is that, at some future point, we will have forgotten what it means to hold this person accountable in this situation for this particular horrible deed.

Let's pursue this just a bit further, depressing as it is, because the elimination of the possibility of judgment, the evacuation of the very capacity of judging, would spell the end of the human subject as a self-respecting, accountable being. Judging is a sign, a mark, of our respect for the dignity of others and ourselves. We are surrounded by various strategies of exculpation—ways to evade responsibility for a situation or an outcome should one happen to be a member of an "oppressed" or "victimized" group. In a recent book, The Alchemy of Race and Rights , the author, Patricia Williams, plays the victim card to achieve both ends simultaneously. Acknowledging that the Tawana Brawley accusations in the now-notorious 1988 scandal were part of a hoax, Williams suggests that that doesn't really matter. For Brawley was a victim of "some unspeakable crime." "No matter how she got there. No matter who did it to her—and even if she did it to herself." That is, even if Brawley injured herself, "her condition was clearly the expression of some crime against her, some tremendous violence, some great violation that challenges comprehension." Brawley was the victim of a "meta-rape," and this secures both her victim status and legitimates the power plays of those who cynically manipulated the situation. These latter escape judgment; and Brawley cannot be judged either. But the "society" that somehow "did" this to her on a "meta" level becomes responsible given the prejudice that in a "racist" society all African Americans are victims of the dominant "metanarrative." Consider the alternative view of black possibility and responsibility noted by Stephen Carter:

> We must never lose the capacity for judgment, especially the capacity to judge ourselves and our people . . . . Standards of morality matter no less than standards of excellence. There are black people who commit heinous crimes, and not all of them are driven by hunger and neglect . . . . We are not

automatons. To understand all may indeed be to forgive all, but no civilization can survive when the capacity for understanding is allowed to supersede the capacity for judgment. Otherwise, at the end of the line lies a pile of garbage: Hitler wasn't evil, just insane.

"When the capacity for understanding is allowed to supersede the capacity for judgment"-let the words linger for a moment. Then conjure with the teaching of Jesus: "Judge not that ye be not judged," this, of course, from the Sermon on the Mount. These, too, are words I grew up with. And I pondered them, wondering if my mother's "judgmental" attitude was compatible with Jesus' injunction. We were also told: "There but for the grace of God go I." We were told to "walk around in the other guy's shoes" before we judged severely or before we judged at all. Squaring this with Grandma's dismissive "Russki" was no easy matter. I sometimes repaired to Lincoln, one of my childhood heroes. I especially loved the magnificent Second Inaugural, "With malice toward none, with charity for all . . ." Those words I could square with judgment. Malice and judgment; the punitive and the fair are not the same. Lincoln had, after all, insisted that the nations were under God's judgment, and our terrible Civil War, the war he was prosecuting in terms of "unconditional surrender," was our punishment for chattel slavery. Lincoln was no value-free, laid-back kind of guy: compassion with judgment, this framed his life and work. "Judge not" is, then, not an injunction to spineless acceptance but a caution against peremptory legalisms that leave no space for acts of compassion and witness.

I have also found helpful the discussion of the lively British philosopher, Mary Midgley. In her book Can't We Make Moral Judgments? Midgley notes our contemporary search for a nonjudgmental politics and quotes all those people who cry, in effect, "But surely it's always wrong to make moral judgments." We are not permitted to make anyone uncomfortable, to be "insensitive." Yet moral judgment of "some kind," says Midgley, "is a necessary element to our thinking." Judging involves our whole nature—it isn't just icing on the cake of self-identity. Judging makes it possible for us to "find our way through a whole forest of possibilities."

Midgley argues that Jesus was taking aim at sweeping condemnations and vindictiveness: he was not trashing the "whole faculty of judgment." Indeed, Jesus is making the "subtle point that while we cannot possibly avoid judging, we can see to it that we judge fairly, as we would expect others to do to us." This is part and parcel, then, of justice as fairness, as a discernment about a particular case and person and deed. Subjectivism in such matters—of the "I'm okay, you're okay," variety—is a cop-out, a way to stop forming and expressing moral judgments altogether. This strange suspension of specific moments of judgment goes hand-in-glove, of course, with an often violent rhetoric of condemnation of whole categories of persons, past and present—that all-purpose villain, the Dead White European Male, comes to mind.

Perhaps this is the point at which we might recall Tocqueville's warnings about "What Sort of Despotism Democratic Nations Have to Fear," for Tocqueville's worst-case scenario has quite a bit to do with judging or, better put, no longer being able to distinguish the better from the worse, the excellent from the mediocre, slavishness from self-responsibility. Democratic despotism, according to Tocqueville, would have a "different character" from the tyranny of the Old World. "It would be more widespread and milder; it would degrade men rather than torment them." Thus, Tocqueville sees citizens withdrawing into themselves, circling around one another in pursuit of "the petty and banal pleasures with which they glut their souls." The exercise of genuine free choice becomes rarer, the activity of free will occurs "within a narrower compass, and little by little robs each citizen of the proper use of his own faculties." The words Tocqueville uses to describe this state of things are "hinder . . . restrain . . . enervate . . . stultify." Losing over time the "faculty of thinking, feeling, and acting for themselves," these citizens "slowly fall below the level of humanity." Tocqueville nowhere talks about collapse of the faculty of judgment in a specific sense but that, surely, is much of what is at stake. Judging is central to, indeed constitutive of, both our self-identity and our sociality: it helps us to disentangle, analyze, separate, discern and, in so doing, puts us smack dab in a world of others—not apart, not above, not below, but among.

Told that, if we are "powerful" we cannot judge others but can only be judged, and on the other hand that if we are "powerless" we can judge totally but cannot be judged—since the "powerful" by definition "don't get it"-we fall into an intellectual laziness that is itself ethically corrupt and corrupting. As Midgley notes, Jesus' message was: do not stone people, do not cast them out, do not write them off. His target was punitive self-righteousness. With such self-righteousness now a major cottage industry, are we in the danger zone imagined by Tocqueville? That is the question to which sober reflection on judging leads us—or at least where it should.

From *First Things*, October 1994 by Jean Bethke Elshtain. Copyright © 1994 by First Things. Reprinted by permission.

Discussion Question(s)

1. Why, according to Elshtain, has judgment taken on a "bad odor" in American society? Does this argument hold across all areas of American culture, including sport? That is, are we hesitant to judge in sport or are we too judgmental in sport?

2. What is the distinction between judgment and prejudice? Why does Elshtain think the distinction is so important?

3. According to Elshtain, what does good judgment look like?

Selection #2: Matt Bowen, *Chicago Tribune*, "Bounties part of game across the NFL," March 2, 2012.

Read the article here: https://www.chicagotribune.com/sports/ct-xpm-2012-03-02-ct-spt-0304-bowen-nfl-20120304-story.html

Introduction: In this short essay Matt Bowen, who played strong safety in the NFL for seven seasons, argues that bounties are a common and accepted practice in professional football. More importantly he hints that it morally acceptable because everyone in the NFL knows about it, accepts it, and does it.

Bounties are payments made to players for "big hits" which cause injury to an opposing team's players. In 2012 the New Orleans Saints were embroiled in the "bountygate" scandal which exposed a coach led system of financially compensating Saints players for injuring opponents. This system included payments for "'Knockouts' [which] were worth $1,500 and 'cart-offs' [which were worth] $1,000." Payments were "doubled or tripled for the playoffs" (ESPN.com news services, 2012).

Discussion Question(s)

1. "Some day, when my three sons grow up, I will make clear to them that this league isn't for everyone. No doubt, it can be downright disgusting living by a win-at-all-costs mentality. It's a fundamental part of the NFL's culture that isn't talked about outside of team facilities." Is the preceding quote relativistic? Why or why not?

2. Is Bowen conflating normative and descriptive claims in his defense/description of bounties in the NFL?

3. How might the arguments made in Chapter 1 (pp. 12–14) regarding the limitations of a "just win" philosophy poke holes in Bowen's argument?

Selection #3: Justin P. McBrayer, *The New York Times*, "Why our Children Don't think there are Moral Facts," March 2, 2015. © 2015 The New York Times.

http://opinionator.blogs.nytimes.com/2015/03/02/why-our-children-dont-think-there-are-moral-facts/?_r=1

> **Introduction:** This selection examines the tacit relativism which is being commonly taught to elementary school children across the United States. Although the word epistemology is never used by the author, or ever found in the school lessons he examines, it is clear that what is at issue is the question, "what can be known?" Are facts and opinions different things? Can values ever become facts by being objectively true? Are our moral beliefs mere opinions, or is McBrayer right to insist that "at least some moral claims are true"?

What would you say if you found out that our public schools were teaching children that it is not true that it's wrong to kill people for fun or cheat on tests? Would you be surprised?

I was. As a philosopher, I already knew that many college-aged students don't believe in moral facts. While there are no national surveys quantifying this phenomenon, philosophy professors with whom I have spoken suggest that the overwhelming majority of college freshmen in their classrooms view moral claims as mere opinions that are not true or are true only relative to a culture.

What I didn't know was where this attitude came from. Given the presence of moral relativism in some academic circles, some people might naturally assume that philosophers themselves are to blame. But they aren't. There are historical examples of philosophers who endorse a kind of moral relativism, dating back at least to Protagoras who declared that "man is the measure of all things," and several who deny that there are any moral facts whatsoever. But such creatures are rare. Besides, if students are already showing up to college with this view of morality, it's very unlikely that it's the result of what professional philosophers are teaching. So where is the view coming from?

A few weeks ago, I learned that students are exposed to this sort of thinking well before crossing the threshold of higher education. When I went to visit my son's second grade open house, I found a troubling pair of signs hanging over the bulletin board. They read:

Fact: Something that is true about a subject and can be tested or proven.

Opinion: What someone thinks, feels, or believes.

Hoping that this set of definitions was a one-off mistake, I went home and Googled "fact vs. opinion." The definitions I found online were substantially the same as the one in my son's classroom. As it turns out, the Common Core standards used by a majority of K-12 programs in the country require that students be able to "distinguish among fact, opinion, and reasoned judgment in a text." And the Common Core institute provides a helpful page full of links to definitions, lesson plans and quizzes to ensure that students can tell the difference between facts and opinions.

So what's wrong with this distinction and how does it undermine the view that there are objective moral facts?

First, the definition of a fact waffles between truth and proof—two obviously different features. Things can be true even if no one can prove them. For example, it could be true that there is life elsewhere in the universe even though no one can prove it. Conversely, many of the things we once "proved" turned out to be false. For example, many people once thought that the earth was flat. It's a mistake to confuse truth (a feature of the world) with proof (a feature of our mental lives). Furthermore, if proof is required for facts, then facts become person-relative. Something might be a fact for me if I can prove it but not a fact for you if you can't. In that case, $E=MC^2$ is a fact for a physicist but not for me.

But second, and worse, students are taught that claims are either facts or opinions. They are given quizzes in which they must sort claims into one camp or the other but not both. But if a fact is something that is true and an opinion is something that is believed, then many claims will obviously be both. For example, I asked my son about this distinction after his open house. He confidently explained that facts were things that were true whereas opinions are things that are believed. We then had this conversation:

> Me: "I believe that George Washington was the first president. Is that a fact or an opinion?"
> Him: "It's a fact."
> Me: "But I believe it, and you said that what someone believes is an opinion."
> Him: "Yeah, but it's true."
> Me: "So it's both a fact and an opinion?"
> The blank stare on his face said it all.

How does the dichotomy between fact and opinion relate to morality? I learned the answer to this question only after I investigated my son's homework (and other examples of assignments online). Kids are asked to sort facts from opinions and, without fail, every value claim is labeled as an opinion. Here's a little test devised from questions available on fact vs. opinion worksheets online: are the following facts or opinions?

— Copying homework assignments is wrong.
— Cursing in school is inappropriate behavior.
— All men are created equal.
— It is worth sacrificing some personal liberties to protect our country from terrorism.
— It is wrong for people under the age of 21 to drink alcohol.
— Vegetarians are healthier than people who eat meat.
— Drug dealers belong in prison.

The answer? In each case, the worksheets categorize these claims as opinions. The explanation on offer is that each of these claims is a value claim and value claims are not facts. This is repeated ad nauseum: any claim with good, right, wrong, etc. is not a fact.

In summary, our public schools teach students that all claims are either facts or opinions and that all value and moral claims fall into the latter camp. The punchline: there are no moral facts. And if there are no moral facts, then there are no moral truths.

The inconsistency in this curriculum is obvious. For example, at the outset of the school year, my son brought home a list of student rights and responsibilities. Had he already read the lesson on fact vs. opinion, he might have noted that the supposed rights of other students were based on no more than opinions. According to the school's curriculum, it certainly wasn't true that his classmates deserved to be treated a particular way—that would make it a fact. Similarly, it wasn't really true that he had any responsibilities—that would be to make a value claim a truth. It should not be a surprise that there is rampant cheating on college campuses: If we've taught our students for 12 years that there is no fact of the matter as to whether cheating is wrong, we can't very well blame them for doing so later on.

Indeed, in the world beyond grade school, where adults must exercise their moral knowledge and reasoning to conduct themselves in the society, the stakes are greater. There, consistency demands that we acknowledge the existence of moral facts. If it's not true that it's wrong to murder a cartoonist with whom one disagrees, then how can we be outraged? If there are no truths about what is good or valuable or right, how can we prosecute people for crimes against humanity? If it's not true that all humans are created equal, then why vote for any political system that doesn't benefit you over others?

Our schools do amazing things with our children. And they are, in a way, teaching moral standards when they ask students to treat one another humanely and to do their schoolwork with academic integrity. But at the same time, the curriculum sets our children up for doublethink. They are told that there are no moral facts in one breath even as the next tells them how they ought to behave.

We can do better. Our children deserve a consistent intellectual foundation. Facts are things that are true. Opinions are things we believe. Some of our beliefs are true. Others are not. Some of our beliefs are backed by evidence. Others are not. Value claims are like any other claims: either true or false, evidenced or not. The hard work lies not in recognizing that at least some moral claims are true but in carefully thinking through our evidence for which of the many competing moral claims is correct. That's a hard thing to do. But we can't sidestep the responsibilities that come with being human just because it's hard.

That would be wrong.

Discussion Question(s)

1. According to McBrayer, what is the proper way to understand the difference between fact and opinion?

2. Why does McBrayer think it is unlikely that college philosophy professors are to blame for the popularity of relativism among college students?

3. How, according to McBrayer, does the conflation of fact and opinion end up encouraging moral relativism?

Suggested Readings

Guttmann, A. (1978; 2004). Chapter 2: From ritual to record. In A. Guttmann, *From ritual to record: The nature of modern sports* (pp. 15–55). New York, NY: Columbia University Press.

McWorter, J. H. (2015, July 17). *How dare you say that! The evolution of profanity*. Retrieved January 21, 2016, from www.wsj.com: http://www.wsj.com/articles/how-dare-you-say-that-the-evolution-of-profanity-1437168515

Midgely, M. (1981, 2003). Trying out one's new sword. In M. Midgely, *Heart and mind: The varieties of moral experience* (pp. 80–87). New York, NY: Routledge.

Simon, R. L. (1997, June 27). The paralysis of 'absolutophobia'. *Chronicle of Higher Education*, B5–B6.

Bibliography

Andersson, H. (2008, July 13). *China "is fueling war in Darfur".* Retrieved January 26, 2016, from www.bbc.com: http://news.bbc.co.uk/2/hi/africa/7503428.stm

Applebaum, A. (2008, March 24). *Boycott Beijing.* Retrieved January 28, 2016, from www.slate.com: http://www.slate.com/articles/news_and_politics/foreigners/2008/03/boycott_beijing.html

Benedict, R. (1934). Anthropology and the abnormal. *The Journal of General Psychology*, 10, 59–82.

Blitz, R., & McGregor, R. (2008, April 25). *Olympics chief tells West not to hector China.* Retrieved January 28, 2016, from www.ft.com: http://www.ft.com/intl/cms/s/0/c4d86cf2-12f3-11dd-8d91-0000779fd2ac.html#axzz3yO001gHD

Burleigh, M. (2005). *Earthly powers: The clash of religion and politics in Europe, from the French Revolution to the Great War.* New York, NY: Harper Perennial.

Burns, J. F. (2008, April 7). *Protests of China make Olympic torch relay an obstacle course.* Retrieved January 26, 2016, from www.nytimes.com: http://www.nytimes.com/2008/04/07/world/europe/07torch.html

Dikötter, F. (2015). *The tragedy of liberation: A history of the Chinese revolution 1945-1957.* New York, NY: Bloomsbury Press.

ESPN.com news services. (2005, March 18). *McGwire admits nothing; Sosa and Palmeiro deny use.* Retrieved January 26, 2016, from www.espn.com: http://espn.go.com/mlb/news/story?id=2015420

ESPN.com news services. (2012, March 4). *NFL: Saints defense had 'bounty' fund.* Retrieved January 11, 2016, from espn.com: http://espn.go.com/nfl/story/_/id/7638603/new-orleans-saints-defense-had-bounty-program-nfl-says

Feser, E. (2015, September 8). *The absolute truth about relativism.* Retrieved January 20, 2016, from edwardfeser.blogspot.com: http://edwardfeser.blogspot.com/2015/09/the-absolute-truth-about-relativism.html

Finnis, J. (1980). *Natural law and natural rights.* New York, NY: Oxford University Press.

Herodotus. (1952). The history of Herodotus. In R. M. Hutchins (Ed.), *Great books of the Western world* (G. Rawlingson, Trans.). Chicago, IL: University of Chicago Press.

International Olympic Committee. (2013). *Olympic charter.* Lausanne, Switzerland: International Olympic Committee.

Jacobs, A. (2008, August 13). *Specter of arrest deters demonstrators in China.* Retrieved January 26, 2016, from www.nytimes.com: http://www.nytimes.com/2008/08/14/sports/olympics/14protest.html

James, W. (1896/1956). The will to believe. In W. James, *The will to believe and other essays in popular philosophy; human immortality* (pp. 1–32). New York, NY: Dover Publications.

Jian, M. (2013, May 21). *China's brutal one-child policy.* Retrieved January 26, 2016, from www.nytimes.com: http://www.nytimes.com/2013/05/22/opinion/chinas-brutal-one-child-policy.html?_r=0

Labott, E. (2008, September 19). *U.S.: Chinese targeted religious groups before Olympics.* Retrieved January 28, 2016, from www.cnn.com: http://edition.cnn.com/2008/WORLD/asiapcf/09/19/china.religion.report/

MacIntyre, A. (1984). *After virtue* (2nd ed.). Notre Dame, IN: University of Notre Dame Press.

MacIntyre, A. (2009). *God, philosophy, universities: A selective history of the Catholic philosophical tradition.* Lanham, MD: Rowman & Littlefield Publishers Inc.

McCann, M. (2019, October 7). *Analyzing the fallout between the NBA and China after Daryl Morey's Tweet.* Retrieved November 14, 2019, from www.si.com: https://www.si.com/nba/2019/10/07/nba-china-hong-kong-daryl-morey-tweet

Midgely, M. (1981; 2003). *Heart and mind: The varieties of moral experience.* New York, NY: Routledge.

Moody-Adams, M. (1997). *Fieldwork in familiar places: Morality, culture, and philosophy.* Cambridge, MA: Harvard University Press.

Montaigne, M. d. (1948). Of cannibals. In M. d. Montaigne, *The complete essays of Montaigne* (D. M. Frame, Trans., pp. 150–159). Stanford, CA: Stanford University Press.

Simon, R., Torres, C., & Hager, P. (2015). *Fair play: The ethics of sport* (4th Ed.). Boulder, CO: Westview Press.

Timmons, M. (2013). *Moral theory: An introduction* (2nd ed.). New York, NY: Rowman & Littlefield.

U.S. Department of Education. (2015, April). *Title IX and sex discrimination.* Retrieved from www2.ed.gov: https://www2.ed.gov/about/offices/list/ocr/docs/tix_dis.html

Walt, V. (2008, July 16). *Why nobody's boycotting Beijing.* Retrieved January 28, 2016, from www.time.com: http://content.time.com/time/world/article/0,8599,1823561,00.html

Chapter 4

Utilitarianism

"Football has been subverted into a made-for-television event. Everything is so clear. Except it's not. The third dimension is what makes it real, violent, and dangerous. Consuming the product through a television screen, at a safe distance, dehumanizes the athlete and makes his pain unreal. *The more you watch it, the less real it becomes, until the players are nothing more than pixelated video game characters to be bartered and traded.*"

—Nate Jackson, former NFL tight-end[1]

Students will be able to:

1. Define utilitarianism in general as well the specific difference between act and rule utilitarianism.
2. Explain how quantitative and qualitative hedonism differ.
3. Summarize the strengths and weaknesses of utilitarianism.
4. Identify and evaluate practical examples of utilitarian thinking and behavior in sport.
5. Articulate how one's ethical commitments (utilitarian or otherwise) are bound up in a web of other philosophical commitments and assumptions.

Utilitarianism is a form of **consequentialism**. Consequentialists hold that the rightness or wrongness of any given moral action should be evaluated based on the results (consequences) of the action. It follows from this consequentialist commitment that actions are not intrinsically right or wrong. The good action is the most useful action. That is, actions are not right or wrong in principle. They are to be judged not on the type of act they are, but rather on the outcomes that this or that action procures. For the consequentialist (and the utilitarian), the ends always justify the means.

Utilitarianism is a hedonistic version of consequentialism. Utilitarians argue that the rightness of any given action should be determined by the principle that we should seek the greatest good for the greatest number, with good being understood as pleasure and evil understood as pain. Any *means* which can be shown to generate the

Utilitarianism: The consequentialist moral theory which argues that one should maximize pleasure by pursuing the "greatest good for the greatest number."

Consequentialism: Any moral theory which bases right action not upon the intrinsic nature of the act but rather upon the consequences any action produces or is likely to produce.

---

[1] Jackson, *Slow Getting Up*, page 158 [Emphasis added].

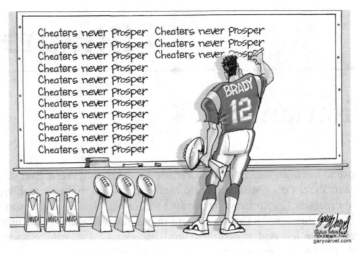

Do the ends justify the means?
By permission of Gary Varvel and Creators Syndicate, Inc.

Act Utilitarianism: The form of utilitarianism which focuses on evaluating the balance of pleasures or pains produced by any particular action.

Rule Utilitarianism: The form of utilitarianism which focuses on which rules will best promote the greatest good. In contrast to act utilitarians, rule utilitarians are not interested in what should be done in any particular case, but instead are focused on which general rules will—taken in aggregate—lead to the greatest good for the greatest number (e.g., "even if prohibitions against PEDs won't produce maximized pleasure in every specific instance, they will in most cases").

end of the most pleasure for the most people should be pursued. Hence the name utilitarianism, for the usefulness or "utility" of any action is determinative. All moral action should be judged solely by the pleasures or pains it produces. As such, a pithy way to summarize the philosophy of utilitarianism is the phrase "maximize pleasure."

To properly evaluate the philosophy of utilitarianism will require three steps. First, we will need to review the major thinkers and types of utilitarianism. This section will examine the work of Jeremy Bentham, the founder of utilitarianism, as well as Bentham's disciple John Stuart Mill. Mill modified Bentham's theory in an effort to respond to Bentham's critics. We will then conclude this section by considering the distinction between the two most prominent variations of utilitarianism, which are known as **act utilitarianism** and **rule utilitarianism**. In the second section of the chapter we will discuss the strengths and weaknesses of utilitarianism. Why are many people attracted to it? Why do others find it not only problematic but even morally dangerous? Finally, we will close the chapter by considering sports ethics in light of utilitarianism. Is the maxim "the greatest good for the greatest number" a sufficient guide by which to lead a good life and treat others well?

Bentham's Quantitative Hedonism

Quantitative Hedonism: The form of hedonism which bases the evaluation of pleasure simply in terms of the amount (quantity) of pleasure produced. For the quantitative hedonist, only the amount of pleasure produced matters.

Jeremy Bentham lived in England in the late 18th and early 19th Century. Bentham advocates a straight-forward version of utilitarianism. He is not interested in qualifications or deviation from the implications of his theory. Bentham (2007) argues that "Nature has placed mankind under the governance of two sovereign masters, pain and pleasure. It is from them alone to point out what we ought to do, as well as what we shall do" (p. 1). In so doing he is advocating for a form of **quantitative hedonism**. What one *does* is irrelevant to the matter. As Bentham (1830) argues, "Prejudice apart, the game of push-pin is of equal value with the arts and sciences of music and poetry. If the game of push-pin furnish more pleasure, it is more valuable than either." (p. 206).

His theory endorses the idea that it is *the amount of pleasure* produced, not the *type of activity* or action, which is the key determinative factor in deciding what we ought to do.[2]

Because Bentham advocates a quantitative hedonism, he argues that the utilitarian should justify any decision made by adding up the pleasures and pains produced. That is, one should quantify the value of each pleasure and pain produced by any given action to see which of the actions will produce the most pleasure. This creates something akin to a "moral balance sheet" where one's assets are weighed against one's liabilities. When this "moral balance sheet" shows that the good (pleasure) produced outweighs the bad (pain) produced, then the action is morally sanctioned.[3] In fact, most utilitarians would say the action is morally required.

Is ethics simply a matter of "maximizing pleasure"?
©sergign/Shutterstock.com

Of course, to quantify pleasure and pain is easier said than done. Something that sounds plausible in principle may actually be unworkable in practice. Bentham (2007) is not unaware of this objection. He suggests using the following categories to accurately gauge the quantitative value of any pleasure or pain; "(1) Its intensity. (2) Its duration. (3) Its certainty or uncertainty. (4) Its propinquity [proximity] or remoteness. (5) Its fecundity [will it be recurring]. (6) Its purity [its likelihood of not being followed by pain]. . . (7) Its extent; that is, the number of persons to whom it *extends*" (p. 30).

What might this look like in practice? Let us focus on a practical problem in the world of sport to try and test Bentham's methodology. Imagine that you are the Athletics Director at a small NCAA Division I university, let us call it "Bentham University" (BU). ESPN approaches you with a $750,000 contract to move your upcoming season's rivalry game against your arch-rival "Kant State University" (KSU) from Saturday afternoon to Tuesday night. What, according to quantitative utilitarianism, should you do?

---

[2] This is why (generally speaking) the "greatest number" matters to any utilitarian calculus. Because in many, though not necessarily all circumstances, the amount of pleasure will be increased when factoring in the impact of any of our decisions on other people.

[3] In an instance where one is weighing more than one option, one would simply apply the utilitarian calculus to both (all) options and then choose the option which has greater balance of pleasure produced.

Table 1. Should Bentham University Accept the Mid-Week Game?

Pleasures	Pains
$750,000 (which can be used to procure various forms of pleasure for your athletes; food, travel, uniforms, etc.)	BU Players will miss class on Tuesday. (Which would not have happened on Saturday)
Increased Fun/Enjoyment for the fans due to the spectacle created by a nationally televised night game.	KSU players will miss class on Tuesday as well as on any necessary travel days.
Increased exposure for the University due to the national reach of broadcast and the university promos run during the broadcast	Students on campus will be distracted (and may also skip class) on the day of the game.

The first step would be to identify the possible actions. In this case you can either accept the check and move the game or you can decline the check and keep the game on Saturday. The next step would be to begin identifying pleasures and pains. What should we identify on each side of this balance sheet? Here is my initial account of the goods and harms produced. See if you agree.

Let us assume that the list above is a more or less accurate measure of the pleasures and pains produced. The next step would be quantify these goods so that a sum of the goods produced can be compared to the sum of the evils produced. In doing so we should take Bentham's categories of evaluation into account (e.g., intensity, duration, etc.). What might this look like?

Looking at Bentham's seven categories suggests in this instance that duration, fecundity and extent are the most pertinent variables. The $750,000, for instance, would seem to produce durable, fecund and widely dispersed pleasure. This is because the money will procure goods for the athletes (such as better food or travel or facilities) which will in turn generate better programs and more winning, which in turn will make fans happier, etc. Not only is the initial pleasure gained by the money widely dispersed (all athletes), the pleasure will likely endure and compound. As such, if zero utils (the "unit" used by utilitarians) is a baseline/pleasure-neutral value and one hundred is a perfect score of "absolute pleasure," it would seem that the "money" produced should be valued very highly. Let us say 75 utils.

What of the fun and excitement produced? Here the duration is relatively short but the extent is wide. Not only will the 35,000 fans enjoy the game more, so will the national TV audience which would not have access to this game otherwise. As such, it seems clear that "fun" should be valued less than the money on the grounds that although the extent is very large the duration is fleeting. Nevertheless, a lot of pleasure will be produced, so we will value "fun" at 50 utils.

The final pleasure produced is "exposure." Here, in addition to duration, fecundity, and extent, we should consider Bentham's fourth category of "remoteness," for the pleasures produced by exposure will likely not be immediate. Considering these categories we see that exposure will likely lead to increased enrollment (or at least applications) which is likely to compound to increased revenue, which could lead to better facilities, better faculty compensation, etc. It is also worth mentioning that exposure will likely make recruiting easier for your Athletics Department because more young athletes will know about your school and will be excited by the prospect of playing on television, etc.

How then should we value "exposure"? The potential extent is wide, as is the potential fecundity, as is the potential duration. However, given the remoteness of these possibilities and the likelihood that not all of them will bear fruit, it seems clear we should value it less than either "fun" or "money." We will give it 25 utils.

Now we must turn our attention to the pains produced. As with pleasure, we will use a 100 point scale with zero being "pain-neutral" and 100 being "absolute pain." Again it seems clear that duration, fecundity and extent are the most pertinent of Bentham's categories. How then might we quantify the pains produced in this situation?

If we consider the missed class by the BU football team you should notice that the duration and extent is small. There are roughly one hundred players as compared to millions watching the game. These players are only missing one additional day of class during a semester which is four months long. The pain generated seems small by comparison. As with duration and extent, so, arguably, with fecundity. After all, if the pain generated from missed class were likely to compound upon itself, we would expect to find universities hesitant to ever excuse students from their courses. But we find just the opposite. Not only do athletes routinely get excused from courses for travel and games, so do member of other university sponsored activities (drama, choir, band, etc.). It appears then that although the harm is real, it is of a short duration, a small extent and will not generate ongoing pain. Therefore, we will value "BU missed class" at 10 utils.

The next pain is very similar to the first, except this time we're considering the KSU football team's missed class. Everything from the previous analysis of BU would apply here with a slightly longer duration due to the necessary travel time. In the worst case scenario this would add two additional days (one to BU and one home to KSU). As such, since the duration is tripled and the fecundity and extent will be roughly the same as BU, we will value the pain produced by "KSU missed class" at 30 utils.

The final pain to evaluate is "distraction," by which we mean that the game may cause students to not pay attention in class or even skip class to party, tailgate, drink, etc. Here we should add in Bentham's third category of "uncertainty." Why? Because although the duration, extent and fecundity will all likely be relatively small (on the same grounds as was established with the BU and KSU football teams), it seems likely that on game day many students *will* go to class and many student *will* pay attention, which means that the

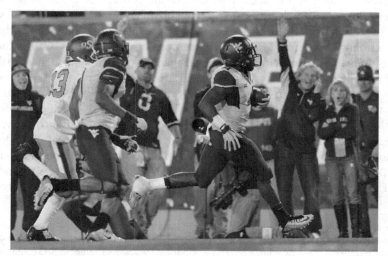

Can "mid-week" football games be morally justified?
©Aspen Photo/Shutterstock.com

game will, at worst, *encourage* students to be "distracted." It is therefore uncertain that distraction will cause significant pain. Even after acknowledging a relatively larger extent—due to the fact that the student body is larger than the football team—it only seems fair to value the pain produced by "distraction" no higher than "BU missed class." Therefore we will value the pain produced by "distraction" at 10 utils.

The final step is to add up the value of the pleasures and pains produced. Here we see that the pleasures generate a value of 150 while the pains generate a value of only 50. As a result, the utilitarian calculus indicates that taking the money to play a mid-week game is justified because it will generate far more pleasure than pain.[4] Is that right?

Table 2. Valuation of the Goods/Harms Produced by the BU vs. KSU mid-week Game

Pleasures	Value	Pains	Value
$750,000 (which can be used to procure various forms of pleasure for your athletes; food, travel, uniforms, etc.)	75	BU Players will miss class on Tuesday. (Which would not have happened on Saturday)	10
Increased Fun/Enjoyment for the fans due to the spectacle created by a nationally televised night game.	50	KSU players will miss class on Tuesday as well as on any necessary travel days.	30
Increased exposure for the University due to the national reach of broadcast and the university promos run during the broadcast.	25	Students on campus will be distracted (and may also miss/skip class) on the day of the game.	10
Totals:	150		50

A common criticism of this type of analysis is that Bentham's endorsement of quantitative utilitarianism ends ups endorsing a crude hedonism which results in nothing more than decadence. You should remember the concept of crude hedonism from Chapter 2. In essence, such critics are using Bentham's claim that "push-pin is as good as poetry" against him by insisting that some goods are inherently higher than others. That is, any amount of "poetry" would always trump "push-pin." This is because the beauty and profundity of poetry is inherently better than childish pursuits such as pushpin.

Put in contemporary terms we might say that any amount of "friendship" always trumps any amount of "sex, drugs, and rock & roll" or that any amount of "Shakespeare" always trumps any amount of "pornography." Similarly, in this specific case one might argue that since a university is purportedly in the business of education, that any amount of unnecessary "missed class" always trumps any amount of "revenue." The educational mission should always trump money. How should a utilitarian respond to such criticism? Bentham stuck to his guns and insisted that the quantity of pleasure and not the type of pleasure was what mattered. His disciple John Stuart Mill took a different tack.

---

[4] We are assuming that a calculus run on the option of turning down the mid-week game would produce a mirror result (e.g. the loss of $750,000 would become a pain of the same value, staying an extra day in class would be a pleasure of the same value, etc.). This is important because as Timmons (2013) points out: "Utilitarianism is a maximizing theory, and we are to perform the action with the highest utility. So we must calculate the utilities of the alternative actions open to us in some situation" (p. 119).

J.S. Mill's Qualitative Hedonism

John Stuart Mill was an English philosopher and economist who lived from 1806 to 1873. Although he agreed with Bentham's general principle that moral decisions should be based in their utility, he disagreed with Bentham's assertion that we should only take the quantity of pleasure into account. As Mill (1998) insists, "It would be absurd that while, in estimating all other things, quality is considered as well as quantity, the estimation of pleasure should be supposed to depend on quantity alone" (p. 56).

Mill's point is that human experience shows that in all areas of life (including pleasure) we take both the quantity (amount) of the good and the quality (type) of good into account. This idea can be made more explicit. Mill intends to reform Bentham's claim by pointing out that only counting the amount of pleasure means that one will necessarily end up "comparing apples to oranges." Think of it this way: How many apples do you need to get an orange? 100? 500? 1000? The question is absurd. No *amount* of apples (one good) will ever get you an orange (another good). The two goods are incommensurate. Which means, Mill argues, utilitarianism cannot be mere quantitative hedonism.

Qualitative Hedonism:
The form of hedonism which bases the evaluation of pleasure both in terms of the amount (quantity) and type (quality) of pleasure produced. For the qualitative hedonist, both the amount and type of pleasure produced matter.

No amount of apples (one good) will ever get you an orange (another good).
Kuznetsov Alexey/Shutterstock.com

Moreover, Mill (1998) believes that we all know not only that goods are often incommensurate, we also all know how to adjudicate between the higher and lower goods.

> "Now it is an unquestionable fact that those who are equally acquainted with, and equally capable of appreciating and enjoying, both [the higher and lower pleasures], do give a most marked preference to the manner of existence which employs their higher faculties. Few human creatures would consent to be changed into any of the lower animals, for a fullest allowance of the beast's pleasures; no intelligent human being would consent to be a fool . . . It is better to be a human being dissatisfied than a pig satisfied; better to be Socrates dissatisfied than a fool satisfied" (pp. 56–57).

How might these insights modify our previous utilitarian calculus regarding the midweek football game between BU and KSU? Arguably it would alter the balance significantly. It would all depend on whether we think there are any qualitative differences between the pleasures (or pains). If, as was briefly outlined above, we take universities to be in the business of education, then we might argue that attending class is a higher good

It is better to be a human being dissatisfied than a pig satisfied.
©Patrik Jech/Shutterstock.com

than any of the other goods listed. Which would mean that it would trump "money," "fun," and "exposure" no matter how much of each of these pleasures is on offer. No amount of "education" should ever be sacrificed at the altar of "lower goods." As a result, the opportunity to host a mid-week game should be turned down. Is that right?

Act versus Rule Utilitarianism

So far we have been considering the classical forms of utilitarianism advanced by Bentham and Mill. Each philosopher advances a version of what is known as Act-utilitarianism. Act-utilitarians are concerned with applying the principle "maximize pleasure" to our individual choices. That is, before making any significant choice, one should balance the pleasure and pains likely to be produced by that choice against the pleasures and pains of any other possible choices. One should then choose the option which promotes "the greatest good for the greatest number."[5] Although Bentham and Mill disagree on how to calculate the greatest good, they each endorse the principle of utility as a way to guide individual actions.[6]

Rule-utilitarians, in contrast, are not interested in evaluating particular acts. Instead they promote the idea that we should follow the rules which best promote the greatest good for the greatest number. As the philosopher William Frankena (1973) puts it, "the question is not which *action* has the greatest utility, but which *rule* has" (p. 39). To stick with our example, a rule utilitarian might agree with the claim that "universities should always promote education." However they would do so only on the grounds that such a rule will lead to the "best consequences" (Frakena, 1973, p. 39). As a result, the rule utilitarian would not be overly interested in any particular case, such as our calculus in

---

[5] Of course, the nature of life means that we will not always have time to do the type of strict utilitarian calculus Bentham suggests. But as Bentham (2007) points out, although such calculation may not always be "strictly pursued" it may always be "kept in view" (p. 31).

[6] There is some controversy over whether Mill is a consistent Act-utilitarian. Some argue that he is a rule utilitarian. It is worth bearing in mind that this controversy is anachronistic. As Schefczyk (n.d.) points out, "the distinction between rule and act utilitarianism had not yet been introduced in Mill's days" (para. 22).

Table 2, unless it somehow indicated that the rule was *generally* not conducive to the greatest good. The rule utilitarian is interested in the most useful general principle not the most useful action in this or that particular case.

The Strengths of Utilitarianism

What then are the strengths of utilitarian philosophy? Why are intelligent people convinced of its truth? We will consider three strengths. The first strength is that there is something intuitive about considering the consequences of our actions. We want our actions to lead to good results. In fact you might argue that we expect good actions to lead to good consequences. Insofar as utilitarians take the consequences of our actions seriously they would seem to be on solid ground. It is a strength of utilitarianism that its defenders recognize that at least one of the reasons that we do good things is *because we want good results.*

The second strength of utilitarianism is for many people the most important. Why? Because the second strength is that utilitarianism is flexible to the situation. In contrast to other theories that bind us to specific action by prescribing ("tell the truth") or proscribing ("don't lie"), utilitarianism allows us to evaluate the circumstances rather than slavishly follow rigid rules. This is obviously true of act-utilitarianism where the situation dictates action and where the only rule to follow is to "maximize pleasure." Yet, it is also true, to a great extent, of rule utilitarianism. Why? Because although rule utilitarians are constrained from modifying rules simply to fit one specific circumstance, the rules are still open to modification. Again, as with Act-utilitarians, the only permanent rule is "maximize pleasure." Every other rule that the Rule-utilitarian promotes is merely pragmatic. Its value exists only because the rule is *useful* for maximizing pleasure. As Frankena (1973) insists, "Rules must be selected, maintained, revised and replaced on the basis of their utility and not any other basis" (p. 39). For the Rule-utilitarian, flexibility comes from the fact that every rule other than "maximize pleasure" is merely procedural and therefore ultimately up for debate. Should a more efficient means to maximizing pleasure become convincing (or convenient) the existing rule should *necessarily* be abandoned. Many find this flexibility attractive because ethical situations often seem to fall outside of any set of absolute rules.

The final strength of utilitarianism is one we considered in Chapter 2 and that is that hedonism seems plausible. Pleasure does seem to be a real good. Pain does seem to be bad. It would make sense then that utilitarians desire to promote those actions or rules which will promote the most pleasure for the most people. Moreover, given the amount of suffering in the world, it seem that any theory which spurs concern for the suffering of others is a moral advance. The utilitarian philosopher Peter Singer (1995) puts the idea this way: "From this perspective, we can see that our own sufferings and pleasures are very like the sufferings and pleasures of others; and that there is no reason to give less consideration to the sufferings of others, just because they are 'other'" (p. 222). Maximizing pleasure and reducing pain is simple common sense.

What, if anything, is wrong with this view? The key controversial assumption of the utilitarians is not that pleasure is good. The key controversial assumption is that pleasure is the only *intrinsic* good. Critics of utilitarianism insist that it is highly questionable that pleasure is something we should pursue for its own sake. As I argued in Chapter 2, this position seems dubious because pleasure is, as Aristotle pointed out,[7] always attendant to

---

[7] See *Nicomachean Ethics* Book X (Aristotle, 2002).

some other good(s). As I (2012) have said elsewhere, "Activity trumps sensation. As rational animals, humans need to *be* in a certain way not merely *feel* certain things. Our embodiment demands recognition of the reality that the human good is more than [pleasurable] states of consciousness." (p. 182). Sport (and life) is about *being* not merely about *feeling*. As I argued in Chapter 2, "We want to *play baseball*, not merely *feel* the pleasures involved."

Furthermore, real compassion for the suffering of others relies on particularity. That is, compassion is grounded in relationships. Compassion is born of community not measurement or calculation. For:

> "Community is a co-mingling of particulars that have realized human vulnerability and interconnectedness. It is this interconnectedness that is the antidote to the rationality and cold empiricism that results from a purely utilitarian conception of duty. Names and faces make all the difference" (Twietmeyer, 2007, p. 205).

Real concern for others is born of love. Contrary to Singer, genuine concern for others cannot be based in a pleasure/pain calculus. As a result, hedonism is mistaken. Of course, if this is right, then utilitarianism is also mistaken. If so, we should expect that other weaknesses in the theory can be identified. What are these weaknesses?

The Weaknesses of Utilitarianism

Even after setting aside the dubious status of hedonism, several weaknesses of utilitarianism can be identified. Again, as with the strengths, we will consider three. First, how are we to accurately quantify the good? How do we know what the goods are, that we have identified all of them, and that we have correctly valued their worth? This criticism is based in the idea that, even given Bentham's seven categories (intensity, duration, etc.), any valuation of pleasures and pains will still be subjective.

Consider our example of the mid-week game; one might identify different pleasures and pains from the one's we've identified, one might agree with all of the pleasure and pains identified, yet value them differently and thereby tip the scales in the opposite

Is missing class a pleasure or a pain?
©wavebreakmedia/Shutterstock.com

direction. Worse yet, one might even disagree that a pain is actually a pain. A student, for instance, may see "missed class" as another pleasure. There is nothing in Bentham's seven categories for quantifying pleasures that can say that the student is wrong. Whose measure, then, should we use?[8]

This problem of identifying goods well enough to accurately quantify them is further complicated by the fact that there are limits to our knowledge.[9] As a result it is often (perhaps always) unclear what the full set of consequences of our actions (or rules) will be. Certainly it is not unheard of for any action or rule to have "unintended consequences." But for a consequence to be unintended it would have to be unforeseen, which means it could not ever be part of the utilitarian calculus upon which the decision was justified in the first place. But this means that the calculus was not an accurate measure of the pleasures and pains produced and cannot therefore be a sound justification of the action. The implications of this insight are dire for utilitarianism. For if this criticism is right and generally applicable, then it would follow that we could *never* know enough to decide what the "greatest good" really is.

The second weakness of utilitarianism is related to the first and applies most directly to act-utilitarianism. In the first weakness the focus was on our knowledge (or lack thereof). In this criticism, however, the focus is on the relationship between cause and effect. What the critics allege is that the line between cause and effect is not always clear. The point is twofold. First, it is often hard to establish what effects follow from our choices (as we discussed in weakness one). Second, the apparent effects of our decisions (causes) can often seem to justify the necessity of making unjust choices.[10]

For instance, imagine that you are a recent graduate of your university's sports ethics course. Since it used this textbook you are well grounded in moral theory and have become convinced of the truth of utilitarianism. After graduating you take a job as the manager of a local recreation center. This is good news for you because you are also a single parent of two children. After a few months on the job, the owner of the recreation center propositions you. He demands that you have sex with him to keep your job. Furthermore, knowing your utilitarian inclinations—for he's seen you reading Bentham at lunch—he points out that the greatest good will be served by you agreeing to his proposal. For in doing so, you will keep your job and thereby be able to provide for your children. Providing for your children is clearly the greater good. It is more durable, more fecund and has a greater extent. In comparison, the pains involved in giving in to his demands are rather small. Is it not clear that you should agree? Is it not also clear that should you turn down the proposition that you would be to blame for being fired (at least insofar as you did not choose the greater good)? That is, the effect (firing) was

---

[8] MacIntyre's (1984) criticism here is damning: "For different pleasures and different happinesses are to a large degree incommensurable: there are no scales of quality or quantity on which to weight them. Consequently appeal to the criteria of pleasure will not tell me whether to drink or swim and appeal to those of happiness cannot decide for me between the life of a monk and that of a soldier. To have understood the polymorphous character of pleasure and happiness is of course to have rendered those concepts useless for utilitarian purposes…" (p. 64).

[9] One way utilitarians have attempted to get around this problem is by arguing for "expected consequences" (See Timmons Chapter 5 for a discussion). According to this theory we ought to do our pleasure/pain calculus based upon what knowledge we have at hand. Actions which *expect* to maximize utility are therefore justified. Yet, it seems that such a modification would do serious damage to utilitarianism as such. If fact, it could be argued it undermines the larger theory by changing it from a theory of "maximizing pleasure" to a theory of "maximizing calculation". That is, any action is justified if the sums are neat and tidy (they align with the presumed rather than actual facts).

[10] For classic cases of this objection see: (Ross, 1930, 2002) and (Nathanson, n.d.)

caused by *your* unwillingness to give in to your boss, even though the calculus showed that the greatest good was served by doing so?[11] You have, therefore, no one to blame but yourself.

Many would argue that such reasoning is profoundly mistaken. No one should ever be put in a situation where they have to choose between losing their job or giving in to a sexual **quid pro quo**. This is exactly why we have sexual harassment laws! But notice what was said. This should *never* happen. To say such things is to imply that such behavior is intrinsically evil. That is, such propositions are always wrong (independent of the consequences). Yet, if one intrinsic evil can be identified, might there be more?

This question leads directly into the third weakness of utilitarianism. In utilitarianism, *there are no intrinsically wrong actions*. None. There are only good or bad results. Everything—even human beings—can and should be used as a means to the goal of maximizing pleasure. The wrongness of cheating, lying, using performance enhancing drugs, sexism, racism, even rape and murder, is contingent upon a pleasure/pain calculus justifying that any given behavior will generate more pain than pleasure. If the utilitarian is being consistent, he would have to admit that should the right situation come along, all of the actions just listed could be justified. To be fair, the utilitarian could also insist that such circumstances are extremely rare. But that is the best he can say (and his saying so is contingent upon—as we saw with weakness #1—*his valuation* of the pleasures and pains produced).[12]

The result, the critic would argue, is that utilitarianism can justify all kinds of evil, as long as the actor(s) involved *say to themselves* that the good produced outweighs the "evil" required. What others would consider "evil" must be considered by the utilitarian solely on the grounds of its usefulness (utility). For the utilitarian, actions and rules are only "evil" if they are not the most useful actions or rules. Nonetheless, is it not the case that we often want to say that at least some actions (e.g., "cheating" or "racism" or "murder") are never justified? How can this be right if, as the utilitarian surmises, every action/rule can only be justified by its consequences?

Similarly, critics allege that utilitarians will often fail to live up to their own standard. Instead of maximizing pleasure, once one has adopted a consequentialist attitude (free of any intrinsic evils), it may be very tempting to use an "ends justify the means" position but only apply it to one's self. After all, what pleasure could possibly be higher (quantitatively or qualitatively) than my own?!? Utilitarianism, in practice, then becomes "the greatest pleasure for me . . . by any means necessary" (See the Singer reading in this chapter for a good example of how this can play out in sport). The result, so the critic alleges, is that human beings gain an easy rationalization for their own selfish behavior, by hiding it under the guise of utilitarianism.[13] The result is the crass, selfish and shallow ethic that "If it feels good, do it."

Quid Pro Quo: A Latin phrase meaning "something for something." When used in reference to sexual harassment, it describes actions where some good (such as employment, a raise, etc.) is used as an enticement or threat for the procurement of sexual favors (e.g., "sleep with me or you're fired").

---

[11] The rule utilitarian could of course argue that such behavior (sexual quid pro quos) could never be a general rule by which to promote the greatest good. In doing so they would seem to be able to avoid the criticism. However, they wouldn't actually be prohibiting the rule on moral grounds beyond usefulness, which means the rule could always be changed. Many, will find such conditional (and therefore tepid) condemnation of the behavior unsatisfactory.

[12] An alternative valuation of the pleasure and pains may, of course, turn such "evils" into "goods".

[13] In reviewing this point, the philosopher and mathematician David Berlinski (Hoover Institution, 2011) points to a famous quote from the 18th Century English literary critic Dr. Samuel Johnson who opined that "All the laws of heaven and earth are insufficient to restrain men from their crimes." If this is true Berlinksi argues, then "surely relaxing the laws of heaven and earth shall not dispose men to better behavior" (p. 10).

Calvin and Hobbes

Utilitarian Responses

How do utilitarians respond to such criticism? One strategy would be to point out that the critics are far too pessimistic. People can, with sound education and an emphasis on reason, learn to think about the greater good. Moreover, people are basically good.[14] In fact, a utilitarian might argue that we only tend to be pessimistic about human behavior because of traditionalist moral "hang-ups" that are not actually justifiable on a pleasure/plain calculus. Utilitarians also often argue that hard cases can be found in the other direction. That is, there are hard cases that support utilitarianism. Isn't lying, for example, sometimes justified, if it will save someone from hurt feelings or save a life? Finally, insofar, as people only look out for themselves they are not being utilitarians! Utilitarianism demands the greater good; not mere pleasure for the self, but maximized pleasure.

How then should this argument be settled? I find the weaknesses of utilitarianism far more convincing than its strengths. Although considering the consequences when making moral decisions can be valuable, I do not see how utility can be the basis or sole criterion for moral action. This is true regarding our actions in sport, as well as our actions in general. The good is larger than pleasure. Right and wrong are more than usefulness. You will, of course, have to evaluate utilitarianism for yourself. As you do so, you must engage both sides of the argument. Utilitarianism may be wrong as I have surmised, but there are

---

[14] It is worth pointing out that this is a metaphysical claim. As we saw in Chapter 1, ethics and metaphysics implicate one another.

certainly smart people who have defended it. Therefore, to call yourself educated requires understanding the arguments both for and against the theory. Even if one is convinced that utilitarianism is deeply mistaken, one must recognize and evaluate the point of view of its supporters before one can take ownership of their own reasoned position.

Utilitarianism & Sport

It should be apparent now how often utilitarianism (or some similar form of consequentialism) makes an appearance in sport. Every time one argues that the ends justify the means one is making a consequentialist argument. Examples of this type of thinking in sport are not hard to identify. We see it in clichés such as "Winning isn't everything, it is the only thing!" Utilitarianism is also a driving force behind the ever increasing commercialization of sport. As former NFL player Nate Jackson points out in the epigraph to this chapter, professional sports players themselves are often commodified by owners and fans alike. Nevertheless the same sort of utilitarian analysis is often used by players as well. It can commonly be found in the rationales offered by athletes looking to justify this or that moral decision. Utilitarianism has even been offered in academic sport philosophy as a serious justification for otherwise morally dubious action.[15]

Here are three more quick examples of how pervasive utilitarian thinking is in sport. There are, of course, many others. As you read them, ask yourself if the utilitarian rationale offered makes sense. Are pleasures and pains the only things that need to be taken into account when making ethical decisions?

The first example is quite similar to the mid-week game dilemma we've already considered. In 2005, the NCAA voted to add a 12th football came to the college football schedule. Despite the added pressure this would add to student-athletes both academically and physically, the additional revenue was impossible to resist. This is because, "For football powers such as Michigan, Ohio State and Tennessee, which play in 100,000-seat stadiums that dwarf the typical NFL venue, an extra home game could mean more than $3 million per year in additional revenue" (Clarke, 2005, para. 5).

Money (and what it would procure) was clearly considered the greatest good. Is that not plausible? After all, that money will be put to good use, supporting minor (often women's) sports, paying for scholarships, etc. Don't such goods outweigh any additional harms created by adding one game to the season? Yet, as Bob Eno, an advocate of intercollegiate athletic reform pointed out, the "motivation for having intercollegiate athletics is supposed to be for educational enhancement" (Clarke, 2005, para. 13). Can it really be said that the added practice, travel, competitive, physical and academic pressures created by another game will further the purported educational *mission* of the university and its athletics programs? Moreover, should students ever be used as a means to the end of greater profits?

The second example is the recent FIFA decision to expand the men's World Cup to 48 teams (from 32) beginning in 2026. Although FIFA President Gianni Infantino insists it was done because "Football is more than Europe and South America; football is global," (Conn, 2017, para. 4) it seem likely that the true motivating factor was not what's good for global soccer, but rather, money. This can be inferred from problems that the new format creates regarding competitive integrity and interest, as well as from the estimates

---

[15] In *The "hand of God"?: Essays in the philosophy of sports*, Claudio Tamburinni (2000) argues that Diego Maradona's infamous handball goal in the 1986 World Cup is a case of "blameful right doing" because "After its occurrence, encounters between the Argentinean and the English national football teams are marked by enhanced competitive character" (p. 32). The good generated by an enhanced rivalry outweighs the harms created by cheating. "Therefore, his goal should be placed on a moral par with other actions (such as diving, intimidating interventions and others), that—though performed for morally suspect motivations—add to the hedonic quality of the sports performance and increase the enjoyment of the public" (p. 32).

that it will "generate around $1bn more income, and $640m profit, from greater television rights and sponsorship" (Conn, 2017, para 3).

As regards competitive integrity, critics of the expansion have worried that the larger tournament will create "less intrigue in regional qualifying, more ho-hum pairings in the first round and odd, three-team groups" (Goff, 2019, para. 20). If these criticisms are on target, then it seems clear the "greater good" of profit, has won the day, even at the cost of watering down and cheapening the integrity of the competition.

Finally, consider this account of a conversation between Lance Armstrong and *New York Times* reporter Juliet Macur (2014) from her book *Cycle of Lies.* The conversation occurred after Armstrong's lies and PED use had been exposed in 2013:

> "He isn't sorry for lying. Not for the original lie or any other in the cycle of lies that followed. 'We all would have lied,' he says. 'You would have lied'.
>
> In 1999, he sat in front of reporters at the Tour and made his first denial of doping. After that, he says, he could never turn back—he had to keep denying. But, really, he says, everybody would have done what he did. You, me, the guy down the street—if it meant you could win the Tour de France, anybody and everybody would have denied doping. In Lance Armstrong's moral universe, anyone will sell his or her soul to win" (p. 402).

As usual, the importance of philosophy comes into focus. For it is clear that Armstrong's claim that victory, fame, and money justify lying is a utilitarian claim, which is bound up in other philosophical commitments. His view of the good, his view of moral truth, even his confusion of normative and descriptive ethics comes into play. The take home point is this: our evaluation of utilitarianism does not occur in a vacuum. Instead it relies upon, as Macur puts it, a "moral universe," a moral universe built upon all of our philosophical commitments. Can those philosophic commitments be justified? I have argued that the moral universe described by utilitarianism does not ultimately mesh with reality. As the sole or principal guide to moral action utilitarianism cannot be justified. Will a commitment to following the rules, a commitment to doing our duty, do any better?

In Lance Armstrong's moral universe, anyone will sell his or her soul to win.
©Freederric Legrand – COMEO/Shutterstock.com

PHILOSOPHIC SELECTIONS

Selection #1: Jeremy Bentham, *"An Introduction to the Principles of Morals and Legislation."*

http://www.econlib.org/library/Bentham/bnthPML1.html#Chapter I, Of the Principle of Utility; http://www.econlib.org/library/Bentham/bnthPML4.html#Chapter IV, Value of a Lot of Pleasure or Pain, How to be Measured

Introduction: Whatever one thinks of Jeremy Bentham particularly or utilitarianism in general, it is clear that he cannot be charged with being milquetoast or unclear. Bentham articulates his principles and then doggedly sticks to them. In this brief selection from "An introduction to the Principles of Morals and Legislation" he lays out several key points. First, he argues that all ethical decisions are reducible to a hedonic calculus. Second, he insists that the "value" (quantity) of pleasure is what matters. Finally, he gives the "circumstances" (e.g., intensity, duration, etc.) by which an accurate measure of the pleasures involved in any moral calculus can be made.

I.1

Nature has placed mankind under the governance of two sovereign masters, pain and pleasure. It is for them alone to point out what we ought to do, as well as to determine what we shall do. On the one hand the standard of right and wrong, on the other the chain of causes and effects, are fastened to their throne. They govern us in all we do, in all we say, in all we think: every effort we can make to throw off our subjection, will serve but to demonstrate and confirm it. In words a man may pretend to abjure their empire: but in reality he will remain subject to it all the while. The principle of utility*6 recognizes this subjection, and assumes it for the foundation of that system, the object of which is to rear the fabric of felicity by the hands of reason and of law. Systems which attempt to question it, deal in sounds instead of sense, in caprice instead of reason, in darkness instead of light.

I.2

But enough of metaphor and declamation: it is not by such means that moral science is to be improved.

I.3

II. The principle of utility is the foundation of the present work: it will be proper therefore at the outset to give an explicit and determinate account of what is meant by it. By the principle of utility is meant that principle which approves or disapproves of every action whatsoever, according to the tendency it appears to have to augment or diminish the happiness of the party whose interest is in question: or, what is the same thing in other words, to promote or to oppose that happiness. I say of every action whatsoever, and therefore not only of every action of a private individual, but of every measure of government.

I.4

III. By utility is meant that property in any object, whereby it tends to produce benefit, advantage, pleasure, good, or happiness, (all this in the present case comes to the same thing) or (what comes again to the same thing) to prevent the happening of mischief, pain, evil, or unhappiness to the party whose interest is considered: if that party be the community in general, then the happiness of the community: if a particular individual, then the happiness of that individual.

VALUE OF A LOT OF PLEASURE OR PAIN, HOW TO BE MEASURED

IV.1

I. Pleasures then, and the avoidance of pains, are the ends that the legislator has in view; it behoves him therefore to understand their value. Pleasures and pains are the instruments he has to work with: it behoves him therefore to understand their force, which is again, in other words, their value.

IV.2

II. To a person considered by himself, the value of a pleasure or pain considered by itself, will be greater or less, according to the four following circumstances:

1. Its intensity.
2. Its duration.
3. Its certainty or uncertainty.
4. Its propinquity or remoteness.

IV.3

III. These are the circumstances which are to be considered in estimating a pleasure or a pain considered each of them by itself. But when the value of any pleasure or pain is considered for the purpose of estimating the tendency of any act by which it is produced, there are two other circumstances to be taken into the account; these are,

IV.4

5. Its fecundity, or the chance it has of being followed by sensations of the same kind: that is, pleasures, if it be a pleasure: pains, if it be a pain.

IV.5

6. Its purity, or the chance it has of not being followed by sensations of the opposite kind: that is, pains, if it be a pleasure: pleasures, if it be a pain.

IV.6

These two last, however, are in strictness scarcely to be deemed properties of the pleasure or the pain itself; they are not, therefore, in strictness to be taken into the account of the value of that pleasure or that pain. They are in strictness to be deemed properties only of the act, or other event, by which such pleasure or pain has been produced; and accordingly are only to be taken into the account of the tendency of such act or such event.

IV.7

IV. To a number of persons, with reference to each of whom to the value of a pleasure or a pain is considered, it will be greater or less, according to seven circumstances: to wit, the six preceding ones; viz.

1. Its intensity.
2. Its duration.

3. Its certainty or uncertainty.
4. Its propinquity or remoteness.
5. Its fecundity.
6. Its purity.
   And one other; to wit:
7. Its extent; that is, the number of persons to whom it extends; or (in other words) who are affected by it.

IV.8

V. To take an exact account then of the general tendency of any act, by which the interests of a community are affected, proceed as follows. Begin with any one person of those whose interests seem most immediately to be affected by it: and take an account.

IV.9

1. Of the value of each distinguishable pleasure which appears to be produced by it in the first instance.

IV.10

2. Of the value of each pain which appears to be produced by it in the first instance.

IV.11

3. Of the value of each pleasure which appears to be produced by it after the first. This constitutes the fecundity of the first pleasure and the impurity of the first pain.

IV.12

4. Of the value of each pain which appears to be produced by it after the first. This constitutes the fecundity of the first pain, and the impurity of the first pleasure.

IV.13

5. Sum up all the values of all the pleasures on the one side, and those of all the pains on the other. The balance, if it be on the side of pleasure, will give the good tendency of the act upon the whole, with respect to the interests of that individual person; if on the side of pain, the bad tendency of it upon the whole.

IV.14

6. Take an account of the number of persons whose interests appear to be concerned; and repeat the above process with respect to each. Sum up the numbers expressive of the degrees of good tendency, which the act has, with respect to each individual, in regard to whom the tendency of it is good upon the whole: do this again with respect to each individual, in regard to whom the tendency of it is good upon the whole: do this again with respect to each individual, in regard to whom the tendency of it is bad upon the whole. Take the balance which if on the side of pleasure, will give the general good tendency of the act, with respect to the total number or community of individuals concerned; if on the side of pain, the general evil tendency, with respect to the same community.

IV.15

VI. It is not to be expected that this process should be strictly pursued previously to every moral judgment, or to every legislative or judicial operation. It may, however, be always kept in view: and as near as the process actually pursued on these occasions approaches to it, so near will such process approach to the character of an exact one.

IV.16

VII. The same process is alike applicable to pleasure and pain, in whatever shape they appear: and by whatever denomination they are distinguished: to pleasure, whether it be called good (which is properly the cause or instrument of pleasure) or profit (which is distant pleasure, or the cause or instrument of distant pleasure,) or convenience, or advantage, benefit, emolument, happiness, and so forth: to pain, whether it be called evil, (which corresponds to good) or mischief, or inconvenience, or disadvantage, or loss, or unhappiness, and so forth.

IV.17

VIII. Nor is this a novel and unwarranted, any more than it is a useless theory. In all this there is nothing but what the practice of mankind, wheresoever they have a clear view of their own interest, is perfectly conformable to. An article of property, an estate in land, for instance, is valuable, on what account? On account of the pleasures of all kinds which it enables a man to produce, and what comes to the same thing the pains of all kinds which it enables him to avert. But the value of such an article of property is universally understood to rise or fall according to the length or shortness of the time which a man has in it: the certainty or uncertainty of its coming into possession: and the nearness or remoteness of the time at which, if at all, it is to come into possession. As to the intensity of the pleasures which a man may derive from it, this is never thought of, because it depends upon the use which each particular person may come to make of it; which cannot be estimated till the particular pleasures he may come to derive from it, or the particular pains he may come to exclude by means of it, are brought to view. For the same reason, neither does he think of the fecundity or purity of those pleasures.

IV.18

Thus much for pleasure and pain, happiness and unhappiness, in general. We come now to consider the several particular kinds of pain and pleasure.

"An Introduction to the Principles of Morals and Legislation" by Jeremy Bentham. Public Domain.

Discussion Question(s)

1. Is Bentham right that happiness is synonymous with pleasure? Does sport offer a counter-example in its "no pain no gain" ethos? That is, does suffering for a good cause sometimes lead to happiness? Can pain and struggle be satisfying?
2. Bentham seems quite confident that pleasures can be quantified if we take variables such as intensity and duration into account. Is he right?
3. What pleasures, besides money (or winning), should utilitarian sport managers use as part of their moral calculus? Why?

Selection #2: J.S. Mill, *Utilitarianism*, Chapter 2

http://www.gutenberg.org/files/11224/11224-h/11224-h.htm#CHAPTER_II

Introduction: John Stuart Mill attempted to defend utilitarianism from the charge of debauchery by arguing that both the quality (type) of pleasure and the quantity (amount) of pleasure matters in utilitarian decision making. As such, Mill urges his readers to recognize that we ought to "give a most marked preference to the manner of existence which employs the higher faculties." Utilitarianism, rightly understood is not about crude hedonism. Just as a low amount of a higher-quality good is better than any amount of a lower-quality good, so too it is "better to be a human being dissatisfied than a pig satisfied."

The creed which accepts as the foundation of morals, Utility, or the Greatest Happiness Principle, holds that actions are right in proportion as they tend to promote happiness, wrong as they tend to produce the reverse of happiness. By happiness is intended pleasure, and the absence of pain; by unhappiness, pain, and the privation of pleasure. To give a clear view of the moral standard set up by the theory, much more requires to be said; in particular, what things it includes in the ideas of pain and pleasure; and to what extent this is left an open question. But these supplementary explanations do not affect the theory of life on which this theory of morality is grounded—namely, that pleasure, and freedom from pain, are the only things desirable as ends; and that all desirable things (which are as numerous in the utilitarian as in any other scheme) are desirable either for the pleasure inherent in themselves, or as means to the promotion of pleasure and the prevention of pain.

Now, such a theory of life excites in many minds, and among them in some of the most estimable in feeling and purpose, inveterate dislike. To suppose that life has (as they express it) no higher end than pleasure—no better and nobler object of desire and pursuit—they designate as utterly mean and grovelling; as a doctrine worthy only of swine, to whom the followers of Epicurus were, at a very early period, contemptuously likened; and modern holders of the doctrine are occasionally made the subject of equally polite comparisons by its German, French, and English assailants.

When thus attacked, the Epicureans have always answered, that it is not they, but their accusers, who represent human nature in a degrading light; since the accusation supposes human beings to be capable of no pleasures except those of which swine are capable. If this supposition were true, the charge could not be gainsaid, but would then be no longer an imputation; for if the sources of pleasure were precisely the same to human beings and to swine, the rule of life which is good enough for the one would be good enough for the other. The comparison of the Epicurean life to that of beasts is felt as degrading, precisely because a beast's pleasures do not satisfy a human being's conceptions of happiness. Human beings have faculties more elevated than the animal appetites, and when once made conscious of them, do not regard anything as happiness which does not include their gratification. I do not, indeed, consider the Epicureans to have been by any means faultless in drawing out their scheme of consequences from the utilitarian principle. To do this in any sufficient manner, many Stoic, as well as Christian elements require to be included. But there is no known Epicurean theory of life which does not assign to the pleasures of the intellect; of the feelings and imagination, and of the moral sentiments, a much higher value as pleasures than to those of mere sensation. It must be admitted, however, that utilitarian writers in general have placed the superiority of mental over bodily pleasures chiefly in the greater permanency, safety, uncostliness, &c., of the former—that is, in their circumstantial advantages rather than in their intrinsic nature. And on all these points utilitarians have fully proved their case; but they might have taken the other, and, as it may be called, higher ground, with entire consistency. It is quite compatible with the principle of utility to recognise the fact, that some kinds of pleasure are more desirable and more valuable than others. It would be absurd that while, in estimating all other things, quality is considered as well as quantity, the estimation of pleasures should be supposed to depend on quantity alone.

If I am asked, what I mean by difference of quality in pleasures, or what makes one pleasure more valuable than another, merely as a pleasure, except its being greater in amount, there is but one possible answer. Of two pleasures, if there be one to which all or almost all who have experience of both give a decided preference, irrespective of any feeling of moral obligation to prefer it, that is the more desirable pleasure. If one of the two is, by those who are competently acquainted with both, placed so far above the other that they prefer it, even though knowing it to be attended with a greater amount of discontent, and would not resign it for any quantity of the other pleasure which their nature is capable of, we are justified in ascribing to the preferred enjoyment a superiority in quality, so far outweighing quantity as to render it, in comparison, of small account.

Now it is an unquestionable fact that those who are equally acquainted with, and equally capable of appreciating and enjoying, both, do give a most marked preference to the manner of existence which employs their higher faculties. Few human creatures would consent to be changed into any of the lower animals, for a promise of the fullest allowance of a beast's pleasures; no intelligent human being would consent to be a fool, no instructed person would be an ignoramus, no person of feeling and conscience would be selfish and base, even though they should be persuaded that the fool, the dunce, or the rascal is better satisfied with his lot than they are with theirs. They would not resign what they possess more than he, for the most complete satisfaction of all the desires which they have in common with him. If they ever fancy they would, it is only in cases of unhappiness so extreme, that to escape from it they would exchange their lot for almost any other, however undesirable in their own eyes. A being of higher faculties requires more to make him happy, is capable probably of more acute suffering, and is certainly accessible to it at more points, than one of an inferior type; but in spite of these liabilities, he can never really wish to sink into what he feels to be a lower grade of existence. We may give what explanation we please of this unwillingness; we may attribute it to pride, a name which is given indiscriminately to some of the most and to some of the least estimable feelings of which mankind are capable; we may refer it to the love of liberty and personal independence, an appeal to which was with the Stoics one of the most effective means for the inculcation of it; to the love of power, or to the love of excitement, both of which do really enter into and contribute to it: but its most appropriate appellation is a sense of dignity, which all human beings possess in one form or other, and in some, though by no means in exact, proportion to their higher faculties, and which is so essential a part of the happiness of those in whom it is strong, that nothing which conflicts with it could be, otherwise than momentarily, an object of desire to them. Whoever supposes that this preference takes place at a sacrifice of happiness-that the superior being, in anything like equal circumstances, is not happier than the inferior-confounds the two very different ideas, of happiness, and content. It is indisputable that the being whose capacities of enjoyment are low, has the greatest chance of having them fully satisfied; and a highly-endowed being will always feel that any happiness which he can look for, as the world is constituted, is imperfect. But he can learn to bear its imperfections, if they are at all bearable; and they will not make him envy the being who is indeed unconscious of the imperfections, but only because he feels not at all the good which those imperfections qualify. It is better to be a human being dissatisfied than a pig satisfied; better to be Socrates dissatisfied than a fool satisfied. And if the fool, or the pig, is of a different opinion, it is because they only know their own side of the question. The other party to the comparison knows both sides.

It may be objected, that many who are capable of the higher pleasures, occasionally, under the influence of temptation, postpone them to the lower. But this is quite compatible with a full appreciation of the intrinsic superiority of the higher. Men often, from infirmity of character, make their election for the nearer good, though they know it to be the less valuable; and this no less when the choice is between two bodily pleasures, than when it is between bodily and mental. They pursue sensual indulgences to the injury of health, though perfectly aware that health is the greater good. It may be further objected, that many who begin with youthful enthusiasm for everything noble, as they advance in years sink into indolence and selfishness. But I do not believe that those who undergo this very common change, voluntarily choose the lower description of pleasures in preference to the higher. I believe that before they devote themselves exclusively to the one, they have already become incapable of the other. Capacity for the nobler feelings is in most natures a very tender plant, easily killed, not only by hostile influences, but by mere want of sustenance; and in the majority of young persons it speedily dies away if the occupations to which their position in life has devoted them, and the society into which it has thrown them, are not favourable to keeping that higher capacity in exercise. Men lose their high aspirations as they lose their intellectual tastes, because they have not time or opportunity for indulging them; and they addict themselves to inferior pleasures, not because they deliberately prefer them, but because they are either the only ones to which they have access, or the only ones which they are any longer capable of enjoying. It may be questioned whether any one who has remained equally susceptible to both classes of pleasures, ever knowingly and calmly preferred the lower; though many, in all ages, have broken down in an ineffectual attempt to combine both.

From this verdict of the only competent judges, I apprehend there can be no appeal. On a question which is the best worth having of two pleasures, or which of two modes of existence is the most grateful to the feelings, apart from its moral attributes and from its consequences, the judgment of those who are qualified by knowledge of both, or, if they differ, that of the majority among them, must be admitted as final. And there needs be the less hesitation to accept this judgment respecting the quality of pleasures, since there is no other tribunal to be referred to even on the question of quantity. What means are there of determining which is the acutest of two pains, or the intensest of two pleasurable sensations, except the general suffrage of those who are familiar with both? Neither pains nor pleasures are homogeneous, and pain is always heterogeneous with pleasure. What is there to decide whether a particular pleasure is worth purchasing at the cost of a particular pain, except the feelings and judgment of the experienced? When, therefore, those feelings and judgment declare the pleasures derived from the higher faculties to be preferable in kind, apart from the question of intensity, to those of which the animal nature, disjoined from the higher faculties, is susceptible, they are entitled on this subject to the same regard.

Utilitarianism by J.S. Mill. Public Domain.

Discussion Question(s)

1. Do you agree with Mill that ignorance *is not* bliss? Is it better to be unhappy but wise than to be a happy fool? Why?

2. Can the qualitative distinctions Mill wants to add to Bentham's quantitative theory be made objectively? If so, how? Is Mill's suggestion to follow "majority rule" persuasive?

3. What are the qualitatively higher pleasures in sport? Is, for instance, any amount of the "joy of competition" inherently more important than any amount of the "thrill of victory or the agony of defeat"? If so, what would that imply for teams intentionally scheduling "cupcakes" (easy victories) in the pursuit of victory?

Selection #3: Peter Singer, *The Guardian*, "Why is cheating OK in football?," June 29, 2010. Copyright: Project Syndicate, 2010

http://www.theguardian.com/commentisfree/2010/jun/29/cheating-football-germany-goalkeeper

Introduction: Peter Singer argues in this short newspaper column that utilitarianism can only succeed in sport if all those involved can look past their partisanship (and immediate advantage) to the ethical values implied by the utilitarian principle of maximizing pleasure for the greatest number. In particular, he scolds German goalkeeper Manuel Neuer for not thinking about the "greater good" during a key moment of the 2010 World Cup. Is he right to do so? Is the example that Singer recounts real evidence that the adoption of utilitarianism ought to broaden our moral horizons?

Shortly before half-time in the World Cup elimination match between England and Germany on 27 June, the England midfielder Frank Lampard had a shot at goal that struck the crossbar and bounced down onto the ground, clearly over the goal line. The goalkeeper, Manuel Neuer, grabbed the ball and put it back into play. Neither the referee nor the linesman—both of whom were still coming down the field, and poorly positioned to judge—signalled a goal, and play continued.

After the match, Neuer gave this account of his actions: "I tried not to react to the referee and just concentrate on what was happening. I realised it was over the line and I think the way I carried on so quickly fooled the referee into thinking it was not over."

To put it bluntly: Neuer cheated, and then boasted about it.

By any normal ethical standards, what Neuer did was wrong. But does the fact that Neuer was playing football mean that the only ethical rule is "win at all costs"?

In football, that does seem to be the prevailing ethic. The most famous of these incidents was Diego Maradona's goal in Argentina's 1986 World Cup match against England, which he later described as having been scored "a little with the head of Maradona and a little with the hand of God". Replays left no doubt that it was the hand of Maradona that scored the goal. Twenty years later, in a BBC interview, he admitted that he had intentionally acted as if it were a goal, in order to deceive the referee.

Something similar happened last November, in a game between France and Ireland that decided which of the two nations went to the World Cup. The French striker Thierry Henry used his hand to control the ball and pass to a teammate, who scored the decisive goal. Asked about the incident after the match, Henry said: "I will be honest, it was a handball. But I'm not the ref. I played it, the ref allowed it. That's a question you should ask him."

But is it? Why should the fact that you can get away with cheating mean that you are not culpable? Players should not be exempt from ethical criticism for what they do on the field, any more than they are exempt from ethical criticism for cheating off the field, for example by taking performance-enhancing drugs.

Sport today is highly competitive, with huge amounts of money at stake, but that does not mean it is impossible to be honest. In cricket, if a batsman hits the ball and one of the fielders catches it, the batsman is out. Sometimes when the ball is caught the umpire cannot be sure if the ball has touched the edge of the bat. The batsman usually knows and, traditionally, a batsman should "walk"—leave the ground—if he knows he is out.

Some still do. The Australian batsman Adam Gilchrist "walked" in the 2003 World Cup semi-final against Sri Lanka, although the umpire had already declared him not out. His decision surprised some of his team-mates but won applause from many cricket fans.

An internet search brought me just one clear-cut instance of a footballer appearing to doing something equivalent to a batsman walking. In 1996, Liverpool striker Robbie Fowler was awarded a penalty for being fouled by the Arsenal goalkeeper. He told the referee that he had not been fouled, but the referee insisted he take the penalty kick. Fowler did so, but in a manner that enabled the goalkeeper to save it.

Why are there so few examples of such behavior from professional footballers? Perhaps a culture of excessive partisanship has trumped ethical values. Fans don't seem to mind if members of their own team cheat successfully, they only object when the other side cheats. That's not an ethical attitude. (Though, to their credit, many French football followers, from President Nicolas Sarkozy down, expressed their sympathy for Ireland after Henry's handball.)

Yes, we can deal with the problem to some extent by using modern technology or video replays to review controversial refereeing decisions. But while that will reduce the opportunity for cheating, it won't eliminate it, and it isn't really the point. We should not make excuses for intentional cheating in sport. In one important way, it is much worse than cheating in one's private life. When what you do will be seen by millions, revisited on endless video replays, and dissected on television sports programs, it is especially important to do what is right.

How would football fans have reacted if Neuer had stopped play and told the referee that the ball was a goal? Given the rarity of such behavior in football, the initial reaction would no doubt have been surprise. Some German football fans might have been disappointed. But the world as a whole—and every fair-minded German fan, too—would have had to admit that he had done the right thing.

Neuer missed a rare opportunity to do something noble in front of millions of people. He could have set a positive ethical example to people watching all over the world, including the many millions who are young and impressionable. Who knows what difference that example might have made to the lives of many of those watching. Neuer could have been a hero, standing up for what is right. Instead he is just another very skillful, cheating footballer.

First published by Project Syndicate at www.projectsyndicate.org, June 28, 2010; reprinted in Peter Singer, *Ethics in the Real World*, Princeton University Press, 2016.

Discussion Question(s)

1. Singer is a well-known utilitarian. As such, can his condemnation of Neuer actually be reconciled with his ethical commitments? He seems to confidently argue in the piece that Neuer's behavior can be condemned on utilitarian grounds. Singer does so by insisting that Neuer's bad example causes more pain than pleasure. As Singer puts it, "Who knows what difference that [good] example might have made to the lives of many of those watching?" Yet, how do you think Singer would respond to the counter argument that Neuer's own utilitarian calculation came to the opposite conclusion? Isn't an argument such as: "the pleasures of personal glory, winning, happy German fans, etc. far outweigh any pain caused by 'bending the rules' or 'deceiving the referee'" just as plausible as Singer's? Is it possible to reconcile competing accounts of "maximized pleasure"?

Selection #4: Sam Walker, *The Wall Street Journal*, "Sergio Ramos, the World Cup and the benefits of bad Sportsmanship," June 13, 2018.

Retrieved from http://www.wsj.com/articles/the-occasional-brilliance-of-bad-sportsmanship-1528894907

Introduction: In this selection from *The Wall Street Journal*, we see another example of how the utilitarian logic that the "ends justify the means" applies to the sports world. Walker argues that in competitive sporting contexts "bad acts" which "come from a fundamentally good place [and lead to good results]" are morally justifiable. This is the inexorable endpoint of a moral system with no intrinsic goods or evils. Everything is circumstantial and can be justified by the desirability of the consequences procured. As you read this article, consider whether Walker is using utilitarianism appropriately and whether his justification(s) makes sense. That is, does his calculus add up in way that is both plausible and good or does he use and manipulate utilitarian logic to create moral cover for the "justification of all kinds of evil"?

The subject of this column isn't talent, vision, grit, emotional intelligence, radical candor, or any other leadership skill that people aspire to possess. It's about the art of behaving badly.

The World Cup, which opens Thursday in Russia, may be the finest laboratory on Earth for studying leadership's dark side. With a projected audience of 3.2 billion, this tournament will force its 32 team captains to strike a balance between the overwhelming pressure to win and the moral imperative to play fair.

It's glorious when these goals align, but the heaviest burden of leadership comes when they don't—when the captain has to choose one or the other.

"Can Sergio Ramos' deliberate injury of Mohamed Salah (seen here) be justified on utilitarian grounds? If so, does that mean that Walker is right to call it a good example of leadership?"

VI-Images/Getty Images Sport/Getty Images

Last month, while captaining his club team, Real Madrid, Sergio Ramos (who will also lead Spain at the World Cup) made just such a decision. With the Champions League final knotted in a scoreless tie, the 32-year-old defender pinned the arm of Liverpool's top scorer, Mohamed Salah, in the crook of his own, then drove his body to the turf. Mr. Salah left the match with a shoulder injury.

Across the globe, people responded to Real Madrid's 3-1 victory with explosive outrage. They saw Mr. Ramos's violent tackle as the embodiment of everything that's wrong with sports and accused him of hurting the Egyptian on purpose. His status as captain for both club and country made the optics exponentially worse.

Within days, 500,000 people had signed a petition calling Mr. Ramos "an awful example to future generations" and urging the sport's governing bodies to punish him retroactively.

There's no doubt Mr. Ramos will be lustily booed in Russia and that some people will never forgive him. The more provocative question is whether he'd even hesitate to do it again.

When England's upper classes brought organized sports to prominence, they yoked them to a behavioral code that's come to be known as "sportsmanship." To this day, we teach our children that it's not whether you win or lose—it's how you play the game.

Violations of this code, which are common at the World Cup, can provoke outsize anger. Many French fans will never forgive their former captain, Zinedine Zidane, for head-butting an Italian player in a fit of pique during the final minutes of the 2006 final. His subsequent ejection effectively destroyed his team's chances of winning. (Mr. Zidane, incidentally, was Mr. Ramos's manager during the Champions League final.)

Leaders in business and other competitive fields are sometimes felled by bad behavior, too. Last year, reports of aggressive tactics and a toxic workplace culture prompted Uber's board to oust Travis Kalanick, its hard-charging chief executive. A viral video that showed Mr. Kalanick engaged in a heated argument with a driver didn't help.

The tricky thing about aggressive leadership is that no right-minded person believes it's 100% negative. We wouldn't be talking about Uber if Mr. Kalanick hadn't thrown a few elbows while expanding into hundreds of new markets. The real issue isn't the leader's instinct to do aggressive things; it's our confusion about when it's appropriate.

Before passing judgment on any example, there are four tests to apply. The first one is identifying the motive.

Starting in the 1960s, researchers began to separate aggression into different flavors. The most common variety is "hostile" aggression, which is driven by a desire to hurt or punish someone. This motive is entirely negative. A second flavor, however, involves an action that may look hostile, but is chiefly done to achieve a worthwhile goal. That's what researchers call "instrumental" aggression.

Studies performed on athletes have shown that when they take the field they enter a "game frame" where the rules of sport supersede the everyday rules of society. They might do things in competition they would never do anywhere else. Athletes understand what spectators, who live in the real world, often don't: The rules of sports aren't laws per se, but guidelines subject to interpretation by the officials.

That's also true in the workplace, where behavioral norms will vary and the board or HR department has the final say.

Unlike Mr. Zidane's impulsive head-butt, there's no evidence that Mr. Ramos's tackle was a hostile act. Though Mr. Salah has yet to publicly forgive him, Mr. Ramos hovered over him afterward and says the two men have traded messages. Viewed this way—as strategic rather than malicious—his tackle seems to fit squarely in the "instrumental" category.

The second test is whether an ugly play actually helped the team win—and whether the leader got away with it.

The elite sports captains profiled in my recent book, "The Captain Class," uniformly described the nasty things they did in competition as cold-blooded, calculated acts. Through experience, and by studying the referees, they hoped to commit "intelligent fouls" that fell just inside the line—even if the fans found them excessive.

Mr. Ramos's tackle met this standard, too. Taking out Liverpool's best player helped his team and the referees didn't sanction him for it.

The third test is a matter of timing. Did the potential reward outweigh the risk of failure?

Mr. Ramos surely knew that a rough tackle could lead to his ejection. In this case, however, the consequences of losing paled in comparison to the prize at hand. By winning, Real Madrid edged closer to legend: It's only the fourth team in history to collect three straight European titles.

The final test is whether a leader's aggressiveness stays confined to the field—and again, Mr. Ramos sails through. He might want to abandon his dream of becoming a rapper, but he's no troublemaker.

From the outside looking in, Mr. Ramos's tackle might seem no more thoughtful than Mr. Zidane's head-butt. The difference is that the latter was disastrous, pointless, hot-blooded and thoroughly hostile. The former was the work of a committed leader.

No matter what business they're in, exceptional leaders care more about the team's results than how their individual contributions might be judged. They're-exceptional because they don't care if you hate them.

What sets Sergio Ramos's foul apart is that it was purposeful, calculated, intelligent, selfless, well timed and not indicative of how he behaves in the real world. It also worked.

I realize this is confusing. These rules shouldn't apply to amateur forms of competition where the point is helping kids, or students, develop broadly acceptable teamwork skills. The last message we want to send to young people is that cheaters prosper.

But here's the inconvenient truth about leaders: Some bad acts come from a fundamentally good place.

—*Mr. Walker, a former reporter and editor at The Wall Street Journal, is the author of "The Captain Class: The Hidden Force That Creates the World's Greatest Teams" (Random House).*

Discussion Question(s)

1. Is Walker's phrase "aggressive leadership" accurate? Or, is he using euphemism to hide and soften the kinds of actions he is defending?

2. What are Walker's "four tests" for evaluating whether an act of "bad sportsmanship" is justifiable? Do you find them convincing? Why? Why not?

3. What do you make of this quote: "These rules shouldn't apply to amateur forms of competition where the point is helping kids, or students, develop broadly acceptable teamwork skills. The last message we want to send to young people is that cheaters prosper." Does Walker's point hold? Will limiting "bad sportsmanship" to the realm of big-time sport keep children from getting the message that "cheaters prosper"?

Suggested Readings

Booth, D. (2009). Pleasure and physical education philosophy. *Quest, 61*(2), 133–153.

Nielsen, K. (1972). Against moral conservatism. *Ethics, 82*(3), 219–231.

Twietmeyer, G. (2012). The merits and demerits of pleasure in kinesiology. *Quest, 64*(3), 177–186.

Wertheim, L. J., & Dohrmann, G. (2006, March 13). Going big time. *Sports Illustrated, 104*(11), 62–69.

Bibliography

Aristotle. (2002). *Nicomachean ethics.* (J. Sachs, Trans.) Newburyport, MA: Focus Publishing.

Bentham, J. (1830). *The rationale of reward.* London, UK: Robert Heward.

Bentham, J. (2007). *An introduction to the principles of morals and legislation.* Mineola, NY: Dover Publications.

Clarke, L. (2005, April 29). *College football gets 12th game.* Retrieved February 18, 2016, from www.washingtonpost.com: http://www.washingtonpost.com/wp-dyn/content/article/2005/04/28/AR2005042801872.html

Conn, D. (2017, January 10). *Fifa's Infantino claims 48-team World Cup will boost football worldwide.* Retrieved June 4, 2019, from theguardian.com: https://www.theguardian.com/football/2017/jan/10/fifa-vote-expand-world-cup-48-teams-from-2026

Frankena, W. K. (1973). *Ethics.* Englewood Cliffs, NJ: Prentice-Hall.

Goff, S. (2019, March 17). *2022 World Cup was already flawed. Expanding it would make things worse.* Retrieved June 4, 2019, from washingtonpost.com: https://www.washingtonpost.com/sports/2019/03/17/world-cup-was-already-flawed-expanding-it-would-make-thing-worse/?utm_term=.8cce12baddd2

Hoover Institution. (2011, August 26). *David Berlinski interview on August 26, 2011.* Retrieved February 16, 2016, from www.hoover.org: http://media.hoover.org/sites/default/files/documents/David_Berlinski_transcript.pdf

Jackson, N. (2013). *Slow getting up: A story of NFL survival from the bottom of the pile.* New York, NY: Harper Collins.

MacIntyre, A. (1984). *After virtue* (2nd ed.). Notre Dame, IN: University of Notre Dame Press.

Macur, J. (2014). *Cycle of lies: The fall of Lance Armstrong.* New York, NY: Harper Collins.

Mill, J. S. (1998). *Utilitarianism.* New York, NY: Oxford University Press.

Nathanson, S. (n.d.). *Act and rule utilitarianism.* Retrieved February 19, 2016, from Internet Encyclopedia of Philosophy: http://www.iep.utm.edu/util-a-r/#SSSH4aii1

Ross, W.D. (1930, 2002). *The right and the good.* New York, NY: Oxford University Press.

Schefczyk, M. (n.d.). *John Stuart Mill: Ethics.* Retrieved February 12, 2016, from Internet Encyclopedia of Philosophy: http://www.iep.utm.edu/mill-eth/#H5

Singer, P. (1995). *How are we to live? Ethics in an age of self-interest.* Amherst, NY: Prometheus Books.

Tamburrini, C. (2000). *The "Hand of God"?: Essays in the philosophy of sports.* Göteburg, Sweden: Acta Universitatis Gothoburgensis.

Timmons, M. (2013). *Moral theory: An introduction* (2nd ed.). New York, NY: Rowman & Littlefield.

Twietmeyer, G. (2007). Suffering play: Can play and games be defended in a suffering world? *Quest, 59*(2), 201–211.

Twietmeyer, G. (2012). The merits and demerits of pleasure in kinesiology. *Quest, 64*(3), 177–186.

Chapter 5

Deontological Ethics

"*No one is above the rules*. Unfortunately, some people will try to break *the rules*—but to ensure a fair system, *the rules and the consequences have to apply to everyone*. Our goal is to further strengthen our culture of personal responsibility and individual accountability." —NCAA.com[1]

Students will be able to:

1. Distinguish the difference between utilitarian theories and deontological theories of ethics.
2. Explain how Kantian ethics and Intuitionism differ from each other.
3. Explain Kant's two formulations of the Categorical Imperative as well as Ross' seven Prima Facie duties.
4. Summarize the strengths and weaknesses of the various forms of deontological ethics.
5. Identify and evaluate how deontological theories which focus on rules and duties intersect with different theories of sport such as formalism, conventionalism, and broad internalism.

In contrast to utilitarianism and other forms of consequentialism, deontological ethics is not focused on pleasure, outcomes or consequences. Instead deontologists are interested in duty, and the rules such duties imply. In fact, **deontology** simply means "the study of duty." Moral rules play a central role in deontological ethics, for the rules allows us to see our duties clearly. These rules also allow us to judge our actions based upon their congruence to duty rather than outcomes. That is, the deontologist is interested in the rightness of one's act independent of the result(s). This rightness is determined by following through on our obligations rather than in calculations regarding the consequences of our actions.

In examining deontology, we will follow a format similar to that used to examine utilitarianism in the last chapter. We will begin by reviewing the position of the 18th Century German philosopher Immanuel Kant (pronounced Kahn-t) who argues that reason illuminates our duties and that once these duties have been identified we should follow them *categorically*. That is, **categorical duties** admit of no exceptions. For instance,

Deontology: "The study of duty." Any ethical theory which considers duty—as well as the rules which such duties imply—as the proper guide to how we ought to behave.

Categorical Duties: Duties which admit of no exceptions (e.g., if we have a duty to be honest, we should *always* tell the truth. Period. Consequences be damned.)

---

[1] http://www.ncaa.org/about/what-we-do/fairness-and-integrity [Emphasis added].

Intuitionism: A deontological theory of ethics which emphasizes *prima facie* rather than categorical duties.

if telling the truth is a duty, we should always tell the truth. Period. No qualifications and no exceptions. As we will see, although Kant's admirers like the uncompromising nature of his position, his critics have found Kant's ethics to be too inflexible.

One deontological alternative to Kant's strict understanding of duty is the work of the 20th Century English philosopher W.D. Ross, who argued for a deontological position commonly known as **intuitionism**. According to Ross, although our duties are categorical in the sense of being objectively true independent of their utility, the application of our duties, especially when two or more duties come into conflict, relies upon a prudential evaluation of the circumstances. To put it more succinctly, for Ross, while the existence of our duties is categorical, a specific duty's relevance to any given situation is not. Instead, the application of relevant duties relies on sound judgment.

After considering these two philosophers we will then review the strengths and weaknesses of deontology. In doing so, we will have the opportunity to contrast deontological ethics with utilitarianism. The chapter will then close with an assessment of the value of deontological ethics for sport. How well does an emphasis on duties and rules fit with sport? Metaphysically, one might argue that the nature of sport is a function of the rules that make up the games we play. If that's true, what, if anything, does that imply about the moral import of rule following in sport? What impact—for good or ill—would deontological ethics have on the practice and performance of sport? Finally, if deontology is an appropriate way to approach sports ethics, which understanding of deontology should be pursued? Would a "sports deontologist" be better off following Kant or Ross?

Kant and the Categorical Imperative

For Kant, as we have seen, ethics is a function of rationally recognizing our duties and then following through on those obligations categorically. The obligations which reason identifies are universally valid. All human beings are bound by such duties. For an action to have moral worth it cannot proceed from selfishness, nor from utilitarian purposes, nor even from emotion, but only from duty. Moral value flows from a motivation which is disinterestedly fixed on the rightness of the action rather than the results or feelings the action will produce.

Kant (1785/2011) explains this idea clearly when discussing the duty to avoid suicide. Most men preserve their lives out of "anxious care." There is no *moral* value[2] in such behavior, because, "They preserve their life *as duty requires*, no doubt, but not *because duty requires*" (p. 4). Kant's point is simple. Although the behavior in this instance is good and coincidentally reflects what duty requires, the motivation to not kill oneself was not a rational recognition of duty but rather a desire for this or that aspect of life (pleasure, family, etc.).

In contrast, if someone found themselves in a state of "hopeless sorrow" and yet found a way to continue to preserve "his life without loving it—not from inclination [desire] or fear, but from duty—then his maxim has moral worth" (p. 4). This action, like all others done from duty, is praiseworthy because there is a clear indication that one acted not out of emotion, or selfishness, or consequentialism, but rather from the sober recognition of right reason, which points out what our obligations are.

---

[2] Doing good things for other reasons can be "honorable" and even worthy of "praise" due to the "public utility" such actions generate (p. 4). Kant's point is not that such actions are bad, but that they are not strictly moral actions, because they don't flow from duty.

How far does Kant take this idea? To the very end. Even beneficence (doing good to others) must result, if it is to have moral worth, from duty:

> "To be beneficent when we can is a duty; and besides this, there are many minds so sympathetically constituted that, without any other motive of vanity or self-interest, they find a pleasure in spreading joy around them, and can take delight in the satisfaction of others so far as it is their own work. But I maintain that in such a case an action of this kind, however proper, however amiable it may be, has nevertheless no true moral worth, but is on a level with other inclinations . . . For the maxim lacks the moral import, namely, that such actions be done from duty, not from inclination" (p. 4).

Kant wants a disinterested morality based in reason and reason alone. Moral action is dependent upon one's *autonomous will,* which recognizes through reason the universal laws which are our duty. Ethics is based in reason, not outcomes, experience, emotion *or even external compulsion.* We are bound by a universal duty because our "own will" recognizes the truth of certain duties. This autonomous will recognizes that "he is only bound to act in conformity with his own will; a will, however which is designed by nature to give universal laws" (p. 29).

To further this goal of a strictly reason based morality Kant puts forward the categorical imperative, which has two formulations.[3] The first formulation states the following: "Act only on that maxim whereby thou canst at the same time will that it should become a universal law" (p. 21). Any moral proposition which logically results in self-contradiction is indefensible. What Kant means by this language is that no maxim (principle) is rationally defensible if it is predicated upon making an exception of ourselves. A pithy way to summarize the practical point of the **first categorical imperative** is therefore simply to say, "don't make an exception of yourself."

A couple of examples, one straight from Kant and one from the world of sport, may help illustrate the point. Kant's most famous example in support of the 1st formulation of the categorical imperative is lying. Kant argues that acknowledging the general benefits or harms of truth telling does little to get to the heart of the matter. That is, to say that lying will "catch up with you" or that "telling the truth allows one to sleep well at night" misses the crucial point. In either instance, one is not focused on duty, but rather on a utilitarian "fear of consequences" (p. 7). This will not suffice. Telling the truth is a duty because to will lying as a universal law would destroy the institution of promises and truth telling. Kant puts the idea this way:

Kant's First Categorical Imperative: "Act only on that maxim whereby thou canst at the same time will that it should become a universal law." To put it succinctly, if a little too crudely, "don't make an exception of yourself."

---

[3] Technically there are two more formulations—each of which are sometimes calls the "third formulation" in philosophic literature. Each receives less attention because they are meant to either synthesize or justify the first two formulations. According to the "autonomy formulation", rational actors should recognize "the idea of the will of every rational being as a universally legislative will" (Kant, 1785/2011 p. 28). The point is simply to re-emphasize Kant's belief that "our status as free rational agents" means that we "are the source of the authority behind the very moral laws that bind us" (Johnson & Cureton, 2016, para. 52). According to the "kingdom of ends" formulation we should "Act according to the maxims of a merely possible kingdom of ends legislating in it universally" (Kant, 1785/2011, pp. 33–34). What this essentially means is that we should act as if all members of the society are rationally willing universal law (imperative #1) and treating others as ends rather than mere means (imperative #2). Doing so will bring us closer to the ideal and just society. As Jankowiak (n.d.) puts it, "A kingdom of ends can be thought of as a sort of perfectly just utopian ideal in which all citizens of this kingdom freely respect the intrinsic worth of the humanity in all others because of an autonomously self-imposed recognition of the bindingness of the universal moral law for all rational agents" (para. 85).

"Then I presently become aware that while I can will the lie, I can by no means will that lying should be a universal law. For with such a law there would be no promises at all, since it would be in vain to allege my intention in regard to my future actions to those who would not believe this allegation, or if they over-hastily did so, would pay me back in my own coin.[4] Hence my maxim, as soon as it should be made a universal law, would necessarily destroy itself" (p. 7).

Is lying always wrong?
Tibor Bognar/Getty Images

Something similar could be said about performance-enhancing drug (PED) use in sport. One cannot will that their use become a universal law. At least not if: (A) the logic of PED use is predicated on the notion of getting an advantage on other competitors. (B) The logic of sport is safe and fair competition.[5] For if one willed that all competitors used PEDs there would be no advantage to any user. At which point one would have the same level playing field that existed before PED use, but with all the health risks and side effects that come along with usage. Yet it would make no rational sense to will that a level playing field with harms/side effects become the universal law when one could easily have the same level playing field without these harms. PED use only makes sense within the logic of "making an

---

[4] This idiom means: To treat another the same way they treated you.
[5] This may not always be the case. As Simon, ET. Al (2015) point out, "Some athletes might consider other issues. For example, some might believe that a universally higher level of competition generated by using steroids more than compensate for the health risks" (p. 98).

exception of one's self" and therefore conflicts with the 1st formulation of the categorical imperative. For to will PED use as a universal law would destroy the cheater's advantage as well as destroy safe competition. This is why PED use is almost always a clandestine affair. The point is not to institutionalize a new practice as "universal" but rather to covertly gain an advantage at the expense of others. To take PEDs is to treat one's competitors as a mere means to the end of victory.

The **2nd formulation of the categorical imperative** builds on this idea. Here Kant argues, contra the utilitarians, that human beings have inherent value. He says, "So act as to treat humanity, whether in thine own person or in that of any other, in every case as an end withal, never as means only" (p. 27). The point is that human beings are of intrinsic worth. Human beings should not be considered "merely as a means to be arbitrarily used" by others (p. 26). Human beings, due to their rational nature, should be valued simply for their own sake.[6]

An interesting question, for our purposes, follows. Does sport ever encourage treating human beings as mere means to other ends (e.g., winning, money, power, or prestige)? Although it would be difficult to establish how common such behavior is, it is safe to say that it occurs. Here is but one example, from the book *League of Denial* (Fainaru-Wada & Fainaru, 2013). The story, from 2002, recounts how New England Patriots linebacker Ted Johnson was told to return to practice even though his head coach knew he was still suffering from a concussion:

> "Four days after the injury, still groggy, he took the practice field wearing a noncontact red jersey. Before a set of running drills, however, an assistant trainer handed him a blue jersey—essentially an order to get out and hit. Johnson knew right away the switch had been made not by the team's medical staff but by the Patriots' head coach, Bill Belichick. He feared that if he refused, he'd lose his job and his $1.1 million salary. 'I'm sitting there going, 'God, do I put this thing on?' he said. He added that such intimidation is common in the NFL. 'That day it was Bill Belichick and Ted Johnson,' he said. 'But it happens all the time.'
>
> Johnson got hit in the head on the first play, leaving him dazed. When he reported the second concussion to a trainer after practice, the Pats sent him to Massachusetts General Hospital.
>
> 'You played God with my health,' Johnson said he later told Belichick. 'You knew I shouldn't have been cleared to play, and you gave me the blue jersey anyway'" (pp. 213–214).

If such behavior is common—as Johnson alleges—then Kant's maxim would seem to be a valuable way to check such behavior. Human beings are of inherent value. Despite appearances to the contrary, any success that comes at the cost of human dignity or human life is no success at all.

Kant's Second Categorical Imperative: "So act as to treat humanity, whether in thine own person or in that of any other, in every case as an end withal, never as means only." Human beings have intrinsic worth and should always be treated as such.

---

[6] "The foundation of this principle is: *rational nature exists as an end in itself*. Man necessarily conceives his own existence as being so: so far then this is a *subjective* principle of human actions. But every other rational being regards its existence similarly, just on the same rational principle that holds for me: that it is at the same time an objective principle, from which as a supreme practical law all laws of the will must be capable of being deduced" (Kant, 1785/2011, p. 26).

"You knew I shouldn't have been cleared to play, and you gave me the blue jersey anyway."
Boston Globe/Getty Image

In circumstances such as this, Kant's insistence on categorically following our duties can seem quite attractive. Compromising on or making exceptions regarding things such as player health is hard to justify on moral grounds. Nevertheless not all circumstances are this clear cut. Compromise may often be called for. If this is true, how can Kant deal with such circumstances? Moreover many circumstances would seem to lead to situations where our duties are, or at least appear to be, in conflict. Are there not at least some circumstances where I might need to ignore one duty in service of another? How should such decisions be made? Are there not, for instance, situations where I would need to lie in order to save a life or protect someone? But if that is so, then Kant is wrong. What then should be done?

Ross, Prima Facie Duties and Intuitionism

Ross attacks deontology from a very different perspective than Kant. Whereas Kant grounds duty in reason and believes that our duties can be rationally justified, Ross grounds duty in our intuitive grasp of moral reality. In so doing, he argues that our duties are axiomatic. That is, they can have and need no further justification.[7]

---

[7] This is an important contrast to Kant. Kant (1785/2011) assumes that autonomy demands that duty originates, "as a law from his own will" (p. 29). Ross (1930, 2002) on the other hand seems to endorse the heteronomy [external sources of obligation] which Kant denies. "The moral order expressed in these propositions is just as much a part of the fundamental nature of the universe (and, we may add, of any possible universe in which there are moral agents at all) as is the spatial or numerical structure expressed in the axioms of geometry or arithmetic" (pp. 29–30).

"It [duty] is self-evident just as a mathematical axiom, or the validity of a form of inference, is evident . . . In both cases we are dealing with propositions that cannot be proved, but that just as certainly need no proof" (Ross, 1930, 2002, pp. 29–30).

Ross also differs from Kant regarding whether our duties are categorically binding. In contrast to Kant, Ross argues that our duties are **prima facie**. By which he means that although our duties are objectively valid, their application depends on the particulars of any given situation. They are generic principles that need specific application.

Prima Facie Duties:
A set of objectively valid duties whose specific application depends on the particular circumstances one finds oneself in. When two or more prima facie duties come into conflict (e.g., justice and self-improvement), one must prudentially prioritize one duty over another.

Yet, the term *prima facie* can be confusing. This is because in everyday language it usually means something akin to "first impression" or even "superficial." However, as the *Oxford English Dictionary* points out, it also means "acceptable unless [or until] contradicted."[8] This is clearly the meaning Ross has in mind. For he believes our duties are binding unless or until they are in conflict with some other duty. Ross identifies the following prima facie duties; fidelity (honesty), reparation (making up for past wrongs), gratitude (acknowledging our debt to others), justice (giving others what they deserve), beneficence (looking to help/do good to others), self-improvement (to be one's best), and non-maleficence (avoid harming others).

By arguing for taking the situation into account, Ross is not endorsing relativism. He is trying to overcome the rigidity of the Kantian system. We must do our duty, our prima facie duties are binding upon each of us, but *which* duty is binding at any given time is dependent upon the relevant details of the situation. Moreover, our prima facie duties can only be overridden by another more relevant prima facie duty. As such our *prima facie duty* regards what is right in principle, while our *actual duty* is what is right in practice, given the particular situation. Frankena (1973) puts the idea this way:

"'Every rule has exceptions,' that is, every rule of actual duty has exceptions. But there still may be and are, Ross contends, exceptionless rules of prima facie duty. Something is a prima facie duty if it is a duty other things being equal, that is, if it would be an actual duty if other moral considerations did not intervene" (p. 26).

Of course, things are not always equal. What then are we to do when our prima facie duties conflict? Here Ross is cautious. As Ross (1930, 2002) insists, "For the estimation of the comparative stringency of these prima facie obligations no general rules can, so far as I can see, be laid down" (p. 41). Such caution is admirable and frustrating at the same time.

This is admirable because, following Aristotle (2002), Ross (1930, 2002) recognizes that "the decision rests with perception" (p. 42, 1109b23). That is, ethics as a practical matter necessarily relies on judgment not merely slavishly following rules. When prima facie duties conflict we can, for example, override the duty of fidelity (lie) if it means serving the duty of beneficence, by saving a life. What this means is that the character of the actor plays a vital role. Ethics is not mathematics and we will only get ourselves in trouble if we pretend that it is. Timmons (2013) offers a valuable explanation of what Ross means in this regard:

"To say that one prima facie duty is more stringent [more relevant to the given situation] than another, competing prima facie duty is not, however, to say that the latter prima facie duty is somehow canceled out or 'silenced'. Rather, the

---

[8] http://www.oed.com/view/Entry/151264?redirectedFrom=prima+facie#eid

idea is that in such situations, one prima facie duty overrides other, competing prima facie duties. Consequently, in cases where one has a prima facie that is overridden, this fact about the situation may generate a further prima facie duty. For instance, in the case where I ought to break my promise to you in order to help an accident victim, the fact that my prima facie duty to keep my promise is overridden (but not cancelled) means that I now have a new prima facie duty of reparation—to do what is necessary to make it up to you" (p. 252).

Nevertheless, Ross' hesitance to tell us how to prioritize our prima facie duties is found by many to be frustrating because it is unclear in many instances of prima facie conflict how one might come to a reasoned position on what ought to be done, which will generate common or even individual assent.

Consider the example from Chapter 2, that of "stopping to help injured runner." You may remember it as a conflict between "supererogatory acts" (those that go above and beyond the call of duty) and the "law of love" (the obligation to love our neighbors as ourselves). However, it can also be looked at from the perspective of Ross' account of prima facie duties. In fact, one might argue that in any dilemma regarding stopping to help an injured runner there is an inherent conflict between the prima facie duties of beneficence and self-improvement. How ought such conflicts be reconciled?

One might argue that beneficence should trump self-improvement, for the life and safety of the runner is more important than maximizing your performance. Moreover one might say that self-improvement in the broadest sense will itself be actualized if you can cultivate the virtue of selflessness necessary to see that beneficence is always more important than a definition of self-improvement that hinges on "victory." If that is true, then there is no conflict at all.

Perhaps you find this reasoning persuasive. Nevertheless two problems for Ross' theory remain. First, what if we complicate the matter? For instance by; making the injury to the competitor minor, or by putting Olympic qualification on the line, or by positing that all runners promised to each other before the race not to stop for a fallen comrade. What then should be done? At least some of these qualifications—by altering the balance between prima facie duties or by bringing new prima facie duties into the situation—will likely cause greater controversy over what ought to be done. How then do we know what the *right* thing to do is?

How then do we know what the right thing to do is?
Wally McNamee/Getty Images

Second, no general principle can be gathered from this specific instance, even if the reasoning put forth for this or that specific course of action were universally accepted. This is because each new prima facie conflict must be adjudicated on its own merits. Perhaps that is Ross' point. Character is key. As he said, "no general rules . . . can be laid down" and the "decision rests with perception." Yet, if this is the case, one might ask if Ross' intuitionism really points beyond itself to the necessity of virtue ethics (a topic which we will examine in Chapter 6). If that is right, then perhaps deontology should be abandoned?

The Strengths of Deontological Ethics

At this point, the strengths of deontological ethics should be coming into focus. Here, we will concentrate on three. First, deontology is a theory of obligations rather than calculations. Duty not outcomes is what matters. Second, deontology is based in reason not emotion. Feelings and inclinations take a back seat to doing what we ought, whether or not we feel like doing it. If you believe that good human behavior relies on the cultivation of responsibility, this is no small matter. Third, deontological ethics takes human beings seriously. Human beings are ends in themselves and are not merely servants of the greatest good for the greatest number.

Another way to describe the first strength would be to say that deontological ethics are not wishy-washy. There is no wavering or calculation regarding what should be done. We should do our duty. Always. This is the case for both Kant and Ross. Whereas Kant is categorical, Ross simply stresses that what our duty actually is in any given situation will require prudential judgment. This is why our duties are prima facie, because they are binding in all situations unless a more relevant duty can make a greater claim upon us. Deontological thinking is very attractive to those who are convinced that moral clarity is necessary for human beings to behave well. For such advocates, to equivocate regarding our principles is likely to lead to moral indifference or even moral abuse. Rules and duties, in contrast, compel us to do the right thing even when we would rather not.

It is because of the power of duty to compel us to do the right thing even when we would rather not that reason trumps emotion. Squeamishness, fear, cowardice, despair, lust, etc. can cloud our thinking and dampen our motivation to do the right thing. Therefore, the insistence of Kant that actions should be "done from duty, not from inclination" is a great

One of Kant's strengths is that he insists that human beings are not mere means to other ends. Therefore, they should not be used [or objectified] as such.
William West/AFP/Getty Image.

boon to ethics. For disinterested reason can calmly and objectively establish impartial grounds for what we ought to do. By ignoring emotion and soberly submitting to reason we will learn best how to avoid "making an exception of ourselves."

Finally, deontological ethics requires that human being are ends in themselves. This means that contrary to utilitarianism human beings cannot be mere elements of a larger cost benefit analysis. Each human beings has intrinsic worth. That is, they are good simply for being a human being. For anyone concerned about utilitarians reducing human beings to mere producers or inhibitors of a greater pleasure/pain calculus, Kant's insistence that human beings should in "every case" be treated as "an end" and "never as a means only" will be extremely attractive.

The Weaknesses of Deontological Ethics

There are, of course, also weaknesses to deontological ethics. Again we will consider three. First, deontological ethics—at least in its Kantian form—is based in reason not emotion. In contrast to those who find this a strength, critics allege that it makes ethics too cold and impersonal. Second, Kant's categorical imperative has been criticized for being both too broad and for being tacitly dependent upon utilitarianism. What critics mean here is that the categorical imperative allows for universal maxims that are logically consistent but trivially important, and that all maxims rely upon some argument to the effect that "the *results* of this or that behavior prove that the behavior cannot be universalized." In so doing they are actually dependent upon the principle "maximize pleasure." Finally, deontological ethics has been criticized for being rigid and inflexible. Obviously, this criticism is again usually targeted at Kant and his categorical conception of ethical duty. However, the criticism can also be leveled at Ross in the sense that his alleged solution (prima facie duties whose application depend upon judgment) may indirectly confirm the weakness of deontology by posting the necessity of character to any functioning deontological theory. This confirms the weakness of deontology because *character* is at the heart not of deontology, but of virtue ethics.

The first weakness of deontology is centered on the idea that Kant's exclusive focus on reason hampers ethical practice and can even lead to absurdity. Recall that when we examined "reason not emotion" as a strength it was posited that "fear," "lust" and so forth often cloud our moral judgment. A critic could acknowledge this and still counter that "love," "compassion," and "sympathy" often strengthen our moral resolve. Our inclinations often spur right action. Why shouldn't such actions be of moral worth?

From this point of view, Kant's problem is not that he thinks reason is important for sound ethical thinking. Every serious person will agree. His problem is that he excludes emotion. Kant's mistake is that he sees reason versus emotion as an either/or proposition; either we act from reason or we act from emotion. But this is a false dichotomy! We should take both reason and emotion into account. To divorce reason from emotion is to prioritize one aspect of human life at the expense of all the others.[9] This is, according

---

[9] A similar criticism is worth brief mention here. Kant's emphasis on "autonomy" and "self-legislation" has been held to be self-contradictory, as well as the precursor to a moral anarchy dominated by decadence and libertinism. The self-contradictory criticism results from Kant's claim that universal duty can be derived from the will alone. A self-determined law would seem to be anything but universal. The concern regarding anarchy results from the deification of man's will implicit in Kant's insistence on autonomy, as well as from the idea that man's end is found in himself rather than an objective external standard such as nature or God. According to the classical philosophical tradition (Plato, Aristotle, the Scholastics), "In no sense are we the source of the nature that determines our ends, including the end of reason itself; God alone is that. Hence nature, and ultimately God—rather than the individual reason of the moral agent—are what ground the content and obligatory force of the moral law" (Feser, 2010, para. 4).

Does Kant, like the Tin-man, need a heart?
John Springer Collection/Corbis Historical/Getty Images

to critics, impractical and will lead to absurdity. A contemporary of Kant, Friedrich Schiller, satirically put the point this way:

> "I like to serve my friends but unfortunately I do so by inclination. And so I am bothered by the thought that I am not virtuous . . . There is no other way but this! You must seek to despise them. And do with repugnance what duty bids you" (Wood, 1999, p. 28).

If such criticism is at all warranted it should be clear that Kant's system, whatever its merits, is too cold and impersonal to be a fully effective guide to leading a good life.

The second weakness of deontological ethics again focuses on Kant. Here the criticism is that the categorical imperative is too broad, and that any defense of it implicitly relies upon utilitarianism. By arguing that the categorical imperative is too broad, critics mean two things. First, it allows for trivial assertions. Second, it allows for immoral ones. On the first count, Frankena (1973) alleges that "When alone in the dark, whistle" seems "to be a maxim one can will to be a universal law" (p. 32). The implication is this: if the categorical imperative allows for such trivialities, how can it be a serious guide for what we ought to do? On the second count, MacIntyre (1984) asserts that, "there is not even any inconsistency in willing a universe of egoists all of whom live by this [self-serving] maxim" (p. 46). The implication here is that the categorical imperative allows for the willing of profoundly immoral universal laws.[10]

---

[10] If we return to the PED use example from earlier in the chapter, you may recall it was rested upon two assumptions including the idea that "The logic of sport is safe and fair competition". But it is unclear, given an ethics of autonomous will, why one couldn't construct a rationally consistent alternative that could be universalized on Kant's terms (e.g., maximize performance by any means necessary).

J.S. Mill also criticizes the ability of the categorical imperative to function as Kant supposed. But instead of arguing that it was too broad, Mill (1998) alleges that the categorical imperative was not self-sufficient. Kant's categorical imperative does not show any "contradiction" in the adoption of "the most outrageously immoral rules of conduct" (p. 30). All Kant demonstrates "is that the consequences of their universal adoption would be such as no one would choose to incur" (p. 30). That is, the categorical imperative relies upon utilitarianism to actually arrive at *just* maxims.

Finally, there is perhaps the most common criticism of deontological ethics. Again this applies most especially to its Kantian form. The critics here allege that deontological ethics cannot deal with the messiness of real life. In categorically saying we should do our duty, Kant and his followers are too rigid. Circumstances will often conspire to make it clear, for example, that we ought to "lie" if it will "save a life" or "protect a friend". At the very least, it is clear that Kant's insistence on categorical duty allows for no consideration of the *situation*. Yet, as Ross' version of deontology makes manifest, our duties should only be considered categorical if they are prima facie duties. Of course, as already mentioned, it is unclear that such a move saves deontology. Critics may say that everything Ross does to save Kant ultimately relies on virtue ethics rather than deontology, which, if true, means that it is no defense of deontology at all.

Deontologist Responses

Noteworthy if not always compelling responses have been made to all of these criticisms. Regarding the first criticism, defenders of Kant usually point to the fact that Kant (1785/2011) did not deny the goodness of actions motivated by inclination. Any such action, "deserves praise" and could be "honourable". The fact that they were not motivated by duty simply makes them less worthy of "esteem" (p. 4). As philosopher Marcia Baron (2006) insists, "A much more Kantian reading [contrary to Schiller] is simply that in acting from duty, the man gives himself a higher worth than does the person who never acts from duty . . . " (p. 82).

Responses have also been offered regarding the criticisms of the categorical imperative. Here, defenders of the categorical imperative point out that Kant meant to address moral questions rather than (trivial) non-moral questions (Frankena, 1973) and that Kant (1785/2011) insisted that egoism could not be universalized because in doing so one would "deprive himself of all hope of the aid he [naturally] desires" (p. 23). This natural desire means egoism cannot be universally willed. At the very least then, Kant's defenders would argue that MacIntyre's specific criticism fails.[11] Regarding Mill's criticism of Kant, Frankena's (1973) explanation seems decisive.

> "It is often alleged that Kant is being utilitarian in these arguments. . . This is a mistake. He is not arguing that one must keep one's promises because the results of everyone's breaking them when convenient or advantageous to themselves would be so bad as to be intolerable. This is how a rule-utilitarian would run the argument. Kant, however, is contending that one cannot even will such a maxim to be acted on, because in so doing, one would be involved in a contradiction of the will; one would be willing both that it be possible to make promises and have them credited (else why make them?) and that everyone be free to break promises to suit his own purposes" (p. 31).

---

[11] MacIntyre's (1984) rejoinder would insist that Kant's argument is inconsistent with this larger project. For "considerations of convenience [such as the 'the hope of the aid he [naturally] desires'] would in any case be to introduce just that prudential reference to happiness which Kant aspires to eliminate from all considerations of morality" (p. 46).

In response to the final criticism, defenders of deontology have insisted that adaptation to the situation *is* possible. This is most obviously the case for Ross' system of prima facie duties, but even Kant has had his defenders on this score. Timmons (2013) for example argues that "particular facts about concrete situations . . . play a role in Kant's considered view" (p. 236).[12] Moreover, Timmons insists, that Kant's 2nd categorical imperative anticipates Ross. This is because when two duties come into conflict the 2nd categorical imperative implies that "it is the duty that most respects humanity as an end in itself that one is morally obligated to perform" (p. 236). This suggests, according to Timmons, that even a Kantian could lie to protect a life.

What then should be made of deontology as an ethical theory? Here is what I would say. Although deontology is superior to utilitarianism, the theory is still found wanting. The insistence on duty is persuasive for two reasons. First, because it compels us to do the right thing rather than calculate consequences. In allowing for any action, if it produces good consequences, utilitarianism opens a Pandora's Box which allows for all kinds of evil to be called good. *That deontology recognizes and avoids this problem is to its great credit.* Second, deontology compels us to do the right thing even when we do not want to. To turn this point to sport, we could say, for example, that even after a tough loss to a bitter rival one ought to shake hands. Insofar as an ethics of duty encourages such behavior, it is a good thing.

Yet, I can't help but agree with Schiller. Kant's ethics are too cold. Ethics isn't just reason, but also the cultivation of sentiment and virtue. We are taught to do the right thing by example more so than we are by argument. Moreover, reason—and therefore the will—are not "autonomous" and never have been. This is an Enlightenment fiction. We are all dependent upon and bound to tradition and inheritance (MacIntyre, 1990; Polanyi, 1962; Polanyi & Prosch, 1975; Berger & Luckmann, 1966). Finally, although Ross does much to rectify the problems of Kantian ethics, he does so, as we shall see in the next chapter, by relying implicitly and explicitly on an Aristotelean ethic of virtue.

We are taught to do the right thing by example more so than we are by argument.
©Bobby Johnson/Shutterstock.com

---

[12] "However, a subject may have, in a rule he prescribes to himself, two *grounds* of obligation (*rationes obligandi*) one or the other of which is not sufficient to put him under obligation (*rationes obligandi non obligantes*), so that one of them is not a duty. – When two such grounds conflict with each other, practical philosophy says, not that the stronger obligation takes precedence (*fortior obligation vincut*) but that the stronger *ground of obligation* prevails (*fortiori obligandi ratio vincut*)" (Kant, The metaphysics of morals, 1996, pp. 16–17).

It is worth noting then, as we close this section, our recurring theme: you will have to evaluate these arguments for yourself. As always there are plausible arguments and smart people on each side. It is your responsibility to evaluate them in the pursuit of truth. Not simply so that you can understand, but for the twin purposes of living well and treating others as you ought.

Deontology and Sport?

In closing the chapter, let us consider two way that deontology affects sport. First, there are several theoretical issues that have been examined by sport philosophers regarding the precise relationship between rules and the nature of sport. Here again we see the interdependence of metaphysics and ethics. For claims about the nature of sport, such as "sports are defined by their rules," will necessarily impact how we should behave in sport. Second, there is the practical level of rules and rule enforcement. This issue raises many questions: What obligations, if any, do we have to the rules? On what grounds does the authority to enforce the rules exist? How should discipline for rules violations be handled in sport? Should all rules violations be treated the same? Is following the rules always a duty? If so, should intentionally breaking the rules (as, for instance, in intentionally fouling to stop the clock late in a basketball game) always be considered immoral? We will only have space for a brief sketch of each of these ideas, but if you are intrigued by this introduction you can find a fuller treatment of many of these issues in some of the suggested readings.

The Nature of Sport?

Formalism: A theory of sport which argues that sport is defined by its constitutive rules.

There are three common views regarding the nature of sport. The first view is called **formalism**. According to the theory of formalism, "games are a product of their constitutive rules" (Kretchmar, 2015, p. 11). The rules define the game and, as such, the player

How should rules violations be adjudicated in sport? (This cartoon is contrasting the original punishment Ray Rice got for domestic assault against the intended punishment for Tom Brady's involvement in 'Deflategate').
Dan Wasserman Editorial cartoon/Boston Globe/TNS

is bound by those rules if they choose to play it. To fail to play by the rules, is to fail to play the game, which means cheaters, by definition, cannot win (since in intentionally breaking the rules they fail to play game). This claim, that cheaters cannot win, is known as the **logical incompatibility thesis**. Clearly, there are parallels between formalism and categorical versions of deontology.

Despite the intuitive pull of some of these ideas, formalism is not without problems. First, how do we know that the rules, as we find them, are *good* rules? To formalistically turn to the rules to adjudicate the normative value of the rules simply begs the question. Second, how should a formalist deal with moral issues that fall outside the written rules? Such problems generated significant pressure for alternative accounts of sport. As with deontology, formalism has often been criticized for being too inflexible.

The second theory of sport is called **conventionalism**. According to conventionalists, formalism's insistence upon the rules is too strict. It is therefore better to understand sport as a function of the "ethos" of the practice community. That is, sport is best understood by looking at the commonly accepted norms of the athletes, coaches and administrators that make up any given sport, not merely the rules. This understanding allows for the importance of rules without being slavishly bound by them. This is why conventionalists believe that intentionally fouling (breaking a rule) at the end of a basketball game is ok. It is an accepted practice. Everyone in the practice community knows about it and endorses it. Therefore, conventionalists insist that rules must be understood within the wider context of "ethos".

Conventionalism also takes seriously the social and cultural aspects of sport. As sport philosopher William J. Morgan (2015) reminds us, "conventions of language, etiquette, and courtesy are inescapable features of our lives". Similarly the conventions of sport "can scarcely be ignored once engaged" (p. 37). Unfortunately this insistence on "accepted practice" has opened conventionalism to the criticism that it is relativistic. That is, in abandoning rules, it lacks, according to critics, all normative force.[13] To simply say "that everyone does it" does not prove that the practice is good.

The perceived inadequacy of these two theories has spurred interest in a third theory of sport known as **broad internalism** (or **interpretivism**). According to broad internalists, rules are useful, but it is the "the point and purposes that underlie the game" (Simon, Torres, & Hager, 2015, p. 33), that are most relevant. This is because although the rules help define those purposes, the rules serve the larger purposes of sport. We engage in baseball to participate in the central excellences of the game (e.g., stolen bases, home runs, double plays, etc.). We do not play baseball simply to follow its rules. Nor are these central excellences/**internal goods** mere conventions.[14] Therefore the rules and their adjudication must be seen in the light of these larger purposes for sport.

Logical Incompatibility Thesis: A theory based in formalism which says that since games are a product of their rules and since cheaters break rules intentionally, then it follows that cheaters cannot really win, because by breaking the rules, they are not actually playing the game. A game cannot be won by someone who is not playing it. As such, cheating and winning are "logically incompatible."

Conventionalism: A theory of sport which argues that in addition to rules one must pay attention to the "ethos" of the practice community. Conventionalists argue that focusing on the norms, habits, "unwritten rules," and customs of any given practice community (e.g., players, coaches, administrators, and fans) is the best way to understand sport.

Broad Internalism (Interpretivism): A theory of sport which emphasizes the central excellences (internal goods) of any given sport as the best way to understand sport. This is because the internal goods clarify the "points and purposes that underlie the game." Rules are important, but as means (to further our access to internal goods) not as ends in themselves.

Internal Goods: The central excellences of any given sport, which cannot be achieved outside the practice of that sport. For an in-depth discussion/review of internal goods see Chapter 1 pp. 13–14.

---

[13] Morgan's (2015) "deep conventionalism" has challenged this notion: "For, if that were true [conventional standards had no normative force], it would mean that we could somehow plausibly distinguish between what such a community thinks is the purpose of sport and what it *really* is. But I don't think any such distinction can be plausibly made since, after all, what is the aim of sport and what standards we should use to evaluate actions within its precincts are not things we discover but rather things we create. And because we, the relevant practice communities, are the ones who created them, it seems strange, to say the least, that we could be wholly wrong about what we created" (p. 50).

[14] An important contemporary debate in sport philosophy regards this very question; whether these "points and purposes of the game" can be said to be universally true or whether they too are culturally bound conventions.

Rule Enforcement?

How might such theories, in concert with the deontological ideas discussed in this chapter, impact the practical issue of rule enforcement in sport? Let us focus on one example.[15] Consider this classic case from sport philosopher John Russell's (1999) important paper *Are Rules All an Umpire Has to Work With?* This paper neatly summarizes how the distinction between categorical duties and prima facie duties can play out in sport.

In the article Russell points out that it is commonly held that "the rules of a contest are fully authoritative" (p. 27). As such, umpires (and other officials) are "never to step outside the rules that are officially laid down to govern the conduct of games" (p. 27). In Kantian language, you could call this the "categorical position". Umpires should follow and enforce the rules. Period. In contrast to the categorical position, Russell advocates for the necessity of "discretion" by umpires because of the "untidiness of rules" (p. 27). In Ross' language you could call this the "prima facie position". As a result:

> "umpires can legitimately use their authority to clarify and resolve ambiguities in rules, to add rules, and *even at times to overturn or ignore certain rules*, and that the exercise of such discretion is governed by *principles underlying the games* themselves and by an ideal of the integrity of games" (p. 28) [Emphasis Added].

To illustrate the truth of this position, Russell recounts several "hard cases" (p. 28) from the history of baseball. For our purposes, it will suffice to focus on just one. He recounts a baseball game from the late 19th Century where a runner—upon scoring—turned around and interfered with the catcher. In doing so, he allowed two subsequent runners to score by interfering with what would have been a close play at the plate. "The rules [at the time] said nothing explicitly to prohibit non-baserunners from interfering with fielders" (p. 28). Moreover, the player who interfered with the catcher was no longer a baserunner after scoring, which would seem to imply that his interference was legal. What should the umpire do?

In this instance the umpire ignored the rule. He declared the first runner to cross after interference out and disallowed the next runner's run. Russell commends this discretion on the grounds that "Any other decision would have invited a nine-inning-long wrestling match. Umpire Curry's exercise of discretion . . . preserved the good conduct and integrity of the game" (p. 28).

Russell's position would usually—and rightly in my view—be understood as a clear case of broad internalism. For the umpire's actions undoubtedly had the "point and

---

[15] Here is another, jurisdiction. By which I mean: how much power, latitude and authority should sport officials and administrators have to make and enforce rules? What power should the NFL have, for example, to discipline its players for off the field conduct? How should the Ray Lewis domestic abuse scandal or the Deflategate scandal be adjudicated? Why? Recently, the sport philosopher, Bogdan Ciomaga (2013) argued, along broadly Kantian lines, for a "principle of autonomy, according to which obligations should be imposed on participants in sport only if they are necessary to protect the rights of the participants or if they are derived from the choices of participants" (p. 20). Given the modern emphasis on negative freedom this will sound well and good to many, but notice that he does not base his reasoning in the nature of human beings as Aristotle would (e.g., man is by nature a "political animal"), nor does he ground authority in some natural order larger than the autonomous will. There is no standard of justice outside the will to which decisions are beholden. This is deeply Kantian, and, the critic would worry, susceptible to abuse. In other words, it is an open question whether such a position can hold and avoid descending into bureaucratic despotism, as different autonomous wills impose their definition of "rights" and "choice" under the guise of "reason". Even "pluralism" is an imposition.

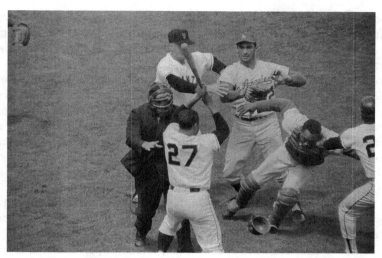

Any other decision would have invited a nine-inning-long wrestling match.
Bettmann/Getty Images

purposes that underlie the game" at heart. However, as we've already seen, an alternative but parallel reading is possible. Russell's position aligns well with Ross, intuitionism and prima facie duties. For both Russell and Ross endorse the idea that our duty to follow the rules is subordinate to larger over-arching principles (prima facie duties) which are normatively binding without being in-and-of-themselves prescriptive for any given situation. This is why Russell says discretion is necessary and Ross insists that the "the decision rests with perception."

Similar to Ross' insistence on the prima facie duties of fidelity, etc., Russell recommends four principles by which umpire discretion should be exercised. First, rules should be understood to serve the central excellences of sport. Second, rules should be understood to serve "competitive balance" (p. 35), by which Russell means the "competition should be designed to provide fair and meaningful opportunities" (p. 36). Third, rules should be understood to promote "sportsmanship" (p. 36). Finally, Russell argues that rules should be understood to be in service of preserving the "good conduct of games" (p. 36). In both of these latter instances, Russell essentially means that things such as "delay tactics" (e.g., refusing to throw a pitch) which fall outside the rules should not be tolerated simply because the rules are silent in their regard.

Of course, Russell runs into the same problem as Ross. For discretion, like prima facie duties, relies upon judgment. As Russell admits, "we need, then, some way of determining the force of the relevant principles in deliberation" (p. 37). Yet, as Ross points out "no such general rules . . . can be laid down," for this is exactly what discretion means; the ability to make right judgments by relying on more than "any set of rules" can by themselves provide.[16]

This insight also has important implications for the limits of technological "solutions" to refereeing decisions and mistakes. If Russell and Ross are right, then any vision

---

[16] Russell (1999) tries to answer this problem by insisting that the rules "ought to be bound by some notion of integrity" (p. 38). Here he is following Dworkin (1986) who uses integrity in a technical sense meaning something akin to "always promote justice". Nevertheless, judgment (even assuming integrity) remains necessary.

of "robo-umps" simply replacing (rather than supplementing) humans is naive and will prove ultimately unworkable. For robots cannot, by definition, have "discretion" programmed into them, for the same reason that Ross insists that rules cannot be written to adjudicate between prima facie duties.

Moreover the programmers themselves will be baking all kinds of their own prior discretionary choices into their programming rules as regards things such as precision (where do we draw the lines for a strike), accuracy (how much margin of error is tolerable), etc. As journalist, Nathan Washatka (2019) points out, "It doesn't matter how strict our definition is—determining whether an action on the field meets that definition is an act of interpretation" (para. 9). It also important to realize that *where* the decision is made, does not affect the fact *that* a decision was made. Relocating the judgment one step removed from the umpire on the field does not remove the judgment. Or again, to take that discretion out of the hands of the umps and put it into the hands of computer scientists does not eliminate, but only masks the discretion involved, under the supposed "objectivity" of science (Kagan, 2018).

The bottom line is that rule enforcement in sport relies upon discretion. For instance, in baseball the strike zone relies upon judgment, as decisions on "check swings" or what counts as the "bottom of the knee" (the MLB standard for the bottom of the strike zone) show.[17] All of this suggests that character is key. If so, let us turn our attention directly to virtue ethics and see whether an ethic of character ought to be pursued.

"If Russell and Ross are right then 'robo-umps' will ultimately prove unworkable, for even the strike zone is a judgment call."
© mTaira/Shutterstock.com

---

[17] For further information on the practical and philosophic issues involved in the issue of "robo-umps" see (Collins, 2019; Boyle, Et. al, 2018).

PHILOSOPHIC SELECTIONS

Selection #1: Immanuel Kant, "Fundamental Principles of the Metaphysic of Morals."

http://www.gutenberg.org/cache/epub/5682/pg5682-images.html

Introduction: Immanuel Kant is universally considered by both admirers and critics as one of the greatest philosophers of the modern era. In this selection from the *Fundamental Principles of the Metaphysic of Morals*, Kant reviews the relationship between reason, duty, and will. He also introduces the categorical imperative. For Kant, duty is supreme. Reason identifies and defends it, while will must be conformed to it.

Nothing can possibly be conceived in the world, or even out of it, which can be called good, without qualification, except a good will. Intelligence, wit, judgement, and the other talents of the mind, however they may be named, or courage, resolution, perseverance, as qualities of temperament, are undoubtedly good and desirable in many respects; but these gifts of nature may also become extremely bad and mischievous if the will which is to make use of them, and which, therefore, constitutes what is called character, is not good. It is the same with the gifts of fortune. Power, riches, honour, even health, and the general well-being and contentment with one's condition which is called happiness, inspire pride, and often presumption, if there is not a good will to correct the influence of these on the mind, and with this also to rectify the whole principle of acting and adapt it to its end. The sight of a being who is not adorned with a single feature of a pure and good will, enjoying unbroken prosperity, can never give pleasure to an impartial rational spectator. Thus a good will appears to constitute the indispensable condition even of being worthy of happiness.

There are even some qualities which are of service to this good will itself and may facilitate its action, yet which have no intrinsic unconditional value, but always presuppose a good will, and this qualifies the esteem that we justly have for them and does not permit us to regard them as absolutely good. Moderation in the affections and passions, self-control, and calm deliberation are not only good in many respects, but even seem to constitute part of the intrinsic worth of the person; but they are far from deserving to be called good without qualification, although they have been so unconditionally praised by the ancients. For without the principles of a good will, they may become extremely bad, and the coolness of a villain not only makes him far more dangerous, but also directly makes him more abominable in our eyes than he would have been without it.

A good will is good not because of what it performs or effects, not by its aptness for the attainment of some proposed end, but simply by virtue of the volition; that is, it is good in itself, and considered by itself is to be esteemed much higher than all that can be brought about by it in favour of any inclination, nay even of the sum total of all inclinations. Even if it should happen that, owing to special disfavour of fortune, or the niggardly provision of a step-motherly nature, this will should wholly lack power to accomplish its purpose, if with its greatest efforts it should yet achieve nothing, and there should remain only the good will (not, to be sure, a mere wish, but the summoning of all means in our power), then, like a jewel, it would still shine by its own light, as a thing which has its whole value in itself. Its usefulness or fruitlessness can neither add nor take away anything from this value. It would be, as it were, only the setting to enable us to handle it the more conveniently in common commerce, or to attract to it the attention of those who are not yet connoisseurs, but not to recommend it to true connoisseurs, or to determine its value.

There is, however, something so strange in this idea of the absolute value of the mere will, in which no account is taken of its utility, that notwithstanding the thorough assent of even common reason to the idea, yet a suspicion must arise that it may perhaps really be the product of mere high-flown fancy, and that we may have misunderstood the purpose of nature in assigning reason as the governor of our will. Therefore we will examine this idea from this point of view.

In the physical constitution of an organized being, that is, a being adapted suitably to the purposes of life, we assume it as a fundamental principle that no organ for any purpose will be found but what is also the fittest and best adapted for that purpose. Now in a being which has reason and a will, if the proper object of nature were its conservation, its welfare, in a word, its happiness, then nature would have hit upon a very bad arrangement in selecting the reason of the creature to carry out this purpose. For all the actions which the creature has to perform with a view to this purpose, and the whole rule of its conduct, would be far more surely prescribed to it by instinct, and that end would have been attained thereby much more certainly than it ever can be by reason. Should reason have been communicated to this favoured creature over and above, it must only have served it to contemplate the happy constitution of its nature, to admire it, to congratulate itself thereon, and to feel thankful for it to the beneficent cause, but not that it should subject its desires to that weak and delusive guidance and meddle bunglingly with the purpose of nature. In a word, nature would have taken care that reason should not break forth into practical exercise, nor have the presumption, with its weak insight, to think out for itself the plan of happiness, and of the means of attaining it. Nature would not only have taken on herself the choice of the ends, but also of the means, and with wise foresight would have entrusted both to instinct.

And, in fact, we find that the more a cultivated reason applies itself with deliberate purpose to the enjoyment of life and happiness, so much the more does the man fail of true satisfaction. And from this circumstance there arises in many, if they are candid enough to confess it, a certain degree of misology, that is, hatred of reason, especially in the case of those who are most experienced in the use of it, because after calculating all the advantages they derive, I do not say from the invention of all the arts of common luxury, but even from the sciences (which seem to them to be after all only a luxury of the understanding), they find that they have, in fact, only brought more trouble on their shoulders, rather than gained in happiness; and they end by envying, rather than despising, the more common stamp of men who keep closer to the guidance of mere instinct and do not allow their reason much influence on their conduct. And this we must admit, that the judgement of those who would very much lower the lofty eulogies of the advantages which reason gives us in regard to the happiness and satisfaction of life, or who would even reduce them below zero, is by no means morose or ungrateful to the goodness with which the world is governed, but that there lies at the root of these judgements the idea that our existence has a different and far nobler end, for which, and not for happiness, reason is properly intended, and which must, therefore, be regarded as the supreme condition to which the private ends of man must, for the most part, be postponed.

For as reason is not competent to guide the will with certainty in regard to its objects and the satisfaction of all our wants (which it to some extent even multiplies), this being an end to which an implanted instinct would have led with much greater certainty; and since, nevertheless, reason is imparted to us as a practical faculty, i.e., as one which is to have influence on the will, therefore, admitting that nature generally in the distribution of her capacities has adapted the means to the end, its true destination must be to produce a will, not merely good as a means to something else, but good in itself, for which reason was absolutely necessary. This will then, though not indeed the sole and complete good, must be the supreme good and the condition of every other, even of the desire of happiness. Under these circumstances, there is nothing inconsistent with the wisdom of nature in the fact that the cultivation of the reason, which is requisite for the first and unconditional purpose, does in many ways interfere, at least in this life, with the attainment of the second, which is always conditional, namely, happiness. Nay, it may even reduce it to nothing, without nature thereby failing of her purpose. For reason recognizes the establishment of a good will as its highest practical destination, and in attaining this purpose is capable only of a satisfaction of its own proper kind, namely that from the attainment of an end, which end again is determined by reason only, notwithstanding that this may involve many a disappointment to the ends of inclination.

We have then to develop the notion of a will which deserves to be highly esteemed for itself and is good without a view to anything further, a notion which exists already in the sound natural understanding, requiring rather to be cleared up than to be taught, and which in estimating the value of our actions always takes the first place and constitutes the condition of all the rest. In order to do this, we will take the notion of duty, which includes that of a good will, although implying certain subjective restrictions and hindrances. These, however, far from concealing it, or rendering it unrecognizable, rather bring it out by contrast and make it shine forth so much the brighter.

I omit here all actions which are already recognized as inconsistent with duty, although they may be useful for this or that purpose, for with these the question whether they are done from duty cannot arise at all, since they even conflict with it. I also set aside those actions which really conform to duty, but to which men have no direct inclination, performing them because they are impelled thereto by some other inclination. For in this case we can readily distinguish whether the action which agrees with duty is done from duty, or from a selfish view. It is much harder to make this distinction when the action accords with duty and the subject has besides a direct inclination to it. For example, it is always a matter of duty that a dealer should not over charge an inexperienced purchaser; and wherever there is much commerce the prudent tradesman does not overcharge, but keeps a fixed price for everyone, so that a child buys of him as well as any other. Men are thus honestly served; but this is not enough to make us believe that the tradesman has so acted from duty and from principles of honesty: his own advantage required it; it is out of the question in this case to suppose that he might besides have a direct inclination in favour of the buyers, so that, as it were, from love he should give no advantage to one over another. Accordingly the action was done neither from duty nor from direct inclination, but merely with a selfish view.

On the other hand, it is a duty to maintain one's life; and, in addition, everyone has also a direct inclination to do so. But on this account the of anxious care which most men take for it has no intrinsic worth, and their maxim has no moral import. They preserve their life as duty requires, no doubt, but not because duty requires. On the other band, if adversity and hopeless sorrow have completely taken away the relish for life; if the unfortunate one, strong in mind, indignant at his fate rather than desponding or dejected, wishes for death, and yet preserves his life without loving it—not from inclination or fear, but from duty—then his maxim has a moral worth.

To be beneficent when we can is a duty; and besides this, there are many minds so sympathetically constituted that, without any other motive of vanity or self-interest, they find a pleasure in spreading joy around them and can take delight in the satisfaction of others so far as it is their own work. But I maintain that in such a case an action of this kind, however proper, however amiable it may be, has nevertheless no true moral worth, but is on a level with other inclinations, e.g., the inclination to honour, which, if it is happily directed to that which is in fact of public utility and accordant with duty and consequently honourable, deserves praise and encouragement, but not esteem. For the maxim lacks the moral import, namely, that such actions be done from duty, not from inclination. Put the case that the mind of that philanthropist were clouded by sorrow of his own, extinguishing all sympathy with the lot of others, and that, while he still has the power to benefit others in distress, he is not touched by their trouble because he is absorbed with his own; and now suppose that he tears himself out of this dead insensibility, and performs the action without any inclination to it, but simply from duty, then first has his action its genuine moral worth. Further still; if nature has put little sympathy in the heart of this or that man; if he, supposed to be an upright man, is by temperament cold and indifferent to the sufferings of others, perhaps because in respect of his own he is provided with the special gift of patience and fortitude and supposes, or even requires, that others should have the same—and such a man would certainly not be the meanest product of nature—but if nature had not specially framed him for a philanthropist, would he not still find in himself a source from whence to give himself a far higher worth than that of a good-natured temperament could be? Unquestionably. It is just in this that the moral worth of the character is brought out which is incomparably the highest of all, namely, that he is beneficent, not from inclination, but from duty.

To secure one's own happiness is a duty, at least indirectly; for discontent with one's condition, under a pressure of many anxieties and amidst unsatisfied wants, might easily become a great temptation to transgression of duty. But here again, without looking to duty, all men have already the strongest and most intimate inclination to happiness, because it is just in this idea that all inclinations are combined in one total. But the precept of happiness is often of such a sort that it greatly interferes with some inclinations, and yet a man cannot form any definite and certain conception of the sum of satisfaction of all of them which is called happiness. It is not then to be wondered at that a single inclination, definite both as to what it promises and as to the time within which it can be gratified, is often able to overcome such a fluctuating idea, and that a gouty patient, for instance, can choose to enjoy what he likes, and to suffer what he may, since, according to his calculation, on this occasion at least, he has not sacrificed the enjoyment of the present moment to a possibly mistaken expectation of a happiness which is supposed to be found in health. But even in this case, if the general desire for happiness did not influence his will, and supposing that in his particular case health was not a necessary element in this calculation, there yet remains in this, as in all other cases, this law, namely, that he should promote his happiness not from inclination but from duty, and by this would his conduct first acquire true moral worth.

It is in this manner, undoubtedly, that we are to understand those passages of Scripture also in which we are commanded to love our neighbour, even our enemy. For love, as an affection, cannot be commanded, but beneficence for duty's sake may; even though we are not impelled to it by any inclination- nay, are even repelled by a natural and unconquerable aversion. This is practical love and not pathological- a love which is seated in the will, and not in the propensions of sense- in principles of action and not of tender sympathy; and it is this love alone which can be commanded.

The second proposition is: That an action done from duty derives its moral worth, not from the purpose which is to be attained by it, but from the maxim by which it is determined, and therefore does not depend on the realization of the object of the action, but merely on the principle of volition by which the action has taken place, without regard to any object of desire. It is clear from what precedes that the purposes which we may have in view in our actions, or their effects regarded as ends and springs of the will, cannot give to actions any unconditional or moral worth. In what, then, can their worth lie, if it is not to consist in the will and in reference to its expected effect? It cannot lie anywhere but in the principle of the will without regard to the ends which can be attained by the action. For the will stands between its a priori principle, which is formal, and its a posteriori spring, which is material, as between two roads, and as it must be determined by something, it that it must be determined by the formal principle of volition when an action is done from duty, in which case every material principle has been withdrawn from it.

The third proposition, which is a consequence of the two preceding, I would express thus Duty is the necessity of acting from respect for the law. I may have inclination for an object as the effect of my proposed action, but I cannot have respect for it, just for this reason, that it is an effect and not an energy of will. Similarly I cannot have respect for inclination, whether my own or another's; I can at most, if my own, approve it; if another's, sometimes even love it; i.e., look on it as favourable to my own interest. It is only what is connected with my will as a principle, by no means as an effect—what does not subserve my inclination, but overpowers it, or at least in case of choice excludes it from its calculation—in other words, simply the law of itself, which can be an object of respect, and hence a command. Now an action done from duty must wholly exclude the influence of inclination and with it every object of the will, so that nothing remains which can determine the will except objectively the law, and subjectively pure respect for this practical law, and consequently the maxim[1] that I should follow this law even to the thwarting of all my inclinations.

Thus the moral worth of an action does not lie in the effect expected from it, nor in any principle of action which requires to borrow its motive from this expected effect. For all these effects—agreeableness of one's condition and even the promotion of the happiness of others—could have been also brought about by other causes, so that for this there would have been no need of the will of a rational being; whereas it is in this alone that the supreme and unconditional good can be found. The pre-eminent good which we call moral can therefore consist in nothing else than the conception of law in itself, which certainly is only possible in a rational being, in so far as this conception, and not the expected effect, determines the will. This is a good which is already present in the person who acts accordingly, and we have not to wait for it to appear first in the result.[2]

---

[1] A maxim is the subjective principle of volition. The objective principle (i.e., that which would also serve subjectively as a practical principle to all rational beings if reason had full power over the faculty of desire) is the practical law.

[2] It might be here objected to me that I take refuge behind the word respect in an obscure feeling, instead of giving a distinct solution of the question by a concept of the reason. But although respect is a feeling, it is not a feeling received through influence, but is self-wrought by a rational concept, and, therefore, is specifically distinct from all feelings of the former kind, which may be referred either to inclination or fear, What I recognise immediately as a law for me, I recognise with respect. This merely signifies the consciousness that my will is subordinate to a law, without the intervention of other influences on my sense. The immediate determination of the will by the law, and the consciousness of this, is called respect, so that this is regarded as an effect of the law on the subject, and not as the cause of it. Respect is properly the conception of a worth which thwarts my self-love. Accordingly it is something which is considered neither as an object of inclination nor of fear, although it has something analogous to both. The object of respect is the law only, and that the law which we impose on ourselves and yet recognise as necessary in itself. As a law, we are subjected too it without consulting self-love; as imposed by us on ourselves, it is a result of our will. In the former aspect it has an analogy to fear, in the latter to inclination. Respect for a person is properly only respect for the law (of honesty, etc.) of which he gives us an example. Since we also look on the improvement of our talents as a duty, we consider that we see in a person of talents, as it were, the example of a law (viz., to become like him in this by exercise), and this constitutes our respect. All so-called moral interest consists simply in respect for the law.

But what sort of law can that be, the conception of which must determine the will, even without paying any regard to the effect expected from it, in order that this will may be called good absolutely and without qualification? As I have deprived the will of every impulse which could arise to it from obedience to any law, there remains nothing but the universal conformity of its actions to law in general, which alone is to serve the will as a principle, i.e., I am never to act otherwise than so that I could also will that my maxim should become a universal law. Here, now, it is the simple conformity to law in general, without assuming any particular law applicable to certain actions, that serves the will as its principle and must so serve it, if duty is not to be a vain delusion and a chimerical notion. The common reason of men in its practical judgements perfectly coincides with this and always has in view the principle here suggested. Let the question be, for example: May I when in distress make a promise with the intention not to keep it? I readily distinguish here between the two significations which the question may have: Whether it is prudent, or whether it is right, to make a false promise? The former may undoubtedly of be the case. I see clearly indeed that it is not enough to extricate myself from a present difficulty by means of this subterfuge, but it must be well considered whether there may not hereafter spring from this lie much greater inconvenience than that from which I now free myself, and as, with all my supposed cunning, the consequences cannot be so easily foreseen but that credit once lost may be much more injurious to me than any mischief which I seek to avoid at present, it should be considered whether it would not be more prudent to act herein according to a universal maxim and to make it a habit to promise nothing except with the intention of keeping it. But it is soon clear to me that such a maxim will still only be based on the fear of consequences. Now it is a wholly different thing to be truthful from duty and to be so from apprehension of injurious consequences. In the first case, the very notion of the action already implies a law for me; in the second case, I must first look about elsewhere to see what results may be combined with it which would affect myself. For to deviate from the principle of duty is beyond all doubt wicked; but to be unfaithful to my maxim of prudence may often be very advantageous to me, although to abide by it is certainly safer. The shortest way, however, and an unerring one, to discover the answer to this question whether a lying promise is consistent with duty, is to ask myself, "Should I be content that my maxim (to extricate myself from difficulty by a false promise) should hold good as a universal law, for myself as well as for others?" and should I be able to say to myself, "Every one may make a deceitful promise when he finds himself in a difficulty from which he cannot otherwise extricate himself?" Then I presently become aware that while I can will the lie, I can by no means will that lying should be a universal law. For with such a law there would be no promises at all, since it would be in vain to allege my intention in regard to my future actions to those who would not believe this allegation, or if they over hastily did so would pay me back in my own coin. Hence my maxim, as soon as it should be made a universal law, would necessarily destroy itself...

...In this problem we will first inquire whether the mere conception of a categorical imperative may not perhaps supply us also with the formula of it, containing the proposition which alone can be a categorical imperative; for even if we know the tenor of such an absolute command, yet how it is possible will require further special and laborious study, which we postpone to the last section.

When I conceive a hypothetical imperative, in general I do not know beforehand what it will contain until I am given the condition. But when I conceive a categorical imperative, I know at once what it contains. For as the imperative contains besides the law only the necessity that the maxims[3] shall conform to this law, while the law contains no conditions restricting it, there remains nothing but the general statement that the maxim of the action should conform to a universal law, and it is this conformity alone that the imperative properly represents as necessary.

There is therefore but one categorical imperative, namely, this: Act only on that maxim whereby thou canst at the same time will that it should become a universal law.

Now if all imperatives of duty can be deduced from this one imperative as from their principle, then, although it should remain undecided what is called duty is not merely a vain notion, yet at least we shall be able to show what we understand by it and what this notion means.

Since the universality of the law according to which effects are produced constitutes what is properly called nature in the most general sense (as to form), that is the existence of things so far as it is determined by general laws, the imperative of duty may be expressed thus: Act as if the maxim of thy action were to become by thy will a universal law of nature.

We will now enumerate a few duties, adopting the usual division of them into duties to ourselves and ourselves and to others, and into perfect and imperfect duties.[4]

1. A man reduced to despair by a series of misfortunes feels wearied of life, but is still so far in possession of his reason that he can ask himself whether it would not be contrary to his duty to himself to take his own life. Now he inquires whether the maxim of his action could become a universal law of nature. His maxim is: "From self-love I adopt it as a principle to shorten my life when its longer duration is likely to bring more evil than satisfaction." It is asked then simply whether this principle founded on self-love can become a universal law of nature. Now we see at once that a system of nature of which it should be a law to destroy life by means of the very feeling whose special nature it is to impel to the improvement of life would contradict itself and, therefore, could not exist as a system of nature; hence that maxim cannot possibly exist as a universal law of nature and, consequently, would be wholly inconsistent with the supreme principle of all duty.

2. Another finds himself forced by necessity to borrow money. He knows that he will not be able to repay it, but sees also that nothing will be lent to him unless he promises stoutly to repay it in a definite time. He desires to make this promise, but he has still so much conscience as to ask himself: "Is it not unlawful and inconsistent with duty to get out of a difficulty in this way?" Suppose however that he resolves to do so: then the maxim of his action would be expressed thus: "When I think myself in want of money, I will borrow money and promise to repay it, although I know that I never can do so." Now this principle of self-love or of one's own advantage may perhaps be consistent with my whole future welfare; but the question now is, "Is it right?" I change then the suggestion of self-love into a universal law, and state the question thus: "How would it be if my maxim were a universal law?" Then I see at once that it could never hold as a universal

[3] A maxim is a subjective principle of action, and must be distinguished from the objective principle, namely, practical law. The former contains the practical rule set by reason according to the conditions of the subject (often its ignorance or its inclinations), so that it is the principle on which the subject acts; but the law is the objective principle valid for every rational being, and is the principle on which it ought to act that is an imperative.

[4] It must be noted here that I reserve the division of duties for a future metaphysic of morals; so that I give it here only as an arbitrary one (in order to arrange my examples). For the rest, I understand by a perfect duty one that admits no exception in favour of inclination and then I have not merely external but also internal perfect duties. This is contrary to the use of the word adopted in the schools; but I do not intend to justify there, as it is all one for my purpose whether it is admitted or not.

law of nature, but would necessarily contradict itself. For supposing it to be a universal law that everyone when he thinks himself in a difficulty should be able to promise whatever he pleases, with the purpose of not keeping his promise, the promise itself would become impossible, as well as the end that one might have in view in it, since no one would consider that anything was promised to him, but would ridicule all such statements as vain pretences.

3. A third finds in himself a talent which with the help of some culture might make him a useful man in many respects. But he finds himself in comfortable circumstances and prefers to indulge in pleasure rather than to take pains in enlarging and improving his happy natural capacities. He asks, however, whether his maxim of neglect of his natural gifts, besides agreeing with his inclination to indulgence, agrees also with what is called duty. He sees then that a system of nature could indeed subsist with such a universal law although men (like the South Sea islanders) should let their talents rest and resolve to devote their lives merely to idleness, amusement, and propagation of their species- in a word, to enjoyment; but he cannot possibly will that this should be a universal law of nature, or be implanted in us as such by a natural instinct. For, as a rational being, he necessarily wills that his faculties be developed, since they serve him and have been given him, for all sorts of possible purposes.

4. A fourth, who is in prosperity, while he sees that others have to contend with great wretchedness and that he could help them, thinks: "What concern is it of mine? Let everyone be as happy as Heaven pleases, or as he can make himself; I will take nothing from him nor even envy him, only I do not wish to contribute anything to his welfare or to his assistance in distress!" Now no doubt if such a mode of thinking were a universal law, the human race might very well subsist and doubtless even better than in a state in which everyone talks of sympathy and good-will, or even takes care occasionally to put it into practice, but, on the other side, also cheats when he can, betrays the rights of men, or otherwise violates them. But although it is possible that a universal law of nature might exist in accordance with that maxim, it is impossible to will that such a principle should have the universal validity of a law of nature. For a will which resolved this would contradict itself, inasmuch as many cases might occur in which one would have need of the love and sympathy of others, and in which, by such a law of nature, sprung from his own will, he would deprive himself of all hope of the aid he desires...

... Now I say: man and generally any rational being exists as an end in himself, not merely as a means to be arbitrarily used by this or that will, but in all his actions, whether they concern himself or other rational beings, must be always regarded at the same time as an end. All objects of the inclinations have only a conditional worth, for if the inclinations and the wants founded on them did not exist, then their object would be without value. But the inclinations, themselves being sources of want, are so far from having an absolute worth for which they should be desired that on the contrary it must be the universal wish of every rational being to be wholly free from them. Thus the worth of any object which is to be acquired by our action is always conditional. Beings whose existence depends not on our will but on nature's, have nevertheless, if they are irrational beings, only a relative value as means, and are therefore called things; rational beings, on the contrary, are called persons, because their very nature points them out as ends in themselves, that is as something which must not be used merely as means, and so far therefore restricts freedom of action (and is an object of respect). These, therefore, are not merely subjective ends whose existence has a worth for us as an effect of our action, but objective ends, that is, things whose existence is an end in itself; an end moreover for which no other can be substituted, which they should subserve merely as means, for otherwise nothing whatever would possess absolute worth; but if all worth were conditioned and therefore contingent, then there would be no supreme practical principle of reason whatever.

If then there is a supreme practical principle or, in respect of the human will, a categorical imperative, it must be one which, being drawn from the conception of that which is necessarily an end for everyone because it is an end in itself, constitutes an objective principle of will, and can therefore serve as a universal practical law. The foundation of this principle is: rational nature exists as an end in itself. Man necessarily conceives his own existence as being so; so far then this is a subjective principle of human actions. But every other rational being regards its existence similarly, just on the same rational principle that holds for me: so that it is at the same time an objective principle, from which as a supreme practical law all laws of the will must be capable of being deduced. Accordingly the practical imperative will be as follows: So act as to treat humanity, whether in thine own person or in that of any other, in every case as an end withal, never as means only. We will now inquire whether this can be practically carried out. . . .

. . . Looking back now on all previous attempts to discover the principle of morality, we need not wonder why they all failed. It was seen that man was bound to laws by duty, but it was not observed that the laws to which he is subject are only those of his own giving, though at the same time they are universal, and that he is only bound to act in conformity with his own will; a will, however, which is designed by nature to give universal laws. For when one has conceived man only as subject to a law (no matter what), then this law required some interest, either by way of attraction or constraint, since it did not originate as a law from his own will, but this will was according to a law obliged by something else to act in a certain manner. Now by this necessary consequence all the labour spent in finding a supreme principle of duty was irrevocably lost. For men never elicited duty, but only a necessity of acting from a certain interest. Whether this interest was private or otherwise, in any case the imperative must be conditional and could not by any means be capable of being a moral command. I will therefore call this the principle of autonomy of the will, in contrast with every other which I accordingly reckon as heteronomy.

The conception of the will of every rational being as one which must consider itself as giving in all the maxims of its will universal laws, so as to judge itself and its actions from this point of view—this conception leads to another which depends on it and is very fruitful, namely that of a kingdom of ends.

By a kingdom I understand the union of different rational beings in a system by common laws. Now since it is by laws that ends are determined as regards their universal validity, hence, if we abstract from the personal differences of rational beings and likewise from all the content of their private ends, we shall be able to conceive all ends combined in a systematic whole (including both rational beings as ends in themselves, and also the special ends which each may propose to himself), that is to say, we can conceive a kingdom of ends, which on the preceding principles is possible.

For all rational beings come under the law that each of them must treat itself and all others never merely as means, but in every case at the same time as ends in themselves. Hence results a systematic union of rational being by common objective laws, i.e., a kingdom which may be called a kingdom of ends, since what these laws have in view is just the relation of these beings to one another as ends and means.

Discussion Question(s)

1. Is Kant right to emphasize reason over emotion? Why or why not?
2. What do you make of the two formulations of the categorical imperative? Are they good guides to moral action? Can you think of an example in sport where the 2nd formulation might apply?
3. Is Kant's "kingdom of ends" possible in sport? Can we make real progress toward a sporting culture which recognizes universal moral duties and which respects the intrinsic worth of athletes, coaches, administrators, and fans? If so, what about the present state of affairs would need to change?

Selection #2: W.D. Ross, "The Right and the Good," Chapter 2.

http://www.ditext.com/ross/right2.html#14

Introduction: W.D. Ross is interested in how obligation works in the day–to–day world. That is, he believes that our duties are real and binding upon us but that as a practical matter, we have to adjudicate which of our duties is incumbent upon us at *this* time, given *this* situation. To do this well, Ross argues, we must cultivate "perception," or what Aristotle called "prudence/practical wisdom." Such perception will allow us to recognize "our particular duty in particular circumstances."

II
What Makes Right Acts Right?

The real point at issue between hedonism and utilitarianism on the one hand and their opponents on the other is not whether 'right' means 'productive of so and so'; for it cannot with any plausibility be maintained that it does. The point at issue is that to which we now pass, viz. whether there is any general character which makes right acts right, and if so, what it is. Among the main historical attempts to state a single characteristic of all right actions which is the foundation of their rightness are those made by egoism and utilitarianism. But I do not propose to discuss these, not because the subject is unimportant, but because it has been dealt with so often and so well already, and because there has come to be so much agreement among moral philosophers that neither of these theories is satisfactory. A much more attractive theory has been put forward by Professor Moore: that what makes actions right is that they are productive of more *good* than could have been produced by any other action open to the agent.[1]

This theory is in fact the culmination of all the attempts to base rightness on productivity of some sort of result. The first form this attempt takes is the attempt to base rightness on conduciveness to the advantage or pleasure of the agent. This theory comes to grief over the fact, which stares us in the face, that a great part of duty consists in an observance of the rights and a furtherance of the interests of others, whatever the cost to ourselves may be. Plato and others may be right in holding that a regard for the rights of others never in the long run involves a loss of happiness for the agent, that 'the just life profits a man'. But this, even if true, is irrelevant to the rightness of the act. As soon as a man does an action *because* he thinks he will promote his own interests thereby, he is acting not from a sense of its rightness but from self-interest.

---

[1] I take the theory which, as I have tried to show, seems to be put forward in *Ethics* rather than the earlier and less plausible theory put forward in *Principia Ethica*. For the difference, cf. my pp. 8–11.

To the egoistic theory hedonistic utilitarianism supplies a much-needed amendment. It points out correctly that the fact that a certain pleasure will be enjoyed by the agent is no reason why he ought to bring it into being rather than an equal or greater pleasure to be enjoyed by another, though, human nature being what it is, it makes it not unlikely that he will try to bring it into being. But hedonistic utilitarianism in its turn needs a correction. On reflection it seems clear that pleasure is not the only thing in life that we think good in itself, that for instance we think the possession of a good character, or an intelligent understanding of the world, as good or better. A great advance is made by the substitution of 'productive of the greatest good' for 'productive of the greatest pleasure'.

Not only is this theory more attractive than hedonistic utilitarianism, but its logical relation to that theory is such that the latter could not be true unless it were true, while it might be true though hedonistic utilitarianism were not. It is in fact one of the logical bases of hedonistic utilitarianism. For the view that what produces the maximum pleasure is right has for its bases the views

- that what produces the maximum good is right, and
- that pleasure is the only thing good in itself.

If they were not assuming that what produces the maximum *good* is right, the utilitarians' attempt to show that pleasure is the only thing good in itself, which is in fact the point they take most pains to establish, would have been quite irrelevant to their attempt to prove that only what produces the maximum *pleasure* is right. If, therefore, it can be shown that productivity of the maximum good is not what makes all right actions right, we shall *a fortiori* have refuted hedonistic utilitarianism.

When a plain man fulfils a promise because he thinks he ought to do so, it seems clear that he does so with no thought of its total consequences, still less with any opinion that these are likely to be the best possible. He thinks in fact much more of the past than of the future. What makes him think it right to act in a certain way is the fact that he has promised to do so—that and, usually, nothing more. That his act will produce the best possible consequences is not his reason for calling it right. What lends colour to the theory we are examining, then, is not the actions (which form probably a great majority of our actions) in which some such reflection as 'I have promised' is the only reason we give ourselves for thinking a certain action right, but the exceptional cases in which the consequences of fulfilling a promise (for instance) would be so disastrous to others that we judge it right not to do so. It must of course be admitted that such cases exist. If I have promised to meet a friend at a particular time for some trivial purpose, I should certainly think myself justified in breaking my engagement if by doing so I could prevent a serious accident or bring relief to the victims of one. And the supporters of the view we are examining hold that my thinking so is due to my thinking that I shall bring more good into existence by the one action than by the other. A different account may, however, be given of the matter, an account which will, I believe, show itself to be the true one. It may be said that besides the duty of fulfilling promises I have and recognize a duty of relieving distress,[2] and that when I think it right to do the latter at the cost of not doing the former, it is not because I think I shall produce more good thereby but because I think it the duty which is in the circumstances more of a duty. This account surely corresponds much more closely with what we really think in such a situation. If, so far as I can see, I could bring equal amounts of good into being by fulfilling my promise and by

---

[2] These are not strictly speaking duties, but things that tend to be our duty, or *prima facie* duties. Cf. pp. 19–20.

helping some one to whom I had made no promise, I should not hesitate to regard the former as my duty. Yet on the view that what is right is right because it is productive of the most good I should not so regard it.

There are two theories, each in its way simple, that offer a solution of such cases of conscience. One is the view of Kant, that there are certain duties of perfect obligation, such as those of fulfilling promises, of paying debts, of telling the truth, which admit of no exception whatever in favour of duties of imperfect obligation, such as that of relieving distress. The other is the view of, for instance, Professor Moore and Dr. Rashdall, that there is only the duty of producing good, and that all 'conflicts of duties' should be resolved by asking 'by which action will most good be produced?' But it is more important that our theory fit the facts than that it be simple, and the account we have given above corresponds (it seems to me) better than either of the simpler theories with what we really think, viz. that normally promise-keeping, for example, should come before benevolence, but that when and only when the good to be produced by the benevolent act is very great and the promise comparatively trivial, the act of benevolence becomes our duty.

In fact the theory of 'ideal utilitarianism', if I may for brevity refer so to the theory of Professor Moore, seems to simplify unduly our relations to our fellows. It says, in effect, that the only morally significant relation in which my neighbours stand to me is that of being possible beneficiaries by my action.[3] They do stand in this relation to me, and this relation is morally significant. But they may also stand to me in the relation of promisee to promiser, of creditor to debtor, of wife to husband, of child to parent, of friend to friend, of fellow countryman to fellow countryman, and the like; and each of these relations is the foundation of a *prima facie* duty, which is more or less incumbent on me according to the circumstances of the case. When I am in a situation, as perhaps I always am, in which more than one of these *prima facie* duties is incumbent on me, what I have to do is to study the situation as fully as I can until I form the considered opinion (it is never more) that in the circumstances one of them is more incumbent than any other; then I am bound to think that to do this *prima facie* duty is my duty *sans phrase* in the situation.

I suggest '*prima facie* duty' or 'conditional duty' as a brief way of referring to the characteristic (quite distinct from that of being a duty proper) which an act has, in virtue of being of a certain kind (e.g. the keeping of a promise), of being an act which would be a duty proper if it were not at the same time of another kind which is morally significant. Whether an act is a duty proper or actual duty depends on *all* the morally significant kinds it is an instance of. The phrase '*prima facie* duty' must be apologized for, since

1. it suggests that what we are speaking of is a certain kind of duty, whereas it is in fact not a duty, but something related in a special way to duty. Strictly speaking, we want not a phrase in which duty is qualified by an adjective, but a separate noun.

2. '*Prima*' facie suggests that one is speaking only of an appearance which a moral situation presents at first sight, and which may turn out to be illusory; whereas what I am speaking of is an objective fact involved in the nature of the situation, or more strictly in an element of its nature, though not, as duty proper does, arising from its whole nature.

I can, however, think of no term which fully meets the case. 'Claim' has been suggested by Professor Prichard. The word 'claim' has the advantage of being quite a familiar one

---

[3] Some will think it, apart from other considerations, a sufficient refutation of this view to point out that I also stand in that relation to myself, so that for this view the distinction of oneself from others is morally insignificant.

in this connexion, and it seems to cover much of the ground. It would be quite natural to say, 'a person to whom I have made a promise has a claim on me', and also, 'a person whose distress I could relieve (at the cost of breaking the promise) has a claim on me'. But (1) while 'claim' is appropriate from their point of view, we want a word to express the corresponding fact from the agent's point of view—the fact of his being subject to claims that can be made against him; and ordinary language provides us with no such correlative to 'claim'. And (2) (what is more important) 'claim' seems inevitably to suggest two persons, one of whom might make a claim on the other; and while this covers the ground of social duty, it is inappropriate in the case of that important part of duty which is the duty of cultivating a certain kind of character in oneself. It would be artificial, I think, and at any rate metaphorical, to say that one's character has a claim on oneself.

There is nothing arbitrary about these *prima facie* duties. Each rests on a definite circumstance which cannot seriously be held to be without moral significance. Of *prima facie* duties I suggest, without claiming completeness or finality for it, the following division.[4]

1. Some duties rest on previous acts of my own. These duties seem to include two kinds,
    A. those resting on a promise or what may fairly be called an implicit promise, such as the implicit undertaking not to tell lies which seems to be implied in the act of entering into conversation (at any rate by civilized men), or of writing books that purport to be history and not fiction. These may be called the duties of fidelity.
    B. Those resting on a previous wrongful act. These may be called the duties of reparation.

2. Some rest on previous acts of other men, i.e. services done by them to me. These may be loosely described as the duties of gratitude.[5]

3. Some rest on the fact or possibility of a distribution of pleasure or happiness (or of the means thereto) which is not in accordance with the merit of the persons concerned; in such cases there arises a duty to upset or prevent such a distribution. These are the duties of justice.

4. Some rest on the mere fact that there are beings in the world whose condition we can make better in respect of virtue, or of intelligence, or of pleasure. These are the duties of beneficence.

5. Some rest on the fact that we can improve our own condition in respect of virtue or of intelligence. These are the duties of self-improvement.

6. I think that we should distinguish from (4) the duties that may be summed up under the title of 'not injuring others'. No doubt to injure others is incidentally to fail to do them good; but it seems to me clear that non-maleficence is apprehended as a duty distinct from that of beneficence, and as a duty of a more stringent character. . .

---

[4] I should make it plain at this stage that I am *assuming* the correctness of some of our main convictions as to *prima facie* duties, or, more strictly, am claiming that we know them to be true. To me it seems as self-evident as anything could be, that to make a promise, for instance, is to create a moral claim on us in someone else. Many readers will perhaps say that they do nor know this to be true. If so, I certainly cannot prove it to them; I can only ask them to reflect again, in the hope that they will ultimately agree that they also know it to be true. The main moral conviction of the plain man seem to me to be, not opinions which it is for philosophy to prove or disprove, but knowledge from the start; and in my own case I seem to find little difficulty in distinguishing these essential convictions from other moral convictions which I also have, which are merely fallible opinions based on an imperfect study of the working for good or evil of certain institutions or types of action.

[5] For a needed correction of this statement, cf. see Ross (1930/2002).

...Something should be said of the relation between our apprehension of the prima facie rightness of certain types of act and our mental attitude towards particular acts. It is proper to use the word 'apprehension' in the former case and not in the latter. That an act, qua fulfilling a promise, or qua effecting a just distribution of good, or qua returning services rendered, or qua promoting the good of others, or qua promoting the virtue or insight of the agent, is prima facie right, is self-evident; not in the sense that it is evident from beginning of our lives, or as soon as we attend to the proposition for the first time, but in the sense that when we have reached sufficient mental maturity and have given sufficient attention to the proposition it is evident without any need of proof, or of evidence beyond itself. It is self-evident just as a mathematical axiom, or the validity of a form of inference, is evident. The moral order expressed in these propositions is just as much part of the fundamental nature of the universe (and, we may add, of any possible universe in which there were moral agents at all) as is the spatial or numerical structure expressed in the axioms of geometry or arithmetic. In our confidence that these propositions are true there is involved the same trust in our reason that is involved in our confidence in mathematics; and we should have no justification for trusting it in the latter sphere and distrusting it in the former. In both cases we are dealing with propositions that cannot be proved. but that just as certainly need no proof.

... It is worth while to try to state more definitely the nature of the acts that are right. We may try to state first what (if anything) is the universal nature of all acts that are right. It is obvious that any of the acts that we do has countless effects, directly or indirectly, on countless people, and the probability is that any act, however right it be, will have adverse effects (though these may be very trivial) on some innocent people. Similarly, any wrong act will probably have beneficial effects on some deserving people. Every act therefore, viewed in some aspects, will be prima facie right, and viewed in others, prima facie wrong, and right acts can be distinguished from wrong acts only as being those which, of all those possible for the agent in the circumstances, have the greatest balance of prima facie rightness, in those respects in which they are prima facie right, over their prima facie wrongness, in those respects in which they are prima facie wrong—prima facie rightness and wrongness being understood in the sense previously explained. For the estimation of the comparative stringency of these prima facie obligations no general rules can, so far as I can see, be laid down. We can only say that a great deal of stringency belongs to the duties of 'perfect obligation'—the duties of keeping our promises, of repairing wrongs we have done, and of returning the equivalent of services we have received. For the rest, εν τη αισθησειη κρισις[6] This sense of our particular duty in particular circumstances, preceded and informed by the fullest reflection we can bestow on the act in all its bearings, is highly fallible, but it is the only guide we have to our duty.

W.D. Ross, "The Right and the Good". Public Domain.

Discussion Question(s)

1. Do you agree with Ross' assertion that at least some moral truths are as self-evident as a "mathematical axiom"? If he's right and we know the good, why do we so often fail to do it?
2. Explain, in your own words, how Kant's categorical duty to "tell the truth" and Ross' prima facie duty to "honesty" differ.
3. Can you think of a sporting situation where two prima facie duties might come into conflict? How ought such a situation—according to Ross—be resolved?

---

[6] 'The decision rests with perception'. Arist. *Nic. Eth.* 1109 b 23, 1126 b 4.

Selection #3: Rick Reilly, *SI.com*, "Of Mice and Morons," June 5, 2006.

Please read the article here: http://www.si.com/vault/2006/06/05/8379304/of-mice-and-morons

Introduction: What should sport administrators and policy makers be most concerned about? How important are rules and rule-following to well run and just sporting organizations? Which rules or principles should they categorically follow? Which rules or principles should be negotiable? In this short piece from *Sports Illustrated*, columnist Rick Reilly examines the story of Nick End, an NCAA Division III track athlete who was disqualified from the NCAA National Championship Track Meet for rules violations. What rules did Nick violate? Was he accepting cash, cheating in class, or using PEDs? Nope. Nick End was disqualified by a bureaucratic mistake. His coach accidently registered him for the wrong event. Nevertheless, the NCAA refused to consider any possibility of correcting the mistake, even though the error was recognized the very next day.

Discussion Question(s)

1. Does deontology empower bureaucrats? That is, does an adherence to the rules, practically speaking, allow one to wash their hands of "discretion" and ignore common sense?

2. Why do you think the NCAA refused to allow for a correction to be made for such a small error? Is there any truth to Reilly's assertion that: "Nothing ever changes about these small-hearted, rule-worshipping pencil pushers. They can't control the John Dillingers of the world so they take it out on the jaywalkers."?

3. How might the story of Nick End be used to support the claim that "Ross' understanding of prima facie duties is superior to Kant's categorical ethics"? Is such a claim right? Why? Why not?

Selection #4: Nathan Washatka, *Front Porch Republic*, "Robo-umps and Us," May 10, 2019.

https://www.frontporchrepublic.com/2019/05/robo-umps-and-us/

Introduction: Is the strike zone in baseball "objective" or does it rely on the cultivation of "perception"? That is, does baseball (as both the arguments of Ross and Russell discussed in Chapter 5 imply) rely on intuitionism? In this reading, journalist Nathan Washatka argues that calling balls and strikes is one example of how umpires necessarily rely on "discretion." Ross' intuitionism is right, "the decision rests with perception." Washatka argues, therefore, that the desire to cede control of the game to "robo-umps" simply obscures this reality. Judgment is inescapable. The *decision* to eliminate it (via "standardized strike zones", etc.) is but one more judgment, a judgment which would gravely harm rather than improve *our* games.

Robo-umps and Us

There seems to be a growing consensus that machines will one day replace umpires for the purpose of calling balls and strikes in Major League Baseball games. Various pitch-tracking technologies have existed for years, and they're becoming more accurate all the time. MLB has even struck a deal with the independent Atlantic League to serve as a testing ground for "robo-umps." (Though the Atlantic League's implementation of the robo-ump was recently delayed for unspecified reasons.)

The rationale driving the development of automated umpires goes something like this. The human umpires currently judging balls and strikes are generally accurate and generally consistent. But they sometimes make mistakes, and even when they're doing a good job, the results don't always look like one might expect. Umpires affect every pitch of every game, so a bad umpire can lead to unfair games. Even a great umpire could conceivably change the outcome of a game with one bad call. If we have the technology to judge balls and strikes with 100% accuracy, we should use it to ensure that games are not affected by the mistakes of human umpires.

I don't disagree that accuracy is an important goal when it comes to judging balls and strikes. Fans, players, and coaches all long for a world in which umpires make the correct (accurate) call every time.

But I disagree that our collective desire for umpire accuracy should lead us toward a scenario in which balls and strikes are called by machines. I can't claim that robo-umps would be "bad for baseball," since arguing about what's "good" or "bad" for a game is nonsensical. Rather, as is so often the case when new technology promises to correct the errors of human fallibility, I think that robo-umps would be bad for *us*. For everyone. Not just the ones who stand to lose their jobs.

Here is Major League Baseball's definition of the strike zone:

> *The official strike zone is the area over home plate from the midpoint between a batter's shoulders and the top of the uniform pants—when the batter is in his stance and prepared to swing at a pitched ball—and a point just below the kneecap. In order to get a strike call, part of the ball must cross over part of home plate while in the aforementioned area.*

If you had never heard of the game of baseball, this definition would probably strike you as . . . imprecise. For a game in which half-an-inch could, in theory, change the outcome of a game, this definition is awfully whimsical. Inquiring minds may wonder: Where, *exactly*, does a shoulder begin? What happens if some guy wears his pants unusually high or unusually low? How can you find a line "just below the kneecap" if a player is wearing pants? Can a batter assume any stance he wishes, no matter how it might contort the shape or appearance of the strike zone?

I'm only being a little facetious. On the one hand, calling balls and strikes with satisfactory accuracy is not that hard. Millions of children have managed to do it for themselves during tens of millions of games in parks, streets, pastures, and alleyways. For all the imprecision of that definition, we all get the general idea, and it's not difficult to apply the definition to a game.

That said, it's important to recognize a fundamental truth that is obscured behind all the false precision of MLB's definition, a truth further belied by most modern baseball telecasts, in which a strike zone is superimposed during every at-bat: the strike zone is a concept. Its reality is imagined. Yes, home plate is a tangible thing with measurable dimensions. And yes, the batter is really standing there—with real knees, a real waistline, and real shoulders. But the strike zone is *not really there*. We just act like it is.

Officials and umpires in every sport must routinely exercise judgment. Anyone who has watched the NFL in recent years has endured mind-numbing explanations of what constitutes and does not constitute a catch. A "catch" cannot be determined by a machine. It doesn't matter how strict our definition is—determining whether an action on the field meets that definition is an act of interpretation. The same principle holds when an official in a basketball game or soccer match calls a foul, or when boxing judges decide the winner of a fight. They are measuring the action in front of them according to an abstract set of rules.

I've never heard of anyone call for robo-officials in the NBA or NFL. Of course, we *do* hear incessant calls for the expansion of instant replay, all in the name of "getting the calls right." In the case of instant reply, we fantasize that re-watching a given action enough times from enough angles will yield an accurate assessment of that action.

Calls for automated strike zones are slightly different. Here, the theory is that balls and strikes can be judged accurately in an absolute sense. It's not a matter of interpreting action—it's a matter of determining whether a baseball did or did not in fact pass through a defined volume of air.

People sometimes compare automated umpiring to the technology used in tennis to determine whether balls were out of bounds. If you've ever watched a tennis match on television, you've probably seen this technology, in which a computer determines whether a ball touched the line. It's straightforward. The ball was either on the line or it wasn't. Just as importantly, no one questions whether the computer made the right call. Its decisions are authoritative. If such technology can be employed unobtrusively in tennis, the theory goes, why can't we use it in baseball?

Yet the strike zone is different than the lines on a tennis court in one important respect. Namely, *a strike zone has no lines*. A strike zone is not like a football goal line. It is not like a blue line in hockey. It is not like the foul line on a basketball court.

It's more like pornography: you know it when you see it.

The superimposed strike zones that appear on televised baseball games provide the illusion that we viewers can see whether each pitch "really" was a strike or a ball. Like a charlatan in a white coat, that gray box fools us into a false sense of certainty.

Given the vagaries inherent in the definition of a strike, every current pitch tracking system requires a human being to manually set the upper and lower boundaries for each hitter. Picture it: A man sits in a dark room at Angels Stadium in Anaheim. On the television screen before him, he watches Mike Trout stride to the plate and assume his batting stance. Using a dial, the man carefully positions a horizontal line at the bottom of Trout's knee, and another at the midpoint between the top of Trout's shoulder and the top of Trout's pants. It is in reference to these boundaries that the pitch tracking cameras and radar equipment will determine whether each pitch during Trout's at bat is a ball or strike.

Who's to say this man is doing any of this accurately? Why should we accept his judgment more readily than an umpire's? What happens if another man in a different dark room sets the upper and lower boundaries of the strike zone a fraction of an inch higher or lower when Mike Trout plays his next game in Seattle?

In a supreme irony, the accuracy of pitch tracking systems is calibrated by comparing its outputs to the judgment of umpires. We only know whether our computer systems are accurately calling balls and strikes if they seem to align with the best judgment of human umpires. You know—those guys we want to replace, because we don't think they do a good job.

In order to implement an automated strike zone that does not depend on human judgment in any capacity, MLB would have to adopt a so-called "universal strike zone."

A universal strike zone would have fixed boundaries and would be the same for every hitter. It would extend, by one estimate, from 18.29 inches above the ground to 44.08 inches above the ground. This strike zone would be determined by inputting the average heights and shoulder heights and knee heights and waistlines and so forth of baseball players into a computer, calculating the averages, and creating a strike zone for the "average" player.

Whether you're Aaron Judge (6'7") or Jose Altuve (5'6"), the same strike zone would apply. This way, a machine umpiring system would not have to be recalibrated for each hitter. It would not vary according to a hitter's stance. We would have a precise strike zone, and it could be enforced with 100% accuracy.

As I said at the top, I can't argue whether such a change would be good for baseball. There would certainly be repercussions if MLB adopted such a system, many more than I can explore here. My concern is different. It has to do with our willingness to not only cede judgment to machines, but to redefine the terms on which judgment takes place so that "decisions" can more easily be made by machines.

It is intolerable that we should move to create systems around an average of all baseball players when human umpires are perfectly capable of adjusting their interpretation for every hitter. It is intolerable that we should attempt to redefine a functional and imagined boundary in favor of a strictly measured *and yet imperceptible* one. No human on earth is capable of umpiring a universal strike zone; no amount of training could condition the human eye to determine whether a 2.5-inch sphere traveling 99 miles per hour crossed home plate at a height of 18.3 inches (a strike) or at a height a quarter of an inch lower (a ball).

Not only would a universal strike zone make human umpires unnecessary, it would make human umpires impossible.

Baseball is far from the only place where humans have proved ourselves willing to redefine our own experience in an attempt to accommodate the binary logic of computers. Multiple choice tests are handy because they can be graded by machines, whereas written essays or actual human performance must be assessed by a person. Do we really believe that human intelligence is most accurately assessed by filling in bubbles on a piece of paper? Surely not, yet countless facets of our educational system—not to mention billions of dollars in scholarships and state funding—are premised on the assumption that those machine-graded bubbles tell us a lot.

Nearly everything that emerges from Silicon Valley promises to correct for the inefficiencies and irrationality of human behavior. Little thought is usually given to the question of whether something ought to be done efficiently, or what might be lost in the drive for efficiency.

A robo-ump provides a simulacrum of human judgment. When we subject the game of baseball, or anything else, to the absolute judgments of machines, we should reasonably wonder what will be lost. The more we seek to root out human judgment and turn it over to machines, the more we deprive ourselves of particularity, freedom, and excellence.

Baseball is only a game, I know. But that's all the more reason to preserve it from the unnecessary intrusion of machine-based constraints and machine-based decision making. If we can't *play* without computers and cameras to help us, what can we do?

Discussion Question(s)

1. Why does Washatka find it ironic that "the accuracy of pitch tracking systems is calibrated by comparing its outputs to the judgment of umpires"?

2. What does Washatka mean when he says "Not only would a universal strike zone make human umpires unnecessary, it would make human umpires impossible"? How is this quote relevant to Ross' and Russell's ideas on "perception/discretion"?

3. Are "robo-umps" a good idea? If not, what, if anything, about Washatka's argument did you find persuasive? If so, what, if anything, does that imply for other sports? Should we desire (at least in principle) "robo-refs" for football or basketball? Why? Why not?

Suggested Readings

Fraleigh, W. P. (2003). Intentional rules violations—one more time. *Journal of the Philosophy of Sport, 30,* 166–176.

Griffioen, A. L. (2015). Why Jim Joyce wasn't wrong: Baseball and the Euthyphro dilemma. *Journal of the Philosophy of Sport, 42*(3), 327–348.

Morgan, W. J. (2012). Broad internalism, deep conventions, moral entrepreneurs, and sport. *Journal of the Philosophy of Sport, 39*(1), 65–100.

Simon, R. L. (2005). The ethics of strategic fouling: A reply to Fraleigh. *Journal of the Philosophy of Sport, 32*(1), 87–95.

Bibliography

Aristotle. (2002). *Nicomachean ethics.* (J. Sachs, Trans.) Newburyport, MA: Focus Publishing.

Baron, M. (2006). Acting from duty. In C. Horn, & D. Schönecker (Eds.), *Groundwork for the Metaphysics of Morals* (pp. 72–92). New York, NY: Walter de Gruyter.

Berger, P., & Luckmann, T. (1966). *The social construction of reality.* New York, NY: Anchor Books.

Boyle, W., O'Rourke, S., Long, J., & Pavlidis, H. (2018, January 28). *Robo strike zone: It's not as simple as you think.* Retrieved August 8, 2019, from baseballprospectus.com: https://www.baseballprospectus.com/news/article/37347/robo-strike-zone-not-simple-think/

Ciomaga, B. (2013). Rules and obligation. *Journal of the Philosophy of Sport, 40*(1), 19–40.

Collins, H. (2019). Applying philosophy to refereeing and umpiring technology. *Philosophies, 4*(2), 21.

Dworkin, R. (1986). *Law's empire.* Cambridge, MA: Harvard University Press.

Fainaru-Wada, M., & Fainaru, S. (2013). *League of denial: The NFL, concussions, and the battle for the truth.* New York, NY: Crown Archetype.

Feser, E. (2010, October 30). *The catastrophic spider.* Retrieved March 16, 2016, from http://edwardfeser.blogspot.com/: http://edwardfeser.blogspot.com/2010/10/catastrophic-spider.html

Frankena, W. K. (1973). *Ethics.* Englewood Cliffs, NJ: Prentice-Hall.

Jankowiak, T. (n.d.). *Immanuel Kant.* Retrieved August 9, 2019, from Internet encyclopedia of philosophy: https://www.iep.utm.edu/kantview/#SH5b

Johnson, R., & Cureson, A. (2016, July 7). *Kant's moral philosophy.* Retrieved August 9, 2019, from Stanford encyclopedia of philopophy: https://plato.stanford.edu/entries/kant-moral/

Kagan, D. (2018, January 23). *The physics of RoboUmp.* Retrieved August 8, 2019, from fangraphs.com: https://tht.fangraphs.com/the-physics-of-roboump/

Kant, I. (1785/2011). *Fundamental principles of the metaphysic of morals* (M. Stapleton, Ed., & T. K. Abbott, Trans.) Kindle edition. https://www.amazon.com/Fundamental-Principles-Metaphysic-Morals-Immanuel-ebook/dp/B0082RB3GS/ref=sr_1_1?s=digital-text&ie=UTF8&qid=1479502282&sr=1-1&keywords=fundamental+principles+of+the+metaphysic+of+morals

Kant, I. (1996). *The metaphysics of morals.* (M. Gregor, Trans.) New York, NY: Cambridge University Press.

Kretchmar, S. (2015). Formalism and sport. In M. McNamee, & W. J. Morgan (Eds.), *Routledge handbook of the philosophy of sport* (pp. 11–21). New York, NY: Routledge.

MacIntyre, A. (1984). *After virtue* (2nd ed.). Notre Dame, IN: University of Notre Dame Press.

MacIntyre, A. (1990). *Three rival versions of moral enquiry: Encyclopedia, genealogy, and tradition.* Notre Dame, IN: University of Notre Dame Press.

Mill, J. S. (1998). *Utilitarianism.* New York, NY: Oxford University Press.

Morgan, W. J. (2015). Conventionalism and sport. In M. McNamee, & W. J. Morgan (Eds.), *Routledge handbook of the philosophy of sport* (pp. 35–52). New York, NY: Routledge.

Polanyi, M. (1962). *Personal knowledge: Towards a post-critical philosophy.* Chicago, IL: The University of Chicago Press.

Polanyi, M., & Prosch, H. (1975). *Meaning.* Chicago, IL: The University of Chicago Press.

Ross, W. D. (1930, 2002). *The right and the good.* New York, NY: Oxford University Press.

Russell, J. (1999). Are rules all an umpire has to work with? *Journal of the Philosophy of Sport, 26*(1), 27–49.

Simon, R., Torres, C., & Hager, P. (2015). *Fair play: The ethics of sport* (4th Ed.). Boulder, CO: Westview Press.

Timmons, M. (2013). *Moral theory: An introduction* (2nd ed.). New York, NY: Rowman & Littlefield.

Washatka, N. (2019, May 10). *Robo-umps and us*. Retrieved August 8, 2019, from frontporchrepublic.com: https://www.frontporchrepublic.com/2019/05/robo-umps-and-us/

Wood, A. W. (1999). *Kant's ethical thought*. New York, NY: Cambridge University Press.

Chapter 6

Virtue Ethics

"For the good are good simply, but the bad are bad in every sort of way."
—Aristotle[1]

Learning Objectives & Outcomes

Students will be able to:

1. Distinguish the difference between virtue theories, utilitarian theories, and deontological theories of ethics.
2. Explain the difference between an ethic of "being" and an ethic of "doing."
3. Identify the Cardinal Virtues and explain how they can be applied to sport.
4. Summarize the strengths and weaknesses of virtue ethics.
5. Identify and evaluate how virtue (or vice) impact the day–to-day practice of sport, as in, for instance, the Penn State or North Carolina scandals.

We turn now to **virtue ethics**, the third and final ethical theory we will consider. Unlike utilitarianism, virtue ethics is not primarily focused on outcomes or consequences. Nor is virtue ethics focused on rules and duties, as is deontology. Instead the virtue ethicist is concerned with the cultivation of the good, the excellent and the noble.[2] By which the virtue ethicist means the development of human character.

Another important way to clarify the difference between virtue ethics on the one hand and utilitarianism and deontology on the other is made clear by philosopher Bernard Mayo's (1958) distinction between an ethics of "**doing**" and an ethics of "**being**." Mayo's point is this: both utilitarianism and deontology are focused on whether or not we've *done* the right thing. Acts are of primary ethical concern. In contrast, Mayo argues, virtue ethics focuses on *being*, that is the character of actor. The heart of the actor is of primary ethical concern. Ethics is a flesh and blood reality rather than a merely theoretical or intellectual evaluation of duties or outcomes.

What is more, Mayo (1958) insists that such an ethic of being has a serious advantage on any ethic of doing. "The point is that an ethics of Being must include this obvious fact, that Being involves Doing; whereas an ethics of Doing, such as I have been

Virtue Ethics: The ethical theory which emphasizes the cultivation of good character traits (i.e., virtues).

"Being vs. Doing": The distinction made between an ethic which focuses on acts (doing the right thing) and an ethic which focuses on character (being the right kind of person).

Arete: The ancient Greek word for the "embodiment of excellence" or "virtue."

---

[1] (Aristotle, *Nicomachean ethics*, 2002, p. 29); 1106b35.
[2] In fact, virtue ethics is sometimes called *aretaic* ethics from the Greek **arete** meaning the "embodiment of excellence" or "virtue".

examining, may easily overlook it" (p. 210). What Mayo means is that *to be* good necessarily requires *doing* good things. In contrast, we all know from experience that the right thing can be done *for the wrong reasons*. We may be mercenaries. We may tell the truth for fear of punishment. We may return a lost item simply in hope of reward. We may play by the rules, only because the referee is watching.

What the virtue ethicist insists upon, therefore, is that although the act itself is important, it is not enough. We must strive to *be* good; to not only have done the right thing, but to have done it for the right reasons. Goodness must be part of who we are, not merely a checklist of do's and don'ts. The German philosopher Josef Pieper (2011) explains the idea this way: "The virtuous person *is* in such a way that, from the innermost tendency of his being, he realizes the good through his actions" (p. 11). Character is key.

The most important name in virtue ethics is the ancient Greek philosopher Aristotle. If one wanted a pithy but essentially accurate summary of Aristotle's ethics, it would be this: "We become what we practice". Our practices cultivate the skills which define our character and our character establishes who we are.

We become what we practice.
SIA KAMBOU/AFP/Getty Images

Therefore, the focus of the chapter will be to briefly introduce and then expand on this Aristotelian conception of ethics. This will then be followed by a quick examination of the classical or cardinal virtues of prudence, justice, courage and temperance. After doing so, we will follow the format established in the previous two chapters. We will review the strengths and weaknesses of virtue ethics and then close the chapter by addressing the relevance of virtue ethics for sport. Is virtue ethics a superior way to assess ethical action in sport when compared to utilitarianism or deontology? Let us examine this question.

Aristotle's Nicomachean Ethics

Aristotle's most important ethical work is called the *Nicomachean Ethics,* so named after his son (or perhaps his father) each of whom were named Nicomachus. For the purpose of brevity it is also sometimes referred to simply as the *Ethics*. In introducing you to the work, we will focus most of our attention on the beginning of the text where Aristotle lays out the key principles of his ethics. Although we cannot review the whole of the *Nicomachean Ethics* here, it is well worth reading in its entirety.

There are at least five important foundational ideas that need to be understood when considering the *Nicomachean Ethics*. The first is one we introduced in Chapter 1, the distinction between intrinsic and extrinsic goods. The second, is that ethics is social and tied to our nature. The third, is the concept of virtue itself, which Aristotle defines as those excellences that are in accord with our nature. The fourth, is the importance of habit. Finally we must consider Aristotle's method for identify the virtues, that is, the idea of the mean.

As I am sure you recall, intrinsic goods are those goods we pursue for their own sake (such as play or friendship or love). In contrast, extrinsic goods are those goods which we value for their utility (such as working out, trips to the dentist, or dieting). They are good, but they are good because they get us something else. They are not good in and of themselves. We all pursue what we perceive to be the good. As Aristotle (2002) insists in the first line of the *Ethics*, "Every art and every inquiry, and similarly every action and pursuit, is thought to aim at some good; and for this reason the good has rightly been declared to be that at which all things aim"(1094a).[3]

The good is that at which all things aim.
Randy Belice/National Basketball Association/Getty Images

---

[3] 1094a refers to the Bekker numbers, a cross-translation referencing system for Aristotle's texts. For copyright and consistency reasons the translation generally used in this text is from W.D. Ross (1994–2009). However the Sachs (2002) translation is arguably superior. Hence the Bekker numbers. Once one settles on a translation one can then find the relevant citation in which ever translation they prefer.

Eudaimonia: The ancient Greek word for "happiness" or "human flourishing." Aristotle argues that eudaimonia is that good at which "all other goods aim."

Yet, ultimately, Aristotle argues, even those goods we commonly ascribe intrinsic status to actually aim at something beyond themselves (1097b20). Aristotle's preeminent good is happiness. The Greek word here is **eudaimonia**, which is often also translated as "human flourishing." Aristotle's point is that even those goods we normally think of as intrinsic goods are pursued for the sake of happiness. We desire love, friendship, play, etc. because we believe those things significantly contribute to happiness.

But if this right, a critic might reply, Aristotle has not told us very much. Everyone knows human beings aim at happiness, but what exactly does Aristotle mean by happiness? Aristotle anticipates this objection. In response, he acknowledges disagreement over the definition of happiness, and then offers three common candidates for what happiness consists of; pleasure, honor and contemplation.[4]

In assessing these options, Aristotle quickly dismisses pleasure. He acknowledges that pleasure is good, but rejects pleasure as the goal of life on grounds similar to those already used to criticize hedonism in Chapters 2 and 4. The good is larger than pleasurable sensations. More surprisingly, he argues that honor is also insufficient. This is the case primarily because honor:

> "seems too superficial to be what we are looking for, since it is thought to depend on those who bestow honour rather than on him who receives it, but the good we divine to be something proper to a man and not easily taken from him" (1994–2009, 1095b25).

Aristotle's point is that honor depends upon other people and that popularity is an inconsistent guide to the good. We may, on occasion, receive praise for doing evil and scorn for doing good.[5] We may also hesitate to do good because we are more concerned with our reputation (and the honor that depends upon it) than we are with the good, the true or the beautiful. It should be clear then, through the process of elimination, that Aristotle settles on contemplation as the proper goal of human life. This is because Aristotle believes happiness is to live in accord with our nature.

This leads into our second foundational idea. Ethics is social and based in human nature. What does this mean? Let us look at each point individually. First, ethics is social. Aristotle (1994–2009) insists that all of our actions naturally impact more than ourselves "since man is born for citizenship" (1097b12). That is, human beings are born into, and beholden to a community. Ethics is not merely personal but a matter "of how we ought to order our life together" (Neuhaus, 2009, p. 45). Our actions, for good or ill, profoundly influence other people.

Second, ethics is based in human nature. By this Aristotle means that the good of a thing always relies upon an assessment of its nature or purpose. Consider a knife or a piece of sports equipment such as a baseball bat or glove. How do you know what is a good knife or a good bat or a good glove? Aristotle insists that any coherent answer will necessarily rely upon a claim about the nature of that thing. That is: "a good knife is sharp because knifes are (by nature) meant for cutting." Similarly we know a bat is meant for hitting and glove is meant for catching. Any claims to goodness will inevitably rely on such assertions. Ethics and metaphysics, at least for Aristotle, go hand in hand.

---

[4] A further question you should consider as you analyze these three options from 2,500 years ago is this: are these alternative definitions of happiness still common today?

[5] Dante (2002) makes the same point regarding the difference between reputation and reality this way in the *Inferno*: "Up there how many think themselves great kings/Who will be stuck like swine here in this sty, [Hell]/ Leaving a name to spit on in contempt" (Canto 8, lines 49–51).

Our actions, for good or ill, profoundly influence other people.
Vivien Killilea/Getty Images and Entertainment/Getty Images

Aristotle claims that what is true of objects is also true of living things. To know a good human being, we have to first know what a human being is. What then is the nature of human beings? Aristotle (1994–2009) answers the question this way:

"Or as eye, hand, foot, and in general each of the parts evidently has a function, may one lay it down that man similarly has a function apart from all these? What then can this be? Life seems to be common even to plants, but we are seeking what is peculiar to man. Let us exclude, therefore, the life of nutrition and growth. Next there would be a life of perception, but it also seems to be common even to the horse, the ox, and every animal. There remains, then, an active life of the element that has a rational principle . . ." (1097b30).

It is reason which is most human. Therefore, it is contemplation, not pleasure or honor, which is the surest road to human happiness, for in contemplation we exercise our powers of reason in pursuit of human excellence (1098ab10-20).

This insight regarding the importance of human nature to ethics points to our third and fourth foundational Aristotelian ideas; virtue and habit. As Aristotle scholar Joe Sachs (2002) points out, virtue (arete in Greek) "means the excellence that makes anything an outstanding specimen of its kind, especially well fitted to its ends" (p. 5). Since we have already seen that Aristotle argues that human beings are "rational animals" it follows that human virtue will be those excellences which are in accord with reason. Moreover, given our social nature, virtue must be cultivated within us by the community. As Aristotle (1994–2009) famously insists: "Neither by nature, then, nor contrary to nature do the virtues arise in us; rather we are adapted by nature to receive them, and are made perfect by habit" (1103a25). We have a natural capacity to take on virtue, but must be taught to do so.[6]

---

[6] Frankena (1973) explains the idea this way: "Virtues are dispositions or traits that are not wholly innate; they must all be acquired, at least in part, by teaching and practice, or perhaps, by grace" (p. 63).

This inculcation is not a matter of theoretical argumentation or of abstract concepts but rather of practice. We become better people by cultivating the virtues within us by doing virtuous things. This is what Aristotle means by habit; the cultivation of a good character traits through practice. Virtue is of course, to some degree dependent on our natural aptitudes, talents and proclivities, but like any other skill based area of human endeavor, our aptitudes can whither or flower based upon how they are exercised and in what type of environment they are sown.

Moreover, habits, once established, are very hard to change. It is for this reason that Aristotle emphasizes the importance of moral education: "Hence we ought to have been brought up in a particular way from our very youth, as Plato says, so as both to delight in and to be pained by the things that we ought; for this is the right education." (1104b10). Sound ethical practice is therefore a process of maturation and growth which should be started in youth and which should continue throughout life.

Ethics is not mere routine. Nor is habituation meant to make us passive. Lecture, theory and scolding, can, at best, identify the virtues that ought to be pursued. However, the actual possession of virtue relies on the active cultivation of character traits through the training and disciplining of our natural potential. Again, we *become* what we practice. Just as a sport skill can become "second nature" through sound repetition and practice, virtue, with sound repetition and practice, becomes "second nature" within us. It is for this reason that Aristotle argues that habit allows us to develop "moral skill" or perhaps better put "moral fitness." The Greek here is **hexis** or "active condition" (Aristotle, *Nicomachean ethics,* 2002). Habit allows for the "active condition" of *being* "just" or "honest", from which we can then lead our lives. Just as we can be "in shape" or "out of shape" physically, we can be "in shape" or "out of shape" morally.

Consider soccer training as an analogy. To cultivate the skills of the game you must practice soccer skills, you must practice soccer skills often and you must practice soccer skills well. Skill at dribbling, shooting (with your weak foot), heading, trapping, etc. can only come through extended participation, careful correction and insistence on excellent technique. Theory, though not unimportant, will do very little to actually procure the skills. Little by little, through dedication, repetition and correction you will become a soccer player. That is, you will have cultivated the skills to the point that you no longer have to focus on doing them but can live from that skillful foundation towards the soccer game. Moreover, when you execute those skills in the game, your skills (built on the foundation of habit) must flow naturally. Rote repetition of the drills will not suffice in a game situation. Instead, you must live through those skills towards the particular situation of the game. Habit allows such skill to become an "active condition" whereby you can call forth the soccer skills, that is the virtues, necessary to perform well.

Of course this means skill development is central to sound performance. When you first start to play, you need to think about (and focus on) how to dribble or shoot. This lack of skill seriously hampers your ability to perform, adapt, and judge what the situation calls for. One cannot see, let alone execute, the "appropriate pass" when one's focus is consumed in simply dribbling the ball. Upon *becoming* a soccer player things change. Your skills free you to exercise your nature in pursuit of the larger purposes of the game of soccer and the needs of the particular situation.

Yet, the skills are not an end in themselves. They exist to allow to you play soccer well. Soccer is not a game about dribbling, per se. It is a game which uses the skill of dribbling (among others) in pursuit, as we saw in the last chapter's discussion of broad internalism, of the larger "point and purposes that underlie the game" (Simon, Torres, & Hager, 2015, p. 33). To do so, one must, through habituation, learn to dribble so well that one can do so without focusing on it. The skill has simply become part of who you are.

Hexis: The ancient Greek word which means "active condition." Just as a tennis player is light on their feet and can react to the course of play because of the habituation and skills they've developed, so too an ethical person can prudentially react with good character because, via habituation, they developed the "active condition" of being "light on their feet" morally.

Similarly, we become ethical people through dedication, repetition and correction in pursuit of good character. If you want to be an honest person, practice telling the truth. If you want to be a courageous person, then be willing to suffer for the sake of the good. Aristotle (1994–2009) explains the point this way: "For the things we have to learn before we can do them, we learn by doing them, e.g. men become builders by building and lyre-players by playing the lyre; so too we become just by doing just acts, temperate by doing temperate acts, brave by doing brave acts" (1103a35). We practice good things, we discipline ourselves morally, just as soccer players discipline themselves athletically, so that we may become virtuous people.

We become just by doing just things.
Steve Sykes/Getty Images Sport/Getty Images

This brings us to the final foundational Aristotelian concept, **the mean**. Aristotle uses this idea as a way to identify what the virtues are. That is, they are found at neither extreme, each of which is a vice. One extreme is excess, while the other is deficiency. For example, courage is neither foolhardy (excessive) nor cowardly (deficient). Instead it is the just right recognition of proper action. To be courageous one must be willing to confront something fearful without recklessness (which is unlikely to accomplish anything) and without fainthearted inaction (which is guaranteed to accomplish nothing).

This sometimes encourages students to think that what Aristotle is after is a careful and blasé mediocrity, where enthusiasm and commitment are the enemy of virtue. Such an interpretation seriously misunderstands Aristotle's point. He is not insisting on indifference, nor is he insisting on mathematically balancing vices, so that courage becomes 50% foolhardiness mixed in with 50% cowardice. Rather he is pointing out that the mean condition, in being "just right," should always be exercised. That is, once we have identified courage (or any other virtue) two thing will become clear. First it is a mean condition between two extremes and second we cannot have too much of it. Courage, as with any virtue, *is always in season*. Although excess and deficiency are necessary for understanding the type of thing a virtue is, they are not necessary for the application of any particular virtue to life. This is why Aristotle says that "in respect of its substance and the definition which states its essence virtue is a mean, with regard to what is best and right an extreme" (1107a10).

How then ought Aristotle's *Ethics* be summarized? In contrast to the utilitarians he believes that pleasure is an insufficient guide to right action. Pleasure attends goods but is

The Mean: The "just right" condition between two extremes, each of which is a vice. For instance, the virtue of courage is neither foolhardy (excessive) nor cowardly (deficient).

not itself the good. In contrast to the deontologists, Aristotle is not focused on the rules. This is not because they are unnecessary or unimportant but because they are insufficient. Instead the moral life is dedicated to human excellence, through the cultivation of those character traits, those virtues, which lead to happiness. This cultivation is a communal project. We need to *become* good people and we cannot do so without relying on those communities (such as teams, schools and families) to which we belong.[7] If this is right, sport is an inherently moral institution engaged in an inherently moral project. What implications does this have for sport?

The Cardinal Virtues

The Cardinal Virtues: The hinge or key virtues (prudence, justice, courage, temperance) around which all other good character traits turn.

According to the classical and medieval tradition to which Aristotle belongs, **the Cardinal Virtues** are prudence, justice, courage and temperance. They are called the cardinal virtues—from the Latin *cardo* or "hinge"—because they are understood to be those virtues around which all the other virtues turn. As such, each of the four Cardinal Virtues is worth a brief but specific examination.

Prudence is often misunderstood. It is not "caution" or "carefulness". Rather it is the ability to see reality for what it is and act accordingly. Aristotle calls this virtue, *phronesis* in the Greek, "practical wisdom." Pieper (1966) explains the idea this way, "He alone can do good who knows what things are like and what their situation is . . . Realization of the good presupposes that our actions are appropriate to the real situation . . ." (p. 10). Ethics is not about feelings, or cleverness, but rather, aligning our actions to the truth. Reality, rather than desire or popularity, defines the good.[8]

Prudence: Also known as "practical wisdom," this virtue is the ability to "see reality for what it is and act accordingly." As such, prudence is the chief of the cardinal virtues, because it allows one to do the "right thing at the right time in the right way for the right reason."

Justice, in turn, is the application of prudence to our interactions with other people. Justice relies upon a recognition of the truth regarding our obligations towards the community. That is, justice "is the notion that each man is to be given what is his due" (Pieper, 1966, p. 44). To be just, we must treat others as we ought.

Justice: The virtue which allows us to give each his due and treat others as we ought.

Even as justice relies on prudence, **courage** relies upon both prudence and justice. Sometimes called fortitude, courage is the "readiness to accept harm for the sake of realizing the good" (Pieper, 2011, p. 23). Prudence, in grounding goodness in reality rather than power, honor, pleasure, or possessions stiffens our moral spines.[9] It reminds us that the good makes demands upon us. This is because the good is real, rather than merely transitory, conventional or fashionable. Similarly, courage relies upon justice. This is because one cannot, by definition, suffer for the sake of *the good,* in pursuit of an unjust cause. Courage demands not only the self-sacrifice of standing up, but standing up for the good, the true and the beautiful.

Courage: Also known as fortitude, this virtue is the willingness to suffer "for the sake of realizing the good."

[7] "After the expulsion of Aristotelianism from our culture there was a period in the eighteenth century when it was commonplace to suggest—on tombstones as well as in philosophical works—that the virtues are nothing but those qualities which we happen to find generally pleasant or useful. The oddity of this suggestion lies in the fact that what we find generally pleasant or useful will depend on what virtues are generally possessed and cultivated in our community" (MacIntyre, 1984, p. 160).

[8] The will ought to be conformed to reality. This is why prudence is the chief virtue, even among the Cardinal Virtues. "The virtue of prudence, on the contrary—being the perfected ability to make decisions in accordance with reality—is the quintessence of ethical maturity (of which, of course, teachability is a great component). And the pre-eminence of prudence over justice, fortitude, and temperance means simply that without maturity truly moral life and action is not possible" (Pieper, 1966, p. 31).

[9] The point is that prudence allows us to see that morality is about reality. It is reality that creates our moral obligations. Pieper (2011) is again useful on this point. "Moralism says: good is what obligation requires, and because obligation requires it. The doctrine of prudence says: good is what accords to reality; it is obligatory because it corresponds to reality" (p. 16).

Finally, we must consider **temperance** or as it is sometimes called moderation. This virtue can be pithily defined as "using things as we ought." It is a proper ordering and use of the goods of the world. Again, this ordering and disciplining of our desires, possessions and actions must be done in reference to the previous virtues. One will not use food or drink or sex or sport rightly if one is unwilling or incapable of prudentially recognizing the reality, the whole, into which each of these good things fits, as a part. Similarly, one cannot be temperate without justice and courage. For justice demands that people are more important than our desires, while courage demands that the good is worth suffering for, which may mean forgoing this or that pleasure or opportunity, because truth is far more important than power, pleasure, honor, or gold.

Temperance: Also known as moderation, this virtue is the "proper ordering and use of the goods of the world."

The Strengths of Virtue Ethics

As with the previous two chapters, we will review three strengths and then three weaknesses. The first strength of virtue ethics is its focus on judgment. Right action, as Ross (following Aristotle) points out, cannot be reduced to merely following rules. The second strength and third strengths of virtue ethics are interrelated and rely upon the recognition of the proper relationship between individual human beings and the culture(s) of which they are a part. The second strength is the importance of culture to ethics. This results from the fact that human beings are born of and beholden to a community which either encourages or discourages human virtue. The third strength is the importance of practice, habit and skill. This results from the fact that virtue is not a bloodless intellectual exercise, nor a detached calculation of "the greatest good," but rather the cultivation of "moral skill," which relies upon commitment, discipline and encouragement.

Right action relies upon judgment, or as a virtue ethicist might put it, prudence allows us to see reality for what it is and then act accordingly. Prudence demands the recognition of reality. A reality which is necessarily wider and deeper than mere rule following can allow for. In essence, prudence demands recognition of the difference between being and doing. Although moral rules are important, they always rely upon the judgment of actor. That is, even in the case where it is obvious that rules should be followed, character is key, for "obviousness" is itself *a judgment*. Sportsmanship, for example, cannot be simply a matter of compulsion. Good sports must act as they do, not out of guilt or rote repetition or threats of sanction, but because they see the good and have learned to embody it. Virtue always trumps duty.

If this is right, then the cultivation of character is one of the chief tasks for any community. Human beings are communal by nature. We inherit and are taught our language our culture and our ethical values. It is to Aristotle's great credit that he doesn't intellectualize morality. Although ethics has an intellectual component due to our rational nature, it is more than that. It is also a matter of how families, institutions and cultures encourage and discourage us to behave. This is what C.S. Lewis (1944, 2001) meant when he argued that:

> "It still remains true that no justification of virtue will enable a man to be virtuous. Without the aid of trained emotions the intellect is powerless against the animal organism. I had sooner play cards against a man who was quite skeptical about ethics, but bred to believe that 'a gentleman does not cheat', than against an irreproachable moral philosopher who had been brought up among sharpers [cheats]" (p. 24).

Ethics is not ultimately an intellectual enterprise but a cultural one. It is, therefore, either a fool's errand or insincerity to insist that moral reform can be bureaucratically achieved through "training" or "education". One such example of either naiveté or duplicity can be found in Florida State University proposing a mandatory course "in social responsibilities" after student-athlete misconduct (Sonnone, 2015). Of course, education and training are a part of human culture. Nevertheless it will be ineffectual because our moral formation is wider, deeper, and longer than "three-credit hours". Moreover, to be good, requires more than knowledge. Therefore, virtue cannot be reduced to a seminar or a guest speaker series. As Aristotle (1994–2009) insists, one does not pursue ethical inquiry "in order to know what virtue is, but in order to become good" (1103b27). Habit, action, and practice trump intellect. Moral skill is always more than knowledge.[10]

This leads into the third and final strength of virtue ethics, its emphasis on habit, for experience and argument both support the claim that we "become what we practice". Moral virtue, once cultivated, is hard, if not impossible, to shake. Moral vice, once spread, is hard, if not impossible, to cure. Ethics depends upon discipline, inheritance and apprenticeship. The development of virtue (moral skill) requires the *right* habits, *sound* tradition and *good* examples, which means that ethics is primarily a matter of practice rather than theory or calculation. Moreover, this practice is not reducible to duty as the deontologist holds, but instead relies on the cultivation of character. It is not enough to *do* good things, we must *be* good.

Moral vice, once spread, is hard, if not impossible, to cure.
Jasper Juinen/DPA/Newscom

Put another way, former NBA All-Star Charles Barkley was wrong . . . he was and is a role model. His example either encourages or inhibits virtue in all others within his reach. Of course, this is true of all human beings not just Charles Barkley, but that only

---

[10] Sport Philosopher Mike McNamee (2008) makes the same point as a way to criticize deontological ethics. "Nevertheless, deontology with its resolute focus on moral reasons is commonly held to be inadequate in terms of moral psychology. It holds, in the classic form of moral cognitivism from Kant and Plato, that merely by knowing the right thing to do one will act in accordance with the dictates of moral reason; moral reasoning and moral action are one. Such a theory holds no space for either weakness of will or for inconsistencies of thought and action" (p. 118).

reinforces the point.[11] Moreover, public figures such as Barkley have a special obligation because of the "unusually great influence they can have on others" (Simon, Torres, & Hager, 2015, p. 234). Ethics is not bloodless moralism, nor is it a cost-benefit analysis. Instead, ethics is about the cultivation of moral skill. Such virtue—like the development of any excellence—takes time, intimacy and experience. Therefore, the cultivation of moral skill is not the realm of "experts" or of "education" or "self-esteem", but of "mom and dad", "apprenticeship", and "discipline". It is not the realm of "government" or "social engineers" but of "teams, churches and neighborhoods". Ethics is part of a living tradition, which is necessarily passed on hand–to–hand from generation to generation.[12]

The Weaknesses of Virtue Ethics

There are, of course, also weaknesses in the theory of virtue ethics. Here are three. Critics have argued that the distinction between being and doing, virtue and duty is a false dichotomy. It is not an either/or situation, but a both/and situation. In fact, virtue ethics needs deontology. Critics have also alleged that virtue ethics lends itself to a kind of relativistic indeterminacy. This is so because virtue ethics doesn't prescribe specific action and leaves too much responsibility to personal judgment. Such flexibility allows for moral chaos under the guise of "prudence". Finally, some critics of virtue ethics have argued that it sets an unreasonably high and therefore inhuman standard. In essence, these critics are alleging that virtue ethics requires saints in a world where sainthood is all but impossible.

Regarding the first criticism Frankena (1973) acknowledges that "morality can hardly be content with a mere conformity to the rules," but then adds "On the other hand, one cannot conceive of traits of character except as including dispositions and tendencies to act in certain ways in certain circumstances" (p. 65). Frankena's point is that while virtues may be necessary, their existence, or at the least the identification of virtues, relies upon the recognition of certain duties or the rightness of certain actions. He therefore proposes that: "we regard the morality of duty and principles and the morality of virtues or traits of character not as rival kinds of morality between which we must choose, but as two complementary aspects of the same morality" (p. 65). Kant and Aristotle are not strange bedfellows after all, for "Being without doing, like faith without works, is dead" (p. 66).

It would seem then that virtue ethics (absent a reliance on deontology) leads to a sort of moral relativism. For the abdication of rules and duties allows for moral chaos or, at least, the paralysis of moral indeterminacy. Who's to say what is right or wrong? But isn't the point of ethics to show us what we ought to do? Timmons (2013) again offers important insight on this point:

> "The standard of right conduct set forth by virtue ethics tells us that an action's rightness or wrongness depends on what a virtuous agent (acting in character)

---

[11] The same point can be made with a spiritual tinge: "All day long we are, in some degree, helping each other to one or other of these destinations. It is in the light of these overwhelming possibilities, it is with the awe and the circumspection proper to them, that we should conduct all our dealings with one another, all friendships, all loves, all play, all politics. There are no *ordinary* people. You have never talked to a mere mortal. Nations, cultures, arts, civilization-these are mortal, and their life is to ours as the life of a gnat. But it is immortals whom we joke with, work with, marry, snub, and exploit-immortal horrors or everlasting splendours" (Lewis, 1949, pp. 45–46).

[12] This is true, even in the case of the radical rejection of inherited morality, for even the rebel—if he wants his cause to endure—needs disciples.

would (or would not) do in some specific situation. A virtuous agent possesses a range of virtues, and in cases where the relevant virtues conflict, there is no super rule or rank ordering of the virtues that determines what the virtuous agent would do. Rather as we have explained, in such cases, the virtuous agent, who, we assume, has practical intelligence, is able to discern which virtue consideration in the situation at hand is most important and act accordingly. Such intelligence or phronesis is not something that can be fully characterized in terms of rules or principles. Thus, according to the objection, the theory fails to yield real guidance in a great many cases" (p. 292).

Therefore, virtue ethics fails—at least by itself—to provide sufficient clarity regarding how we ought to live.

The previous problem of indeterminacy lends further credence to the third and final criticism we will review, that of virtue ethics being an impossible standard. Virtue ethics demands (contrary to any honest person's self-evaluation) standards that are very hard to live up to. Who has not been a coward by, for example, being more concerned about popular opinion than the truth? Who has not failed to treat others as they ought? Who has not succumbed to over indulgence or prudish self-neglect? But if this is right, then virtue ethics demands of us what we cannot offer. But should not a sound moral theory apply to the "real world" and "real people"? Worse yet, virtue ethics demands that we prudentially develop the ability to do the right thing in the right way at the right time and for the right reason. Prudence requires two things; the *ability to see reality for what it is* and *act accordingly*. However, as we have seen, even a brief survey of moral practice shows that a belief in these twin responsibilities is mere idealism. Human being's weaknesses are too common. As such, to live virtuously is, for most human beings anyway, simply not realistic.

Virtue Ethicist Responses

How have virtue ethicists responded to such criticism? Does virtue ethics require deontology to remain coherent? Several responses can be offered. First, virtue ethicists are not bound to deny the importance of duty or rules. Second, to admit the co-dependence of being and doing does little to no harm to virtue ethics, for as Mayo insisted, the point is the priority of Being over Doing not the exclusivity of Being at the expense of Doing. MacIntyre (1990) is quite insightful in this regard.

"Rules and virtues are interrelated. To possess the virtue of justice, for example, involves both a will to give to each person what is due to him or her and a knowledge of how to apply the rules which prevent violations of that order in which each receives his or her due . . . To progress in both moral enquiry and the moral life is then to progress in understanding all the various aspects of that life, rules, precepts, virtues, passions, actions as parts of a single whole. Central to that progress is the exercise of the virtue of prudentia [prudence], the virtue of being able in particular situations to bring to bear the relevant universals and to act so that the universal is embodied in the particular" (p. 139).

The bottom line is this, if virtue (being) is seen as having priority among the two (being and doing), then winning the fight over whether virtue ethics needs deontology, is certainly not a matter of great importance.

What then of the claim that virtue ethics leads to indeterminacy? Two important responses can be made. First, as Timmons (2013) reminds us, "The best response is simply to admit that virtue ethics is limited in this way and then go on to explain that such limits are to be expected given the complexity of moral phenomena" (p. 292). Second, virtue ethics, at least in its classic Aristotelian form, is anything but arbitrary. The virtues are identified as forms of human excellence. This identification is built upon a rigorous (if nonetheless controversial) set of claims about human nature. Ought follows from is. Just as we know a good knife is good because we know that a knife is meant for cutting, so too we know that a good human life is "reasonable" for man is a "rational animal." Therefore, the good life (and moral action) are not arbitrary functions of the autonomous will but rather choices that ought to accord with reason, and thereby, reality.

Turning to the final criticism, I believe it is worth relaying a set questions I have asked my students nearly ever semester since I first taught sports ethics in the summer of 2005. Before I begin, let us remind ourselves what the final criticism was. Proponents of this criticism allege that virtue ethics is an unrealistic standard that requires the moral lives of saints. How, if at all, is this mistaken?

In responding to this charge ask yourself this: In what areas of life do you aim for mediocrity? Love, marriage and family? Are you hoping your spouse and children are thoroughly average or are you hoping that they will be beautiful in every sense of the word? What of your career? Are you hoping for a middling desk job where protecting your stapler is your most important task!?! Are you hoping for a few insignificant achievements? Or are you hoping to excel at work and become a leader or innovator who does great things!?! What of your possessions, free time and recreation? Are you hoping for a mediocre house or car? Do you aim to go on as many run-of-the-mill vacations as possible? Is your dream at the beginning of any sports season (whether as fan or participant) to aim for a .500 record? No! In all of these areas, just like the ones above, you strive for excellence, even when *you know* you will often fail. *Why then, do we so often shrug our shoulders and accept moral mediocrity!?!* No doubt, most of us will fail to be saints. That doesn't mean we should not try![13]

It should be clear from the course of this chapter, that I find virtue ethics more compelling than either utilitarianism or deontology. Per our usual disclaimer, it is worth reiterating that intelligent people have and will continue to disagree with such an assertion. I am convinced they are wrong. They would say the same about me. Of course disagreement, as we saw in Chapter 3, proves nothing beyond disagreement. Therefore, you need, in the light of reason and experience, to evaluate the truth of these arguments for yourselves.

Virtue Ethics and Sport?

What, then, are the implications of virtue ethics for sport? Here are three worth briefly discussing. First, the point and purposes of sport must be larger than money (profit) and victories. Why? Because money is an extrinsic good, and victories, contrary to popular cant, do not endure. We always want to play again tomorrow. Look at it this way. Money, though good, is merely a tool to serve other ends. *But what are*

---

[13] "The only real sadness, the only real failure, the only great tragedy in life, is not to become a saint." (Bloy, 1947, p. 356).

those ends? How soon, upon reflection, do we turn to Aristotle's basic questions! If the good is that at which all things aim, then we must necessarily clarify not only what is good, but what is intrinsically good. It cannot simply be profit or victory.[14]

Second, if ethics is social and habitual then although ethics is not reducible to education, ethics is inherent to education. This is because education is embedded in the nexus of institutions that make up any culture, including both the institutions of formal schooling, as well as the myriad institutions which informally educate as well. Moreover, the cultivation of virtue, depends upon apprenticeship, that is, learning from a living example. Given this reality, athletics is an inherently moral enterprise, since the skills procured and cultivated via participation go far beyond the skills of the game. For example, the conduct, policies, example and ethos of both the institutions and practitioners of sport impact everyone around them in both formal and informal ways. We learn how to "score goals" in sport, but we also learn to be "good or bad sports," etc.

How, then, knowing the impact that athletics has on moral skill development, should it be conducted? How, then, does athletics fit into formal institutions of education? How would interscholastic and intercollegiate athletics best serve "happiness" or "human flourishing"? Again, it seems clear that success in sport must be understood as far more than the relentless pursuit of "profit" or "victory."[15] If logic does not persuade you on this point, then the scandals that have engulfed profitable and victorious schools such as Penn State, Michigan State,[16] North Carolina and Baylor[17] should. What each of these scandals shows is that *how* "victory" is procured is always more important than *that* "victory" was procured. Contrary to the consequentialism promoted by utilitarians, a good end never justifies evil means.

Third, virtue makes a difference. The presence or absence of virtue will be noticed. It is only a matter of when and where. Many if not all of the problems in college athletics just mentioned can be traced back to a lack of courage; an unwillingness to stand up (and suffer for) the good. To illustrate the point, let us quickly examine two of the aforementioned scandals.

---

[14] If one separates winning from the profit motive, one might argue that it could stand as an end in itself. Is it not a form of "excellence"? Why, then, is pursuing victory as an end in itself mistaken? Several reasons can be offered. First, as Aristotle (1097b) and MacIntyre (1984) argue, a good or happy life must be "a life that can be conceived and evaluated as a whole" (p. 205). A naked pursuit of victory absent other goods is therefore perverse. Second, virtue ethics requires that "winning" or any other action is done for the right reason not merely that is it undertaken or procured. Victory is only one measure of excellence. Moreover, victory, procured in the wrong way, may not be excellent at all. Finally, there is the testimony, as we saw in Chapter 1, that a life dedicated to victory is unsatisfying.

[15] In reviewing the work of Erich Fromm, Joseph Pieper (1997) argues movingly in his book *Faith, Hope, Love*, that "it is not simply enough to eat to satiation, not to freeze, to have a roof overhead and everything else that is essential to life." Similarly, victory is not enough. Instead we also need "the sweetness of life and the happiness of life", which necessarily comes not from achievement or "victory" but rather from the affirmation of love. That is, the assertion by another: "How good that you exist" (p. 175)!

[16] Michigan State employed Dr. Larry Nassar as an osteopathic sports doctor. During that time he sexually assaulted scores of women under the guise of giving them "examinations". The first reports of his misbehavior occurred in 1997 and then continued to accumlate. Despite this knowledge, University officials, at several levels, allowed him to continue to assault girls under the cover of "medicine" until 2016. For more information on this scandal, see (Kozlowski, 2018).

[17] The Baylor University athletics department was credibly accused of covering up (and refusing to investigate) allegations made by women on campus of being sexually assaulted or raped by players on the University's football team. For a brief introduction to the scandal, see (Lavigne, 2018).

According to the best evidence (Smith, 2016), at the crucial moment of his professional career, if not his life, Joe Paterno bureaucratically washed his hands of the Sandusky Scandal by merely reporting the incident to his "superiors." The problem with this course of action being that Joe Paterno was de facto if not de jure the most powerful man on Penn State's campus and had been for decades. In fact the record shows that when he thought something was important, or was going to affect his program, he had a long history of asserting his will and getting his way.[18] Yet, when the chips were down, courage was in short supply. It would appear that "Success with honor" (Penn State's athletic "motto") became more important than the truth.[19]

Now consider the University of North Carolina. In *the twenty years* in which "paper courses" designed to keep athletes eligible existed at the University, there must have been myriad "Jiminy Cricket" moments. That is, there must have been any number of times where pangs of conscience suggested to one or another person who was involved that participating in such academic fraud was wrong. Why then did it continue? Because no one had the courage to try and stop it. No one was willing to risk their job or their reputation to put an end to academic fraud. The bottom line seems to be that national titles were more important than academic integrity. As a consequence,

©2010 Kevin Siers. Distributed by King Features Syndicate, Inc.

---

[18] This included both laudable and questionable interventions. On the laudable side, for example, is the fact that because "the Paterno family and others contributed a substantial endowment, possibly several hundred thousand dollars, the Classics Department [at Penn State] was saved from extinction" (Smith, 2016, p. 115). On the questionable side two examples jump out. First, Paterno's scolding of his superiors, including the President and athletics director, among others, when they came to his home after the dismal 2004 season to "ask him to retire" (Smith, 2016, p. 122). The second was his long battle in the mid-2000s with Vicky Triponey and Penn State's Office of Student Affairs over whether he or the university had the authority to discipline football players for wrongdoing (including alleged criminal acts).

[19] Aristotle's point about honor being dependent upon other people is particularly apropos here.

academic fraud became rationalized to the point that it could be nonchalantly discussed via email as this brief quote of the *Cadwalader Report* (Wainstein, Jay III, & Kukowski, 2014) shows:

> "In addition to Reynolds' grade guidance, our email review disclosed several instances where Boxill [a women's basketball advisor and sports ethics professor] made specific grade suggestions for her women's basketball players. In September 2008, for example, Boxill forwarded a paper on behalf of one of her players, to which Crowder [a Afro-American Studies secretary] responded that '[a]s long as I am here, I will try to accommodate as many favors as possible,' presumably signaling her willingness to grant grade requests up to the point of her retirement. As to that particular student's paper, Crowder then said "Did you say a D will do for [the basketball player]? I'm only asking because 1. no sources, 2, it has absolutely nothing to do with the assignments for that class and 3. it seems to me to be a recycled paper. She took [another class] in spring of 2007 and that was likely for that class." Boxill replied "Yes, a D will be fine; that's all she needs. I didn't look at the paper but figured it was a recycled one as well, but I couldn't figure out from where" (p. 40).

Is it fair to criticize the actors at PSU and UNC for their lack of courage? I believe it is. First, because it is merely a diagnosis: backbone is in short supply. I am far from convinced that I carry the requisite amount of virtue to consistently act courageously in such circumstances. I hope I would, but know myself well enough to know I might not. The same would likely be said by all of us. Yet, that admission does not raise doubts about the accuracy of the diagnosis. In this instance at least, the actors involved were weighed upon the scales and found wanting.[20]

Second, the point is not sanctimoniousness but a note caution; "there but for the grace of God go I!" For example, I have little doubt that in many ways Joe Paterno was a good man, perhaps a better man than I. But the fact that he did many good things *only sharpens the warning.* Even good men, if not vigilant, can fail. This is why it is called a *tragic* flaw. As MacIntyre (1984) has insisted "Yet, notoriously the cultivation of truthfulness, justice and courage will often, the world being what it contingently is, bar us from being rich or famous or powerful" (p. 196). If that is right, then we must clearly and consistently place virtue above not only rules, duties and outcomes, *it must also be placed above riches, power and fame.*

---

[20] They were challenged by the situation to show courage and failed. The "measure of the man" revealed "moral fault". See Daniel 5:27 for the origin of the phrase.

PHILOSOPHIC SELECTIONS

Selection #1: Aristotle, *Nicomachean Ethics*, Book I, Book II.

http://classics.mit.edu/Aristotle/nicomachaen.html

Introduction: Aristotle's *Nicomachean Ethics* is an examination of how the cultivation of virtue allows for human flourishing. In this selection, from the first two books of the *Ethics*, Aristotle focuses on the nature of the good, on the nature of happiness, and on the nature of virtue. He then turns his attention to how "we become what we practice." Here he argues that moral virtue (and vice) are the result of cultivated habits and skills. Ethics is not primarily about knowledge (we usually know what the right thing to do is), rather ethics is about being the right kind of person (one who has cultivated the moral skills necessary to live well and treat others as we ought).

1

Every art and every inquiry, and similarly every action and pursuit, is thought to aim at some good; and for this reason the good has rightly been declared to be that at which all things aim. But a certain difference is found among ends; some are activities, others are products apart from the activities that produce them. Where there are ends apart from the actions, it is the nature of the products to be better than the activities. Now, as there are many actions, arts, and sciences, their ends also are many; the end of the medical art is health, that of shipbuilding a vessel, that of strategy victory, that of economics wealth. But where such arts fall under a single capacity as bridle-making and the other arts concerned with the equipment of horses fall under the art of riding, and this and every military action under strategy, in the same way other arts fall under yet others in all of these the ends of the master arts are to be preferred to all the subordinate ends; for it is for the sake of the former that the latter are pursued. It makes no difference whether the activities themselves are the ends of the actions, or something else apart from the activities, as in the case of the sciences just mentioned.

2

If, then, there is some end of the things we do, which we desire for its own sake (everything else being desired for the sake of this), and if we do not choose everything for the sake of something else (for at that rate the process would go on to infinity, so that our desire would be empty and vain), clearly this must be the good and the chief good. Will not the knowledge of it, then, have a great influence on life? Shall we not, like archers who have a mark to aim at, be more likely to hit upon what is right? If so, we must try, in outline at least, to determine what it is, and of which of the sciences or capacities it is the object. It would seem to belong to the most authoritative art and that which is most truly the master art. And politics appears to be of this nature; for it is this that ordains which of the sciences should be studied in a state, and which each class of citizens should learn and up to what point they should learn them; and we see even the most highly esteemed of capacities to fall under this, e.g., strategy, economics, rhetoric; now, since politics uses the rest of the sciences, and since, again, it legislates as to what we are to do and what we are to abstain from, the end of this science must include those of the others, so that this end must be the good for man. For even if the end is the same for a single man and for a state, that of the state seems at all events something greater and more complete whether to attain or to preserve; though it is worthwhile to attain the end merely for one man, it is finer and more godlike to attain it for a nation or for city-states. These, then, are the ends at which our inquiry aims, since it is political science, in one sense of that term.

3

Our discussion will be adequate if it has as much clearness as the subject-matter admits of, for precision is not to be sought for alike in all discussions, any more than in all the products of the crafts. Now fine and just actions, which political science investigates, admit of much variety and fluctuation of opinion, so that they may be thought to exist only by convention, and not by nature. And goods also give rise to a similar fluctuation because they bring harm to many people; for before now men have been undone by reason of their wealth, and others by reason of their courage. We must be content, then, in speaking of such subjects and with such premises to indicate the truth roughly and in outline, and in speaking about things which are only for the most part true and with premises of the same kind to reach conclusions that are no better. In the same spirit, therefore, should each type of statement be received; for it is the mark of an educated man to look for precision in each class of things just so far as the nature of the subject admits; it is evidently equally foolish to accept probable reasoning from a mathematician and to demand from a rhetorician scientific proofs.

Now each man judges well the things he knows, and of these he is a good judge. And so the man who has been educated in a subject is a good judge of that subject, and the man who has received an all-round education is a good judge in general. Hence a young man is not a proper hearer of lectures on political science; for he is inexperienced in the actions that occur in life, but its discussions start from these and are about these; and, further, since he tends to follow his passions, his study will be vain and unprofitable, because the end aimed at is not knowledge but action. And it makes no difference whether he is young in years or youthful in character; the defect does not depend on time, but on his living, and pursuing each successive object, as passion directs. For to such persons, as to the incontinent, knowledge brings no profit; but to those who desire and act in accordance with a rational principle knowledge about such matters will be of great benefit.

These remarks about the student, the sort of treatment to be expected, and the purpose of the inquiry, may be taken as our preface.

4

Let us resume our inquiry and state, in view of the fact that all knowledge and every pursuit aims at some good, what it is that we say political science aims at and what is the highest of all goods achievable by action. Verbally there is very general agreement; for both the general run of men and people of superior refinement say that it is happiness, and identify living well and doing well with being happy; but with regard to what happiness is they differ, and the many do not give the same account as the wise. For the former think it is some plain and obvious thing, like pleasure, wealth, or honor; they differ, however, from one another—and often even the same man identifies it with different things, with health when he is ill, with wealth when he is poor; but, conscious of their ignorance, they admire those who proclaim some great ideal that is above their comprehension. Now some thought that apart from these many goods there is another which is self-subsistent and causes the goodness of all these as well. To examine all the opinions that have been held were perhaps somewhat fruitless; enough to examine those that are most prevalent or that seem to be arguable.

Let us not fail to notice, however, that there is a difference between arguments from and those to the first principles. For Plato, too, was right in raising this question and asking, as he used to do, 'are we on the way from or to the first principles?' There is a difference, as there is in a race-course between the course from the judges to the turning-point and the way back. For, while we must begin with what is known, things are objects of knowledge in two senses—some to us, some without qualification. Presumably, then, we must begin with things known to us. Hence anyone who is to listen intelligently to lectures about what is noble and just, and generally, about the subjects of political science must have been brought up in good habits. For the fact is the starting-point, and if this is sufficiently plain to him, he will not at the start need the reason as well; and the man who has been well brought up has or can easily get starting points. And as for him who neither has nor can get them, let him hear the words of Hesiod:

> Far best is he who knows all things himself;
>
> Good, he that hearkens when men counsel right;
>
> But he who neither knows, nor lays to heart
>
> Another's wisdom, is a useless wight.

5

Let us, however, resume our discussion from the point at which we digressed. To judge from the lives that men lead, most men, and men of the most vulgar type, seem (not without some ground) to identify the good, or happiness, with pleasure; which is the reason why they love the life of enjoyment. For there are, we may say, three prominent types of life—that just mentioned, the political, and thirdly the contemplative life. Now the mass of mankind are evidently quite slavish in their tastes, preferring a life suitable to beasts, but they get some ground for their view from the fact that many of those in high places share the tastes of Sardanapallus. A consideration of the prominent types of life shows that people of superior refinement and of active disposition identify happiness with honor; for this is, roughly speaking, the end of the political life. But it seems too superficial to be what we are looking for, since it is thought to depend on those who bestow honor rather than on him who receives it, but the good we divine to be something proper to a man and not easily taken from him. Further, men seem to pursue honor in order that they may be assured of their goodness; at least it is by men of practical wisdom that they seek to be honored, and among those who know them, and on the ground of their virtue; clearly, then, according to them, at any rate, virtue is better. And perhaps one might even suppose this to be, rather than honor, the end of the political life. But even this appears somewhat incomplete; for possession of virtue seems actually compatible with being asleep, or with lifelong inactivity, and, further, with the greatest sufferings and misfortunes; but a man who was living so no one would call happy, unless he were maintaining a thesis at all costs. But enough of this; for the subject has been sufficiently treated even in the current discussions. Third comes the contemplative life, which we shall consider later.

The life of money-making is one undertaken under compulsion, and wealth is evidently not the good we are seeking; for it is merely useful and for the sake of something else. And so one might rather take the aforenamed objects to be ends; for they are loved for themselves. But it is evident that not even these are ends; yet many arguments have been thrown away in support of them. Let us leave this subject, then.

6

We had perhaps better consider the universal good and discuss thoroughly what is meant by it, although such an inquiry is made an uphill one by the fact that the Forms have been introduced by friends of our own. Yet it would perhaps be thought to be better, indeed to be our duty, for the sake of maintaining the truth even to destroy what touches us closely, especially as we are philosophers or lovers of wisdom; for, while both are dear, piety requires us to honor truth above our friends.

The men who introduced this doctrine did not posit Ideas of classes within which they recognized priority and posteriority (which is the reason why they did not maintain the existence of an Idea embracing all numbers); but the term 'good' is used both in the category of substance and in that of quality and in that of relation, and that which is per se, i.e., substance, is prior in nature to the relative (for the latter is like an off shoot and accident of being); so that there could not be a common Idea set over all these goods. Further, since 'good' has as many senses as 'being' (for it is predicated both in the category of substance, as of God and of reason, and in quality, i.e., of the virtues, and in quantity, i.e., of that which is moderate, and in relation, i.e. of the useful, and in time, i.e., of the right opportunity, and in place, i.e. of the right locality and the like), clearly it cannot be something universally present in all cases and single; for then it could not have been predicated in all the categories but in one only. Further, since of the things answering to one Idea there is one science, there would have been one science of all the goods; but as it is there are many sciences even of the things that fall under one category, e.g. of opportunity, for opportunity in war is studied by strategics and in disease by medicine, and the moderate in food is studied by medicine and in exercise by the science of gymnastics. And one might ask the question, what in the world they mean by 'a thing itself', is (as is the case) in 'man himself' and in a particular man the account of man is one and the same. For in so far as they are man, they will in no respect differ; and if this is so, neither will 'good itself' and particular goods, in so far as they are good. But again it will not be good any the more for being eternal, since that which lasts long is no whiter than that which perishes in a day. The Pythagoreans seem to give a more plausible account of the good, when they place the one in the column of goods; and it is they that Speusippus seems to have followed.

But let us discuss these matters elsewhere; an objection to what we have said, however, may be discerned in the fact that the Platonists have not been speaking about all goods, and that the goods that are pursued and loved for themselves are called good by reference to a single Form, while those which tend to produce or to preserve these somehow or to prevent their contraries are called so by reference to these, and in a secondary sense. Clearly, then, goods must be spoken of in two ways, and some must be good in themselves, the others by reason of these. Let us separate, then, things good in themselves from things useful, and consider whether the former are called good by reference to a single Idea. What sort of goods would one call good in themselves? Is it those that are pursued even when isolated from others, such as intelligence, sight, and certain pleasures and honors? Certainly, if we pursue these also for the sake of something else, yet one would place them among things good in themselves. Or is nothing other than the Idea of good in itself? In that case the Form will be empty. But if the things we have named are also things good in themselves, the account of the good will have to appear as something identical in them all, as that of whiteness is identical in snow and in white lead. But of honor, wisdom, and pleasure, just in respect of their goodness, the accounts are distinct and diverse. The good, therefore, is not some common element answering to one Idea.

But what then do we mean by the good? It is surely not like the things that only chance to have the same name. Are goods one, then, by being derived from one good or by all contributing to one good, or are they rather one by analogy? Certainly as sight is in the body, so is reason in the soul, and so on in other cases. But perhaps these subjects had better be dismissed for the present; for perfect precision about them would be more appropriate to another branch of philosophy. And similarly with regard to the Idea; even

if there is some one good which is universally predicable of goods or is capable of separate and independent existence, clearly it could not be achieved or attained by man; but
we are now seeking something attainable. Perhaps, however, some one might think it
worthwhile to recognize this with a view to the goods that are attainable and achievable;
for having this as a sort of pattern we shall know better the goods that are good for us,
and if we know them shall attain them. This argument has some plausibility, but seems
to clash with the procedure of the sciences; for all of these, though they aim at some good
and seek to supply the deficiency of it, leave on one side the knowledge of the good. Yet
that all the exponents of the arts should be ignorant of, and should not even seek, so
great an aid is not probable. It is hard, too, to see how a weaver or a carpenter will be
benefited in regard to his own craft by knowing this 'good itself', or how the man who
has viewed the Idea itself will be a better doctor or general thereby. For a doctor seems
not even to study health in this way, but the health of man, or perhaps rather the health
of a particular man; it is individuals that he is healing. But enough of these topics.

7

Let us again return to the good we are seeking, and ask what it can be. It seems different in
different actions and arts; it is different in medicine, in strategy, and in the other arts likewise. What then is the good of each? Surely that for whose sake everything else is done. In
medicine this is health, in strategy victory, in architecture a house, in any other sphere something else, and in every action and pursuit the end; for it is for the sake of this that all men
do whatever else they do. Therefore, if there is an end for all that we do, this will be the good
achievable by action, and if there are more than one, these will be the goods achievable by
action.

So the argument has by a different course reached the same point; but we must try to
state this even more clearly. Since there are evidently more than one end, and we choose
some of these (e.g. wealth, flutes, and in general instruments) for the sake of something
else, clearly not all ends are final ends; but the chief good is evidently something final.
Therefore, if there is only one final end, this will be what we are seeking, and if there are
more than one, the most final of these will be what we are seeking. Now we call that which
is in itself worthy of pursuit more final than that which is worthy of pursuit for the sake
of something else, and that which is never desirable for the sake of something else more
final than the things that are desirable both in themselves and for the sake of that other
thing, and therefore we call final without qualification that which is always desirable in
itself and never for the sake of something else.

Now such a thing happiness, above all else, is held to be; for this we choose always for
self and never for the sake of something else, but honor, pleasure, reason, and every virtue we choose indeed for themselves (for if nothing resulted from them we should still
choose each of them), but we choose them also for the sake of happiness, judging that by
means of them we shall be happy. Happiness, on the other hand, no one chooses for the
sake of these, nor, in general, for anything other than itself.

From the point of view of self-sufficiency the same result seems to follow; for the final
good is thought to be self-sufficient. Now by self-sufficient we do not mean that which
is sufficient for a man by himself, for one who lives a solitary life, but also for parents,
children, wife, and in general for his friends and fellow citizens, since man is born for
citizenship. But some limit must be set to this; for if we extend our requirement to
ancestors and descendants and friends' friends we are in for an infinite series. Let us
examine this question, however, on another occasion; the self-sufficient we now define
as that which when isolated makes life desirable and lacking in nothing; and such we
think happiness to be; and further we think it most desirable of all things, without being

counted as one good thing among others—if it were so counted it would clearly be made more desirable by the addition of even the least of goods; for that which is added becomes an excess of goods, and of goods the greater is always more desirable. Happiness, then, is something final and self-sufficient, and is the end of action.

Presumably, however, to say that happiness is the chief good seems a platitude, and a clearer account of what it is still desired. This might perhaps be given, if we could first ascertain the function of man. For just as for a flute-player, a sculptor, or an artist, and, in general, for all things that have a function or activity, the good and the 'well' is thought to reside in the function, so would it seem to be for man, if he has a function. Have the carpenter, then, and the tanner certain functions or activities, and has man none? Is he born without a function? Or as eye, hand, foot, and in general each of the parts evidently has a function, may one lay it down that man similarly has a function apart from all these? What then can this be? Life seems to be common even to plants, but we are seeking what is peculiar to man. Let us exclude, therefore, the life of nutrition and growth. Next there would be a life of perception, but it also seems to be common even to the horse, the ox, and every animal. There remains, then, an active life of the element that has a rational principle; of this, one part has such a principle in the sense of being obedient to one, the other in the sense of possessing one and exercising thought. And, as 'life of the rational element' also has two meanings, we must state that life in the sense of activity is what we mean; for this seems to be the more proper sense of the term. Now if the function of man is an activity of soul which follows or implies a rational principle, and if we say 'so-and-so-and 'a good so-and-so' have a function which is the same in kind, e.g. a lyre, and a good lyre-player, and so without qualification in all cases, eminence in respect of good-ness being added to the name of the function (for the function of a lyre-player is to play the lyre, and that of a good lyre-player is to do so well): if this is the case, and we state the function of man to be a certain kind of life, and this to be an activity or actions of the soul implying a rational principle, and the function of a good man to be the good and noble performance of these, and if any action is well performed when it is performed in accordance with the appropriate excellence: if this is the case, human good turns out to be activity of soul in accordance with virtue, and if there are more than one virtue, in accordance with the best and most complete.

But we must add 'in a complete life.' For one swallow does not make a summer, nor does one day; and so too one day, or a short time, does not make a man blessed and happy.

Let this serve as an outline of the good; for we must presumably first sketch it roughly, and then later fill in the details. But it would seem that any one is capable of carrying on and articulating what has once been well outlined, and that time is a good discoverer or partner in such a work; to which facts the advances of the arts are due; for any one can add what is lacking. And we must also remember what has been said before, and not look for precision in all things alike, but in each class of things such precision as accords with the subject-matter, and so much as is appropriate to the inquiry. For a carpenter and a geom-eter investigate the right angle in different ways; the former does so in so far as the right angle is useful for his work, while the latter inquires what it is or what sort of thing it is; for he is a spectator of the truth. We must act in the same way, then, in all other matters as well, that our main task may not be subordinated to minor questions. Nor must we demand the cause in all matters alike; it is enough in some cases that the fact be well established, as in the case of the first principles; the fact is the primary thing or first principle. Now of first principles we see some by induction, some by perception, some by a certain habituation, and others too in other ways. But each set of principles we must try to investigate in the natural way, and we must take pains to state them definitely, since they have a great influence on what follows. For the beginning is thought to be more than half of the whole, and many of the questions we ask are cleared up by it.

8

We must consider it, however, in the light not only of our conclusion and our premises, but also of what is commonly said about it; for with a true view all the data harmonize, but with a false one the facts soon clash. Now goods have been divided into three classes, and some are described as external, others as relating to soul or to body; we call those that relate to soul most properly and truly goods, and psychical actions and activities we class as relating to soul. Therefore our account must be sound, at least according to this view, which is an old one and agreed on by philosophers. It is correct also in that we identify the end with certain actions and activities; for thus it falls among goods of the soul and not among external goods. Another belief which harmonizes with our account is that the happy man lives well and does well; for we have practically defined happiness as a sort of good life and good action. The characteristics that are looked for in happiness seem also, all of them, to belong to what we have defined happiness as being. For some identify happiness with virtue, some with practical wisdom, others with a kind of philosophic wisdom, others with these, or one of these, accompanied by pleasure or not without pleasure; while others include also external prosperity. Now some of these views have been held by many men and men of old, others by a few eminent persons; and it is not probable that either of these should be entirely mistaken, but rather that they should be right in at least some one respect or even in most respects.

With those who identify happiness with virtue or someone virtue our account is in harmony; for to virtue belongs virtuous activity. But it makes, perhaps, no small difference whether we place the chief good in possession or in use, in state of mind or in activity. For the state of mind may exist without producing any good result, as in a man who is asleep or in some other way quite inactive, but the activity cannot; for one who has the activity will of necessity be acting, and acting well. And as in the Olympic Games it is not the most beautiful and the strongest that are crowned but those who compete (for it is some of these that are victorious), so those who act win, and rightly win, the noble and good things in life.

Their life is also in itself pleasant. For pleasure is a state of soul, and to each man that which he is said to be a lover of is pleasant; e.g. not only is a horse pleasant to the lover of horses, and a spectacle to the lover of sights, but also in the same way just acts are pleasant to the lover of justice and in general virtuous acts to the lover of virtue. Now for most men their pleasures are in conflict with one another because these are not by nature pleasant, but the lovers of what is noble find pleasant the things that are by nature pleasant; and virtuous actions are such, so that these are pleasant for such men as well as in their own nature. Their life, therefore, has no further need of pleasure as a sort of adventitious charm, but has its pleasure in itself. For, besides what we have said, the man who does not rejoice in noble actions is not even good; since no one would call a man just who did not enjoy acting justly, nor any man liberal who did not enjoy liberal actions; and similarly in all other cases. If this is so, virtuous actions must be in themselves pleasant. But they are also good and noble, and have each of these attributes in the highest degree, since the good man judges well about these attributes; his judgement is such as we have described. Happiness then is the best, noblest, and most pleasant thing in the world, and these attributes are not severed as in the inscription at Delos.

Most noble is that which is justest, and best is health;

But pleasantest is it to win what we love.

For all these properties belong to the best activities; and these, or one—the best—of these, we identify with happiness.

Yet evidently, as we said, it needs the external goods as well; for it is impossible, or not easy, to do noble acts without the proper equipment. In many actions we use friends and riches and political power as instruments; and there are some things the lack of which takes the luster from happiness, as good birth, goodly children, beauty; for the man who is very ugly in appearance or ill-born or solitary and childless is not very likely to be happy, and perhaps a man would be still less likely if he had thoroughly bad children or friends or had lost good children or friends by death. As we said, then, happiness seems to need this sort of prosperity in addition; for which reason some identify happiness with good fortune, though others identify it with virtue.

9

For this reason also the question is asked, whether happiness is to be acquired by learning or by habituation or some other sort of training, or comes in virtue of some divine providence or again by chance. Now if there is any gift of the gods to men, it is reasonable that happiness should be god-given, and most surely god-given of all human things inasmuch as it is the best. But this question would perhaps be more appropriate to another inquiry; happiness seems, however, even if it is not god-sent but comes as a result of virtue and some process of learning or training, to be among the most godlike things; for that which is the prize and end of virtue seems to be the best thing in the world, and something godlike and blessed.

It will also on this view be very generally shared; for all who are not maimed as regards their potentiality for virtue may win it by a certain kind of study and care. But if it is better to be happy thus than by chance, it is reasonable that the facts should be so, since everything that depends on the action of nature is by nature as good as it can be, and similarly everything that depends on art or any rational cause, and especially if it depends on the best of all causes. To entrust to chance what is greatest and most noble would be a very defective arrangement.

The answer to the question we are asking is plain also from the definition of happiness; for it has been said to be a virtuous activity of soul, of a certain kind. Of the remaining goods, some must necessarily pre-exist as conditions of happiness, and others are naturally co-operative and useful as instruments. And this will be found to agree with what we said at the outset; for we stated the end of political science to be the best end, and political science spends most of its pains on making the citizens to be of a certain character, viz. good and capable of noble acts.

It is natural, then, that we call neither ox nor horse nor any other of the animals happy; for none of them is capable of sharing in such activity. For this reason also a boy is not happy; for he is not yet capable of such acts, owing to his age; and boys who are called happy are being congratulated by reason of the hopes we have for them. For there is required, as we said, not only complete virtue but also a complete life, since many changes occur in life, and all manner of chances, and the most prosperous may fall into great misfortunes in old age, as is told of Priam in the Trojan Cycle; and one who has experienced such chances and has ended wretchedly no one calls happy.

10

Must no one at all, then, be called happy while he lives; must we, as Solon says, see the end? Even if we are to lay down this doctrine, is it also the case that a man is happy when he is dead? Or is not this quite absurd, especially for us who say that happiness is an activity? But if we do not call the dead man happy, and if Solon does not mean this, but that one can then safely call a man blessed as being at last beyond evils and misfortunes, this also affords matter for discussion; for both evil and good are thought to exist for a dead man, as much as for one who is alive but not aware of them; e.g., honors and dishonors and the good or bad fortunes of children and in general of descendants. And this also presents a problem; for though a man has lived happily up to old age and has had a death worthy of his life, many reverses may befall his descendants—some of them may be good and attain the life they deserve, while with others the opposite may be the case; and clearly too the degrees of relationship between them and their ancestors may vary indefinitely. It would be odd, then, if the dead man were to share in these changes and become at one time happy, at another wretched; while it would also be odd if the fortunes of the descendants did not for some time have some effect on the happiness of their ancestors.

But we must return to our first difficulty; for perhaps by a consideration of it our present problem might be solved. Now if we must see the end and only then call a man happy, not as being happy but as having been so before, surely this is a paradox, that when he is happy the attribute that belongs to him is not to be truly predicated of him because we do not wish to call living men happy, on account of the changes that may befall them, and because we have assumed happiness to be something permanent and by no means easily changed, while a single man may suffer many turns of fortune's wheel. For clearly if we were to keep pace with his fortunes, we should often call the same man happy and again wretched, making the happy man out to be chameleon and insecurely based. Or is this keeping pace with his fortunes quite wrong? Success or failure in life does not depend on these, but human life, as we said, needs these as mere additions, while virtuous activities or their opposites are what constitute happiness or the reverse.

The question we have now discussed confirms our definition. For no function of man has so much permanence as virtuous activities (these are thought to be more durable even than knowledge of the sciences), and of these themselves the most valuable are more durable because those who are happy spend their life most readily and most continuously in these; for this seems to be the reason why we do not forget them. The attribute in question, then, will belong to the happy man, and he will be happy throughout his life; for always, or by preference to everything else, he will be engaged in virtuous action and contemplation, and he will bear the chances of life most nobly and altogether decorously, if he is 'truly good' and 'foursquare beyond reproach'.

Now many events happen by chance, and events differing in importance; small pieces of good fortune or of its opposite clearly do not weigh down the scales of life one way or the other, but a multitude of great events if they turn out well will make life happier (for not only are they themselves such as to add beauty to life, but the way a man deals with them may be noble and good), while if they turn out ill they crush and maim happiness; for they both bring pain with them and hinder many activities. Yet even in these nobility shines through, when a man bears with resignation many great misfortunes, not through insensibility to pain but through nobility and greatness of soul.

If activities are, as we said, what gives life its character, no happy man can become miserable; for he will never do the acts that are hateful and mean. For the man who is truly good and wise, we think, bears all the chances life becomingly and always makes the best of circumstances, as a good general makes the best military use of the army at his command and a good shoemaker makes the best shoes out of the hides that are given him; and so with all other craftsmen. And if this is the case, the happy man can never become miserable; though he will not reach blessedness, if he meet with fortunes like those of Priam.

Nor, again, is he many-colored and changeable; for neither will he be moved from his happy state easily or by any ordinary misadventures, but only by many great ones, nor, if he has had many great misadventures, will he recover his happiness in a short time, but if at all, only in a long and complete one in which he has attained many splendid successes.

When then should we not say that he is happy who is active in accordance with complete virtue and is sufficiently equipped with external goods, not for some chance period but throughout a complete life? Or must we add 'and who is destined to live thus and die as befits his life'? Certainly the future is obscure to us, while happiness, we claim, is an end and something in every way final. If so, we shall call happy those among living men in whom these conditions are, and are to be, fulfilled but happy men. So much for these questions.

11

That the fortunes of descendants and of all a man's friends should not affect his happiness at all seems a very unfriendly doctrine, and one opposed to the opinions men hold; but since the events that happen are numerous and admit of all sorts of difference, and some come more near to us and others less so, it seems a long—nay, an infinite—task to discuss each in detail; a general outline will perhaps suffice. If, then, as some of a man's own misadventures have a certain weight and influence on life while others are, as it were, lighter, so too there are differences among the misadventures of our friends taken as a whole, and it makes a difference whether the various suffering befall the living or the dead (much more even than whether lawless and terrible deeds are presupposed in a tragedy or done on the stage), this difference also must be taken into account; or rather, perhaps, the fact that doubt is felt whether the dead share in any good or evil. For it seems, from these considerations, that even if anything whether good or evil penetrates to them, it must be something weak and negligible, either in itself or for them, or if not, at least it must be such in degree and kind as not to make happy those who are not happy nor to take away their blessedness from those who are. The good or bad fortunes of friends, then, seem to have some effects on the dead, but effects of such a kind and degree as neither to make the happy unhappy nor to produce any other change of the kind.

12

These questions having been definitely answered, let us consider whether happiness is among the things that are praised or rather among the things that are prized; for clearly it is not to be placed among potentialities. Everything that is praised seems to be praised because it is of a certain kind and is related somehow to something else; for we praise the just or brave man and in general both the good man and virtue itself because of the actions and functions involved, and we praise the strong man, the good runner, and so on, because he is of a certain kind and is related in a certain way to something good and important. This is clear also from the praises of the gods; for it seems absurd that the gods should be referred to our standard, but this is done because praise involves a reference, to something else. But if praise is for things such as we have described, clearly what applies to the best things is not praise, but something greater and better, as is indeed obvious; for what we do to the gods and the most godlike of men is to call them blessed and happy. And so too with good things; no one praises happiness as he does justice, but rather calls it blessed, as being something more divine and better.

Eudoxus also seems to have been right in his method of advocating the supremacy of pleasure; he thought that the fact that, though a good, it is not praised indicated it to be better than the things that are praised, and that this is what God and the good are; for by reference to these all other things are judged. Praise is appropriate to virtue, for as a result of virtue men tend to do noble deeds, but encomia are bestowed on acts, whether of the body or of the soul. But perhaps nicety in these matters is more proper to those who have made a study of encomia; to us it is clear from what has been said that happiness is among the things that are prized and perfect. It seems to be so also from the fact that it is a first principle; for it is for the sake of this that we all do all that we do, and the first principle and cause of goods is, we claim, something prized and divine.

13

Since happiness is an activity of soul in accordance with perfect virtue, we must consider the nature of virtue; for perhaps we shall thus see better the nature of happiness. The true student of politics, too, is thought to have studied virtue above all things; for he wishes to make his fellow citizens good and obedient to the laws. As an example of this we have the lawgivers of the Cretans and the Spartans, and any others of the kind that there may have been. And if this inquiry belongs to political science, clearly the pursuit of it will be in accordance with our original plan. But clearly the virtue we must study is human virtue; for the good we were seeking was human good and the happiness human happiness. By human virtue we mean not that of the body but that of the soul; and happiness also we call an activity of soul. But if this is so, clearly the student of politics must know somehow the facts about soul, as the man who is to heal the eyes or the body as a whole must know about the eyes or the body; and all the more since politics is more prized and better than medicine; but even among doctors the best educated spend much labor on acquiring knowledge of the body. The student of politics, then, must study the soul, and must study it with these objects in view, and do so just to the extent which is sufficient for the questions we are discussing; for further precision is perhaps something more laborious than our purposes require.

Some things are said about it, adequately enough, even in the discussions outside our school, and we must use these; e.g., that one element in the soul is irrational and one has a rational principle. Whether these are separated as the parts of the body or of anything divisible are, or are distinct by definition but by nature inseparable, like convex and concave in the circumference of a circle, does not affect the present question.

Of the irrational element one division seems to be widely distributed, and vegetative in its nature, I mean that which causes nutrition and growth; for it is this kind of power of the soul that one must assign to all nurslings and to embryos, and this same power to full grown creatures; this is more reasonable than to assign some different power to them. Now the excellence of this seems to be common to all species and not specifically human; for this part or faculty seems to function most in sleep, while goodness and badness are least manifest in sleep (whence comes the saying that the happy are not better off than the wretched for half their lives; and this happens naturally enough, since sleep is an inactivity of the soul in that respect in which it is called good or bad), unless perhaps to a small extent some of the movements actually penetrate to the soul, and in this respect the dreams of good men are better than those of ordinary people. Enough of this subject, however; let us leave the nutritive faculty alone, since it has by its nature no share in human excellence.

There seems to be also another irrational element in the soul-one which in a sense, however, shares in a rational principle. For we praise the rational principle of the continent man and of the incontinent, and the part of their soul that has such a principle, since it urges them aright and towards the best objects; but there is found in them also another element naturally opposed to the rational principle, which fights against and resists that principle. For exactly as paralyzed limbs when we intend to move them to the right turn on the contrary to the left, so is it with the soul; the impulses of incontinent people move in contrary directions. But while in the body we see that which moves astray, in the soul we do not. No doubt, however, we must none the less suppose that in the soul too there is something contrary to the rational principle, resisting and opposing it. In what sense it is distinct from the other elements does not concern us. Now even this seems to have a share in a rational principle, as we said; at any rate in the continent man it obeys the rational principle and presumably in the temperate and brave man it is still more obedient; for in him it speaks, on all matters, with the same voice as the rational principle.

Therefore the irrational element also appears to be two-fold. For the vegetative element in no way shares in a rational principle, but the appetitive and in general the desiring element in a sense shares in it, in so far as it listens to and obeys it; this is the sense in which we speak of 'taking account' of one's father or one's friends, not that in which we speak of 'accounting for a mathematical property. That the irrational element is in some sense persuaded by a rational principle is indicated also by the giving of advice and by all reproof and exhortation. And if this element also must be said to have a rational principle, that which has a rational principle (as well as that which has not) will be twofold, one subdivision having it in the strict sense and in itself, and the other having a tendency to obey as one does one's father.

Virtue too is distinguished into kinds in accordance with this difference; for we say that some of the virtues are intellectual and others moral, philosophic wisdom and understanding and practical wisdom being intellectual, liberality and temperance moral. For in speaking about a man's character we do not say that he is wise or has understanding but that he is good-tempered or temperate; yet we praise the wise man also with respect to his state of mind; and of states of mind we call those which merit praise virtues.

Book II

1

Virtue, then, being of two kinds, intellectual and moral, intellectual virtue in the main owes both its birth and its growth to teaching (for which reason it requires experience and time), while moral virtue comes about as a result of habit, whence also its name (ethike) is one that is formed by a slight variation from the word ethos (habit). From this it is also plain that none of the moral virtues arises in us by nature; for nothing that exists by nature can form a habit contrary to its nature. For instance the stone which by nature moves downwards cannot be habituated to move upwards, not even if one tries to train it by throwing it up ten thousand times; nor can fire be habituated to move downwards, nor can anything else that by nature behaves in one way be trained to behave in another. Neither by nature, then, nor contrary to nature do the virtues arise in us; rather we are adapted by nature to receive them, and are made perfect by habit.

Again, of all the things that come to us by nature we first acquire the potentiality and later exhibit the activity (this is plain in the case of the senses; for it was not by often seeing or often hearing that we got these senses, but on the contrary we had them before we used them, and did not come to have them by using them); but the virtues we get by first exercising them, as also happens in the case of the arts as well. For the things we have to learn before we can do them, we learn by doing them, e.g. men become builders by building and lyre players by playing the lyre; so too we become just by doing just acts, temperate by doing temperate acts, brave by doing brave acts.

This is confirmed by what happens in states; for legislators make the citizens good by forming habits in them, and this is the wish of every legislator, and those who do not effect it miss their mark, and it is in this that a good constitution differs from a bad one.

Again, it is from the same causes and by the same means that every virtue is both produced and destroyed, and similarly every art; for it is from playing the lyre that both good and bad lyre-players are produced. And the corresponding statement is true of builders and of all the rest; men will be good or bad builders as a result of building well or badly. For if this were not so, there would have been no need of a teacher, but all men would have been born good or bad at their craft. This, then, is the case with the virtues also; by doing the acts that we do in our transactions with other men we become just or unjust, and by doing the acts that we do in the presence of danger, and being habituated to feel fear or confidence, we become brave or cowardly. The same is true of appetites and feelings of anger; some men become temperate and good-tempered, others self-indulgent and irascible, by behaving in one way or the other in the appropriate circumstances. Thus, in one word, states of character arise out of like activities. This is why the activities we exhibit must be of a certain kind; it is because the states of character correspond to the differences between these. It makes no small difference, then, whether we form habits of one kind or of another from our very youth; it makes a very great difference, or rather all the difference.

2

Since, then, the present inquiry does not aim at theoretical knowledge like the others (for we are inquiring not in order to know what virtue is, but in order to become good, since otherwise our inquiry would have been of no use), we must examine the nature of actions, namely how we ought to do them; for these determine also the nature of the states of character that are produced, as we have said. Now, that we must act according to the right rule is a common principle and must be assumed-it will be discussed later, i.e. both what the right rule is, and how it is related to the other virtues. But this must be agreed upon beforehand, that the whole account of matters of conduct must be given in outline and not precisely, as we said at the very beginning that the accounts we demand must be in accordance with the subject-matter; matters concerned with conduct and questions of what is good for us have no fixity, any more than matters of health. The general account being of this nature, the account of particular cases is yet more lacking in exactness; for they do not fall under any art or precept but the agents themselves must in each case consider what is appropriate to the occasion, as happens also in the art of medicine or of navigation.

But though our present account is of this nature we must give what help we can. First, then, let us consider this, that it is the nature of such things to be destroyed by defect and excess, as we see in the case of strength and of health (for to gain light on things imperceptible we must use the evidence of sensible things); both excessive and defective exercise destroys the strength, and similarly drink or food which is above or below a certain amount destroys the health, while that which is proportionate both produces and increases and preserves it. So too is it, then, in the case of temperance and courage and the other virtues. For the man who flies from and fears everything and does not stand his ground against anything becomes a coward, and the man who fears nothing at all but goes to meet every danger becomes rash; and similarly the man who indulges in every pleasure and abstains from none becomes self-indulgent, while the man who shuns every pleasure, as boors do, becomes in a way insensible; temperance and courage, then, are destroyed by excess and defect, and preserved by the mean.

But not only are the sources and causes of their origination and growth the same as those of their destruction, but also the sphere of their actualization will be the same; for this is also true of the things which are more evident to sense, e.g. of strength; it is produced by taking much food and undergoing much exertion, and it is the strong man that will be most able to do these things. So too is it with the virtues; by abstaining from pleasures we become temperate, and it is when we have become so that we are most able to abstain from them; and similarly too in the case of courage; for by being habituated to despise things that are terrible and to stand our ground against them we become brave, and it is when we have become so that we shall be most able to stand our ground against them.

3

We must take as a sign of states of character the pleasure or pain that ensues on acts; for the man who abstains from bodily pleasures and delights in this very fact is temperate, while the man who is annoyed at it is self-indulgent, and he who stands his ground against things that are terrible and delights in this or at least is not pained is brave, while the man who is pained is a coward. For moral excellence is concerned with pleasures and pains; it is on account of the pleasure that we do bad things, and on account of the pain that we abstain from noble ones. Hence we ought to have been brought up in a particular way from our very youth, as Plato says, so as both to delight in and to be pained by the things that we ought; for this is the right education.

Aristotle, *Nicomachean Ethics*. Public Domain.

Discussion Question(s)

1. Is Aristotle's conception of human nature plausible? Is reason what most makes us human? If so, how might that insight impact sport?
2. Can Aristotle's conception of "happiness" as "contemplation" be reconciled with a life dedicated to sport, play and games? If so, how? If not, why not?
3. Speculate on how most athletes, coaches and fans think and behave. Do they generally see "happiness" in terms of "pleasure," "honor," or "contemplation"? Why? How might someone who is convinced that Aristotle is right, convince others to view sport as more than "pleasure" or "honor"?

Selection #2: Lee Lowenfish, *Branch Rickey*, Chapter 17: "An historic meeting in Brooklyn," pp. 371–384.

Introduction: In this chapter from Lee Lowenfish's biography of *Branch Rickey*, we get an account of Rickey's first meeting with Jackie Robinson. Robinson, who had been a standout athlete at UCLA, broke Major League Baseball's color barrier in 1947 after he was signed by Rickey to a professional contract with the Brooklyn Dodgers. This meeting and its aftermath vividly display the impact that virtues— such as courage—can have in the world of sport. As you read the historical details of this meeting between these two men, consider how and why Rickey and Robinson had the courage to act, when so many others could not or would not do so.

Shortly after V-J Day Branch Rickey called Clyde Sukeforth into his Brooklyn office. Sukeforth, a taciturn native of Maine, was one of the most trusted members of Rickey's inner circle. A former backup Major League catcher, he played for ten seasons in the Major Leagues before his career was curtailed because of a hunting accident. He retired with a .264 ʙᴀ and .331 sᴀ in 1,237 at-bats, and by the 1940s he had become a valuable jack-of-all-trades for the Dodgers as scout, pitching coach, Minor League instructor, and manager. Earlier in the 1945 season, at age forty-three, Sukeforth had even caught some games for the Dodgers when Leo Durocher's squad was strapped for healthy bodies.

Of all Rickey's evaluators Sukeforth was the only one who had yet to see Jackie Robinson in action. To get another independent viewpoint about the player's abilities and limitations, Rickey told him to go to Chicago, where Robinson would be playing for the Kansas City Monarchs against the Chicago Lincoln Giants. Knowing George Sisler's reservation that Robinson might not have a Major League shortstop's arm, Rickey advised Sukeforth to carefully observe his throwing. "If you like what you see, Clyde, bring him back with you to Brooklyn," Rickey said. "If he can't get away from his team, well, maybe I will come out and see him." The scout made a mental note that if Branch Rickey would be willing to travel to Chicago to see the player in person, his own mission was not merely about looking to sign a prospect for the Brooklyn Brown Dodgers. "This could be the real thing," Sukeforth thought.[1]

On August 24, 1945, Sukeforth arrived at Comiskey Park in Chicago and introduced himself to Robinson as a scout for Mr. Branch Rickey, who was running the Brooklyn Brown Dodgers of the new United States League. Sukeforth said that Mr. Rickey was interested in him and would like to evaluate his throwing arm. Robinson had scarcely heard of Branch Rickey and was understandably suspicious of strangers peddling him baseball stories (as he had discovered at the bogus Boston Red Sox tryout). Anyway, he was injured, having hurt his shoulder stumbling on the ground going into the shortstop hole, and would be unable to play for a few days. "Don't make a regular throw," Sukeforth told Robinson. "Just field a fungo grounder and make an underhand toss to first."[2] The player consented to make a few throws from shortstop to the scout, who, dressed in street clothes, caught the tosses at first base. Since Robinson couldn't play for about a week, Rickey's emissary invited him to come to Brooklyn to meet his boss.

Robinson did not know what to make of Sukeforth's proposition, but he accepted the scout's invitation to get more acquainted at Sukeforth's hotel after the Negro League game. As they entered Chicago's Stevens Hotel late that evening, Sukeforth slipped a little money to the elevator operator to allow Robinson to accompany him in the passenger elevator and not endure the indignity of having to use the freight elevator.[3] As they began to get to know each other, Sukeforth was immediately impressed by Robinson's intelligence, directness, and seriousness. The scout asked him about his army experience, and Robinson mentioned that an old football ankle injury contributed to his discharge but that it posed no problem in playing baseball.

Sukeforth told Robinson that he was heading out on another scouting trip to Toledo, but that if the player were interested, he should meet him in Toledo and they would go to Brooklyn together. Injured, and not thrilled at the chaotic conditions in the Negro Leagues, where he had been playing only since April, Robinson agreed. He told Monarchs manager Frank Duncan that he had to go away on a private business matter. Duncan had not been happy when his shortstop left to try out for the Red Sox in April and was less pleased now, but since he couldn't really stop the player from going, he just urged him to return to the Monarchs as soon as possible.

---

[1] Clyde Sukeforth as told to Donald Honig, "Oh! They Were a Pair," reprinted in Tygiel, ed., *The Jackie Robinson Reader*, 67 (originally published in Honig, *Baseball: When the Grass Was Real*).
[2] Mann, *The Jackie Robinson Story*, 28.
[3] Rampersad, *Jackie Robinson: A Biography*, 125.

Robinson met Sukeforth at the Toledo ballpark, and after the game the two men headed for the train station. The scout asked for two seats together in the same Pullman sleeper car. "Yes, together," Sukeforth told the ticket seller. At daybreak Sukeforth asked Robinson if he wanted to have breakfast, but the player said that "he'd eat with the boys," meaning the Pullman porters.[4] When they arrived in New York, Sukeforth went to a hotel in Brooklyn and Robinson went to the Theresa Hotel on 125th Street in Harlem, one of the better-known lodgings in the black community.

At ten o'clock the next morning, Tuesday August 28, 1945, Clyde Sukeforth and Jackie Robinson entered Branch Rickey's fourth-floor office at the Dodgers team headquarters on 215 Montague Street in downtown Brooklyn. Rickey was seated behind a large mahogany desk in a luxurious leather swivel chair, a legacy from former general manager Larry MacPhail. Above him was a giant elk head, a hunting memento given to MacPhail by pitcher Curt Davis.[5] Framed on the walls were photos of Rickey's granddaughters, Caroline and Nancy Rickey (Branch Rickey Jr.'s daughters), Leo Durocher, and the late Charley Barrett, and a portrait of Abraham Lincoln. Off to the side in an illuminated tank were some goldfish, nervously swimming back and forth, exhibiting an uneasiness that Robinson later said matched his own.[6]

In introducing the player to his boss, Clyde Sukeforth said, "Mr. Rickey, this is Jack Roosevelt Robinson of the Kansas City Monarchs. I think he is the Brooklyn kind of player." Branch Rickey rose from his seat, placing his omnipresent cigar in his left hand while offering Robinson a warm handshake. Rickey sat down and "just stared and stared, . . . stared at him as if he was trying to get inside the man," remembered Sukeforth, the only eyewitness to the meeting. "And Jack stared right back at him. Oh, they were a pair, those two! I tell you, the air in that office was electric."[7]

Rickey finally broke the silence. As we have seen, he usually gave a third degree to any potential employee, finding out as quickly as possible about a person's family background, religion, job experience, marital status, ambition, intelligence, and ability to think and express oneself on one's feet. At the Robinson interview, however, Branch Rickey changed the order around, asking immediately, "Do you have a girl?" "I think so," came the reply. "What do you mean, 'I think so'?" Rickey retorted. "Well, a ballplayer's life keeps him away from home so much that I don't know if she is still waiting for me," Robinson said. "Do you love her?" Rickey asked. "Oh, yes, Mr. Rickey, I love her very much. Rachel's a very special girl." "Well, marry her!" Rickey said to a man he had met only moments earlier. "A man needs a wife and a good home, especially when he has a man's work to do."

Rickey went on to ask Robinson about his church affiliations, and he was elated to learn that Robinson was a God-fearing, church-going Protestant. Rickey may have asked Robinson the name of his pastor, and he might have recognized the name of the Reverend Karl Downs, who, seven years earlier in Chicago, had attended with Rickey in Chicago a two hundredth anniversary commemoration of John Wesley's conversion. When Robinson told Rickey that he didn't drink, the executive's eyes lit up approvingly. (Once, while on a double date with a Kansas City Monarch teammate, Robinson threw a glass of whiskey into a lighted fire-place to dramatize the dangers of alcohol.)[8] If the subject of Robinson's birthday came up, Rickey undoubtedly would have been pleased that the

---

[4] Sukeforth as told to Honig, "Oh! They Were a Pair," 69.
[5] Taylor, "Borough Defender—I," 21.
[6] Mann, *Branch Rickey: American in Action*, 220.
[7] Sukeforth as told to Honig, "Oh! They Were a Pair," 69. See also an interview with Clyde Sukeforth by Gene Karst, Branson MO radio station KSOZ, 1978. I am indebted to the late Gene Karst for sharing this tape with me.
[8] Rampersad, *Jackie Robinson: A Biography*, 118.

ballplayer was born on the same day as Branch Rickey Jr., January 31, but five years later, in 1919. He was not young for a potential Major Leaguer, Rickey thought, but he was young enough.

Rickey next inquired about Robinson's situation in the Negro Leagues. "Are you under contract to the Kansas City Monarchs?" "No, sir, we don't have contracts," Robinson gave the answer that Rickey already knew, but he wanted to make sure. "Do you have any agreements—written or oral—about how long you will play for them?" "No, none at all. Just pay day to pay day," Robinson answered.

After he finished with his barrage of questions, Branch Rickey suddenly looked deep into Jack Robinson's eyes. "Do you know why you were brought here?" he asked. "Something about the Brown Dodgers and a new Negro league?" Robinson replied tentatively. "No, that isn't it," Rickey exclaimed. "I want you to play for the Brooklyn Dodgers organization. Perhaps on Montreal to start with."

"Montreal? Play for Montreal?" Robinson exclaimed. He did not like the life in the Negro Leagues, he was openly critical of it, and once he proved a success in the big leagues in 1947, he wrote scathingly in *Ebony* magazine about the poor working conditions and dissolute behavior in the Negro Leagues.[9] He was eager to escape the second-class conditions of the segregated leagues, but he didn't expect an offer to aim directly for the Major Leagues.

If the opportunity to make the Major Leagues and become a race pioneer in the process overwhelmed and excited Robinson, he wasn't prepared for the next stage in the momentous meeting. "I know you're a good ballplayer," Rickey exclaimed. "What I don't know is whether you have the guts." When physically challenged Robinson always was quick to defend his manhood. He told Rickey that he wasn't afraid of anybody or anything on a playing field. Rickey interrupted. "I'm looking for a ball player with guts enough not to fight back," he roared.

Branch Rickey, the dramatic actor manqué, Lionel Barrymore playing Thaddeus Stevens, began to describe vividly and act out physically the threats Robinson would endure as the first black player in twentieth-century Major League Baseball. Rickey took off his jacket and got down on the floor, imitating a base runner sliding into second, kicking Robinson in the shins, imitating the actions of a racist opponent barreling into Robinson with spikes vengefully high. He probably shouted the "n" word and voiced other epithets that opponents would yell at Robinson. He asked the stunned athlete how he would react when white waiters wouldn't serve him on the road, railroad conductors turned their backs on him, and other situations of discrimination in America arose that Rickey deplored but felt that he could change through the actions of a great black baseball player. The key to the success, Rickey stressed, was that Robinson could not fight back against the indignities.

Suddenly, the passionate executive pulled out of his desk drawer a heavily marked passage from one of his favorite books, Giovanni Papini's *The Life of Christ*. Papini (1881–1956) had been a Harvard student of William James, the philosopher-psychologist who wrote "The Moral Equivalent of War," one of Rickey's favorite essays. Papini had been an atheist, but in researching his history of the life of Jesus Christ, he had became an enthusiastic convert to Christianity. Papini's book had moved Rickey to order copies for all his children one Christmas.[10]

---

[9] Robinson, "What's Wrong with the Negro Leagues," 16–18. In September 1947 Robinson and his wife and infant son appeared on the cover of *Ebony* with the caption "Family Man."
[10] Interview with Jane Rickey Jones, Elmira NY, August 1999.

Branch Rickey read Jackie Robinson the words from Jesus that Papini had underscored: "Ye have heard that it hath been said, An eye for an eye, and a tooth for a tooth: But I say unto you, That ye resist not evil: But whosoever shall smite thee on thy cheek, turn to him the other also." After listening to Branch Rickey's amazing mixture of oratory and psychodrama, Jack Roosevelt Robinson said simply, "I have two cheeks, Mr. Rickey. Is that it?" Rickey nodded with deep satisfaction.

The executive did not yet know the extent of Jackie Robinson's competitiveness and will to win, which Rickey would later compare to Ty Cobb's. Yet, after their initial Brooklyn meeting of almost three hours Rickey's intuition told him he had found his man. Branch Rickey sensed in Jackie Robinson everything that he wanted in a race pioneer—great talent, fierce competitiveness, good personal and family values, and a commitment to uplift his race. Clyde Sukeforth remembered that when Robinson promised Rickey at the end of the interview that he would provoke no racial incident, "Well, I thought the old man was going to kiss him."[11]

"Nobody will ever know the hell Robinson went through in those [first] seasons," Rickey told *Newsweek* sports columnist John Lardner ten years later. "He has never opened his face about it, about the details. He never will. Proud man. When *he* made it, it was made."[12] For his part Robinson was immediately won over by Rickey's compelling combination of competitiveness and spirituality. He recalled that at their first meeting, his, "piercing eyes looked at me with such meticulous care, I felt almost naked," but once he got to know him, he felt that "he was like a piece of mobile armor, and he would throw himself and his advice in the way of anything likely to hurt me."[13]

Robinson was captivated by Rickey's recounting of a favorite "trouble ahead, trouble ahead" story about an old Ohio couple taking their first railroad trip. They were afraid that their train would not make it through the mountains and would plunge over a precipice. Yet they reached their destination safely, and Rickey told Robinson, "That's the way it is with most trouble ahead in this world, Jackie—if we use the common sense and courage God gave us. But you've got to study the hazards and build wisely."[14]

As their initial meeting drew to a close, Rickey reached into his drawer and offered Robinson a standard Minor League contract for a player assigned to the Dodgers' highest-classification team, the Montreal Royals in the International League. He would receive $600 a month, and also a $3,500 signing bonus, a relatively high figure from Branch Rickey, a man who loathed the concept of bonuses for unproven talent. Yet he rightly saw Robinson as a special case and expected that he was getting a bargain as a baseball businessman.

At the end of their historic first meeting, Branch Rickey's last words were to admonish Jackie Robinson to follow strict secrecy about their meeting. Robinson could tell his family and his fiancee, Rachel Isum, but no one else. Rickey had not yet decided on when to announce "The Young Man from the West" as his race pioneer.

Ideally, Rickey wanted to wait until the end of the regular college football season in late November or even until after the bowl games on New Year's Day. Local New York City politics, however, forced him to move up his timetable. During the summer of 1945 an End Jim Crow in Baseball Committee, supported by Communist New York City councilman Benjamin B. Davis, was picketing the three Major League ballparks with photographs of

---

[11] Sukeforth as told to Honig, "Oh! They Were a Pair," 70. See also Lincoln, "A Conversation with Clyde Sukeforth," 72–73.

[12] Lardner, "The Old Emancipator," pt. 1, 88 (emphasis in original).

[13] Robinson as told to Smith, *Jackie Robinson: My Own Story*, 21; United Press International obituary for Branch Rickey, *Columbus (Ohio) Dispatch*, December 10, 1965, 2A.

[14] J. Robinson, "Trouble Ahead Needn't Bother You," 239.

dead and wounded black soldiers. Underneath the graphic pictures was the caption "Good enough to die for their country but not good enough to play for organized baseball."[15]

New York City mayor Fiorello LaGuardia also wanted positive action on racial equality. Unlike the late President Franklin Roosevelt, LaGuardia had decided not to run for a fourth term as mayor, but the onetime Italian immigrant wanted to add a farewell laurel of improved race relations to his progressive legacy. LaGuardia urged all three local Major League teams to join his Committee for Unity, which had been established in the wake of the Harlem race riots in 1943, and to make a pledge to conform to the Ives-Quinn antidiscrimination law and sign black players as soon as possible.

Branch Rickey for the Dodgers and Larry MacPhail for the Yankees had pledged their teams' willingness to join the Committee for Unity, but the Giants' Horace Stoneham, who had inherited the team from his father Charles Stoneham in 1936, rejected the mayor's appeal in no uncertain terms. He denounced the "professional do-gooders" on LaGuardia's committee for interfering with the private enterprise of the baseball business. Although Larry MacPhail did agree to give the Yankees' tacit support to a call for integration, he privately supported Stoneham. MacPhail wanted no part of a committee made up of what he also branded as "social and political drum-beaters."[16]

The executive director of the Committee for Unity, New York University sociology professor Daniel K Dodson, hoped that Branch Rickey would view things differently and was delighted when he hit it off immediately with the paternal Brooklyn executive. Once again Rickey struck up a friendship with a man of similar background and convictions. The sociologist Dodson, the son of poor white sharecroppers, was raised in the small Texas town of Mt. Vernon and had attended McMurry College, a small Texas school named after a Methodist bishop. After earning a master's degree from Southern Methodist University in Dallas, he obtained his doctorate at New York University. Dodson belonged to the Christ Methodist Church in New York and was active in the Boy Scouts, the Girl Scouts, and the YMCA. His views on education were similar to Rickey's in that he believed that true learning occurred less from "erudition" than through "community involvement."[17]

Branch Rickey found in Daniel Dodson such a kindred spirit that, after the baseball executive's investigators performed a background check on the sociologist to make sure he had no left-wing tinge in his back-ground, he brought him into his confidence. He told Dodson about the Dodgers' already advanced scouting of black players and confided that at least one and possibly several black players would be signed before the start of the 1946 season. The two men discussed in detail the least painful way to reveal the breaking of the color line in baseball to players, fans, owners, and the society at large. Dodson thought that the sooner Rickey made his decision public, the better prepared everyone would be for the dramatic change in the 1946 season. To allow sufficient time for the white players to adjust to the new working conditions, the sociologist suggested that the end of the 1945 baseball season might be the ideal time for the announcement. Dodson also forewarned Rickey that Mayor LaGuardia wanted quick action on ending discrimination, preferably before the November election.[18]

---

[15] Tygiel, *Baseball's Great Experiment*, 69.

[16] Dan W. Dodson, "The Integration of Negroes in Baseball," *Journal of Educational Sociology* (October 1954), reprinted in Tygiel, ed. *The Jackie Robinson Reader*, 158; Mann, *The Jackie Robinson Story*, 23.

[17] *New York World-Telegram and Sun*, February 21, 1964, clipping in the Dodson Papers, New York University Bobst Library.

[18] Dodson, "The Integration of Negroes in Baseball," 162–63.

Rickey preferred waiting until after the election for he too, like his fellow baseball owners, had an aversion to being labeled a "do-gooder." However, circumstances hastened Rickey's announcement. Early in October 1945 the LaGuardia Committee on Unity issued what it called a "tentative proposal submitted purely on the basis of discussion." The report listed the pros and cons of prospective racial integration in baseball. Problems of acceptance in the South during spring training and among southern players year-round were noted. Difficulties in hotel arrangements in border cities were also mentioned, but the working draft concluded forcefully that there was "little doubt that New York City's baseball public would certainly support the integration of Negroes on the basis of their abilities. There was never a more propitious moment than the present, when we are just concluding a terrible World War to suppress the theory of racial superiority, to put our house in order."[19]

When Rickey learned from Dodson that Mayor LaGuardia planned to make baseball integration the subject of his regular Sunday afternoon radio address on October 18, 1945, the baseball executive decided that he must act quickly. He implored Dodson to use his influence on the mayor to postpone his talk on racial justice because, shortly, there would be favorable news on integration in baseball. Dan Dodson had not known Branch Rickey for very long, but he put his reputation on the line when he convinced LaGuardia to change the subject for his weekly radio remarks. The mayor chose to devote his Sunday radio talk to a general plea for patriotism and community service instead of a call for specific actions on behalf of racial equality.[20]

Branch Rickey hurriedly got in touch with Jackie Robinson, who, fortunately, was in New York, preparing to leave soon for ten weeks of winter baseball in Venezuela. Rickey instructed Robinson to go to Montreal for a press conference on Tuesday, October 23, 1945. He would be accompanied by Branch Rickey Jr., director of the Dodgers' Minor League operations.

Shortly before the blockbuster announcement, Branch and Jane Rickey dropped in for a social visit with their friends broadcaster Lowell Thomas and his wife on Quaker Hill, north of New York City. When Rickey confided to Thomas the news of the forthcoming signing, the broadcaster was aghast. According to Rickey's oldest daughter, Mary Rickey Eckler, who was also visiting that day, Lowell Thomas predicted, "Branch, all hell will break loose!" The Dodgers president disagreed. "No, Lowell," he said. "All heaven will rejoice."[21]

On the afternoon of Tuesday, October 23, 1945, the press corps in Montreal gathered for a "major announcement." They had no idea what the news would be, although many writers hoped that it would involve the hiring of Babe Ruth as the new manager of the local team. The scribes nodded hello to team co-owner Hector Racine and greeted Branch Rickey Jr., who had been to Montreal many times in his role as farm director. They were stunned when in strode athletic, black Jack Roosevelt Robinson, who was introduced as the newest member of the Brooklyn Dodgers organization. The writers were told that Robinson would have every chance to make the Montreal Royals in the upcoming 1946 season.

Scheduling Robinson's first professional season in Montreal was a wise strategy because there was no deep tradition of white racism in Canada, which had relatively few

[19] Polner, *Branch Rickey: A Biography*, 171.
[20] Polner, *Branch Rickey: A Biography*, 172.
[21] Sam Roberts, "Faster than Jackie Robinson: Branch Rickey's Sermons on the Mound," *New York Times*, April 13, 1997, sec. 4, 7; interview with Mary Rickey Eckler, Sebastopol CA, July 2000.

people of color. Even so, the reporters in attendance were astounded by the announcement. AI Parsley of the *Montreal Herald* wrote the next day: "This Robinson is definitely dark. His color is the hue of ebony. By no means can he be called a brown bomber or a chocolate soldier."[22] ("The Brown Bomber" was the nickname of heavyweight champion Joe Louis, who was deliberately being promoted as a mild-mannered, unthreatening figure in contrast to the defiantly black, white-womanizing Jack Johnson.)

Genuinely gifted in his public speaking, Jack Robinson was poised and modest in his comments. "Of course, I can't begin to tell you how happy I am that I am the first member of my race in organized baseball," he said. "I can only say I'll do my very best to come through in every manner."[23] For his part Branch Rickey Jr. made it a point to mention how thorough the Dodgers' scouting had been in discovering Robinson, even noting the figure of $25,000 spent on the project. (Harold Parrott later suggested that mentioning the money was a way for Rickey Sr. to refute the ongoing allegations in the tabloids that he was "El Cheapo.")[24] Branch Jr. noted: "Undoubtedly [we] will be criticized in some sections of the United States where racial prejudice is rampant." He said that the Dodgers were "not inviting trouble, but they won't avoid it if it comes." Branch Jr. admitted that "some players now with us may even quit," he also predicted that "they'll be back in baseball after they work a year or two in a cotton mill."[25]

The reaction of Rickey's colleagues in the baseball business ranged from skeptical to positively vitriolic. For Judge William Bramham, president of the National Association, the governing body of the Minor Leagues, breaking the color line was a serious breach of American social mores. Speaking from his office in Durham, North Carolina, the Minor League chief denounced Rickey as one of "those of the carpetbagger stripe of the white race" who "under the guise of helping" are really using black people "for their own selfish interests that retard the race." Bramham added sarcastically: "Father Divine will have to look to his laurels, for we can expect Rickey Temple to be in the course of construction in Harlem soon."[26] Clark Griffith and Larry MacPhail added their critical voices, denouncing Rickey's move as a selfish act by a notoriously manipulative colleague.

Most players were noncommittal, although, as the younger Rickey predicted, many southern-born players did not take the news easily and resented the reference to returning to the cotton mills if they didn't like the new development. Privately, many of Robinson's future teammates on the Dodgers were worried about the competition of a black man for their jobs as well as about bad reactions from racially conservative people back home. The aptly named Dixie Walker said, "As long as he isn't with the Dodgers, I'm not worried."[27] Bob Feller, ace pitcher for the Cleveland Indians, opined that on the basis of playing some exhibition games against Robinson, he "couldn't foresee any future" for him. He is "so tied up in the shoulders and couldn't hit an inside pitch to save his neck," Feller said. "If he were a white man I doubt they would even consider him as big league material."[28]

The pitcher's critique was shared by *Daily News* columnist Jimmy Powers, coiner of the "El Cheapo" epithet against Rickey, which he was beginning to use with ever-greater frequency. Powers dismissed Robinson's chances as "1,000 to 1." If Robinson weren't

[22] Tygiel, *Baseball's Great Experiment*, 72.
[23] Rampersad, *Jackie Robinson: A Biography*, 129.
[24] Parrott, *The Lords of Baseball*, 98.
[25] Tygiel, *Baseball's Great Experiment*, 72.
[26] Tygiel, *Baseball's Great Experiment*, 79·
[27] Mann, *The Jackie Robinson Story*, 150.
[28] Rampersad, *Jackie Robinson: A Biography*, 130.

black, he wrote, he would have been assigned to class C. As the Robinson saga evolved into a major story, Powers impugned any possible humanitarian motive of Rickey's, even using the loaded metaphor that readers not be misled by a man who claims to "have a heart big as a watermelon."[29]

Rickey didn't think that most of the writers would be as vitriolic as Powers, but he was acutely aware that the press coverage of the Robinson breakthrough would be crucial to its success. He hired the respected New York sportswriter Frank Graham to survey his colleagues' reaction to the signing.[30] Most scribes viewed Robinson's signing with an open mind, although they also expressed some skepticism and fear of the uncharted waters Rickey and Robinson were entering.

Two reactions, one white and one black, definitely encouraged the executive. In a column titled "Rickey Explodes a Bomb," the *New York Herald-Tribune's* AI Laney wrote about Jimmie Odoms, a retired Pullman porter, and big baseball fan, who swept the floors of the newspaper's office. A close follower of the Negro Leagues, Odom praised Rickey for his strategy of integration. "Pick out just one good boy. Put him in the minors and let him come up," Odoms said, predicting, "He gonna make it and when he do, . . . the stars ain't gonna fall . . . . They'll be plenty kids ready to try it after Robinson makes good."[31] With words that warmed Branch Rickey's staunch Republican heart, Sam Lacy of the *Baltimore Afro-American* wrote: "Alone, Robinson represents a weapon far more potent than the combined forces of all our liberal legislation."[32]

Rickey was also heartened by the thoughts of Hearst newspaper columnist Bill Corum, who urged in the *New York Journal-American* that Robinson's signing not become "a cause celebre" but should be welcomed by "common sense." Corum and Rickey shared the bonds of a small-town Midwest upbringing (the writer hailed from Boonville, Missouri) and their participation in the Chemical Warfare Service of World War I, when Corum was the youngest and Rickey was the oldest major in the same cause. "Good luck to Rickey! Good luck to Robinson!" Corum concluded his column. "Good luck to baseball, which may be a little slow on the uptake, but which usually gets around to doing the sensible thing in the long run."[33]

Reaction within the Negro League community was generally favorable. Although it has been said that he was embittered by not being selected as the pioneer, Satchel Paige was gracious at the news of Robinson's selection. "They didn't make a mistake by signing Robinson," Paige said. "They couldn't have picked a better man."[34] Negro American League president J. B. Martin also praised Rickey. "I feel that I speak the sentiment of 15 million Negroes in America who are with you one hundred per cent," Martin said. "[We] will always remember the day and date of this great event."[35]

Other Negro league officials were more critical, especially the co-owners of the Kansas City Monarchs, J. L. Wilkinson and Thomas Baird, who were understandably upset that Rickey had signed Robinson without compensating the Monarchs in any way. Baird said sharply, "Rickey reminds me of the man who walked into the room with a rope and at the end of the rope was a horse."[36] The Monarchs owners even contemplated suing

---

[29] Tygiel, *Baseball's Great Experiment*, 74.

[30] Polner, *Branch Rickey: A Biography*, 173.

[31] AI Laney, *New York Herald Tribune*, October 25, 1945, 26.

[32] Tygiel, *Baseball's Great Experiment*, 75.

[33] Corum, *Off and Running*, 232.

[34] Rowan with Robinson, *Wait till Next Year*, 123.

[35] Rampersad, *Jackie Robinson: A Biography*, 131.

[36] Quoted in Lowenfish, "Sport, Race and the Baseball Business," 10.

Rickey for stolen property, but they were quickly dissuaded by other Negro League officials, who didn't want it to appear that they were standing in the way of Robinson's and other black players' advancement.

The combative Rickey insisted that he did nothing wrong in his signing of Robinson. "There is no Negro league as such, as far as I am concerned," he repeated defiantly, maintaining the same stance he had taken since he had condemned the Negro Leagues in May 1945 as "zones in the form of a racket."[37] However, in the future, as he made plans to soon sign more Negro League players (two of them destined to be great Brooklyn stars, catcher Roy Campanella of the Baltimore Elite Giants and nineteen-year-old pitcher Don Newcombe of the Newark Eagles), the executive made certain that the black players put into writing the lack of contractual agreements with their Negro League teams.[38]

As Thanksgiving 1945 neared, Rickey looked back at the momentous year with a sense of relief and anticipation. The war at last was over and, as he had predicted and felt in every fiber of his heart and mind, the Allies had won over the forces of totalitarianism and darkness. The human cost of war always pained the idealist in Branch Rickey, but he accepted the sad reality that in war as in sports, "You have to pay the price."

He did worry about the shape of the peace to come. As a fervent, idealistic, anti-Communist Christian, Rickey foresaw threats from expanding Communism in Europe and Asia, and it is likely that he foresaw by the end of 1945 how fearful and paralyzing the "Cold War" would become. Yet, on the level he was most acquainted with, youth and sports, Rickey was guardedly optimistic. "I am sometimes quite anxious about the period of transition these young folks will need to go through," he wrote to Franklin P. Cole, his minister at the Church-of-the-Gardens in Forest Hills, who was still on active duty as an army chaplain, "but they have a way of coming out on top."[39]

Most of all Branch Rickey was happy that his sons-in-law had all returned unharmed from the war. One of them, Robert Terry Jones, a Burroughs School graduate from St. Louis who married Rickey's second-oldest daughter, Jane, would be going, so to speak, into the family business as business manager and radio announcer for the Dodgers' Fort Worth franchise in the double-A Texas League. Bob Jones liked to refer to himself, kiddingly, as "Mr. Jane Rickey Jones," because, though he may have married a Rickey daughter, the enormous vital presence of Branch and Jane Rickey was always there. Mary Rickey's husband, John Eckler, also liked to call himself, at times, Mr. Mary Rickey Eckler.[40]

Bob Jones earned the rank of colonel in the military, but he was not a career soldier and was eagerly looking forward to resuming his life as a civilian and a family man. Before he left for Texas, however, Jones was told by one member of the Brooklyn Dodgers organization that he should capitalize on his military status. "I think you should keep the title Colonel," Rickey's partner Walter O'Malley told Jones before he headed south. "No, that's not really my style," Jones replied.[41]

It was not the first or the last time that a Branch Rickey supporter and Walter O'Malley would disagree. There would be friction between the two strong-willed partners starting

[37] Lanctot, *Negro League Baseball*, 281.
[38] Roy Campanella to Branch Rickey, August 6, 1946, Branch Rickey Papers, Library of Congress, Washington DC. There are similar letters from Negro League pitchers John Wright and Roy Partlow in the same folder—July 20 and August 12, 1946, respectively.
[39] Branch Rickey to Franklin Cole, November 16, 1945. Branch Rickey Papers, Library of Congress, Washington DC.
[40] Interview with Robert Jones, Elmira NY, August 1999.
[41] Interview, Robert Jones, August 1999.

in the first postwar season of 1946. However, as the energetic baseball executive prepared at long last for the first full year of peacetime baseball, he could not help but feel elated. The time had finally come to see whether his intense scouting and development of white and black players would succeed. Inevitably, there would be "trouble ahead, trouble ahead," but the ferocious gentleman felt that he was on the verge of a truly major accomplishment in both baseball and the larger American society.

Discussion Question(s)

1. This historical account of the first meeting between Branch Rickey and Jackie Robinson obviously demonstrates the importance of courage. Arguably, however, the other three cardinal virtues are manifest as well. Do you agree? If so, where can one identify prudence, justice and moderation in this account?

2. Which of the Cardinal Virtues is the most important in this specific situation? Why?

3. Why did Rickey insist that "I'm looking for a ball player with guts enough not to fight back"? Why was such nonviolence so important to the success of the integration of Major League baseball?

Selection #3: Gregg Twietmeyer, "The Cardinal Virtues and Kinesiology," 2015, *Quest*, 67, pp. 119–137.

Introduction: In this article, Twietmeyer argues that the Cardinal Virtues are an important but neglected aspect of kinesiology. Kinesiology is the academic discipline which studies physical activity. As such, university kinesiology programs endeavor to produce good physical educators, coaches, athletic trainers, exercise scientists, and sport managers. But what makes a good "coach" or "athletic trainer" and how can kinesiology programs cultivate them? What counts as a successful kinesiology program? How should kinesiology programs define the good? Twietmeyer argues that such questions are impossible to answer until we give "due attention" to prudence, justice, courage, and temperance.

> *Because contrary to the wisdom of the bumper sticker,*
> *it is not enough these days to simply QUESTION AUTHORITY.*
> *You've got to speak with it, too.* (Mali, 2002)

It is clear from the conference theme—Tradition, Transition, and Transformation—that the 2015 NAKHE conference is about addressing both the past and the future. Here is how I would characterize the mission of this year's conference: NAKHE's leaders want to *reflect* upon the past, in hopes of *navigating* the choppy waters of the unsettled present, so as to *chart* a clear path to the future. This is not a new concern. In fact, many of the previous Delphine Hanna Lectures have focused on some aspect of this concern for *charting* a path forward.

Many answers for how this ought to be done have been offered. These include calls for an "enhanced national presence" (Dunn, 2009, p. 277), for the importance of problem solving and "strategic planning" (Buck, 2014, p. 142), and for an "interdisciplinary perspective" (DePauw, 2010, p. 345). Although fine in themselves, focusing on such recommendations is not without danger. For, if taken by themselves, that is, absent first principles, they become essentially technocratic solutions. Technocrats believe that the way forward for kinesiology lies in the implementation of what French sociologist Jacques Ellul (1997) called "technique." Ellul understood technique to be the hyper-rationalization of practices in pursuit of maximal efficiency. So understood, success in kinesiology becomes a matter of things, such as better management and design of curriculum, or of marketing the discipline more effectively, or of improving graduate student formation, or of increased scientific credentials purchased through the publication of ground-breaking research. What the technocratic vision of these proposals has in common is the belief that the future of kinesiology can be assured through better organization. As a result, the chief virtues of kinesiology become utility and efficiency, for they are the means by which we can *demonstrate progress*.[1]

The limitations inherent in this mindset should be apparent, for it constricts truth to that which is tangible and reduces success to productivity. In fact, the pursuit of any larger understanding of truth can seem a time-wasting barrier to progress. As Andrew Hawkins argued in his 2011 Hanna Lecture, "We have become so pragmatic, that asking the big questions seems to get in the way of getting the job done" (p. 261). Ellul (1997) put the same idea this way:

> Technique is the extreme development of means. Everything in the world dom-
> inated by technique is a means and only a means, while the ends have practi-
> cally disappeared. Technique does not develop towards attaining something. It
> develops *because* the world of means has developed. . . . At the same time, there
> is a suppression of meaning, the meaning of existence, the meaning of "why I
> am alive," as technique so vastly develops its power. (p. 40)

Although all of these goals for "reform," or "interdisciplinarity," or "leadership" are fine as far they go, they should not be considered sufficient in and of themselves. If and when they are considered sufficient, kinesiology will have become mere technique. Therefore, a larger vision of the meaning, purpose, and place of kinesiology in the academy and the world at large is necessary. Kinesiologists must be robustly concerned with truth. This *should* be an obvious and uncontroversial point. For even a commitment to the emaciated version of truth I have been describing, assumes a particular understanding of the good, the true, and the beautiful—namely utility and efficiency.

Yet, in the final analysis, the reduction of the good to the productive is incoherent. For if production is to have any real value, it must have an end, a purpose, a *telos* beyond itself.[2] Productivity must be in service of some larger good. Furthermore, just as efficiency is always open to the objection "to what end?" utility is always open to the objection "useful to whom?" Absent some objective conception of truth, utility is impossible to distinguish from the will to power, where calls for efficiency simply mask the desire of the powerful to defend the principle that "might makes right."

Therefore, absent a passionately articulated vision of the common good, grounded in truth, utility and efficiency reign supreme. In such situations, mission statements and visions quickly dissolve into vapid cant, that is, a vague and groundless optimism in

---

[1] What we are progressing toward and why we should want to achieve such progress is rarely defined.

[2] Ron Feingold (2013) made a similar point in his Hanna Lecture when he warned against the increasing calls for accountability and the likelihood that such calls will result in a stunted and emaciated version of success which celebrates "data for data's sake" (p. 387).

progress for progress sake. Once the naiveté and emptiness of such a position is exposed, an explicitly nihilistic philosophy takes its place, where belief, enthusiasm, and passion are either considered passé or mere masks for the will to power.[3] This is, I believe, the condition we will find kinesiology in if we emphasize "technique."[4] Absent first principals, passionately held, we are stillborn.

I intend to propose a different path. Kinesiologists cannot simply rely on technocratic adjustments, or curricular decisions, or growth in research prowess to move the discipline forward. As important as those things can be, and believe me, I know from experience how important they can be, they are not enough. They are necessary to the philosophy of kinesiology but they are not sufficient. So that I am not misunderstood, let me point to two examples of what I mean. One which I have lamented from the outside and one in which I was directly involved.

First, the University of Michigan, my alma mater, has dropped its physical education (PE) major for the fall of 2015 in favor of a non-teaching degree in health and fitness (Camilli-Whisenhunt, 2014). I have no doubt that the leadership of Michigan means well. This is clear from the fact that in an attempt to save the program, Michigan engaged in a vigorous but failed marketing campaign to find more physical education students. Moreover, the fracturing of curricula between different majors within kinesiology made enrollment numbers in the PE program a serious concern. If a PE class is only for PE majors, then it is hard to hold classes once your number of majors drops into the single digits, because you will not have enough other kinesiology students enrolled to justify offering the course. These are real problems that needed to be addressed. Michigan addressed them as best they knew how.

However, I must admit I am nevertheless deeply troubled by the decision. For whatever the motivation, whatever the "situation on the ground," the result is the same: a retreat from the front lines; an abandonment of those most vulnerable and most in need of our teaching, our coaching, and our example; a capitulation, a surrender to cultural trends, in pursuit of greater efficiencies, productivity, and prestige elsewhere; in short, an embrace of technique.

Why do I use such harsh language, when I am admittedly distant from the situation? Because of the weak, shallow and pragmatic rationale used to justify the decision.

It makes little sense to cite government statistics that, "the percentage of schools offering Physical Education at least three days a week has significantly decreased" (University of Michigan School of Kinesiology, n.d.a., p. 1). Similarly, the claim that enrollment in the major has "steadily declined" carries only pragmatic weight (University of Michigan School of Kinesiology, n.d.a., p. 1). After all, the fracturing of curricula was a choice—or set of choices—not an inevitability.

Finally, how can a school that prides itself on consisting of the "leaders and the best" believe that it is in any way relevant that "Michigan State and Albion [College] have discontinued their Physical Education programs" (University of Michigan School of Kinesiology, n.d.a., p. 2)? Whimsically, one might ask: "When has Michigan ever taken their marching orders from Michigan State?!" More seriously, simple logic dictates the following: The fact that something occurs is no evidence of its goodness. "Everybody else is doing it" is simply not a legitimate rationale to drop physical education.

Let me be clear. The curricular and enrollment problems at Michigan were real. As a practical matter, it may have been too late to save the program. Perhaps their hands were tied.

---

[3] One practical result of this is the unwillingness of so many of our students to be committed passionately to anything.
[4] It could be argued that this is the condition we find kinesiology in now.

I do not claim to know. What I do claim is this. As a matter of philosophy and as a matter of precedent, this decision was a disaster.

Why? Because it is a perverse inversion for kinesiologists, of all people, to argue that a lack of physical education in the schools *justifies* dropping the major. The lack of physical education in schools should suggest just the opposite.[5] If you believe what you are doing is important, if physical education is a vital good, then fight! If what we do matters, then these facts regarding disarray and decline are nothing more than a call to action. The solution to low enrollment is in principle simple, even if in practice it is hard. We must recruit more students, we must inspire more students, and we must *LEAD!* Dammit! We have to stop acquiescing! If we do not have pride in our discipline, if we will not stand up for ourselves, no one will![6]

We are fighting an uphill battle. We cannot tire, and, as my second example indicates, we cannot give up. As many of you know, I was trained as a sport philosopher at Penn State University, and I teach at Marshall University. For 7 years at Marshall, I have tried, in both word and deed, to stand up for a well-rounded and broad discipline in which the humanities are taken as seriously as the sciences. Nevertheless, despite all my efforts, I recently had to fight back a proposal to combine our sport ethics and sport law courses. This was put forth as a way to save credits in a time of tight budgets and shrinking faculty lines. In short, it was seen as greater efficiency. It was a change justified not by a sound philosophy of kinesiology but by technique.

To hear such things from one's own department, after years of work, is tiresome and disheartening. It is tempting to throw up one's hands and give in to despair. "How many times," one asks, "must I fight these battles?!?" The answer is as simple as it is hard to put into practice: *as many times as they arise.* So, I stood and I fought. I argued for the vitality of sport ethics in an age of cheating and academic scandals, as well as the vitality of sport law in an age of NCAA lawsuits, concussion lawsuits, and Title IX lawsuits. I argued, therefore, that our students needed more engagement with these sub-disciplines not less. I pointed out that just as one could not do justice to exercise physiology and biomechanics in one course, one could not do justice to sport ethics and sport law in one course. These arguments and the others I raised won the day because *I stood up* and vigorously defended the importance of keeping these classes independent. In fact, I am convinced it was vigor not logic that saved the courses. The point is a modest one. Win or lose, whether the winds are blowing for or against us, we must continue to stand up.

What each of these examples indicates is that the future of kinesiology will rest upon *character*. It is the good or bad *character* of kinesiologists that will shape the future of our discipline. Ultimately it is our virtues and vices, your virtues and vices, and my virtues and vices that will shape the future of the field. The reasons this is so are quite simple. The discipline of kinesiology is not only *made up* of people, the discipline of kinesiology is *about* people. It is *human* movement that we study. *The implications of this truth are wide and deep.* Let me reinforce just one. The success or failure of curricular reform, both in terms of passage and implementation, rises and falls on the good sense, that is, the character, of those faculty and administrators involved.

Kinesiology is dependent upon character. The discipline needs *good* kinesiologists to teach, conduct research, and serve the discipline. It needs a conception of the *good* person by which to cultivate the next generation of *good* sport managers, athletic trainers, exercise scientists, and physical educators. Technocratic efficiencies absent *good* character cannot be

---

[5] Consider, for example, what the reaction would be to statistics that suggested poor literacy in our schools.

[6] Unfortunately, it seems clear that many in the discipline do not see physical education as a vital area of kinesiology.

progress in anything, except perhaps a horrifying progress in evil. After all, efficiency is amoral. A commitment to efficiency alone *cares nothing* for right or wrong.[7]

This, then, is the key question: What is a *good* kinesiologist? I am convinced that the ancient and medieval tradition of the Cardinal Virtues sheds light on this question. The four Cardinal Virtues of prudence, justice, courage, and temperance are so called from the Latin *cardo* meaning "hinge." The Cardinal Virtues are said to be the hinge upon which all the other virtues rest or turn. They are the foundation of *good* character. This, then, is my answer: The good kinesiologist is prudent, just, courageous, and temperate.

Therefore, I believe it is incumbent upon kinesiologists to examine the Cardinal Virtues, in depth, in search of basic understanding and in search of answers to two important practical questions for the field: (a) What do prudence, justice, courage and temperance look like in kinesiology? and (b) How, if at all, can we cultivate and pass on these virtues to those who will quickly follow and then replace us as the caretakers of kinesiology?

To accomplish this goal will require that we proceed in the following manner. First, it will be necessary to individually define, examine, and clarify each of the virtues. Second, within each examination, the virtues will need to be applied to kinesiology. How, for example, does prudence inform kinesiology? Why is prudence necessary to be a good kinesiologist? Finally, I will close by examining the vexing question of whether or not virtue can be taught. Can virtue be cultivated within our discipline, or are such character traits merely innate?

In attempting to illuminate the Cardinal Virtues, I will of course be relying on the broad Platonic, Aristotelian, and Thomistic tradition which identified and cultivated the conception of the Cardinal Virtues. More specifically, I will focus on the work of the great German Thomistic philosopher Josef Pieper whose definitions of the virtues I will follow closely. Yet, before I do so, I must make one brief digression. For in my experience, "Aristotelean literacy," both within the discipline and academy at large, is not what it once was. Scholars are either ignorant of his philosophy or have only been exposed to caricatures. I think it would therefore be wise to lay out the skeletal structure of Aristotle's ethical philosophy. Hopefully, this will avoid any misunderstandings of the relevance of the Cardinal Virtues for leading a life well lived.

Aristotle begins the *Nicomachean Ethics* (2002) by examining the distinction between intrinsic and extrinsic goods. He argued that all actions "aim at some good" (1094a), some of which are ends in themselves and some of which are means to other ends. Ultimately, Aristotle argued, all actions aim at happiness, or as it is sometimes called, "human flourishing." There are three common definitions of happiness: pleasure, honor, and contemplation. Aristotle then rejected the first two options and argued that contemplation is the best definition of happiness, for it best matches up with human beings nature as "rational animals" (1098a).

As rational animals we are called to live in accord with reason by pursuing and cultivating those excellences, that is, those virtues which are in accord with our nature (1098a).

---

[7] "The eighteenth and nineteenth centuries abandoned the idea of spiritual or intellectual happiness in order to have this material happiness, consisting of a certain number of essential consumer goods. And hence, in the nineteenth century, happiness was linked to a well-being obtained by mechanical means, industrial means, production" (Ellul, 1997, pp. 34–35). The key point being—of course—the rejection of the importance of spiritual or intellectual happiness. There is nothing inherently wrong with improving the estate of man. The problem is the reduction of man to his "stomach."

We develop these virtues through habituation. Habit, however, is not an end, but the means by which we produce the *hexis*—the active conditions—which make up our character (1104b). To put it succinctly, if a little too simply, Aristotle argued that we become what we practice. Maturity depends on the development of good habits.

It should be clear then that the stock objection that Aristotle's defense of habit means he is advocating a philosophy which is not self-aware, authentic, or critical is far off the mark, for he is not advocating mindless rote repetition, but rather the development of character through practice. The goal of habituation is to build the skills necessary to live toward the world. Through habituation, we develop the *hexis*, the active condition of *being* prudent, or just, or courageous, or temperate. It is character, not mere reflex, which Aristotle advocated.

Of course, if there is any truth to the Aristotelian position, then it is vital to examine and understand the nature of the virtues we seek to cultivate. For just as one cannot cultivate the skills necessary to be a basketball player, or square dancer, or swimmer, without knowing what basketball, dance, or swimming are, one cannot cultivate prudence without knowing what the virtue of prudence is. It is, therefore, to such an examination of the nature of the Cardinal Virtues that I now turn.

Prudence

> One who does not know how things really are cannot do good; for the good accords with reality. (Pieper, *The Christian Idea of Man*, 2011, p. 13)

Prudence is the ability to see reality for what it is and the willingness to act upon it. As Pieper (1966) insisted, "He alone can do good who knows what things are like and what their situation is" (p. 10). As such, prudence is—even among the other Cardinal Virtues—the "first of the virtues" (Pieper, 2011, p. 13). Prudence, in its very nature, makes the exercise of justice or courage or moderation possible and therefore deserves more attention. Pieper (2011) explained the idea this way:

> The prudent person looks, on the one hand, at the objective reality of things and, on the other hand, at will and action. But he looks first to reality; and by virtue of and on the basis of his knowledge of reality he decides what is to be done and what not, and how it is to be done and how not. And so in truth all virtue is dependent upon prudence. (p. 14)

What then is our prudential situation in kinesiology? What is the objective reality in kinesiology? I would like to make several claims, some of which I am sure will garner wide agreement, and some of which I have little doubt will be controversial. In fact, "the contested nature of claims" is one prudential reality I think must be admitted. But before I digress to defend that claim, let me briefly outline the prudential claims I want to propose regarding kinesiology. Broadly speaking, there are only two. First, as already hinted at, we are temporary caretakers of kinesiology. This insight, though mundane, is important, for it is often forgotten. It is forgotten, I believe, because we are in state of denial about an even more fundamental reality, our own mortality. Second, there are schools of kinesiology. The search for consensus in kinesiology is—generally speaking—a mistake. We do not all believe the same things about kinesiology. Although common ground does exist, and should be pursued where possible, the different schools of kinesiology are irreconcilable. We must not be afraid to passionately defend our convictions, even when doing so implies that others are wrong.

To be a kinesiologist is to be a steward—to recognize one's inheritance, to maintain it, to attempt to improve it, and to pass it on. Stewardship relies on prudence, for good stewardship demands that we distinguish "what it is worth caring about a very great deal, from what it is worth caring about a good deal less, and both from what is not worth caring about at all" (MacIntyre, 2009, p. 178). Recognition of our mortality can help us soberly assess what is worth caring about. Our salaries, positions of authority, honors and awards, our curricular disagreements, our professional jealousies, and personal shortcomings, will all be soon forgotten. In the end, our power, prestige, and reputation mean very little; this is not to say that one should never care about such things. Rather it is to insist that prudence demands that we refuse to care about them a "very great deal."

Many of you may know that the root meaning of the word *secular* is not irreligion, but rather temporality. *To speak of the secular is to speak of the present age, a present age which is—whether we realize it or not—always passing away.* The French philosopher Remi Brague (2013) recently pointed out a less well known but related meaning. Secular can also mean a century, which was understood classically to be the limit of a human lifetime. This is why it was said that no one saw the Roman *ludi saeculares*—or secular games—more than once. For they were only offered once a century. Brague, then expounds on the import of this alternative meaning:

> The ancient usage draws on the fact that a saeculum, a century, is the temporal limit of living memory. It is the halo of possible experience that surrounds the life of the individual. I can keep a remembrance of my grandparents and, more seldom, of my great-grandparents. What my grandfather told me I can tell my grandchildren. I can reach back two generations and forward two, but rarely more, to a period spanning what amounts to a century. (p. 28)[8]

This is, I believe, what Delphine Hanna had in mind when she insisted that "I do not want my biography written. If my work was worthy it is still in progress" (Oberlin College, n.d.). While the impact of what we have done will endure, *what we have done* and *who we are* will, in very short order, be known only to God.[9]

The point could be made another way. Our most important work, be it personal or professional, is to cultivate the next generation, for we all will quickly be replaced. Our culture and our discipline will survive only as long as we are willing to confidently and unapologetically pass on the truths we have inherited.[10] This is an inherently interpersonal task. It is not a matter of technique but of relationships. Ethicist Timothy Fort (1990) put it this way: "[O]ur goal must not be to change everyone, but to be an example to the person working next to us" (p. 25).

We are temporary caretakers of kinesiology. We have inherited the discipline and we will leave it behind. Our vision must extend before and beyond the century of our own lives. What will we leave behind? What should we leave behind? The truth is—and this leads me to my second prudential insight—it depends upon whom you ask. The simple fact is there are different schools of kinesiology.

The first school of kinesiology is *scientific kinesiology*. The premier concern for proponents of this school is the generation of scientific credibility for the discipline through the production and dissemination of data based experimentation. Mark Latash (2008) beautifully summarized this school of kinesiology when he wrote that "The main

---

[8] Brague's overarching point is even more profound: Secular society is impossible . . . .
[9] A profound implication of this insight is that we should act in light of eternity rather than succumb to peer pressure, academic trends, or the "tide of history."
[10] Charles Murray (2012) has amply demonstrated what happens when the transmission of such cultural capital collapses.

challenge of motor control (and kinesiology in general) seems to be turning it into an exact science, just like physics" (p. 27). The emphasis, therefore, is upon hiring the best researchers, for the best labs, to procure the most grant money, all in hopes of proving kinesiology's scientific chops.

This school reaches back into the founding days of physical education, and you can hear echoes or see intimations of it in many of the early leaders of the discipline (Twietmeyer, 2012). Although there is considerable merit to the idea of increasing scientific rigor in kinesiology, it is not without significant limitations. Here, I will only mention one. As philosopher Doug Anderson (2002) has shown, a scientistic philosophy of kinesiology tends to ignore the human components of kinesiology. In the search for "useful generalizations in the form of descriptions, statistical relations, and natural laws" (p. 90), the subjective experience of moving well is lost. As a result, individual experiences are drowned under an avalanche of data. People are reduced to generalizable laws or principles or mechanisms. The cultural foundations, upon which all human endeavors rest, are lost from view.

The second school of kinesiology is *therapeutic kinesiology*. The premier concern for proponents of this school is using kinesiology to solve problems. The emphasis therefore is upon the application of sound management principles to contemporary problems, such as health, self-actualization, and social justice. Solutions will be found by using education to address the sociological, psychological, and cultural roots of inactivity. Scholars in this school tend to focus on socio-cultural issues, such as inclusion and identity, or on public health issues, such as the obesity crisis or the environment.

Again, although there is obvious merit in solving problems, I believe there are significant limitations to this approach, on both the socio-cultural and public health fronts. The primary socio-cultural danger of this approach is an attitude of triumphalist advocacy, where the assumptions of the late post-modern academy regarding human nature, psychology, and morality are not so much argued for, as they are simply taken for granted and then imposed upon others. Such an attitude of presumption ends up being anything but inclusive. Such an attitude inflicts problems upon people, which they themselves do not believe they have (Rittelmeyer, 2014).[11]

As Henrich, Heine, and Norenzayan (2010) have shown, the behavioral science upon which much of this self-confidence rests comes for a very narrow pool of research subjects. In fact, "a randomly selected American undergraduate is more than 4,000 times more likely to be a research participant [in social psychology research] than is a randomly selected person outside the West" (p. 63). Conclusions based on such non-random sampling can hardly be said to be universal. This reality, they argue, indicates that it is the Western, Educated, Industrialized, Rich, and Democratic (WEIRD) societies that are the outliers. WEIRD assumptions may be right, but they should not be presumed as self-evident.[12]

---

[11] This is often the result of identifying "problems" through top-down data-mining: "Much as mountains are climbed, so statistics are used if they are there" (Moynihan, 1965, p. 14).

[12] The danger that must be avoided is over-confidence. The social scientists must learn to turn their lens upon themselves. As Bruno Latour (1993) insightfully pointed out, a sound anthropology must confront not only the beliefs of others which "do not touch us directly" for "we are always critical enough of them" (p. 92). Instead academics must be willing to confront, by *the same critical standards*, their own cherished beliefs which they consider to be "the true knowledge to which [they] adhere totally." If and when this is done, academics will stop endorsing the naïve idea that although: "Error, [and] beliefs, could be explained socially" the "truth remained self-explanatory" (p. 92). Any real explanation must consider both truth and falsity by and through the same standards.

This insight certainly does not disprove any truth claims made from within WEIRD societies, but it does expose the pretense of assuming one's arguments have an unquestionable scientific veneer. As such, therapeutic kinesiologists who take up sociocultural issues should be more sensitive to both traditional and non-Western criticisms. They should take seriously and address the legitimate, even if mistaken, concerns of those whom with they disagree. Finally, they should admit they are not dispassionate social scientists but passionate advocates *who believe in* "critical theory," or "feminism," or what have you.

There are problems on the public health front as well. First, as Kretchmar (2005) pointed out, in a technology-driven society such as ours, physical activity will inevitably be seen as an inefficient and distasteful way to address problems, such as obesity. Instead research will focus on medicinal, surgical, and genetic ways to solve the problem. This is, of course, exactly what we find (Nestlé Group, 2014; Parry, 2014). It seems possible then, that in relatively short order, the claim that exercise is necessary to stay healthy will seem absurd, especially from within the now-dominant "medical view of health."

Most important however, is the limited intrinsic value of health. Health is a vital foundation for all that we do, but it is itself insufficient for human flourishing. No one puts, "I led a healthy life!" on their tombstone. Instead, health, as important as it is, is understood as a means by which we pursue the other goods of life. If kinesiology is going to be a vital rather than tertiary aspect of American education, we must show how we are about goods other than health.

The third school of kinesiology is *ludic,* or *liberal arts, kinesiology.* The premier concern for proponents of this school is the examination and development of kinesthetic skill. The emphasis therefore is upon understanding and building the place of kinesiology in human culture. Kinesiology, though legitimately pursued from different angles and sub-disciplinary perspectives from within this school, *is about one thing:* the importance of physical activity to human flourishing.[13] From the point of view of ludic kinesiology, the problem with the other schools is not science or the desire to solve problems. It is distraction—a shift of focus away from the heart of the discipline. As Ron Feingold insisted in his 2013 Hanna Lecture, we ought to "focus on instilling a love for a physically active lifestyle" (p. 392).

This is, as you might have already suspected, the school I endorse. It is also, I believe, the smallest of the three schools I have mentioned.[14] I endorse ludic kinesiology for theoretical, practical, and idiosyncratic reasons. Here I will expand only on the idiosyncratic, as I believe it ties together my two points regarding prudence in kinesiology and also points toward the next virtue to be examined, justice.

---

[13] Here is what I (Twietmeyer, 2012) am envisioning when I say "physical activity":

> Kinesiology is a human discipline, born of, and reliant upon the embodied, curious, political and rational nature of human beings. The field examines physical activity from a myriad of scholarly perspectives, with physical activity being understood not as an abstract or literal moniker, but rather as the placeholder term for culturally significant and recreative movement forms. Games, play, sport, exercise, dance (among others) are central to who we are and what we do. If physical activity is understood in this way, then the field is as reliant upon "ethics" as much as it is reliant upon "biology." Human *kinesis* is a function of all aspects of the human person whether those aspects are physiological *or just plain logical.* Kinesiology is neither a pure science nor solely a member of the humanities, but rather a field that necessarily encompasses both. (p. 20)

[14] This is a function of the congruence of the first two schools with the utilitarian and technocratic assumptions of our age.

Ludic kinesiology has made my life better. Play, games, and sport have been one of the great reminders to me throughout my life that *life is a good thing*! Running, jumping, kicking, and throwing have been great joys in my life! I grew up in a family where play, games, and sport were central aspects of family life. My father was a physical education teacher, coach, and professor of kinesiology, so we were never far from play opportunities, nor were we ever short on instruction, whether it was to "follow your shot" or "keep your eye on the ball." I grew up in a neighborhood full of unstructured play which included, among other things, capture the flag, driveway basketball, tackle football, laser tag, baseball, ice hockey, and bike soccer. Yet, I also engaged in structured play, be it in physical education class or by participating in youth soccer, baseball, or basketball.

Soccer was my primary organized sport through elementary and middle school. Once I got to high school, my attention shifted to baseball. During my freshman year, I was the starting centerfielder for much of the season. Although it would be hyperbole to say "I hated every minute of it," I was deeply unhappy participating on the team despite the significant playing time I received. Although I am sure that the typical problems of teenage awkwardness and socialization so prominent in the early years of high school played a role, the primary reason was much simpler to identify. For during almost of all my time patrolling center field, I was the DCF, the designated centerfielder; that is, I rarely, if ever, was allowed to hit. How a 9th-grade baseball coach, whose primary goal should have been pedagogy rather than lineup optimization, could rationalize such a decision, I do not know. Suffice it to say that it succeeded in only one thing, *driving me away from the game*.

The point of relaying this story, is neither voyeurism, nor to deliver a scolding. The point is that our behavior toward each other matters.[15] One's enjoyment, disposition, and participation in kinesiology is greatly influenced by the mood, temper, competence, and goals of those women and men in charge of our teams, leagues, parks, and physical education programs. The same is true, of course, regarding our labs, lecture halls, and offices. Sound practice will encourage and build kinesiology, while poor practice will discourage and weaken kinesiology. The fact, for example, that *any* 5-year-old kids, whom are all bubbling with excitement at the idea of running, jumping, kicking, and throwing, become middle-schoolers who sit on the sidelines because they "forgot" their gym clothes tells us something is terribly wrong. Far too often, our practice has been unsound.

Prudence makes clear that kinesiology, and the physical activity of which it is made, is a *cultural reality*, which is passed on from one person and one generation to the next. Furthermore, kinesiology is rooted in the larger culture which either values or denigrates it. Kinesiology cannot be decontextualized from that culture without becoming mere technique. The transmission of culture is necessarily dependent upon authority and tradition. We have to be taught to love kinesiology, but the success of this teaching rises or falls upon how well or how poorly we kinesiologists treat our charges, students, and players. Cultivation of this love in the next generation—even if it damages our reputation—is one of those thing about which we should care a "very great deal."

---

[15] The end of C. S. Lewis's (1949) great sermon *The Weight of Glory* gives this same idea a spiritual perspective:

> All day long we are, in some degree, helping each other to one or other of these destinations. It is in the light of these overwhelming possibilities, it is with the awe and the circumspection proper to them, that we should conduct all our dealings with one another, all friendships, all loves, all play, all politics. There are no ordinary people. You have never talked to a mere mortal. Nations, cultures, arts, civilizationthese are mortal, and their life is to ours as the life of a gnat. But it is immortals whom we joke with, work with, marry, snub, and exploit-immortal horrors or everlasting splendours. (pp. 45–46)

To succeed, we must treat those we hope to convert, as we ought to. We must treat them the way they deserve to be treated. If kinesthetic skill makes for a better life, then to deny that skill to others because of complacency, incompetence, or insecurity is to harm our fellow man. It is to fail to treat him as we ought. If this is right, then the growth of kinesiology relies upon justice.

Justice

Justice is the virtue which accords to each and every man what is his due.
(St. Augustine, 1958, p. 469)

Pieper (1966) began his examination of justice with the insight that "All just order in the world is based on this: that man give man what is his due. On the other hand, everything unjust implies that what belongs to a man is withheld or taken away from him—and once more, not by misfortune, failure of crops, fire or earthquake, but by man" (p. 44). Justice is an inherently relational virtue, which regards our duties to each other (commutative justice), the community's duties to the individual (distributive justice), and the individual's duties to the community (legal justice) (Pieper, 2011).

What, then, given these considerations, does justice demand in kinesiology? Much could be said. I am particularly tempted to discuss the elderly, the infirm, as well as those with disabilities or special needs. However, given the time constraints and the fact that these areas have garnered the attention of others in the discipline, I will focus on only one aspect of distributive justice, what writers have increasingly called the "sports industrial complex" and its relationship to the two prudential insights we have already examined.

The sports industrial complex can be understood as the developing culture of sport in America, which desires the professionalization, commodification, and utilization of all forms of organized sport for the purposes of garnering revenue, attention, power, and prestige. The problem here is not the presence of commercial interests as such, nor is the problem the pursuit of excellence. The problem is an imprudent skewing of priorities. Rather than pursuing excellence for its own sake, we pursue it for the attention, accolades, trophies, or scholarships it will allegedly produce. Rather than pursuing profit as a means to improve the quality, reach, or safety of sport, we use sport merely to maximize revenue. The sports industrial complex turns sport from pastime into technique.

The injustices that result are myriad. In youth sport, children are sifted, categorized, and evaluated too soon.[16] In fact, meaningless evaluations, because they are done so soon, are conducted with the utmost seriousness. What sense, for example, does it make to have a competitive golf tournament—such as the Callaway World Golf Championships—for 6 year olds? This tournament draws participants from around the world, despite the fact that, as ESPN reporter Tom Farrey (2008) pointed out, "the kids are still too young to fill out or tally up a scorecard" (p. 12). The injustice, of course, is that we are not treating children as children.

Children are also unjustly left behind because of this mindset. This results when they do not have the talent or funds necessary to participate on elite, travel, Amateur Athletic Union (AAU), or select teams.

The costs involved are not trivial. The *San Francisco Gate* (Killion, 2013), for example, reported recently that "dues at elite volleyball clubs can run $3,500, with another $3,000 required for travel" (para. 9). As Farrey (2008) pointed out, this mindset, and the costs

---

[16] Worse yet, they are valued not for who they are, but for what they can or cannot procure for the team, coach, or school.

involved, leave behind the "late bloomer, the genetically ordinary, the economically disadvantaged, the child of a one-parent household, the physically and mentally disabled, and the kid who needs exercise more than any other—the clinically obese" (p. 15).[17] Youth sport based on this model shrinks rather than expands access. If the insights of ludic kinesiologists regarding the meaning and joy potentially available in sport and physical activity are correct, then this is a great tragedy.

This mindset is only furthered in big-time college athletics, where the goal of winning, revenue, and attention, justifies greater and greater demands on the athletes as well as a mindset that education is reducible to eligibility (Liber Steeg, Upton, Bohn, & Berkowitz, 2008). Finally, PE, intramurals, and local recreation are denigrated and left behind for sexier, more elite, and prestigious leagues, options, majors, or requirements.

This attitude has all but overrun sport management, where management no longer means administration—in the broad sense of running all aspects of an athletics organization, department, or league—but rather mere business. Consider again my alma mater, the University of Michigan. Their 12-member sport management advisory council is designed to facilitate Michigan's "vision of achieving excellence in undergraduate *sport business* education" (emphasis added; University of Michigan School of Kinesiology, n.d.b., para. 1). The council consists of six professional sport executives, three executives at major sport marketing firms, one TV executive, the president of the Live Nation ticket agency, and a financial manager (University of Michigan School of Kinesiology, n.d.b.). There are no YMCA directors or Ann Arbor parks and recreation employees or adapted sport coaches, nor are there any parents or athletes. The sports industrial complex has not just taken root, it has taken over. Is there any wonder why physical education struggled to maintain itself at Michigan? It does not fit the model being espoused. There is no prestige in teaching "average children" to square dance or to run, throw, and kick well, because prestige is being measured against the standards of technique.[18]

A mindset similar to that of the sports industrial complex can also beset faculty, where the Holy Grail is obtaining a highly paid position in a doctoral-granting research-intensive institution and buying out one's teaching time through grant money and the research prestige that makes the grant money possible. Again, there is nothing wrong in principle with such positions or with grant money. The danger comes when one imprudently puts either above teaching. As Jacques Barzun (1959) lamented nearly 60 years ago, "the highest prize of the teaching profession is: no teaching. For the first time in history, apparently, scholars want no disciples" (p. 130). The problem, of course, if my prudential claims are on target, is not just that our students deserve us, *they need us*. Likewise, if we have any interest in the future of kinesiology, *we need them*. Therefore, as a matter of justice, teaching must be a *focus*.[19]

Challenging the sports industrial complex, at our institutions and within American society at large, will be difficult. There are many who have a vested interest in the status quo. So will insisting on the fundamental human importance of physical education. Too

---

[17] I would add only one more, the child from a large family, which cannot afford the expense or the logistical challenge of providing elite opportunities for multiple children.

[18] Physical education is not the most efficient means to promote a "healthy lifestyle" (University of Michigan School of Kinesiology, n.d.a., para. 9). Technique demands a rationalized, universal, measurable, and bureaucratic approach, which results in "a more comprehensive program" (para. 5) of "health promotion" (para. 9).

[19] According to Polanyi (1962),

> To learn by example is to submit to authority. You follow your master because you trust his manner of doing things even when you cannot analyze and account in detail for its effectiveness . . . . A society which wants to preserve a fund of personal knowledge must submit to tradition. (p. 53)

often we have wilted in the face of skeptical colleagues, scoffing administrators, or a public culture over run with "dumb jock" stereotypes. Nevertheless, justice demands that we find the *courage* to act.

Courage

Stop trusting in man, who has but a breath in his nostrils. Of what account is he?
(Isaiah 2:22, NIV)

Pieper (2011) defined courage succinctly. Courage is the "readiness to accept harm for the sake of realizing the good" (p. 23). It is a willingness to suffer—even unto death, if necessary—for the sake of the truth. This implies something very important. Those who aspire to be courageous must seriously ask themselves the following question: What is worth laying my life down for? Of course, it might be said that the stakes in kinesiology will rarely, if ever, rise to that level. True. But that is the point. If we have not established which goods are worth dying for, how likely is it that we will be willing to suffer lesser indignities, such as lost job opportunities, for the sake of realizing such allegedly trivial goods? The converse is also true, if we are unwilling to suffer relatively minor harms for relatively minor goods, it is safe to say we will refuse to endure great suffering in the defense of the highest goods.[20]

As Pieper (1966) pointed out, it is only with great difficulty that we "divest ourselves from the influence of the prevailing atmosphere" (p. 112). It is much easier to get in line—to go along to get along. This is why it is so important to reflect seriously on one's principles. Because it is hard enough to stand up for the truth, even when we know, in full confidence, what the truth is. What hope is there for courage if we have been paralyzed by doubt?

What role, then, does courage have to play in kinesiology? Obviously courage is applicable in the sorts of situations I have been discussing, regarding standing up for PE, or the humanities in kinesiology, or the willingness to point out the corruptions found in youth or intercollegiate sport. But I can think of three other examples worth brief mention. The first is grade inflation. According to the *New York Times* (Rampell, 2011), "about 43 percent of all letter grades given were A's, an increase of 28 percentage points since 1960" (para. 3). Holding firm against this rising tide of congratulatory mediocrity will require courage.

Second, is the pressure to publish. Studies suggest this pressure has led to an increase in fraud. While hardly the tsunami that is grade inflation, fraudulent research is on the rise. Rates have risen in the sciences from "fewer than 10 fraud retractions for every 1 million studies published" in the 1970s to, "96 retractions per million in 2007" (Associated Press, 2012, para. 2). While this may occasionally require a kinesiology researcher or graduate assistant to find the courage to directly resist participating in fraud, the more likely cause for courage will be whistleblowing, that is, identifying and condemning

---

[20] Discussions of courage always remind me of one of my favorite poems, *The Love Song of J. Alfred Prufrock* (Eliot, 1920):

> Should I, after tea and cakes and ices,
> Have the strength to force the moment to its crisis?
> But though I have wept and fasted, wept and prayed,
> Though I have seen my head (grown slightly bald) brought in upon a platter,
> I am no prophet—and here's no great matter;
> I have seen the moment of my greatness flicker,
> And I have seen the eternal Footman hold my coat, and snicker,
> And in short, I was afraid. (lines 79–86).

fraud when it occurs while serving as reviewers, editors, or colleagues. The integrity of our research, even the most empirical, relies on something that cannot be measured: good character.

Finally, there is the perennial problem in athletic training, that of coaches pressuring trainers over return-to-play decisions. The ethical stakes here have risen with the frightening new evidence regarding the frequency and danger of repeated head trauma in football (Fainaru-Wada & Fainaru, 2013). According to a *chronicle.com* investigation (Wolverton, 2013), 32% of trainers at big-time programs said that coaches had influence "over hiring and firing decisions for their position," while 52% "had felt pressure from football coaches to return a student to play faster than they thought was in his best interest medically" (sidebar). Again character is key, first for the coach and then for the athletic trainer. Just as a good coach needs to be willing to lose games to defend the safety of her athletes, a good athletic trainer needs to be ready to lose his/her job to defend the safety of his/her athletes.

The bottom line regarding courage is this: Truth must come before material success, trendiness, or reputation. As philosopher Alasdair MacIntyre (1984) pointed out, "notoriously the cultivation of truthfulness, justice and courage will often, the world being what it contingently is, bar us from being rich or famous or powerful" (p. 196). Although money, fame, and power are not bad things, they become so when they are considered the most important things. Real success therefore depends upon a *temperate* use of goods, in service of that which truly deserves our love, affection, and devotion.[21]

Temperance

Know Thyself. Nothing in excess. (The Temple at Delphi)

According to Pieper (2011), temperance (or moderation) is a matter of not allowing one's "desire for possessions and enjoyment to become destructive and repugnant to his being" (p. 7). This means that our understanding of human nature is vitally important. To know what is good or bad for a man to do relies upon a previous commitment regarding what a human being is. This is what the injunction "know thyself" at the Temple at Delphi meant. We need to know what we are and what we are not, in order to know what we ought to do. Pieper (2011) puts it this way, "ethics is about a right conception of man" (p. 4).

This is why Aristotle insists on the importance of contemplation to happiness. Man is rational by nature. Therefore, it is incumbent upon human beings to consider good and evil in relationship to "the image of the good person" (Pieper, 2011, p. 4). St. Augustine (1958) took it even further when he insisted that our only real happiness rests in the truth itself, that is, God. For even the most well-lived life will succumb to death while being constantly vulnerable in the meantime to disease, decay, injustice, and misfortune.[22]

Even if one disagrees with either or both of these assertions regarding man's path to happiness, it is easy to recognize the necessity of addressing these metaphysical questions. Ignoring them does not lessen their importance or make them go away. Yet, a pragmatic commitment to efficiency and utility via the means of *technique* leave such questions not only unexamined but incomprehensible. As Ellul (1997) insisted, the emphasis technique places on means necessarily creates a "suppression of meaning" (p. 40).

---

[21] The medieval concepts—see Pieper (2011)—of *Ordo Amoris* (discerning and prioritizing our loves) and *Ordo Timoris* (discerning what is really worth fearing) shed important light on this idea.
[22] See Book XIX, chapter 4.

Despite modern denials of the relevance of temperance,[23] even the most cursory examination of human or personal history clearly indicates that we all struggle with excess, in pleasures such as food and sex, as well as with extrinsic goods like money, possessions, and power. Furthermore, we often tend to react to these problems by swinging from one extreme (excess) to the other extreme of puritanical deficiency. St. Augustine (1958) is again instructive: "The things of earth are not merely good; they are undoubtedly gifts from God" (p. 328). Temperance, therefore, encourages asceticism only insofar as it cures an *abuse* of some good which, *through that abuse*, harms human nature.

One such abuse, common in our technocratic age of progress, merit, growth, and achievement, is the vice of pride. Talking about pride is decidedly out of fashion. However, this vice is real and deeply imprudent. For pride implies something wholly untrue. It implies that "I am the center of the universe." Speaking from experience, I can assure you that pride takes many forms in the academy and kinesiology—most commonly in intellectual impatience with our students, in an unwillingness to admit we were wrong, in an unwillingness to admit we do not know, in an unwillingness to say we are sorry, in an unwillingness to be unpopular, and in an unwillingness to acknowledge our debt to others.

How then do we combat pride? In struggling to combat my own pride, I have tried to follow Pope Benedict's (2009) insights. In *Credo for Today*, he argued quite profoundly that we must achieve a "Copernican revolution in our own lives" by "no longer seeing ourselves as the center of the universe, around which everyone else must turn, because instead of that we have begun to accept quite seriously that we are one of many among God's creatures, all of whom turn around God as their center" (pp. 10–11). Temperance requires recognition of the fact that the good is larger than ourselves or our desires.

Can Virtue Be Taught?

Therefore the virtues come to be present neither by nature nor contrary to nature, but in us who are of such a nature as to take them on . . . (Aristotle, *Nicomachean Ethics*, 1103a25)

Each of us are one among many. Our example matters to those around us. We inherit traditions and pass them on. As such, although we are not mere products of socialization as so much of post-modern theory suggests, socialization does matter. In fact, it matters a great deal. Although one cannot create a great athlete, all aspiring athletes have their natural talents molded and shaped by the coaching they receive and the ensuing habits—whether good or poor—that they develop. Everyone has athletic potential that can be cultivated. It is an inherent part of being human. Similarly, the Cardinal Virtues are an inherent capacity of human beings and must therefore be cultivated.

Are some of us more prone to courage or prudence or justice or moderation than others? Of course. But that makes cultivation more important, not less. For the buttressing of the culture, the cultivation in virtue which we receive may make all the difference

---

[23] From Rieff (1966):

> In fact, evil and immorality are disappearing, as Spencer assumed they would, mainly because our culture is changing its definition of human perfection. No longer the Saint, but the instinctual Everyman, twisting his neck uncomfortably inside the starched collar of culture, is the communal ideal, to whom men offer tacit prayers for deliverance from their inherited renunciations. Freud sought only to soften the collar; others, using bits and pieces of his genius, would like to take it off. (p. 8)

when we are called upon to do the right thing. Just as a good athlete will shoot poorly if taught poor form, a potentially courageous person will, more often than not, embrace timidity if taught to do so.

If this is true, it should be clear why I am convinced that it is virtue that will move kinesiology forward and vice that will hold it back. Technique is not enough. We cannot cultivate virtue if we do not admit the necessity of such cultivation by admitting that we are temporary caretakers of kinesiology. Moreover, there are schools of kinesiology which all advocate incommensurate *prudential* evaluations of the field and its place in the world. It is *imprudent* to pretend otherwise. Claims to truth matter, for the different schools of kinesiology do not and will not cultivate the same things.

I am fully convinced that ludic kinesiology is what should be cultivated in kinesiology. In my experience, this is the minority position. Yet, whether in the minority or the majority, whatever gets put into practice, be it scientific, therapeutic, or ludic kinesiology, each and every school's vision will chart a different path forward. As such, we need to be open and honest about our disagreements. For example, the plausibility and power of my criticisms of the University of Michigan will depend in large part upon which school of kinesiology one subscribes to.

I expect those who are convinced I am wrong to tell me so. I expect those who agree with me to feel free to say so. In all such discussions, whether the commentary and reactions are positive or negative, the goal is *truth*. Rudeness, nor belligerence, nor condescension, nor flattery has any place in kinesiology.

This requires, of course, that we allow space for dissent, that is, for real disagreement, especially on controversial issues. Furthermore, justice demands that kinesiologists acknowledge that we have duties to our fellow man. Duties which we as kinesiologists have often failed to live up to.[24] Making such an admission relies upon courage. For many of our sins are not only unacknowledged, they have popular support. Pointing them out will therefore usually garner criticism rather than praise. Finally, the temperate kinesiologist knows that although his/her job matters, other things matter more. There are more important things than kinesiology. Kinesiology must be seen as, and taught as, a part of a larger whole.

Yet, is not all of this an impossible task? What is the tipping point for institutions? How does one individual change the course of a behemoth? More importantly, an honest look in the mirror quickly inclines one to say something like this, "Given my weaknesses, my vanities, my temper, my despair, my frustrations, and my pride, . . . how can I possibly live up to the standard of the Cardinal Virtues?" Such a critique is biting and powerful, because it cuts to the heart of the matter. All of us who are honest must admit feeling that we, like Hamlet, are not quite up to the job:

> *The time is out of joint. O cursèd spite,*
>
> *That ever I was born to set it right!* (Act 1, Scene 5)[25]

A frank examination seems to show that the problems are too big, that our weaknesses are too strong, that our foolishness is too common, and that our character is too shallow.

---

[24] Our failings are many. Here are a couple that I think are incontrovertible. First, the collapse of physical education is happening on our watch. Second, our defense of physical activity classes as a necessary part of undergraduate core curricula has been far too tepid.

[25] It is similar to the feeling one gets the first time one teaches and sees 40 or 60 or 80 eyeballs looking to you for answers.

Nevertheless our character is vital. The principalities and powers of this world can take many things by force. Our possessions can be taken from us. Our family and friends can be taken from us, as can our reputation, our livelihood, even our very lives. All of these can be taken from us. But our character—that is *always surrendered.* Here is the reality: The future of kinesiology depends upon cultivating rather than surrendering our character. The quality of our coaching and teaching, the integrity of our research, and the health of our discipline all depend upon good kinesiologists. Struggling to be good is something we should care about a "great deal." Given our weaknesses, what then can be done? What answer, if any, can be found? Following Christian tradition, I would point beyond the Cardinal Virtues to the Theological Virtues, to faith, to hope, and to love, . . . but that is, unfortunately, another paper.[26]

Acknowledgment

This lecture is dedicated to my father, Dr. T. Alan Twietmeyer, from whose example I first learned what a *good* kinesiologist *is.*

References

Anderson, D. R. (2002). The humanity of movement or "It's not just a gym class". *Quest, 54*(2), 87–96. doi:10.1080/00336297.2002.10491768

Aristotle. (2002). *Nicomachean ethics* (J. Sachs, Trans.). Newburyport, MA: Focus.

Associated Press. (2012, October 1). *Study: Scientific research fraud on the rise.* Retrieved from http://www.cbsnews.com/news/study-scientific-research-fraud-on-the-rise/

Barzun, J. (1959). *The house of intellect.* New York, NY: Harper and Brothers.

Brague, R. (2013, October). The impossibility of secular society. *First Things* 2013(236), 27–31.

Buck, M. (2014). Leadership for the 21st century. *Quest, 66,* 137–149. doi:10.1080/00336297.2014.895952

Camilli-Whisenhunt, C. (2014, March 20). *Kinesiology will transform PE major to health and fitness emphasis.* Retrieved from http://record.umich.edu/articles/kinesiology-will-transform-pemajor-health-and-fitness-emphasis

DePauw, K. (2010). A journey of many dimensions: Reflections on change and possibility. *Quest, 62,* 335–347. doi:10.1080/00336297.2010.10483653

Dunn, J. M. (2009). The times are a changing: Implications for kinesiology. *Quest, 61,* 268–277. doi:10.1080/00336297.2009.10483615

Eliot, T. S. (1920). Prufrock, and other observations. *Poems.* New York, NY: A. A. Knopf. Retrieved from http://www.bartleby.com/198/1.html

Ellul, J. (1997). *Perspectives on our age: Jacques Ellul speak on his life and work* (rev. ed.) W. H. Venderburg (Ed.), Toronto, Canada: House of Anansi.

Fainaru-Wada, M., & Fainaru, S. (2013). *League of denial: The NFL, concussions, and the battle for the truth.* New York, NY: Crown Archetype.

Farrey, T. (2008). *Game on: How the pressure to win at all costs endangers youth sports, and what parents can do about it.* New York, NY: ESPN.

Feingold, R. S. (2013). Vision in an age of accountability. *Quest, 65,* 385–393. doi:10.1080/00336297.2013.834832

Fort, T. L. (1990, June 15). Who will clean up the mess? *The Chicago Tribune,* Sec. 1, p. 25.

Hawkins, A. (2011). Kinesiology for humans. *Quest, 63,* 249–264. doi:10.1080/00336297.2011.10483679

---

[26] Ellul (1997) stated:

> Christian Hope does not, as is too often said, consist in believing in humanity. It is precisely the contrary. Christian Hope means being convinced that we will not go along completely on our own. It is an affirmation of the love of God . . . . Hope will then simply be the fact that because God is God, because God is love, there is always a future. (p. 89)

Henrich, J., Heine, S. J., & Norenzayan, A. (2010). The weirdest people in the world? *Behavioral and Brain Sciences, 33,* 61–83. doi:10.1017/S0140525X0999152X

Killion, A. (2013, October 18). *Paying to play is new normal for youth athletes.* Retrieved from http://www.sfgate.com/sports/article/Paying-to-play-is-new-normal-for-youth-athletes-4902034.php

Kretchmar, R. S. (2005). *Practical philosophy of sport and physical activity* (2nd ed.). Champaign, IL: Human Kinetics.

Latash, M. L. (2008). Motor control: The heart of kinesiology. *Quest, 60,* 19–30. doi:10.1080/00336297.2008.10483566

Latour, B. (1993). *We have never been modern.* Cambridge, MA: Harvard University Press.

Lewis, C. S. (1949). *The weight of glory: And other addresses.* San Francisco, CA: Harper Collins.

Liber Steeg, J., Upton, J., Bohn, P., & Berkowitz, S. (2008, November 20). *College athletes studies guided toward "major in eligibility".* Retrieved from http://usatoday30.usatoday.com/sports/college/2008-11-18-majors-cover_N.htm

MacIntyre, A. (1984). *After virtue* (2nd ed.). Notre Dame, IN: University of Notre Dame Press.

MacIntyre, A. (2009). *God, philosophy, universities: A selective history of the Catholic philosophical tradition.* Lanham, MD: Rowman & Littlefield.

Mali, T. (2002). *Totally like whatever, you know?* Retrieved from http://www.taylormali.com/poemsonline/totally-like-whatever-you-know/

Moynihan, D. P. (1965). The professionalization of reform. *National Affairs, 1,* 6–16. Retrieved from http://www.nationalaffairs.com/doclib/20080514_issue1theprofessionalization.pdf

Murray, C. (2012). *Coming apart: The state of white America, 1960–2010.* New York: Crown Forum.

Nestlé Group. (2014, November 19). *Unlocking the metabolic 'master switch' to potentially echo exercise effect.* Retrieved from http://www.nestle.com/media/newsandfeatures/ampk-metabolic-master-switch

Oberlin College. (n.d.). *Portrait of a pioneer—unswerving dedication to an ideal brought in a new era of health education for college women.* Retrieved from http://www.oberlin.edu/external/EOG/LucyStonewalk-a-thonTour/Delphine%20Hanna/1957HannaArticle.html

Parry, L. (2014, December 8). *The obesity pill that could replace exercise by turning 'bad' fat to 'good'.* Retrieved from http://www.dailymail.co.uk/health/article-2865581/The-obesity-pill-replace-exercise-Turning-bad-fat-good-step-drug-replace-treadmill-scientists-claim.html

Pieper, J. (1966). *The four cardinal virtues.* Notre Dame, IN: University of Notre Dame.

Pieper, J. (2011). *The Christian idea of man.* South Bend, IN: St. Augustine's.

Polanyi, M. (1962). *Personal knowledge: Towards a post-critical philosophy.* Chicago, IL: University of Chicago Press.

Pope Benedict XVI. (2009). *Credo for today: What Christians believe.* San Francisco, CA: Ignatius.

Rampell, C. (2011, July 14). *A history of college grade inflation.* Retrieved from http://economix.blogs.nytimes.com/2011/07/14/the-history-of-college-grade-inflation/?_r=0

Rieff, P. (1966). *The triumph of the therapeutic: Uses of faith after Freud.* New York, NY: Harper & Row.

Rittelmeyer, H. (2014, February). Bloodless moralism. *First Things 2014*(240), 33–39.

St. Augustine. (1958). *The city of God* (G. G. Walsh, D. B. Zema, G. Monahan, & D. J. Honan, Trans.). New York, NY: Bantam Doubleday.

Twietmeyer, G. (2012). What is kinesiology? Historical & philosophical insights. *Quest, 64,* 4–23. doi:10.1080/00336297.2012.653268

University of Michigan School of Kinesiology. (n.d.a). *PE discontinuance FAQs.* Retrieved from http://www.kines.umich.edu/sites/webservices.itcs.umich.edu.drupal.kinesprod/files/final_pe_discontinuance_faqs.pdf

University of Michigan School of Kinesiology. (n.d.b). *Sport management advisory board.* Retrieved from http://www.kines.umich.edu/programs/sport-management/advisory-board

Wolverton, B. (2013, September 2). *Coach makes the call.* Retrieved from http://chronicle.com/article/Trainers-Butt-Heads-With/141333/

Discussion Question(s)

1. Can you think of an example—besides the ones used in the article—of how prudence or justice or courage or temperance is needed in the world of sport?
2. What does Twietmeyer mean when he argues that "Absent first principals, passionately held, we are stillborn"? What does this point have to do with "technique"?
3. What do you make of Twietmeyer's claim that there are different schools of kinesiology (i.e., scientific, therapeutic, and ludic)? Assuming you are a kinesiology student yourself, speculate on which school of thought dominates in your department. What evidence/arguments can you offer to support your choice? If you are not sure, ask your instructor what they think is the most dominant "school of kinesiology" at your institution.

Suggested Readings

Lewis, C. S. (1944). Men without chests. In C. S. Lewis, *The abolition of man* (pp. 1–26). San Francisco, CA: Harper Collins.
MacIntyre, A. (1984). The nature of the virtues. In A. MacIntyre, *After virtue* (2nd ed.) (pp. 181–203). Notre Dame, IN: University of Notre Dame Press.
McNamee, M. (1995). Sporting practices, institutions, and virtues: A critique and a restatement. *Journal of the Philosophy of Sport*, XXII, 61–82.
Reid, H. L. (2007). Sport and moral education in Plato's Republic. *Journal of the Philosophy of Sport*, 34, 160–175.

Bibliography

Alighieri, D. (2002). *Inferno* (A. Esolen, Trans.). New York, NY: Random House.
Aristotle. (1994–2009). *Nicomachean ethics.* (W. D. Ross, Ed.) Retrieved November 22, 2016, from The internet classics archive: http://classics.mit.edu/Aristotle/nicomachaen.html
Aristotle. (2002). *Nicomachean ethics.* (J. Sachs, Trans.) Newburyport, MA: Focus Publishing.
Bloy, L. (1947). *The woman who was poor: A contemporary novel of the French 'eighties.* (I. Collins, Trans.) New York, NY: Sheed and Ward.
Frankena, W. K. (1973). *Ethics.* Englewood Cliffs, NJ: Prentice-Hall.
Kozlowski, K. (2018, January 19). *What MSU knew: 14 were warned of Nassar abuse.* Retrieved August 13, 2019, from detroitnews.com: https://www.detroitnews.com/story/tech/2018/01/18/msu-president-told-nassar-complaint-2014/1042071001/
Lavigne, P. (2018, July 13). *Baylor University settles Title IX lawsuit in which gang rape by up to 8 football players was alleged.* Retrieved August 13, 2019, from espn.com: https://www.espn.com/college-football/story/_/id/24090683/baylor-university-settles-title-ix-lawsuit-which-gang-rape-8-football-players-was-alleged
Lewis, C. S. (1944, 2001). *The abolition of man.* New York, NY: Harper Collins.
Lewis, C. S. (1949). *The weight of glory: And other addresses.* New York, NY: Harper Collins.
MacIntyre, A. (1984). *After virtue* (2nd ed.). Notre Dame, IN: University of Notre Dame Press.
MacIntyre, A. (1990). *Three rival versions of moral enquiry: Encyclopedia, genealogy, and tradition.* Notre Dame, IN: University of Notre Dame Press.
Mayo, B. (1958). *Ethics and the moral life.* New York, NY: MacMillan & Company.
McNamee, M. (2008). *Sports, virtues and vices: Morality Plays.* New York, NY: Routledge.
Neuhaus, R. J. (2009). *American babylon: Notes of a Christian exile.* New York, NY: Basic Books.
Pieper, J. (1966). *The four cardinal virtues.* Notre Dame, IN: University of Notre Dame.
Pieper, J. (1997). *Faith, hope, love.* San Francisco, CA: Ignatius Press.
Pieper, J. (2011). *The Christian idea of man.* South Bend, IN: St. Augustine's Press.

Simon, R., Torres, C., & Hager, P. (2015). *Fair play: The ethics of sport* (4th ed.). Boulder, CO: Westview Press.

Smith, R. (2016). *Wounded lions: Joe Paterno, Jerry Sandusky and the crisis of Penn State athletics.* Urbana and Chicago, IL: University of Illinois Press.

Sonnone, B. (2015, July 18). *FSU president John Thrasher lays out plan to improve athlete behavior.* Retrieved June 1, 2016, from orlandosentinel.com: http://www.orlandosentinel.com/sports/florida-state-seminoles/chopping-block/os-fsu-president-john-thrasher-improve-athlete-behavior-20150718-post.html

Timmons, M. (2013). *Moral theory: An introduction* (2nd ed.). New York, NY: Rowman & Littlefield.

Wainstein, K. L., Jay III, A. J., & Kukowski, C. D. (2014). *Investigation of irregular classes in the Department of African and Afro-American Studies at the University of North Carolina at Chapel Hill.* New York, NY: Cadwalader, Wickersham & Taft.

Chapter 7

Why be Good?

"Win if you can, lose if you must, but always cheat!"   —*Unknown*[1]

Students will be able to:

1. Distinguish the difference between the intrinsic and extrinsic theories of justice.
2. Explain the "Ring of Gyges" and how it illuminates Plato's/Socrates' understanding of justice as an intrinsic good.
3. Explain Tit for Tat and how it illuminates Singer's extrinsic view of justice.
4. Articulate how the differences between intrinsic and extrinsic theories of justice impact the world of sport (e.g., as regards genetic engineering or gambling in sport).
5. Evaluate whether or not transcendent sporting experiences exist and should be used as evidence in support of an intrinsic theory of justice.

You should recall, that in the last chapter, we gave brief attention to the concept of justice. There we defined it as "treating others as we ought" (Chapter 6, p. 152). You may also recall that in Chapter 1 we gave momentary attention to the relative importance of winning. There we argued that "winning is *a* measure of success, not *the* measure of success" (Chapter 1, p. 14). In this chapter we will delve deeper into these issues, by examining the *nature* of justice. In fact, the nature and purpose of justice is one of the founding and perennial questions of philosophy. When examined from this perspective, it is clear that the problem goes even deeper than the issue of "winning." Instead, the fundamental question is: Why, *precisely*, should we be good at all?

Similarly, in Chapter 2 we focused on theories of good and evil. Although theories of good and evil are also related to the issue, here, the focus will be on *why* we should be just, rather than *what* is good or evil. Therefore, we are asking a related but different question. We are not seeking to define justice or to define good and evil, but rather answer these questions: Why is good preferable to evil? Why should we treat others as we ought? Are our obligations to others, such as "don't cheat" inherent? That is, are they *really* obligations? Or does the nature of our "obligations" to others hinge upon the utility of those obligations in any given situation? That is, can "the situation" or the "outcome" of

---

[1] The origin of this proverb is unclear. It has been used by villains in American professional wrestling many times. Some allege "Gorgeous George" was the first to use it in the 1950s. Whether he is the originator or merely a popularizer of the phrase is unknown.

"cheating" mollify our obligation to avoid it? In sum: Should we do good things simply because they are good, or is the goodness of an action justified by its results?

Applying these issues to sport should make these abstract points more concrete. Let us suppose that we all agree that: "One should tell the truth to the referee, even when he makes a mistake in your favor." Once such an agreement has been settled on, then the definition of the good, at least in this instance, has been resolved. Yet, even if we all agree, there is still an important philosophical question that remains: why is that the case? Why is it *just* to "tell the referee the truth"? Why is it *unjust* to lie to the referee? One argument, let us call it the **intrinsic theory of justice** states that the goodness of "telling the truth" is sufficient unto itself. We ought to tell the truth simply because we realize it *is* good. Virtue, as they say, is its own reward. Come "hell or high water," come victory or defeat, we should do the right thing, simply because it is right. Telling the referee the truth needs no other justification than the fact that it is the truth. It follows from this that one should tell the truth even if doing so means losing the game.

A second argument, call it the **extrinsic theory of justice** states that we ought pursue the good of telling the truth because, at least in the long run, *it will be good for us*. The goodness of the action finds vindication in the consequences telling the truth produces. One might argue, for example, that one's reputation will be improved, that cooperation will be encouraged, that a good example will be set, and so forth. On these grounds, one might even argue (due to such outcomes) that in the long run it will lead to more victories. For example, an enhanced reputation might increase one's ability to recruit. Therefore, from this school of thought, goodness is justified by the outcomes it produces.

Now, you may be thinking to yourself that there is no inherent contradiction between the two schools. As a result, is there really an important disagreement between those who pursue the good intrinsically and extrinsically? For example, one could "tell the referee the truth" simply because truth is good, and yet still reap (and expect) the benefits of the action. Similarly, one could "tell the truth" because one felt it would lead to good results. Yet, even in the case that one is solely motivated extrinsically, the resulting action (telling the truth) is the same. So what is the difference?

The difference matters at the level of principle. In fact, reflection shows that the disagreement between the two schools is larger than it initially appears. Their differences on the level of justification result in important differences in commitment, which then, in turn, can impact practice. The intrinsic school argues that the good, if it really is good, is its own justification. Therefore their commitment to the rightness of any good action (insofar as it really is good) is unassailable.[2] In contrast, because the extrinsic school bases its justification in the consequences of the action, its commitment to the goodness of any action is always contingent. The goodness of the action only depends upon the results that action procures.

In thinking through this issue we will focus on two paradigm examples. The first is the ancient Greek philosopher Plato. Plato, arguably the founder of Western philosophy, was also Socrates' student and Aristotle's teacher. We will examine a section of *The Republic* called the **"Ring of Gyges"** in which Plato (through a dialogue between the characters Socrates and Glaucon) argues that justice should be pursued for its own sake. Justice is an intrinsic good.

The second philosopher, Peter Singer, is from the 20th/21st Century. He argues in his book *How are We to Live?* (1995) that doing good things is good for us. To live a just life is a case of **enlightened self-interest**, by which Singer (1995) means that careful thinking

Intrinsic Theory of Justice: Any answer to the question "Why be good?" which argues that we should treat others as we ought simply because it is good to do so. Justice is its own reward.

Extrinsic Theory of Justice: Any answer to the question "Why be good?" which argues that we should treat others as we ought because of the consequences that behavior generates.

"Ring of Gyges": A short story told by Glaucon in the *The Republic* meant to examine the question: "Should you be good, even in circumstances where you know you will get away with being evil?" That is, are there any good reasons, besides fear of punishment, for being just?

Enlightened Self-Interest: In contrast to 'naked self-interest' which egoistically looks for immediate selfish gain, proponents of enlightened self-interest argue that, even from an egoistic point of view, one's individual good is wrapped up in the good of others.

---

[2] As we have seen with, for instance, W.D. Ross or Aristotle, believing in an intrinsic understanding of justice can still allow for prudential evaluations of what ought to be done. What is not up for debate, however, is the nature of and justification for pursuing the good. As Ross (1930, 2002) insists, the moral order "is self-evident just as a mathematical axiom, or the validity of a form of inference, is evident" (p. 29).

shows us that "Living an ethical life is not self-sacrifice, but rather self-fulfillment." (p. vii). Doing good to others is justified by the fact that it is also doing good for yourself. Justice is good because it is useful.

Therefore, we will proceed as follows. First, we will examine and then analyze the work of Plato and Singer. What do they advocate? What are the strengths and weaknesses of their positions? Are they convincing? After completing this task, we will then close the chapter by applying the insights of Plato and Singer to sport. Why and how does justice fit into the practice and administration of sport? How does sport fit into a good life? Does it matter if we justify the good on intrinsic of extrinsic grounds? What does the practice and administration of sport look like when it is *part* of a good life?

The Ring of Gyges

The story of the Ring of Gyges begins in Book II of *The Republic* (2000). The scene opens with Socrates. He has just finished responding to Thrasymachus, a sophist, who had claimed that "justice is nothing else than the interest of the stronger" (p. 12). Might makes right. To which Socrates replies that "justice is the excellence of the soul" (p. 29). That is, even as the purpose of the eye is to see, the purpose of the soul is to be just.[3] Therefore, the just man lives well. As a result, since he lives well, he will be happy. It follows that injustice can never be more profitable than justice. Although Socrates feels like he has given a satisfactory answer, Glaucon, a friend of Socrates (and brother of Plato), remains unconvinced. Building off of Thrasymachus' skepticism, Glacuon attempts to deepen the challenge to Socrates by telling the story of Gyges.

Does might make right? Or is there more to the good than mere power or success?
Keystone/Stringer/Hulton Archive/Getty Images

---

[3] Notice the affinity between Plato's (Socrates') argument and Aristotle's conception of virtue.

Gyges is a shepherd. One day, while tending his fields, there is an earthquake. After the earthquake ends, Gyges realizes that the earth had opened beneath his feet. Moreover, when he looks down into the crevice he sees that it contains a gold ring. Upon retrieving it, he learns that if he turns it upon his finger the right way, it will make him invisible. "Whereupon he contrived to be chosen one of the messengers who were sent to the court; where as soon as he arrived he seduced the queen, and with her help conspired against the king and slew him, and took the kingdom" (p. 32). Glaucon then asks a deeply serious question: Why should he have done otherwise?

Glaucon's point is that justice, if it is a matter utility, has no place in such a scenario. For example, one might argue, quite plausibly, that one should be just to avoid punishment. Yet, with his newfound power, Gyges has no fear of punishment. *He can do whatever he wants.* Why shouldn't he? Why, absent a fear of retribution, should he or anyone else act justly? As Glaucon asserts "for whenever any one [sic] thinks he can safely be unjust, there he is unjust" (p. 33). Returning to our sport example the idea can be put this way: What, if anything, is wrong with cheating, if *you are certain* you could get away with it?

Glaucon then extends the point by reversing the scenario from one where one safely commits injustice to one where one receives nothing but scorn and condemnation for being just. This is a direct challenge to Socrates' claim that justice, given its nature as an excellence of the soul, naturally leads to happiness.

> "Let him be the best of men, and let him be thought the worst; then he will have been put to the proof; and we shall see whether he will be affected by the fear of infamy and its consequences. And let him continue thus to the hour of his death; being just and seeming to be unjust. When both have reached the uttermost extreme, the one of justice and the other of injustice, let judgment be given which of them is the happier of the two" (p. 33)

Only in such circumstances can we be certain someone pursued justice for its own sake. Yet, can we honestly call the just but forsaken man happy? Never mind the problem of calling someone like Gyges, who "has it all," unhappy. What this counter-argument seems to prove is that what matters is not justice or injustice, but rather appearances. Glaucon puts it this way: "Since then, as philosophers prove, appearance tyrannizes over truth and is lord of happiness, to appearance I must devote myself" (p. 37). But if this is so, justice is not an intrinsic good. We only do good when and if we believe it will be good for us, by, for example, enhancing our reputation. In closing his argument, Glaucon then offers this final challenge to Socrates:

> "Let others praise justice and censure injustice, magnifying the rewards and honors of the one and abusing the other; that in a manner of arguing which, coming from them, I am ready to tolerate, but from you [Socrates] who have spent your whole life in the consideration of this question, unless I hear contrary from your own lips, I expect something better. And therefore, I say, not only prove to us that justice is better than injustice, but show what they either of them do to the possessor of them, which makes the one to be a good and the other evil, whether seen or unseen by gods or men" (p. 39).

Socrates' Response

Socrates offers his direct response much later in the text, after a long but related digression. The middle portion of *The Republic* examines the ideal State on the grounds that the "larger quantity of justice" found in the just state means that identifying the nature of justice "is more easily discernable" (p. 40). Socrates then returns directly to the issue Glaucon proposes in Chapter IX. Why is it better to be just than unjust? Why does anything other than appearances matter?

Socrates begins by positing that it is better for man to be in control of himself than to be subject to his desires. To illustrate how this is the case, Socrates then asks:

> "How would a man profit if he received gold and silver on the condition that he was to enslave the noblest part of him to the worst? Who can imagine that a man who sold his son or daughter into slavery for money, especially if he sold them into the hands of fierce and evil men, would be a gainer, however large the sum which he received" (p. 249)?

Socrates' point is that serving injustice is enslaving oneself. Real freedom is not just *freedom from* constraint, as is so often assumed in modern Western culture. Rather, freedom is also the ability to skillfully exercise one's powers in pursuit of human excellence, which means, since men are rational, the *freedom to* pursue truth.[4] In fact, constraint (at least in the form of discipline) is often necessary for the development of the skills necessary to freely exercise our powers. Therefore, since serving injustice cultivates vices such as "uncontrolled avarice," to deliberately choose to serve injustice, even if it is "profitable," is to be self-destructive. To be just is *to be* what one ought. *Being* good is more important than any consequences.[5] Socrates, therefore asks this rhetorical question:

> "From what point of view, then, and on what ground can we say that a man is profited by injustice or intemperance or other baseness, *which will make him a worse man*, even though he acquire money or power by his wickedness" (p. 250) [Emphasis added]?

The same point is made in the famous scriptural admonition: "What does it profit a man if he gains the whole world and loses his soul?"[6] It is worth noting that each of these formulations of the point assumes a transcendent understanding of good and evil. In so doing, each insists that justice is not something that serves us. Instead, we serve justice. *Justice is the good*, so we cannot actually be successful in opposition to it.

In fact, Socrates takes this point so far as to argue that it is better to be caught and punished for injustice than to get away with it.

> "What shall he profit, if his injustice be undetected and unpunished? He who is undetected only gets worse, whereas he who is detected and punished has the brutal part of his nature silenced and humanized . . . [Therefore] To this nobler purpose the man of understanding will devote the energies of his life" (p. 250).

Is Socrates response to Glaucon convincing? What are the strengths and weaknesses of the Platonic position? For the time being, we will hold off on answering these questions. First, let us turn to a paradigm example of the antithetical position. Then, after hearing the case for the extrinsic position, we will evaluate each school of thought for their strengths and weaknesses.

---

[4] A classic examination of these conceptions of negative and positive freedom can be found in the Isaiah Berlin's (2002) essay *Two Concepts of Liberty*.
[5] Two ongoing and vital political questions arise from this: To what degree do we know what we ought to be and to what degree can we force others to be what we know or "know" they ought to be?
[6] Mark 8:36

Tit for Tat

Peter Singer (1995), a contemporary utilitarian philosopher, argues in the seventh chapter of his text *How Are We to Live?* for an extrinsic understanding of justice. His thesis, as we have already seen, is that "Living an ethical life is not self-sacrifice, but rather self-fulfillment." (p. vii). To support this claim Singer argues in favor of an ethical theory called **Tit for Tat**. Tit for Tat can be accurately summarized in one simple phrase: "cooperate then reciprocate."

In fact, Singer (1995) confidently proclaims that Tit for Tat overturns intrinsic arguments, such as Plato's, regarding the nature of justice:

> "Much of the system of justice can be explained in the same way. Justice is not, as often thought, a sacrosanct moral principle imposed on us by a divine being, nor is it somehow engraved in the bedrock of the universe. Justice is neither more nor less than a set of conceptual tools for making Tit for Tat work in the real world. As such it needs to be used with discretion. 'Let justice be done, though the heavens fall' is an ancient saying, but one that invests justice with a shade too much significance. *How absolute we ought to be will depend on circumstances*" (p. 149) [Emphasis added].

To explain why Tit for Tat makes sense, Singer begins by reviewing a famous thought experiment called the "Prisoner's Dilemma." Imagine, Singer says, that you are languishing in a third-world prison when in walks an interrogator. He offers you the following deal: "Confess against your friend in the next cell and after we use your confession against your friend for a ten year conviction we will let you go free." You protest that he is not your friend and that "you have never met him." "So much the better," says the interrogator, "You should confess immediately since we are offering the same deal to your 'friend' right now." He then continues, "If you refuse to confess, while your 'friend' confesses, then we'll use his confession against you for a ten year conviction." Further discussion indicates that if you both confess, you'll both get eight years. If you both refuse to confess, then they will "turn the screws" on both of you for six months before international pressure will likely result in your release.

What should you do? Is there a solution to the dilemma? Singer argues (for the time being) that there is no clean solution. However, he also insists that the dilemma makes clear that naked self-interest often results, paradoxically, in self-harm. His key point is this: sometimes self-interest leaves us worse off than collective interest. Instead of naked self-interest, Singer proposes that one should pursue what is called enlightened self-interest where one sees that their own good is wrapped up in the good of others.

How does the "Prisoner's Dilemma" point towards enlightened self-interest? It supports enlightened self-interest because naked self-interest would be to rat out the fellow prisoner and get yourself out of prison as fast as possible. However, that logic is just as true for the other prisoner as it is for you! Yet, if you both rat each other out, you will each get eight years and nobody will go free!

What, then, does this thought experiment tell us more generally about justice? Singer argues that it supports Tit for Tat, which again is the theory that in any new encounter between ethical actors, one should begin with cooperation and then respond in kind; good for good and harm for harm. After beginning with cooperation, one should treat others the way they treat you. In endorsing this philosophic position, Singer is saying that justice is circumstantial. The good is a function of utility. The right way to behave, the right way to treat others, depends upon how they treat you. Moreover, this understanding of justice is strategic. It is not a matter of truth, but of efficiency.

Tit for Tat: An extrinsic theory of justice which argues that we should treat others the way they treat us. More specifically, the basic theory of tit for tat is "cooperate, then reciprocate." That is, start with trust and then respond in kind.

Is ethics really all about reciprocation?
Associated Press.

Why does Singer believe in Tit for Tat? He believes in Tit for Tat because he is convinced that he has both theoretical and empirical grounds upon which to stand. On the empirical side, he points to research where the "Prisoner's dilemma," not unlike "Rocks, Paper, Scissors," was played as a game. However in this game, instead of showing "rock" or "paper" one shows "confess" or "not confess" and thereby agrees to "cooperate" or "defect." Singer argues that given multiple rounds and multiple encounters it is clear that Tit for Tat is the best (most effective) strategy for succeeding in Prisoner's Dilemma scenarios.

On the theoretical side, Singer argues that Tit for Tat holds people accountable. Reciprocation rewards good behavior and punishes bad behavior. In doing so, we reward good behavior (cooperation) and punish bad behavior (defection), such as cheating, lying and so forth. If we refused to reciprocate, defection would go unpunished and the cheaters would prosper; a situation, which, at least in the long run, will harm all. Hence, Tit for Tat is a case of enlightened self-interest.

What then should be made of Singer and Tit for Tat? Is it a better way to understand the nature and purpose of justice? What are the strengths and weaknesses of Tit for Tat? How does this extrinsic theory compare to Plato and the intrinsic school?

Plato & Singer: Is Justice Something We Serve or Merely Something We Use?

Since we have just finished examining the basics of Singer's position it seems prudent to reverse the previous order and begin with the strengths and weaknesses of Tit for Tat. Then, when pertinent we can return back to Plato's strengths and weaknesses in light of what we have learned about Singer's extrinsic position. The strengths of Tit for Tat are clear. First, human beings like to see good behavior rewarded and bad behavior punished. As a result, Tit for Tat, at least on the surface, is plausible. We see such reciprocation in sport all the time. The most obvious example of this being the baseball practice of intentionally hitting an opposing batter in response to a slight or some other previous infraction (see the Kirkjian reading in this chapter). Second, Tit for Tat is, in principle at least, simple. It yields clarity rather than confusion. As with utilitarianism, there is only one rule to follow: cooperate then reciprocate. One should reward cooperators and punish defectors. Such simplicity should reduce moral confusion and spur moral action (at least in terms of Tit for Tat).

Yet despite this intuitive force, Tit for Tat is not without problems. Here are four criticisms. First, arguments can be raised about the contrived nature of the evidence that Singer uses; is the Prisoner's Dilemma (upon which he hangs so much weight) realistic? Does the Prisoner's Dilemma accurately mirror ethical encounters in the real world? If not, what moral weight should it have as evidence in favor of Tit for Tat? Second, if one buys Socrates' argument regarding the inherent importance of truth, then one can criticize Tit for Tat on the grounds that it seems to ignore "truth as such" in favor of strategy. But why is such a utilitarian approach correct? Couldn't we say that . . . if you're not guilty you don't confess . . . period? Third, one can argue that Tit for Tat assumes (wrongly) that there are good ("nice") and bad ("mean") people rather than good and bad actions.[7] The criticism here centers on the idea that Tit for Tat focuses on punishment rather than redemption and in doing so ignores the fact that all human beings are guilty of doing "mean" things. The most damning argument, however, is the endless spiral of revenge required by two parties responding to each other in kind. According to Tit for Tat theory, after having been on the end of previous defections, each response will *require* a further defection. How can such a negative spiral be avoided when Tit for Tat demands reciprocation?[8]

Singer (1995) is aware of at least some of these criticisms. To counteract them he argues there are five steps for "doing better with Tit for Tat" (p. 142). The most important of which, for our purposes, is forgiveness. Here he admits that forgiveness "makes it easier to break out of patterns of mutually damaging recriminations" (p. 151). Whether such a concession is enough to save Tit for Tat is a matter of contention. I would argue that Singer soft pedals the importance of forgiveness.[9] Forgiveness is vital. It is not a luxury, a convenience or a matter of "remaining open" (p. 151). Without forgiveness, *you cannot* escape the "downward spiral of revenge" (Fort, 2001, p. 196).

Curiously—almost in passing—Singer recognizes the solution to this and all the other problems with Tit for Tat. He does so when he admits that, "Genuine concern for

---

[7] "If nice animals live in a group with mean ones and behave nicely without discriminating between those animals who return the favor and those who do not, the mean animals gain an advantage. . .We can put this more plainly still. To be nice to someone who is not nice to you is to allow yourself to be a sucker. Where there are suckers, cheats prosper" (Singer, 1995, p. 139).

[8] "More complexly, game theorists have demonstrated that the most effective strategizers in prisoners' dilemma games do not practice just reciprocal altruism. Such a strategy is vulnerable to someone who takes advantage of such trusting behavior. Nor do they practice 'tit-for-tat,' because, while this assures that one will not be taken advantage of, it provides no escape from the downward spiral of revenge. The most effective strategy is something called 'generous tit-for-tat.' In this approach one generally reciprocates the behavior shown, but occasionally one must break out of this reciprocity to treat another as one would like to be treated" (Fort, 2001, pp. 196–197).

[9] After laying out the case that the reciprocal nature of Tit for Tat "keeps out the cheats" (p. 139), Singer (1995) then goes on to say: "This result [keeping out the cheats] amounts to nothing less than an experimental refutation of Jesus's celebrated teaching about turning the other cheek. Most of us think that turning the other cheek is a noble ideal, even if too idealistic. Consequently, we admire those who are prepared to act on it. If they are prepared to be struck on both cheeks, we think, they are the *only* ones who are likely to be worse off. Now we know that this is not so" (p. 139). What, does "turn the other cheek" imply if not forgiveness? Quotes such as this ignore the logical necessity of forgiveness for avoiding negative spirals and suggest that Singer only grudgingly admits the desirability of forgiveness rather than its absolute urgency, even when his own extrinsic system demands it.

others is, then, the complete solution for the Prisoner's Dilemma; it dissolves the dilemma altogether" (p. 147). Unfortunately, instead of building on this point he quickly moves on, because he is convinced genuine concern for others can only be cultivated among one's "family and personal relationships" (p. 148). While I share Singer's concern for community and intimacy, I think he is far too pessimistic regarding what we are capable of regarding strangers. I am also convinced that Singer is also mistaken regarding the nature of our obligation to others.[10]

Instead of writing a chapter on Tit for Tat, Singer should have written a chapter entitled "Genuine Concern for Others." That he did not reveals many of his philosophic commitments including; utilitarianism, **materialism**, hedonism and relativism.[11] Your evaluation of his work will largely depend, just as mine does, upon your prior evaluation of these commitments.

Does Plato stand up any better to scrutiny? It depends, as with Singer, on your prior evaluation of other philosophic positions. That being said, Plato has his strengths, even if the ultimate persuasive power of his argument is debatable. The first strength is his ability to get to the heart of the matter. Through the mouth and character of Socrates, Plato uses questions, doubts and dialectic (careful reasoning and argumentation) to clarify philosophic questions. That is, even if one doesn't like all the answers that Plato arrives at, one still marvels at his ability to define problems and thereby set the course of Western philosophy.

Second, Plato's transcendent account of justice is grounded in reality. Instead of making justice a tool, Plato insists that the good is something we serve because *it is the truth*. If you think courage is in short supply, if you think human beings struggle to do the right thing, if you are convinced that there is objective meaning to the world, then this is no small matter. Plato not only sets a foundation, he points out, even if he missteps at times, the way towards truth. Moreover, it can be argued that even Plato's critics have the same goal in mind (i.e., truth), they simply dispute what the nature of truth is.[12]

Why then has Plato been criticized? Here are three basic claims which we only have the space to sketch in outline. First, Plato's account of justice (and truth) has been accused of being dualistic. By which the critic means that it unnecessarily dichotomizes and prioritizes certain aspects of reality over and above others; soul over body, supernatural over natural, etc. According to critics, not only is this false, it also leads to the denigration of the subordinate aspects of each dichotomy (e.g., neglect of or suspicion towards the body; passive acceptance of the "here and now" in hopes of heaven and so forth).

Second, critics of Plato's dualism have further criticized his philosophy for implying idealism. That is, Plato's theory of justice which is grounded in a transcendent reality focuses on ideas rather than the concrete world. In essence the root criticism is that Plato's philosophy is too theoretical and is therefore impractical. After all, what matters

Materialism: The philosophy which argues that only matter (and material things) exist. Nonmaterial entities or realities such as God, ideas, virtues, etc., are either reducible to material causes or do not exist. For instance, it is not uncommon to hear a materialist argue that, "love is just chemicals in your head."

---

[10] In brief, we ought to treat others well, independent of how they treat us.

[11] "If the universe has not been constructed in accordance with any plan, it has no meaning to be discovered. *There is no value inherent in it*, independently of the existence of sentient beings *who prefer some states of affairs to others*. Ethics is no part of the structure of the universe, *in the way that atoms are*" (Singer, 1995, p. 188) [Emphasis Added].

[12] "At any rate we may say that the search for truth is ultimately the search for Absolute Truth, God, and even those systems of philosophy which appear to refute this statement, e.g. Historical Materialism, are nevertheless examples of it, for they are seeking, even if unconsciously, even if they would not recognize the fact, for the ultimate Ground, the supremely Real. Even if intellectual speculation has at times led to bizarre doctrines and monstrous conclusions, we cannot but have a certain sympathy for and interest in the struggle of the human intellect to attain Truth" (Copleston S.J., 1946/1993, p. 6).

in daily life is the practical results.[13] In support of this criticism, Singer (1995) describes Socrates' answer this way, "It all seems too theoretical, too contrived and [as a result] the dialogue becomes one-sided" (p. 9).[14]

Finally, one could argue that Plato's account of justice is actually extrinsic rather than intrinsic. This argument is made on the grounds that even "harmonizing the soul" is really just a claim about what is "good for" human beings. This criticism seems especially true, when Modern philosophers try describe Plato's point in contemporary terms. For instance, some have argued that "Socrates' answer depends on a notion of mental health" (Pojman & Vaughn, 2011, p. 531). Setting aside the anachronism of the claim, it seems clear that "mental health" is an extrinsic good. We value mental health as an extrinsic good, for the other goods sanity can procure. If that is right, then Plato fails to give an account of justice in which it is really valued for its own sake.

Are these criticisms decisive? I don't think so. It seems to me that the heart of Plato's position hinges upon the plausibility of a transcendent reality. If God and/or Truth exist, then focusing on such "ideas" is hardly idealism. It is simply the recognition of reality, the recognition of the source of all being. Moreover, transcendence may imply order and hierarchy but it certainly does not necessitate "dualism" in the usual pejorative sense, as thinkers such as Aristotle and Aquinas have made clear.[15]

Nor has anyone shown that materialism can give a more compelling account of the cosmos. (Materialism is the theory that all of reality is reducible to matter). In fact, given that materialism cannot account for consciousness, it seem clear that a thoroughgoing materialism *can give no account of reality at all* (Nagel, 2012).[16] Finally, if one gives up modern biases and terminology, then it is clear that Plato intends to say that acting justly is a matter of being what we are intended to be. It is not a crude point of utility and "mental health" but rather about a correspondence between our behavior and Truth. Reality, not convenience, results or desire, determines how we ought to behave. The basic point is this: To really recognize the good is to see that the good cannot be justified upon grounds other than itself. Good consequences are of course preferable, but they alone

---

[13] See for example John Dewey's (1958) *Experience and Nature*. Here is but one sample of Dewey's commitment to reducing truth to pragmatism (what works; efficiency): "But in the practice of science, knowledge is an affair of *making* sure, not of grasping antecedently given sureties. What is already known, what is accepted as truth, is of immense importance; inquiry could not proceed a step without it. But it is held subject to use, and is at the mercy of discoveries which it makes possible. It has to be adjusted to the latter and not the latter to it. When things are defined as instruments, their valued and validity reside in what proceeds from them; consequences not antecedents supply meaning and validity" (p. 154).

[14] What Singer fails to address is that if his criticism of Socrates' answer is correct, then so too is Glaucon's. That is, Singer never accounts for the philosophy of "appearances". Why not simply appear to cooperate with others, when you'll get all the "benefits" that drive Singer's philosophy, along with the freedom to do whatever one wants to do, whenever one wants to do it? Why, on Singer's terms, is that wrong?

[15] Aristotle (2004) argues that the soul is the form of the body. That is, the soul is the life-giving principle of the body. They are two sides of a single organism. "But just as the eyeball and the power of sight are the eye, so here the soul and body are the living thing" (413a15). Similarly, Aquinas (n.d.) argues that Christian resurrection will be an embodied rather than ethereal life. "For it is clear that the soul is naturally united to the body and is departed from it, contrary to its nature and *per accidens*. Hence the soul devoid of its body is imperfect, as long as it is without the body . . . but the soul, since it is part of man's body, is not an entire man, *and my soul is not I*" (p. 197)[Emphasis added].

[16] "The natural internal stance of human life assumes that there is a real world, that many questions, both factual and practical, have correct answers, and that there are norms of thought which, if we follow them, will tend to lead us toward the correct answers to those questions. It assumes that to follow those norms is to respond correctly to values that we apprehend. Mathematics, science and ethics are built on such norms. It is difficult to make sense of all this in traditional naturalistic terms" (Nagel, 2012, p. 72).

To really recognize the good is to see that the good cannot be justified upon grounds other than itself.
©Fam Veld/Shutterstock.com

cannot justify right action. The claim that the good makes upon us is not subject to price, nor outcomes, nor any season. This is why, from within the intrinsic school, the good is simply beautiful.[17] Being good is not a crass calculation of self-benefit (enlightened or otherwise) but a modest submission to reality. Some things *are* simply sacred.

"Why Be Good?" and Sport

Intrinsic and extrinsic theories of justice impact sport in several ways. First, is what might be called the functionary issue. This regards the practical implications that each conception of the nature of justice have upon the actions policies, goals and behaviors prescribed and proscribed in sport. Three areas in sport where the lines between intrinsic and extrinsic justification are starkly drawn and are therefore easy to see are; sex, performance-enhancing drugs (PEDs), and genetic engineering. A second but related issue is more theoretical, though its answer has obvious practical implications. This is the issue of transcendence. Why does sport grab us? Why does it have such power to move us and what does that power suggest? Does sport point beyond itself to a meaningful world, perhaps even to God? Or, is sport merely one more consumer desire to be stoked, manipulated, and satisfied?

The Practical Implications of Intrinsic and Extrinsic Accounts of Justice

How should one explain the astonishing rapidity of the sexual revolution in the Western world? Although an in depth discussion is beyond the purview of this text, it seems, at least in part, to be explained by the tacit understanding among most people that traditional sexual

---

[17] Plato's pupil Aristotle explicitly makes this point in both the *Metaphysics* and *Ethics*. In the *Metaphysics* (2002b), while arguing for a motionless source of all other motions, Aristotle points out that the non-instrumental ground of reality is the beautiful (1072a26). In the *Ethics* (2002a) he asserts that right action is done "for the sake of the beautiful, since this is the end that belongs to virtue" (1115b13).

mores were justified on extrinsic grounds.[18] In crude terms, the argument looks something like this: Just as Gyges' ring made Gyges immune to punishment, the pill (and antibiotics) have made human beings essentially impervious to the consequences of promiscuity or "sexual freedom." Absent such consequences as pregnancy or disease, why should consenting adults not do what they will? In such circumstances, it is clear that without a compelling intrinsic account for the goodness of traditional sexual morality, the traditional view will collapse, for the consequences of breaching that morality have largely disappeared.

The point of this brief exposition, is not to argue that the sexual revolution was good or bad, though that is an important and interesting question. Nor is it to assume or profess that no intrinsic grounds for traditional sexual morality exist.[19] The point is to show one example of how philosophy plays out in the real world. Our commitments, whether wise or foolish, have consequences. The claim being made is this: Whether one extols or laments the fact, the majority of the people in the West are philosophically committed to an extrinsic understanding of sexual morality. This is deeply engrained in our culture. Questions regarding the intrinsic character of sexual activity, or of the effect of such actions on one's character, or of the danger of such behavior "enslaving one's best part to one's worst" are, ironically, like Greek to most people.[20]

For example, the International Olympic Committee (IOC) provided four hundred and fifty thousand condoms, or "42 condoms per athlete" (Caplan-Bricker, 2016, para. 3) at the 2016 Rio de Jeneiro Olympic Games. For the 2018 Winter Games in Pyeongchang the number was 110,000 condoms or approximately, "37 condoms per competitor" (Jimison, 2018, para. 5). Let that sink in. Consider the resources, time and energy involved. Could they have been put to better use? Whatever one thinks about the wisdom of such a decision, it should be clear that it is philosophically based in an extrinsic theory of justice. The good is simply a *function* of fulfilling desires via the procurement or avoidance of certain outcomes and consequences. Nothing more. Nothing less. If an extrinsic understanding of justice is presumed, then as long as those outcomes which are assumed to be desirable are procured and those considered undesirable are avoided, the behavior itself is not and cannot be an issue.

Similarly, discussions of steroids and genetic engineering in sport reveal the difference between intrinsic and extrinsic accounts of justice. For instance, popular arguments against each generally rest upon the extrinsic claim to harm. Steroids and genetic engineering should be avoided, so the popular argument goes, due to the fact that engaging in either form of performance enhancement results in un-safe outcomes for the user or patient. Steroid use, it is said, has well known harmful side-effects, whereas genetic engineering can lead to genetic disease, birth defects, even death (Green, 2007).

Let us assume, for the sake of the argument, that the claim to harm is true in both cases. Each prohibition still rests upon a fragile foundation. Why? Because each prohibition is dependent upon circumstance. Steroids, it has been argued, can be used in effective and safe doses (Brown, 2009). Similarly, genetic engineering proponents argue that it will become safe as knowledge and technology increase (Munthe, 2007). Therefore if safety is the reason to ban genetic engineering, then once it is safe, genetic engineering becomes morally acceptable on both treatment and enhancement grounds. That is, it should be just as licit to genetically improve or select traits such as height, sex, or athleticism (enhancement) as it is to cure a genetic disease (treatment). As with the sexual revolution, if one assumes an extrinsic understanding of justice, then one's attitude

---

[18] For contrasting accounts of the sexual revolution see: Allyn (2001) and Eberstadt (2012).

[19] I, in fact, think that the intrinsic argument for traditional sexual morality (based in the beauty, unitive character, and intimate nature of the act) has the high ground, but that is an argument for another day.

[20] That is they have trouble even conceptualizing such a position as a living, let alone compelling, alternative.

towards PEDs and genetic engineering will (and should) radically shift once the safety concerns have been alleviated.[21]

If the extrinsic case is insufficient to prohibit PEDs or genetic enhancement, can more compelling intrinsic arguments be offered? I think the answer is yes. As regards genetic enhancement, here is but one. Genetic engineering for enhancement purposes commodifies human beings. Such commodification is contrary to our nature as rational animals and therefore contrary to reality. Our rational nature makes us subjects rather than mere objects. Yet, to design your child, to design the next great athlete, or to design the next supermodel is to turn human beings into cattle, or if you prefer, a consumer good. It is to value them not for what they are (a human being) but rather for who they are (tall, blonde, male, female, black, white, strong, intelligent, and so forth) as well as what they will allegedly procure. In such a world human beings no longer have inherent worth and are therefore inherently unequal (see Nietzsche in Chapter 2). As C.S. Lewis (1944, 2001) presciently warned in *The Abolition of Man*, "if man chooses to treat himself as raw material, raw material he will be" (p. 72). To make such a move is not liberation, but as Socrates pointed out, slavery. It is to subordinate reality to the service of utility (e.g. the desires of the parents, or the State, or the scientist).[22]

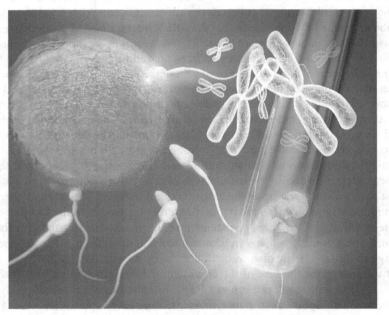

"If man chooses to treat himself as raw material, raw material he will be."
©Giovanni Cancerni/Shutterstock.com

---

[21] That is not to say there are no other arguments (e.g. coercion) or considerations (e.g. access) worthy of our attention in a full ethical analysis. However, it does seem clear that most of the problems dissipate if not disappear once the issue of harm is resolved. For instance, coercion loses moral force if compelling you to take steroids is no different than compelling you to train harder (to compete with me). Similarly, as technology improves drugs and medical interventions will become cheaper, which will alleviate the access problem. Again, we see that opposition, based solely upon extrinsic grounds, is inherently contingent.

[22] "What we call Man's power is, in reality, a power possessed by some men which they may, or may not, allow other men to profit by...From this point of view, what we call Man's power over Nature turns out to be a power exercised by some men over other men with Nature as its instrument" (Lewis, 1944, 2001, pp. 54–55).

What this admittedly cursory (and therefore indecisive) discussion of the ethics of sex, steroids and genetic engineering in sport reveals is this: *If the results are all we have, no claim to justice is secure.* Everything is contingent upon the results procured and the desirability of those results to those in power. Should outcomes or desires change, so too must the conception of justice change with the shifting evaluation of the consequences. As Singer (1995) admits, the application of justice "will depend on circumstances" (p. 149). As a result, sport becomes, in the words of sociologist Jacques Ellul (1997), "technique," a mere means to further efficiency. In sport this utilitarian mindset means that everything is for sale. Everything has a price. Every market must be tapped. Every stream of revenue must be exploited and maximized.

Reflection on the day to day practice of American professionalized sport should quickly show you manifestations of this philosophy at work. Consider, for example, the crass scramble for money exemplified in the growth of naming-rights for stadiums, including such inane names as the Denver Broncos' "Sports Authority Field at Mile High" and the University of Louisville's "KFC Yum Center." Or consider that in 2016 the National Basketball Association (NBA) announced that it would begin selling corporate advertising space on their jerseys for the 2017–2018 season. On uniform advertising was considered necessary despite the fact that league revenue was already "projected to be $7 billion" (Rovell, 2016, para. 5). By the 2018–2019 season 29 of the 30 NBA teams had corporate logos on their jerseys. These advertisements were "generating more than $150 million" a year (Lefton and Lombardo, 2019, para. 2).

Once one assumes this utilitarian mind-set, undergirded by an extrinsic theory of justice, *everything has a price.* Such logic makes the decision to sell uniform advertising inevitable (no matter how superfluous the revenue is and no matter how vulgar the aesthetics are). Given the philosophic commitments ascendant in modern sporting culture, this trend will only grow. In fact, Major League Baseball (MLB) is expected to start selling on-uniform advertising beginning in the 2022 season (Lefton, 2019).

The same logic is also driving all the major American professional sports leagues towards embracing gambling (Ganguli, 2018; Ogus, 2019; Rosen, 2018; Shaikin, 2018). This is even true of MLB, which, given scandals such as Pete Rose and the 1919 Black Sox, has historically kept its distance from sports wagering. No longer. The lust for more revenue is insatiable (see the Brisbee reading in this chapter).

Once the good is reduced to a cost-benefit analysis, leagues will always rationalize coming down on the side of increased revenue. Consider, for example, how MLB Commissioner Rob Manfred describes the selling of proprietary data to MGM Casinos (which will allow the gaming industry to further fix odds in their favor) as a selfless opportunity to serve fans. "Our partnership with MGM will help us navigate this evolving space responsibly, and we look forward to the fan engagement opportunities ahead" (Shaikin, 2018, para. 9). This is a lie, hidden behind corporate speak, buried under euphemism, and then smothered in circumlocution.

A separate but related point can be made regarding the persuasive power of threats and punishments from within an extrinsic theory of justice. Such threats are of limited value because they can inspire no more than calculation. Yet, a cost-benefit analysis does not rule out any given behavior. It simply requires an assessment of the price. In fact, in spite of threats of punishment from leagues or governing bodies, cost-benefit analyses might actually encourage "bad behavior", if the expected benefit (or desire for that benefit) is high enough.

Every stream of revenue must be exploited and maximized.
©jessicakirsh/Shutterstock.com

Consider the case of NCAA Division I "big-time" sport. Threats only work if coaches, administrators, and players think the risk of punishment exceeds the reward. But this is problematic on two levels. First, the amount of power, money, and prestige in big-time college sport is so high that it is tough to tip the scales away from deliberate infractions. Taking the risk seems well worth the likely reward. Similarly, bad behavior will often be tolerated or rationalized by administrators or fans because the costs of real punishment are too high (e.g., fans and administrators don't want to fire a winning coach). How else, for example, can one explain the fact that although coaches of major college programs are routinely fired for not winning enough games, former Louisville men's basketball coach Rick Pitino was not fired until his program was engulfed in its third major ethical scandal, which involved the FBI exposing Louisville as part of a "pay for play" kickback and bribery system between coaches, Adidas and recruited players (Schlabach, 2017). The two previous scandals included Pitino committing adultery, paying for the abortion of the child conceived and using prostitution as an on campus recruiting tool (O'Conner, 2016). He survived all of this despite having a clause in his contract which allowed him to be fired for "acts of moral depravity or misconduct that damages the university's reputation" (*Columbia Daily Tribune*, 2015, para. 4). No such hesitation would have existed if his team had been

CALVIN AND HOBBES © Watterson. Reprinted with permission of ANDREWS MCMEEL SYNDICATION. All rights reserved.

consistently losing games. The second problem with extrinsic threats is one of motivation. If the only motivation in NCAA "big-time" sport is the fear of getting caught, then one will usually feel, like Gyges, impervious to punishment. There simply are not enough NCAA eyes to look over every shoulder. Enforcement, absent virtue, is impossible.

Transcendence and Sport?

Given these limitations to an extrinsic understanding of justice in sport, what can be done? How might an intrinsic account gain traction? It seems to me that the plausibility of an intrinsic account relies upon the claim that sport points beyond itself to the existence of a transcendent reality to which we are beholden. What does this mean and how might it be defended? At its most basic level it simply means that sport is part of a meaningful world. The precise nature of this meaningful world (religious or otherwise) is up for debate. What all proponents of this position would agree on is that the world has purpose and objective value. Such an understanding does not preclude sport practitioners from desiring certain outcomes, or from pursuing commerce or profit, it simply puts each of them in their proper place.

Singer (1995), for his part, discusses "transcendence" at the end of *How are We to Live?*, but he has something very different in mind. In responding to the claim that life is like the Greek **Myth of Sisyphus** (who was condemned by the gods to meaningless toil), he suggests that we must find a transcendent cause in life. But by this term he simply means we must find a "cause that extends beyond the boundaries of the self" (p. 218). We must create our own meaning in the world on the grounds of utility and desire.[23] Then we can reimagine our own Sisyphean struggle, our own lives, as building something worthwhile, something which will survive us, rather than viewing our lives simply as meaningless toil. This is, Singer argues, all we can hope for and more importantly all we need.[24]

This seems to me to be profoundly mistaken. A dead man is still dead. He knows and is nothing. Death, absent some form of transcendent reality, is annihilation. Any meaning *you've created* dies with *you*. After all, *you* created it. Moreover, whatever one leaves behind, even if it has usefulness or subjective meaning to others, will itself crumble and be forgotten. It is only a matter of when. One is reminded of the Latin proverb often found on gravestones, "*Eram quod es; eris quod sum*", which translates as "What you are, I once was, what I am, you will be." Perhaps Singer is right. Perhaps we live in a meaningless world, but if we do, "subjective utilitarian meaning" is no solution.[25]

What then is the intrinsic alternative? As I said before, it is that the world really does a have a transcendent purpose. This is the ground upon which justice rests; its conformity to the real. To paraphrase Aristotle, truth is the "conformity of the mind to reality."

The Myth of Sisyphus: An ancient Greek myth in which Sisyphus is condemned by Zeus to roll a boulder up to the top of hill. Unfortunately the hill's slope and the weight of the boulder are each proportioned in such a way that Sisyphus' muscles always give out as he reaches the top of the hill. As a result, the boulder rolls back down the hill and Sisyphus has to start his toil all over again. The myth is commonly understood to be a metaphor for the human condition, where all of our work and struggles ultimately accomplish nothing and are annihilated by death.

---

[23] "I have been arguing against the view that value depends entirely on my subjective desires. Yet I am not defending the objectivity of ethics in the traditional sense. Ethical truths are not written into the fabric of the universe: to that extent the subjectivist is correct. If there were no beings with desire or preferences of any kind, nothing would be of value and ethics would lack all content. The possibility of being led, by reasoning, to the point of view of the universe provides as much 'objectivity' as there can be" (Singer, 1995, p. 231).

[24] Philosopher Michael Polanyi's (Polanyi & Prosch, 1975) response to such thinking is particularly apropos. "However, the utilitarian calculus cannot demonstrate our commitment to ideals which demand serious sacrifice of us. A man's sincerity in professing his ideals is to be measured rather by the *lack* of prudence he shows in pursuing them. The utilitarian confirmation of unselfishness is not more than a pretense by which traditional ideals are made acceptable to a philosophically skeptical age. Camouflaged as long-term selfishness or 'intelligent self-interest,' the traditional ideals of man are protected from destruction by skepticism" (p. 10).

[25] Philosophically speaking there seems to be only three alternatives; stoicism (heroic resignation), nihilism (the rejection of all values and truth), or transcendence (God, meaning, purpose, etc. are objectively real).

Actions have meaning because they either conform to or reject the truth. Meaningful action is possible because we live in a meaningful world.

Hints of that meaningfulness are all around us in the awesome, terrifying, beautiful, and sublime experiences in our lives. Think of a stunning sunset, a particularly moving piece of art, or the recent burning of Notre Dame Cathedral in Paris. Think of the birth of a child, the death of a loved one, or the self-sacrifice of someone like Mother Theresa. Think of the courage displayed on the beaches of Normandy or by the New York City firefighters on 9/11. Do all such things really amount to nothing? No. In fact, they suggest just the opposite. This or that specific experience of beauty (or its loss) points beyond itself to beauty as such.[26] As the 19th Century psychologist and philosopher William James (1896/1956) suggests, "the best things are the more eternal things, the overlapping things, the things in the universe that throw the last stone, so to speak, and say the final word" (p. 25).

Do all such things really amount to nothing?
©Jerome LABOUYRIE/Shutterstock.com

In fact, sport is one way we have such experiences of beauty and meaning. By "making a nice pass," or "learning to swim" or "catching our second wind" or "losing our self in play" or "sacrificing for the team" we come to recognize *that beauty is real*. This argument is not proof of course, but it is evidence of a meaningful world. The sociologist Peter Berger (1969) describes the idea this way.

> "The experience of joyful play is not something that must be sought on some mystical margin of existence. It can be readily found in the reality of ordinary life. Yet, within this experienced reality it constitutes a signal of transcendence, because its intrinsic intention points beyond itself and beyond man's 'nature' to a 'supernatural' justification" (p. 60).

But if this is right, then justice is something we must discover and to which we are beholden. Justice could never be understood as merely a tool. Profit, competition (winning), marketing and so forth all have their place in sport, but as means not ends. They,

---

[26] Moreover, as we saw in Chapter 2, even the existence of evil can be understood to suggest the existence of a transcendent reality. Meaninglessness would destroy the existence of both good and evil and leave us with nothing more than chaos.

Are our sporting experiences evidence of a transcendent reality?
©sculpies/Shutterstock.com

not justice, are the tools.[27] To be good, profit, competition, marketing, as well as all other instrumental goods in sport, must serve justice.

This chapter, like those that proceeded it, points to the importance of philosophy. Ideas may be refuted, but no idea has an expiration date. The quality of the argument, not its age, is what matters. Nor is history inevitably about progress, moral or otherwise. As such, there is no "wrong side of history." Sometimes good ideas succeed bad ideas, but it is often just the opposite. Both progress and regress, both growth and decay are possible. Only modern prejudice convinces us to believe otherwise. The Englishman Lord Chesterfield (1998) may have said it best when he wrote to his son in 1748 that one ought to, "Speak of the moderns [or ancients] without contempt, and of the ancients [or moderns] without idolatry; judge them all by their merits, but not by their ages" (p. 65).

It should be clear at this point, that one's position on the nature of justice depends, to a great extent, on one's other philosophic commitments. Underneath the surface of this debate are assumptions and commitments regarding many of the questions we have already covered. One's convictions regarding realism/relativism, good and evil and so forth will, for instance, greatly affect your assessment of Plato and Singer. Finally, your commitments ought to be determined by your conviction that they are true, rather than by their utility, popularity, or convenience.[28]

But if this is correct, then we need to understand and carefully examine the arguments as well as our own convictions. Philosophy matters, which means we need to do it well. It impacts all the areas of our lives, including, as we have seen, the world of sport. As this chapter has tried to show, we cannot avoid the question "why be good?" Yet, even if we can satisfactorily answer the question "why be good?" it still remains to be answered how we can put this knowledge to practice. What best promotes ethical behavior? What will encourage people to do the right thing? How might sport play a role? Our eighth and final chapter will attempt to answer these questions.

---

[27] Such assertions are no doubt controversial, but whatever side of the argument you fall on, you should realize that the intrinsic argument, the argument for transcendence, is no more controversial than claims such as Singer's that we live in a meaningless world in which justice is reducible to utility.

[28] As Aristotle (2002a) opined in the *Nicomachean Ethics*, "But no doubt it would be admitted to be better, indeed to be necessary when keeping the truth safe is at stake, even to abandon the things that are one's own, both for other reasons and because we are philosophers; for while both [the truth and one's friends] are loved, it is a sacred thing to give the higher honor to the truth" (1096a17).

PHILOSOPHIC SELECTIONS

Selection #1: Plato, *The Republic*, Book II, Book IX.

http://classics.mit.edu/Plato/republic.3.ii.html; http://classics.mit.edu/Plato/republic.10.ix.html

Introduction: *The Republic* is primarily concerned with justice. What is it to be good and why should any of us actually do good things? Is the good its own justification or should we be good only insofar as doing so is good for us? That is, insofar as doing good leads to good consequences, such as a "happy life" or a "good reputation" or "more victories." Plato (through the mouth of his teacher Socrates) argues that justice is its own reward. We ought to be just simply because in doing so we are serving the good. The good is something we are bound to serve, not something we define, or use at our own convenience.

With these words I was thinking that I had made an end of the discussion; but the end, in truth, proved to be only a beginning. For Glaucon, who is always the most pugnacious of men, was dissatisfied at Thrasymachus' retirement; he wanted to have the battle out. So he said to me: Socrates, do you wish really to persuade us, or only to seem to have persuaded us, that to be just is always better than to be unjust?

I should wish really to persuade you, I replied, if I could.

Then you certainly have not succeeded. Let me ask you now:—How would you arrange goods—are there not some which we welcome for their own sakes, and independently of their consequences, as, for example, harmless pleasures and enjoyments, which delight us at the time, although nothing follows from them?

I agree in thinking that there is such a class, I replied.

Is there not also a second class of goods, such as knowledge, sight, health, which are desirable not only in themselves, but also for their results?

Certainly, I said.

And would you not recognize a third class, such as gymnastic, and the care of the sick, and the physician's art; also the various ways of money-making—these do us good but we regard them as disagreeable; and no one would choose them for their own sakes, but only for the sake of some reward or result which flows from them?

There is, I said, this third class also. But why do you ask?

Because I want to know in which of the three classes you would place justice?

In the highest class, I replied,—among those goods which he who would be happy desires both for their own sake and for the sake of their results.

Then the many are of another mind; they think that justice is to be reckoned in the troublesome class, among goods which are to be pursued for the sake of rewards and of reputation, but in themselves are disagreeable and rather to be avoided.

I know, I said, that this is their manner of thinking, and that this was the thesis which Thrasymachus was maintaining just now, when he censured justice and praised injustice. But I am too stupid to be convinced by him.

I wish, he said, that you would hear me as well as him, and then I shall see whether you and I agree. For Thrasymachus seems to me, like a snake, to have been charmed by your voice sooner than he ought to have been; but to my mind the nature of justice and injustice have not yet been made clear. Setting aside their rewards and results, I want to know what they are in themselves, and how they inwardly work in the soul. If you, please, then, I will revive the argument of Thrasymachus. And first I will speak of the nature and origin of justice according to the common view of them. Secondly, I will show that all men who practise justice do so against their will, of necessity, but not as a good. And thirdly, I will argue that there is reason in this view, for the life of the unjust is after all better far than the life of the just—if what they say is true, Socrates, since I myself am not of their opinion. But still I acknowledge that I am perplexed when I hear the voices of Thrasymachus and myriads of others dinning in my ears; and, on the other hand, I have never yet heard the superiority of justice to injustice maintained by any one in a satisfactory way. I want to hear justice praised in respect of itself; then I shall be satisfied, and you are the person from whom I think that I am most likely to hear this; and therefore I will praise the unjust life to the utmost of my power, and my manner of speaking will indicate the manner in which I desire to hear you too praising justice and censuring injustice. Will you say whether you approve of my proposal?

Indeed I do; nor can I imagine any theme about which a man of sense would oftener wish to converse.

I am delighted, he replied, to hear you say so, and shall begin by speaking, as I proposed, of the nature and origin of justice.

They say that to do injustice is, by nature, good; to suffer injustice, evil; but that the evil is greater than the good. And so when men have both done and suffered injustice and have had experience of both, not being able to avoid the one and obtain the other, they think that they had better agree among themselves to have neither; hence there arise laws and mutual covenants; and that which is ordained by law is termed by them lawful and just. This they affirm to be the origin and nature of justice;—it is a mean or compromise, between the best of all, which is to do injustice and not be punished, and the worst of all, which is to suffer injustice without the power of retaliation; and justice, being at a middle point between the two, is tolerated not as a good, but as the lesser evil, and honoured by reason of the inability of men to do injustice. For no man who is worthy to be called a man would ever submit to such an agreement if he were able to resist; he would be mad if he did. Such is the received account, Socrates, of the nature and origin of justice.

Now that those who practise justice do so involuntarily and because they have not the power to be unjust will best appear if we imagine something of this kind: having given both to the just and the unjust power to do what they will, let us watch and see whither desire will lead them; then we shall discover in the very act the just and unjust man to be proceeding along the same road, following their interest, which all natures deem to be their good, and are only diverted into the path of justice by the force of law. The liberty which we are supposing may be most completely given to them in the form of such a power as is said to have been possessed by Gyges the ancestor of Croesus the Lydian. According to the tradition, Gyges was a shepherd in the service of the king of Lydia; there was a great storm, and an earthquake made an opening in the earth at the place where he was feeding his flock. Amazed at the sight, he descended into the opening, where, among other marvels, he beheld a hollow brazen horse, having doors, at which he stooping and looking in saw a dead body of stature, as appeared to him, more than human, and having nothing on but a gold ring; this he took from the finger of the dead and reascended. Now the shepherds met together, according to custom, that they might send their monthly report about the flocks to the king; into their assembly he came having the ring on his finger, and as he was sitting among them he chanced to turn the collet of the ring inside his hand, when instantly he became invisible to the rest of the company and they began to speak of him as if he were no longer present. He was astonished at this, and again touching the ring he turned the collet outwards and reappeared; he made several trials of the ring, and always with the same result-when he turned the collet inwards he became invisible, when outwards he reappeared. Whereupon he contrived to be chosen one of the messengers who were sent to the court; where as soon as he arrived he seduced the queen, and with her help conspired against the king and slew him, and took the kingdom. Suppose now that there were two such magic rings, and the just put on one of them and the unjust the other; no man can be imagined to be of such an iron nature that he would stand fast in justice. No man would keep his hands off what was not his own when he could safely take what he liked out of the market, or go into houses and lie with any one at his pleasure, or kill or release from prison whom he would, and in all respects be like a God among men. Then the actions of the just would be as the actions of the unjust; they would both come at last to the same point. And this we may truly affirm to be a great proof that a man is just, not willingly or because he thinks that justice is any good to him individually, but of necessity, for wherever any one thinks that he can safely be unjust, there he is unjust. For all men believe in their hearts that injustice is far more profitable to the individual than justice, and he who argues as I have been supposing, will say that they are right. If you could imagine any one obtaining this power of becoming invisible, and never doing any wrong or touching what was another's, he would be thought by the lookers-on to be a most wretched idiot, although they would praise him to one another's faces, and keep up appearances with one another from a fear that they too might suffer injustice. Enough of this.

Now, if we are to form a real judgment of the life of the just and unjust, we must isolate them; there is no other way; and how is the isolation to be effected? I answer: Let the unjust man be entirely unjust, and the just man entirely just; nothing is to be taken away from either of them, and both are to be perfectly furnished for the work of their respective lives. First, let the unjust be like other distinguished masters of craft; like the skilful pilot or physician, who knows intuitively his own powers and keeps within their limits, and who, if he fails at any point, is able to recover himself. So let the unjust make his unjust attempts in the right way, and lie hidden if he means to be great in his injustice (he who is found out is nobody): for the highest reach of injustice is: to be deemed just when you are not. Therefore I say that in the perfectly unjust man we must assume the most perfect injustice; there is to be no deduction, but we must allow him, while doing the most unjust acts, to have acquired the greatest reputation for justice. If he have taken a false step he must be able to recover himself; he must be one who can speak with effect, if any of his deeds come to light, and who can force his way where force is required his courage and strength, and command of money and friends. And at his side let us place the just man in his nobleness and simplicity, wishing, as Aeschylus says, to be and not to seem good. There must be no seeming, for if he seem to be just he will be honoured and rewarded, and then we shall not know whether he is just for the sake of justice or for the sake of honours and rewards; therefore, let him be clothed in justice only, and have no other covering; and he must be imagined in a state of life the opposite of the former. Let him be the best of men, and let him be thought the worst; then he will have been put to the proof; and we shall see whether he will be affected by the fear of infamy and its consequences. And let him continue thus to the hour of death; being just and seeming to be unjust. When both have reached the uttermost extreme, the one of justice and the other of injustice, let judgment be given which of them is the happier of the two.

Heavens! my dear Glaucon, I said, how energetically you polish them up for the decision, first one and then the other, as if they were two statues.

I do my best, he said. And now that we know what they are like there is no difficulty in tracing out the sort of life which awaits either of them. This I will proceed to describe; but as you may think the description a little too coarse, I ask you to suppose, Socrates, that the words which follow are not mine.—Let me put them into the mouths of the eulogists of injustice: They will tell you that the just man who is thought unjust will be scourged, racked, bound—will have his eyes burnt out; and, at last, after suffering every kind of evil, he will be impaled: Then he will understand that he ought to seem only, and not to be, just; the words of Aeschylus may be more truly spoken of the unjust than of the just. For the unjust is pursuing a reality; he does not live with a view to appearances—he wants to be really unjust and not to seem only.

His mind has a soil deep and fertile, Out of which spring his prudent counsels. In the first place, he is thought just, and therefore bears rule in the city; he can marry whom he will, and give in marriage to whom he will; also he can trade and deal where he likes, and always to his own advantage, because he has no misgivings about injustice and at every contest, whether in public or private, he gets the better of his antagonists, and gains at their expense, and is rich, and out of his gains he can benefit his friends, and harm his enemies; moreover, he can offer sacrifices, and dedicate gifts to the gods abundantly and magnificently, and can honour the gods or any man whom he wants to honour in a far better style than the just, and therefore he is likely to be dearer than they are to the gods. And thus, Socrates, gods and men are said to unite in making the life of the unjust better than the life of the just.

I was going to say something in answer to Glaucon, when Adeimantus, his brother, interposed: Socrates, he said, you do not suppose that there is nothing more to be urged?

Why, what else is there? I answered.

The strongest point of all has not been even mentioned, he replied.

Well, then, according to the proverb, 'Let brother help brother'—if he fails in any part do you assist him; although I must confess that Glaucon has already said quite enough to lay me in the dust, and take from me the power of helping justice.

Nonsense, he replied. But let me add something more: There is another side to Glaucon's argument about the praise and censure of justice and injustice, which is equally required in order to bring out what I believe to be his meaning. Parents and tutors are always telling their sons and their wards that they are to be just; but why? not for the sake of justice, but for the sake of character and reputation; in the hope of obtaining for him who is reputed just some of those offices, marriages, and the like which Glaucon has enumerated among the advantages accruing to the unjust from the reputation of justice. More, however, is made of appearances by this class of persons than by the others; for they throw in the good opinion of the gods, and will tell you of a shower of benefits which the heavens, as they say, rain upon the pious; and this accords with the testimony of the noble Hesiod and Homer, the first of whom says, that the gods make the oaks of the just.—

To hear acorns at their summit, and bees I the middle;

And the sheep the bowed down bowed the with the their fleeces. and many other blessings of a like kind are provided for them. And Homer has a very similar strain; for he speaks of one whose fame is—

As the fame of some blameless king who, like a god,

Maintains justice to whom the black earth brings forth

Wheat and barley, whose trees are bowed with fruit,

And his sheep never fail to bear, and the sea gives him fish. Still grander are the gifts of heaven which Musaeus and his son vouchsafe to the just; they take them down into the world below, where they have the saints lying on couches at a feast, everlastingly drunk, crowned with garlands; their idea seems to be that an immortality of drunkenness is the highest meed of virtue. Some extend their rewards yet further; the posterity, as they say, of the faithful and just shall survive to the third and fourth generation.

This is the style in which they praise justice. But about the wicked there is another strain; they bury them in a slough in Hades, and make them carry water in a sieve; also while they are yet living they bring them to infamy, and inflict upon them the punishments which Glaucon described as the portion of the just who are reputed to be unjust; nothing else does their invention supply. Such is their manner of praising the one and censuring the other.

Once more, Socrates, I will ask you to consider another way of speaking about justice and injustice, which is not confined to the poets, but is found in prose writers. The universal voice of mankind is always declaring that justice and virtue are honourable, but grievous and toilsome; and that the pleasures of vice and injustice are easy of attainment, and are only censured by law and opinion. They say also that honesty is for the most part less profitable than dishonesty; and they are quite ready to call wicked men happy, and to honour them both in public and private when they are rich or in any other way influential, while they despise and overlook those who may be weak and poor, even though acknowledging them to be better than the others. But most extraordinary of all is their mode of speaking about virtue and the gods: they say that the gods apportion calamity and misery to many good men, and good and happiness to the wicked. And mendicant prophets go to rich men's doors and persuade them that they have a power committed to them by the gods of making an atonement for a man's own or his ancestor's sins by sacrifices or charms, with rejoicings and feasts; and they promise to harm an enemy, whether just or unjust, at a small cost; with magic arts and incantations binding heaven, as they say, to execute their will. And the poets are the authorities to whom they appeal, now smoothing the path of vice with the words of Hesiod.

Vice may be had in abundance without trouble; the way is smooth and her dwelling-place is near. But before virtue the gods have set toil, and a tedious and uphill road: then citing Homer as a witness that the gods may be influenced by men; for he also says: The gods, too, may he turned from their purpose; and men pray to them and avert their wrath by sacrifices and soothing entreaties, and by libations and the odour of fat, when they have sinned and transgressed. And they produce a host of books written by Musaeus and Orpheus, who were children of the Moon and the Muses—that is what they say—according to which they perform their ritual, and persuade not only individuals, but whole cities, that expiations and atonements for sin may be made by sacrifices and amusements which fill a vacant hour, and are equally at the service of the living and the dead; the latter sort they call mysteries, and they redeem us from the pains of hell, but if we neglect them no one knows what awaits us.

He proceeded: And now when the young hear all this said about virtue and vice, and the way in which gods and men regard them, how are their minds likely to be affected, my dear Socrates,—those of them, I mean, who are quickwitted, and, like bees on the wing, light on every flower, and from all that they hear are prone to draw conclusions as to what manner of persons they should be and in what way they should walk if they would make the best of life? Probably the youth will say to himself in the words of Pindar.

Can I by justice or by crooked ways of deceit ascend a loftier tower which may he a fortress to me all my days? For what men say is that, if I am really just and am not also thought just profit there is none, but the pain and loss on the other hand are unmistakable. But if, though unjust, I acquire the reputation of justice, a heavenly life is promised to me. Since then, as philosophers prove, appearance tyrannizes over truth and is lord of happiness, to appearance I must devote myself. I will describe around me a picture and shadow of virtue to be the vestibule and exterior of my house; behind I will trail the subtle and crafty fox, as Archilochus, greatest of sages, recommends. But I hear some one exclaiming that the concealment of wickedness is often difficult; to which I answer, Nothing great is easy. Nevertheless, the argument indicates this, if we would be happy, to be the path along which we should proceed. With a view to concealment we will establish secret brotherhoods and political clubs. And there are professors of rhetoric who teach the art of persuading courts and assemblies; and so, partly by persuasion and partly by force, I shall make unlawful gains and not be punished. Still I hear a voice saying that the gods cannot be deceived, neither can they be compelled. But what if there are no gods? or, suppose them to have no care of human things—why in either case should we mind about concealment? And even if there are gods, and they do care about us, yet we know of them only from tradition and the genealogies of the poets; and these are the very persons who say that they may be influenced and turned by 'sacrifices and soothing entreaties and by offerings.' Let us be consistent then, and believe both or neither. If the poets speak truly, why then we had better be unjust, and offer of the fruits of injustice; for if we are just, although we may escape the vengeance of heaven, we shall lose the gains of injustice; but, if we are unjust, we shall keep the gains, and by our sinning and praying, and praying and sinning, the gods will be propitiated, and we shall not be punished. 'But there is a world below in which either we or our posterity will suffer for our unjust deeds.' Yes, my friend, will be the reflection, but there are mysteries and atoning deities, and these have great power. That is what mighty cities declare; and the children of the gods, who were their poets and prophets, bear a like testimony.

On what principle, then, shall we any longer choose justice rather than the worst injustice? when, if we only unite the latter with a deceitful regard to appearances, we shall fare to our mind both with gods and men, in life and after death, as the most numerous and the highest authorities tell us. Knowing all this, Socrates, how can a man who has any superiority of mind or person or rank or wealth, be willing to honour justice; or indeed to refrain from laughing when he hears justice praised? And even if there should be some one who is able to disprove the truth of my words, and who is satisfied that justice is best, still he is not angry with the unjust, but is very ready to forgive them, because he also knows that men are not just of their own free will; unless, peradventure, there be some one whom the divinity within him may have inspired with a hatred of injustice, or who has attained knowledge of the truth—but no other man. He only blames injustice who, owing to cowardice or age or some weakness, has not the power of being unjust. And this is proved by the fact that when he obtains the power, he immediately becomes unjust as far as he can be.

The cause of all this, Socrates, was indicated by us at the beginning of the argument, when my brother and I told you how astonished we were to find that of all the professing panegyrists of justice—beginning with the ancient heroes of whom any memorial has been preserved to us, and ending with the men of our own time—no one has ever blamed injustice or praised justice except with a view to the glories, honours, and bene-fits which flow from them. No one has ever adequately described either in verse or prose the true essential nature of either of them abiding in the soul, and invisible to any human or divine eye; or shown that of all the things of a man's soul which he has within him, justice is the greatest good, and injustice the greatest evil. Had this been the universal strain, had you sought to persuade us of this from our youth upwards, we should not have been on the watch to keep one another from doing wrong, but every one would have been his own watchman, because afraid, if he did wrong, of harbouring in himself the greatest of evils. I dare say that Thrasymachus and others would seriously hold the language which I have been merely repeating, and words even stronger than these about justice and injustice, grossly, as I conceive, perverting their true nature. But I speak in this vehement manner, as I must frankly confess to you, because I want to hear from you the opposite side; and I would ask you to show not only the superiority which justice has over injustice, but what effect they have on the possessor of them which makes the one to be a good and the other an evil to him. And please, as Glaucon requested of you, to exclude reputations; for unless you take away from each of them his true reputation and add on the false, we shall say that you do not praise justice, but the appearance of it; we shall think that you are only exhorting us to keep injustice dark, and that you really agree with Thrasymachus in thinking that justice is another's good and the interest of the stronger, and that injustice is a man's own profit and interest, though injurious to the weaker. Now as you have admitted that justice is one of that highest class of goods which are desired indeed for their results, but in a far greater degree for their own sakes—like sight or hearing or knowledge or health, or any other real and natural and not merely conventional good—I would ask you in your praise of justice to regard one point only: I mean the essential good and evil which justice and injustice work in the possessors of them. Let others praise justice and censure injustice, magnifying the rewards and honours of the one and abusing the other; that is a manner of arguing which, coming from them, I am ready to tolerate, but from you who have spent your whole life in the consideration of this question, unless I hear the contrary from your own lips, I expect something better. And therefore, I say, not only prove to us that justice is better than injustice, but show what they either of them do to the possessor of them, which makes the one to be a good and the other an evil, whether seen or unseen by gods and men.

I had always admired the genius of Glaucon and Adeimantus, but on hearing these words I was quite delighted, and said: Sons of an illustrious father, that was not a bad beginning of the Elegiac verses which the admirer of Glaucon made in honour of you after you had distinguished yourselves at the battle of Megara.

'Sons of Ariston,' he sang, 'divine offspring of an illustrious hero.' The epithet is very appropriate, for there is something truly divine in being able to argue as you have done for the superiority of injustice, and remaining unconvinced by your own arguments. And I do believe that you are not convinced—this I infer from your general character, for had I judged only from your speeches I should have mistrusted you. But now, the greater my confidence in you, the greater is my difficulty in knowing what to say. For I am in a strait between two; on the one hand I feel that I am unequal to the task; and my inability is brought home to me by the fact that you were not satisfied with the answer which I made to Thrasymachus, proving, as I thought, the superiority which justice has over injustice. And yet I cannot refuse to help, while breath and speech remain to me; I am afraid that there would be an impiety in being present when justice is evil spoken of and not lifting up a hand in her defence. And therefore I had best give such help as I can . . .

. . . Well, I said, and now having arrived at this stage of the argument, we may revert to the words which brought us hither: Was not some one saying that injustice was a gain to the perfectly unjust who was reputed to be just?

Yes, that was said.

Now then, having determined the power and quality of justice and injustice, let us have a little conversation with him.

What shall we say to him?

Let us make an image of the soul, that he may have his own words presented before his eyes.

Of what sort?

An ideal image of the soul, like the composite creations of ancient mythology, such as the Chimera or Scylla or Cerberus, and there are many others in which two or more different natures are said to grow into one.

There are said of have been such unions.

Then do you now model the form of a multitudinous, many-headed monster, having a ring of heads of all manner of beasts, tame and wild, which he is able to generate and metamorphose at will.

You suppose marvellous powers in the artist; but, as language is more pliable than wax or any similar substance, let there be such a model as you propose.

Suppose now that you make a second form as of a lion, and a third of a man, the second smaller than the first, and the third smaller than the second.

That, he said, is an easier task; and I have made them as you say.

And now join them, and let the three grow into one.

That has been accomplished.

Next fashion the outside of them into a single image, as of a man, so that he who is not able to look within, and sees only the outer hull, may believe the beast to be a single human creature. I have done so, he said.

And now, to him who maintains that it is profitable for the human creature to be unjust, and unprofitable to be just, let us reply that, if he be right, it is profitable for this creature to feast the multitudinous monster and strengthen the lion and the lion-like qualities, but to starve and weaken the man, who is consequently liable to be dragged about at the mercy of either of the other two; and he is not to attempt to familiarize or harmonize them with one another—he ought rather to suffer them to fight and bite and devour one another.

Certainly, he said; that is what the approver of injustice says.

To him the supporter of justice makes answer that he should ever so speak and act as to give the man within him in some way or other the most complete mastery over the entire human creature.

He should watch over the many-headed monster like a good husbandman, fostering and cultivating the gentle qualities, and preventing the wild ones from growing; he should be making the lion-heart his ally, and in common care of them all should be uniting the several parts with one another and with himself.

Yes, he said, that is quite what the maintainer of justice say.

And so from every point of view, whether of pleasure, honour, or advantage, the approver of justice is right and speaks the truth, and the disapprover is wrong and false and ignorant.

Yes, from every point of view.

Come, now, and let us gently reason with the unjust, who is not intentionally in error. 'Sweet Sir,' we will say to him, what think you of things esteemed noble and ignoble? Is not the noble that which subjects the beast to the man, or rather to the god in man; and the ignoble that which subjects the man to the beast?' He can hardly avoid saying yes— can he now?

Not if he has any regard for my opinion.

But, if he agree so far, we may ask him to answer another question: 'Then how would a man profit if he received gold and silver on the condition that he was to enslave the noblest part of him to the worst? Who can imagine that a man who sold his son or daughter into slavery for money, especially if he sold them into the hands of fierce and evil men, would be the gainer, however large might be the sum which he received? And will any one say that he is not a miserable caitiff who remorselessly sells his own divine being to that which is most godless and detestable? Eriphyle took the necklace as the price of her husband's life, but he is taking a bribe in order to compass a worse ruin.'

Yes, said Glaucon, far worse—I will answer for him.

Has not the intemperate been censured of old, because in him the huge multiform monster is allowed to be too much at large?

Clearly.

And men are blamed for pride and bad temper when the lion and serpent element in them disproportionately grows and gains strength?

Yes.

And luxury and softness are blamed, because they relax and weaken this same creature, and make a coward of him?

Very true.

And is not a man reproached for flattery and meanness who subordinates the spirited animal to the unruly monster, and, for the sake of money, of which he can never have enough, habituates him in the days of his youth to be trampled in the mire, and from being a lion to become a monkey?

True, he said.

And why are mean employments and manual arts a reproach Only because they imply a natural weakness of the higher principle; the individual is unable to control the creatures within him, but has to court them, and his great study is how to flatter them.

Such appears to be the reason.

And therefore, being desirous of placing him under a rule like that of the best, we say that he ought to be the servant of the best, in whom the Divine rules; not, as Thrasymachus supposed, to the injury of the servant, but because every one had better be ruled by divine wisdom dwelling within him; or, if this be impossible, then by an external authority, in order that we may be all, as far as possible, under the same government, friends and equals.

True, he said.

And this is clearly seen to be the intention of the law, which is the ally of the whole city; and is seen also in the authority which we exercise over children, and the refusal to let them be free until we have established in them a principle analogous to the constitution of a state, and by cultivation of this higher element have set up in their hearts a guardian and ruler like our own, and when this is done they may go their ways.

Yes, he said, the purpose of the law is manifest.

From what point of view, then, and on what ground can we say that a man is profited by injustice or intemperance or other baseness, which will make him a worse man, even though he acquire money or power by his wickedness?

From no point of view at all.

What shall he profit, if his injustice be undetected and unpunished? He who is undetected only gets worse, whereas he who is detected and punished has the brutal part of his nature silenced and humanized; the gentler element in him is liberated, and his whole soul is perfected and ennobled by the acquirement of justice and temperance and wisdom, more than the body ever is by receiving gifts of beauty, strength and health, in proportion as the soul is more honourable than the body.

Certainly, he said.

To this nobler purpose the man of understanding will devote the energies of his life. And in the first place, he will honour studies which impress these qualities on his soul and disregard others?

Clearly, he said.

In the next place, he will regulate his bodily habit and training, and so far will he be from yielding to brutal and irrational pleasures, that he will regard even health as quite a secondary matter; his first object will be not that he may be fair or strong or well, unless he is likely thereby to gain temperance, but he will always desire so to attemper the body as to preserve the harmony of the soul?

Certainly he will, if he has true music in him.

And in the acquisition of wealth there is a principle of order and harmony which he will also observe; he will not allow himself to be dazzled by the foolish applause of the world, and heap up riches to his own infinite harm?

Certainly not, he said.

He will look at the city which is within him, and take heed that no disorder occur in it, such as might arise either from superfluity or from want; and upon this principle he will regulate his property and gain or spend according to his means.

Very true.

And, for the same reason, he will gladly accept and enjoy such honours as he deems likely to make him a better man; but those, whether private or public, which are likely to disorder his life, he will avoid?

Then, if that is his motive, he will not be a statesman.

By the dog of Egypt, he will! in the city which's his own he certainly will, though in the land of his birth perhaps not, unless he have a divine call.

I understand; you mean that he will be a ruler in the city of which we are the founders, and which exists in idea only; for I do not believe that there is such an one anywhere on earth?

In heaven, I replied, there is laid up a pattern of it, methinks, which he who desires may behold, and beholding, may set his own house in order. But whether such an one exists, or ever will exist in fact, is no matter; for he will live after the manner of that city, having nothing to do with any other.

I think so, he said.

Discussion Question(s)

1. Does Plato's claim that justice is an "excellence of the soul" make sense?
2. What is more important; justice or honor? Why? Can anyone who is just but is thought unjust by everyone else (including family and friends) be happy?
3. If happiness relies upon honor ("reputation") rather than justice ("achievement") then isn't Glaucon right to allege that only "appearances" matter? If not, why?

Selection #2: Peter Singer, 1995, Prometheus Books, *How Are We to Live?*, Chapter 7: "Tit for Tat," pp. 129–153.

Introduction: Peter Singer's *How are We to Live?*, like *The Republic*, is concerned with the nature of justice. However, Singer gives a very different answer. Instead of offering intrinsic grounds for justice, Singer argues that "Living an ethical life is not self-sacrifice, but rather self-fulfillment." Doing good will be good for us. One of the key arguments which Singer offers to support this thesis is called Tit for Tat. According to Tit for Tat, we ought to treat others the way they treat us. In doing so, we hold others to account. This makes it possible for bad behavior to be punished and good behavior to be rewarded. Justice is about the consequences our behavior produces.

Caring for Those Who Care for Us

In World War I, the Allied French and British forces faced the German army across a long front in Northern France. Both sides dug themselves into trenches from which they kept up a bombardment of the other side. When pitched battles were fought,

casualties were enormous. The Allied High Command was willing to take heavy
losses; they reasoned that since there were more French and British, combined, than
Germans, as long as they killed at least one German soldier for every Allied soldier
killed, they would win the war. National feeling and the propaganda of wartime
fuelled hatred of the other side. The commanding officers strove to keep enmity at
fever pitch, in order to keep up the morale of troops who had seen so many of their
comrades die. Yet amidst the hatred, death and mud, an extraordinary system of co-
operation known as 'live and let live' sprang up between Allied and German troops.
Its essence was: I won't try to kill you as long as you don't try to kill me. For considerable periods, in several different sectors of the trenches, the British or French
infantry aimed their shells where they did no harm, and the Germans could be relied
npon to do the same. Troops could relax, and even stroll abont quite openly in range
of enemy machine guns, secure in the knowledge that the person behind the sights
of the gun would not try to kill them. If something did go wrong—perhaps a unit
was replaced by one that had not learned the system, or a zealous commanding offi-
cer decided to show the troops how it should be done—there was immediate
retaliation.[1]

The extraordinary but well—documented existence of the 'live and let live' system
during World War I is eloquent testimony to the possibilities of co-operation in what
might seem to be the most adverse circumstances imaginable. We have already seen
that our biology does not dictate that our ultimate choice be a narrowly selfish one.
On the contrary, the way in which we have evolved has led to the existence of beings
who care directly for their children, for other kin and to some extent for larger groups.
The example of Japan shows how far a culture can reinforce concern for the group.
The aim of this chapter is to show how our evolution has allowed a propensity for
another kind of concern for others, and how human cultures everywhere have developed this aspect of our nature.

In a large, anonymous society that often appears to live by the rule of looking
after number one, it is easy to forget how much of an everyday experience helping
and being helped by others can be in other societies. The contrast became especially
vivid for the inhabitants of Tristan da Cunha, a tiny and remote island in the South
Atlantic Ocean. In 1961 the population of this island consisted of 264 people, mostly
descendants of European sailors, who spoke English and belonged to the Church of
England. Their quiet, agriculturally based life came to an abrupt halt in September
1961 when their island—which consists of the tip of a volcano that rises from the
ocean floor—erupted, spitting out hot ashes. The British Navy evacuated the entire
population and took them to England, where they settled in housing with modern
conveniences and were helped to find work. Within two years, almost all of them
returned to Tristan, despite the burnt-out homes and hard conditions they faced
there. But a few found conditions on the island so difficult that they went back to
England. There they were visited by Peter Munch, an anthropologist who had studied their way of life both on Tristan and in England. He found that those who went
back to England a second time were even more discontented with life there than they
had been on their first forced visit. Then the entire island community had been

---

[1] Tony Ashworth, *Trench Warfare, 1914–1918: The Live and Let Live System*, Holmes and Meier, New York, 1980;
cited by Robert Axelrod, *The Evolution of Cooperation*, Basic Books, New York, 1984, ch. 4.

transplanted; now the few who had chosen to return to England were living among strangers. As one Tristaner said:

> No, the people on Tristan, they's jus' like one family and they live happy and one help t'other, and if I's out in my farm and doin' my potatoes, and someone's finish' his'u, he'll come along an' give me a hand, an' the next day he got something to do, I go 'n give *him* a hand, so we all help 'nother. On Tristan they's jus' like brothers 'n sisters.[2]

To see how these helping relationships work, here is an imaginary example:

Max is a small peasant farmer with a crop ready to harvest. The rainclouds are building on the horizon. Unless Max gets some help, it will rain before he can bring in the harvest. The grain that he has not harvested will spoil. So Max asks Lyn, his neighbour, whose crop is not yet ripe, if she will help him to harvest his crop. In return, he offers to help her when her crop is ready. Max will be better off if Lyn agrees to help him. But will Lyn be better off if she helps? She will, if this means that Max will help her, because she often also has trouble getting her harvest in before it rains. But can she rely on Max's promise to help her? How does she know that, after she has helped him to harvest his crop, he will not stand by and laugh when she asks him for help? If she cannot be even moderately confident that Max will help her, it is not in her interest to help him. She could use her time better by pulling out some weeds that hamper the growth of her crop. Max's problem is that, if he is to get his crop harvested before it spoils, he must somehow get Lyn to believe that if she helps him, he will help her.

In some societies, Max and Lyn could enter into a formal agreement, and, if Max broke the agreement, Lyn would be entitled to some form of compensation or damages. But if Max and Lyn live in a society which lacks such means of making a binding agreement, Max's best chance is to win Lyn's trust. If he has a reputation for being trustworthy, this should not be a problem. How does he get such a reputation? In a small-scale community like Tristan da Cunha, in which everyone knows everyone else, the best way to do this is by actually being trustworthy; that is, by honouring one's commitments to others, and generally being a member of the community in good standing with others.

Max might try to gain a good reputation another way; he might try to deceive others into thinking he is trustworthy when in reality he is not. But—again, in small communities with little change in membership—this is unlikely to work. In those conditions—and they are the conditions that have prevailed for most of the period in which human beings and other social primates have existed—honesty really is the best policy.

In the early eighties Robert Axelrod, an American social theorist, made a remarkable discovery about the nature of co-operation. The full significance of Axelrod's result is still not properly appreciated outside a narrow circle of specialists. It has the potential to change not only our personal lives, but the world of international politics as well.

To understand what Axelrod found, we first need to know something about the problem in which he was interested—a well-known puzzle about co-operation called the

---

[2] This account is taken from the work of Peter Munch, as summarized by Raoul Naroll in *The Moral Order*, Sage Publications, Beverly Hills, Calif., 1983, pp. 125–7. See Peter Munch, *Crisis in Utopia*, New York, Crowell, 1971; the quotation is from Peter Munch, 'Economic Development and Conflicting Values: A Social Experiment in Tristan da Cunha', *American Anthropologist*, 1970, vol. 72, p. 1309.

Prisoner's Dilemma. The name comes from the way in which the puzzle is usually presented: an imaginary choice facing a prisoner. There are many versions. Here is mine:

> You and another prisoner are languishing in separate cells of the Ruritanian Police Headquarters. The police are trying to get you both to confess to plotting against the state. An interrogator comes to your cell, pours you a glass of Ruritanian wine, gives you a cigarette, and in tones of beguiling friendliness, offers you a deal.
>
> 'Confess to the crime!' he says, 'And if your friend in the other cell . . .'
>
> You protest that you have never met the prisoner in the other cell, but the interrogator brushes your objection aside and continues: 'So much the better, then, if he is no friend of yours; for as I was about to say, if you confess, and he does not, we shall use your confession to lock him away for ten years. Your reward will be that you shall go free. On the other hand, if you are so stupid as to refuse to confess, and the 'friend' in the other cell does confess, you will be the one who goes to prison for ten years, and he will be released.'
>
> You think about this for a while, and realize that you don't yet have enough information to decide, so you ask:
>
> 'What if we both confess?'
>
> 'Then, because we didn't really need your confession, you won't go free. But, seeing as how you were trying to help us, you'll each get only eight years.'
>
> 'And if neither of us confesses?'
>
> A scowl passes over the face of your interrogator, and you fear that he is about to strike you. But he controls himself, and grumbles that, then, since they will lack the evidence for a conviction, they won't be able to keep you very long. But then he adds:
>
> 'We don't give up easily. We can still keep you here another six months, interrogating you, before those bleeding hearts at Amnesty International can put enough pressure on our government to get you out of here. So think about it: whether your buddy confesses or not, you'll be better off if you confess than if you don't. And my colleague is telling the other guy the same thing, right now.'
>
> You think over what the interrogator has said and realize that he is right. Whatever the stranger in the other cell does, you will be better off if you confess. For if he does confess, your choice is between confessing too, and getting eight years in gaol, or not confessing, and spending ten years behind bars. On the other hand, if the other prisoner does not confess, your choice is between confessing, and going free, or not confessing, and spending another six months in the cells. So it looks like you should confess. But then another thought occurs to you. The other prisoner is in exactly the same situation as you are. If it is rational for you to confess, it will also be rational for him to confess. So you will both end up with eight years in gaol. Whereas, if neither of you confessed, you would both be free in six months. How can it be that the choice that seems rational for each of you, individually—that is, to confess—will make you both worse off than you would have been if you had decided not to confess? What should you do?

There is no solution to the Prisoner's Dilemma. From a purely self-interested point of view (one that takes no account of the interests of the other prisoner) it is rational for each prisoner to confess—and if each does what it is rational to do from a self-interested point of view, they will each be worse off than they would have been if they had chosen differently. The dilemma proves that when each of us individually chooses what is in our own interest, we can each turn out to be worse off than we would each have been if we had both made a choice that is in our collective interest.

You are unlikely ever to find yourself in the situation of the Ruritanian prisoners, but there are many everyday illustrations of the general rule that the Prisoner's Dilemma proves. Anyone who has spent some time in rush hour traffic knows that, while it may be in your individual interest to take your car to town (since the buses also get held up by the traffic, and they don't run very often anyway) it would be in the interests of everyone if you could all collectively decide to go by bus, since then the bus company could afford to run a much more frequent service, and without the traffic, you would get to work in half the time.

The situation of Max and Lyn, in the example just given, is similar to that of the prisoners in some respects, but different in others. They will both be better off if they co-operate, because otherwise each will lose the grain he or she is unable to reap before it rains. But is it rational for each, individually, to co-operate? If Lyn helps Max with his harvest, and then calls on Max to help her when she needs to get her crop in, Max might be tempted to think that it is not in his interests to help. For he will have already benefited from Lyn's help, and he could more usefully spend his time getting rid of some weeds before he plants his next crop. But now let us put ourselves in Lyn's position. Suppose that Lyn is thinking about whether she should help Max with his harvest. If she realizes that, since Max's harvest will be gathered first, it will not be in his interest to help her with here harvest, and for that reason he may not do so, she will not help him in the first place. Thus, as in the case of the prisoners, both Max and Lyn will be better off if they co-operate, but it is doubtful whether it will be rational for either of them to do so.

If we think of the prisoner's decision *not* to confess as a form of co-operation with the other prisoner—that is, adopting a strategy that means working together, rather than against each other—then it is easy to see the parallel between the Prisoner's Dilemma and what we might call the Peasant's Dilemma. They are both versions of a common problem, the Co-operator's Dilemma. But there is also a crucial difference between the two versions. The Prisoner's Dilemma is a once-in-a-lifetime situation. You and the other prisoner must each decide, just once, whether to co-operate with the other prisoner or not to do so. You and the other prisoner will, presumably, never be in that position again. In that respect, the answer you give to the interrogator in your cell will have no further effects on your life, other than those that the interrogator has spelled out for you. Max and Lyn, on the other hand, are neighbours and are likely to remain neighbours all of their lives. As predictably as the seasons themselves, they will need help to bring in their harvest, not only this year, but for many years to come. This provides a vital additional factor for each of them to take into account when they work out what is in their own interests. Now Max knows that if Lyn helps him, and he does not return the favour, she will surely refuse to help him next year, and probably for many years to come. While Max may get a short-term benefit from the weeding he can do instead of helping Lyn, in the long run he will be much worse off. So it will be in his interest to help Lyn; and Lyn, knowing that this will be the case, will also know that it is in her interest to help Max. Thus the logic of the Co-operator's Dilemma is dramatically different when it is going to be repeated indefinitely, instead of being a one-off situation.

Now we have enough background to see what Axelrod did. He thought of the Prisoner's Dilemma as a game, in which the aim is to spend the least possible time in gaol. To make this work, he set up a round-robin tournament, with many different players. Each player must play the game 200 time with one player. Each game involves deciding whether to co-operate with the other player, by keeping silent, or to defect, and confess. How many years you spend in gaol as a result of that decision depends on what the other player does, in accordance with the offer made to you by the Ruritanian police, as in the story above. The difference is that having done this once, you do it again, and so on. Each time that you do it, the situation is different, because you know what your opponent did before.

Once you have played your 200 games with one player, you move on to the next, and so on, until everyone has played the required number of games with everyone else. At the end, we add up the total number of years each player has spent in gaol.

We can think of a variety of possible strategies that you might adopt in order to win the tournament. For example, you might always keep silent. We could call that strategy Always Co-operate. Or you might adopt the extremely selfish strategy Never Co-operate. You might try a more complicated strategy, say, co-operating for the first ten games, but not co-operating after that. You might also devise a strategy that is sensitive to what your opponent does: for example, co-operate only if the other player has co-operated in the previous game. Axelrod wanted to know if one strategy would generally do better than any other strategy. If it did, maybe it would also be useful in real-life situations, in which we, or our governments, must decide whether to co-operate or not with others who may or may not co-operate themselves. So he announced a Prisoner's Dilemma tournament, along the lines just sketched. Invitations were sent to people carrying out research in areas related to strategies for making decisions. The invitation set out the rules of the competition, and asked entrants to submit, in a form that could be run on a computer, the strategy that they thought would win.

Fourteen entries came in, some of them quite elaborate. The computer pitted them all against each other. The winner turned out to be the shortest and simplest strategy submitted. It went like this:

a. On the first move, co-operate.

b. On every subsequent move, do whatever the other player did on his or her previous move.

This strategy was called Tit for Tat, because it paid the other players back for what they did. If they were nice and co-operated, it co-operated. If they were selfish and did not, they got a selfish, unco-operative response back on the next turn.

That such a childish strategy should win must have caused some discomfort to the many experts who had spent a long time devising much more sophisticated and complicated strategies. Axelrod decided to hold a second, larger tournament, to see if any entrant, knowing that Tit for Tat would be entered again, and knowing how well it had done previously, anyone could come up with a better strategy. This time sixty-two entries were received. The tournament was run. Tit for Tat won again.[3]

Why did Tit for Tat do so well? One reason is that it is what Axelrod calls a 'nice' strategy: by this, he means a strategy which is never the first to try to act in an unco-operative way. Despite being nice, Tit for Tat actually does better than 'mean' strategies that are the first to be selfish. This is not only true of Tit for Tat, in general, in Axelrod's tournament, nice strategies did far better than strategies that were not nice.

This leads to a significant discovery about the role that unselfish behaviour can play in enhancing one's prospects of surviving and leaving descendents. Axelrod shows precisely why beings who act in an unselfish manner can do as well as, or even better than, those who behave completely selfishly. There are three key findings:

1. In doing better for itself, Tit for Tat also helps all other nice strategies to do better. In other words, the total number of years spent in gaol by Tit for Tat *and* other nice strategies against whom Tit for Tat plays will be the minimum possible, because these strategies will all begin by co-operating, and will continue to do so. In general, nice strategies support such other.

---

[3] Robert Axelrod, *The Evolution of Cooperation*, pp. 27–54.

2. In sharp contrast to nice strategies, mean strategies spoil each other's chances of success when they play against each other. Mean strategies playing against each other all end up doing very badly.

3. When nice and mean strategies are matched against each other, nice strategies will do well as long as they are provoked to retaliate by the first selfish action of another.

To understand the significance of these findings for the evolution of unselfish behaviour, we have to stop thinking of them as computer programs or strategies for playing games, and instead think of them as ways in which animals might behave. They would have to be social animals, living in a stable group, with the ability to recognize other members of the group and remember their previous co-operative or unco-operative actions. Human beings, throughout their evolutionary history, have been social animals of this kind. Chimpanzees and gorillas, many species of monkey, elephants, wolves, and several other social mammals would also satisfy these requirements. The question then becomes: if some analogue of the Prisoner's Dilemma occurs quite frequently in real life, would animals be more likely to survive and reproduce if they always go for their own immediate advantage? Or would they do better if they behave 'nicely', giving up some immediate advantage in order to co-operate with another animal?

The answer can be derived from the three key findings above. First, in a group of animals all behaving nicely, each of them would do well. Second, in a group of mean animals, each of them would do badly. Third, and most importantly, when some animals in a group are nice and others are mean, the nice ones would continue to do well, as long as they stop co-operating immediately when they discover that another animal is mean.

The reason for this third conclusion needs to be spelled out more fully. When mean animals interact with nice animals, the mean ones do better on the first encounter, because the nice ones give up their immediate advantage in order to be co-operative, whereas the mean ones do not. But since this is only one encounter, in stable groups it would not make much difference over the long run. It can be outweighed by the fact that, as long as a reasonable proportion of the group are nice, nice animals will do better than mean animals in their second and subsequent encounters with other nice animals, because they will reap the benefits of co-operation, whereas the mean animals will not.

So far, so good. Too good, in fact. Somewhere, in this evolutionary equivalent of the Garden of Eden, the serpent must be lurking. As in the Bible story, innocence opens the way for it. If nice animals live in a group with mean ones and behave nicely without discriminating between those animals who return the favour and those who do not, the mean animals gain an advantage. They benefit from co-operation without giving up anything in return. A vicious spiral commences. Initially the mean animals may be few, but they will now reproduce at a higher rate than the nice ones. Gradually nice animals will meet fewer nice animals, and the chances for reaping the benefits of co-operation will be reduced. In the end, animals who behave nicely will disappear from the group.

We can put this more plainly still. To be nice to someone who is not nice to you is to allow yourself to be a sucker. Where there are suckers, cheats prosper.[4] Conversely, if there are no suckers, cheats do badly. If all nice animals withdraw co-operation as soon as they detect a lack of co-operation on the other side—in other words, as soon as they notice that they are dealing with a cheat—mean animals will have few opportunities to exploit suckers. So the thought that we encountered in Chapter 2—'I don't want to be the only sucker'—is a healthy one. To be a sucker is bad, not only for oneself, but for everyone. Fortunately this

---

[4] The terminology of 'suckers' and 'cheats' comes from R. Dawkins, *The Selfish Gene*, Oxford University Press, Oxford, 1976.

does not mean that we have to be a cheat ourselves in order to do well. The saving element in the situation is that if a proportion of the animals in a group behave in a Tit for Tat kind of way, they can keep out the cheats. Such a society may no longer be paradise, because love and kindness can no longer be unconstrained; but it is still a lot better for all than life in a group dominated by mean animals.

This result amounts to nothing less than an experimental refutation of Jesus's celebrated teaching about turning the other check. Most of us think that turning the other check is a noble ideal, even if too idealistic for this world. Consequently, we admire those who are prepared to act on it. If they are prepared to be struck on both cheeks, we think, they are the *only* ones who are likely to be worse off. Now we know that this is not so. To turn the other check is to teach would-be cheats that cheating pays. There is not much attraction in an ethic of turning the other check if the resulting hardship falls not only on those who allow themselves to be struck, but on everyone else as a whole.

What happens if a group starts off with mostly mean members? Can a virtuous spiral get going? Yes, it can, as long as there is at least a small cluster of nice animals, and they interact mostly with each other. Then they can benefit from co-operating, while not allowing themselves to be exploited. The mean animals will be left to interact mostly with other mean animals, and will do badly. How does the cluster of individuals begin to co-operate? As we have seen, there can be advantages in altruism towards kin, and genes that lead to kin altruism will be favoured by the process of evolution. So initially, members of the cluster might all be related, and co-operation might evolve for that reason. Thus co-operation can emerge even in a world where at first almost everyone acts for immediate, short-term advantage—as happened among the entrenched troops during the World War I. And such co-operation will spread, as long as there is a stable group of people who are better off, as a result of their co-operation, than others who do not co-operate.

This is a striking result. With Tit for Tat, we can spiral in a virtuous direction only. In the right conditions, Tit for Tat behaviour can eliminate mean behaviour, while mean behaviour finds it difficult to dislodge Tit for Tat behaviour. As Axelrod puts it: 'the gear wheels of social evolution have a ratchet.'[5]

It may still seem that we have come very little distance from narrow self-interest. Maybe 'nice' behaviour is advantageous, but if so, aren't those who are being nice merely more enlightened egoists? This objection makes a mistake that is similar to the misunderstanding I mentioned in Chapter 5 in connection with altruism towards kin. Our feelings of love towards our brothers and sisters are no less genuine because we can explain how such feelings evolved: it is still true that we help our siblings because we care about them, not because of the degree of genetic overlap between us. Similarly, the fact that co-operation is the best policy does not mean that those who are co-operative are necessarily being co-operative *because* they desire to gain an advantage. Sometimes this will be true. Presumably it was true in the 'live and let live' system. But at other times it will not be. Some of us just are the kind of beings who develop warm feelings towards those who show kindness towards us.

Consider friendship. Typically, friends help each other. Presumably this usually means that each is better off than he or she would have been without the aid of a friend. So is friendship and all the emotions that belong to it—love, loyalty, solidarity, gratitude and so on—just a charade, a mere cloak thrown over naked self-interest? Of course not. There are some who regard their friends in a calculatingly egoistic way, but most of us do not. Most of us like our friends, and enjoy spending time with them. This turns out to be

---

[5] Robert Axelrod, *The Evolution of Cooperation*, p. 99.

an effective way of bringing about co-operation. Many other animals also co-operate, and also form bonds with other, unrelated members of the group. Between these friends, co-operative behaviour takes place. Some animals share food. Others defend their friends against attack. Chimpanzees and many other primates spend a lot of time grooming each other, removing parasites and dirt from parts that one cannot reach oneself. Our pleasure in being close to our friends may have evolved because it brings us benefits, but friendly feelings are no less genuine for that.

One more point on this topic of friendship and co-operation: in a small, stable society in which everyone knows everyone else, cheats will not prosper. But the less well we know the people with whom we live, work and deal, the greater the opportunities for some of them to benefit by deceit. Richard Christie, a psychologist from Columbia University in New York, developed a way of measuring a character trait he called 'Machiavellianism', which involved the ability to manipulate and deceive others. His work pre-dates the interest in evolutionary explanations of social behaviour, but it shows, as this evolutionary model predicts, that there are some who get on by manipulating and cheating others to their own advantage, and others who will not adopt such tactics. In a test of several hundred Spanish students, it was found that those who showed a high degree of Machiavellianism tended to come from the more industrialized and developed parts of the country. An American study found that Machiavellianism was more pronounced among those who had spent their adolescence in a large city.[6] In ecological terms, we could say that interactions with strangers create a niche for those who can take advantage of the co-operative instincts of others, receiving the benefit of help, but failing to give help themselves when it will no longer benefit them to do so. This niche only exists, however, because many offers to co-operate are genuine. Like a parasitic growth that needs a healthy tree from which to feed, cheats weaken the co-operative bond on which their way of earning a living depends. Thus the cynical view that everyone is in some sense a cheat has the logic of the relationship backwards. If everyone were a cheat, no-one would trust anyone, and there would be no opportunity to cheat.

Doing better with Tit for Tat

In almost every facet of our lives, we are faced with decisions that are structured like repeated versions of the Prisoner's Dilemma. In personal relationships, in business relationships, in politics and in relations between governments, we must decide whether to co-operate with another individual, potential business partner or client, political ally or foreign government. Each side may be tempted to try to reap the benefit of co-operation without paying the price; but if both do it, they will both be worse off than they would have been if they had all co-operated. Axelrod's findings can be applied in ways that make it possible for all parties to achieve better results than they would have achieved otherwise. In the previous section we saw the role played by the elements of Tit for Tat in ensuring its success in the tournaments. Now I shall re-state these elements as rules for use by anyone in a wide variety of everyday situations:

1. *Begin by being ready to co-operate.* Greet the world with a friendly face, think the best of strangers and show kindness towards them, unless you have reason to believe the contrary. Tit for Tat suggests that this will pay off for you as well as for others.

---

[6] Richard Christie and Florence Geis, *Studies in Machiavellianism*, Academic Press, New York, 1970, pp. 318–320, citing studies by A. de Miguel and S. Guterman.

Obviously there are limits to how much one can risk at a first encounter. I often lend books to people whom I do not know well; usually I get them back. Since back issues of academic journals are often impossible to replace, I don't lend them, except to people I know well. In entering into a new business relationship it is equally obvious that risks should be kept low; but whatever the deal that is struck, one should give full value on the assumption that the other party will do the same.

Because Tit for Tat works only when there is likely to be a continuing relationship between you and the other party, both parties can benefit by finding a way to ensure that the relationship between them will be a lasting one. Marriage served precisely this function of providing a basis for a lifetime of wholehearted co-operation, as long as divorce was impossible, socially unacceptable, or very difficult to obtain. The easy, Hollywood-style acceptance of a life involving several divorces and remarriages has undermined this important function of the marriage ceremony. To go through a ceremony of marriage without even intending to make a long-term commitment is utterly pointless, a mere relic of an age in which to have sex without the blessing of the Church was thought to be sinful, and to have children out of wedlock was to disadvantage them. In societies not dominated by conservative forms of religion, these beliefs are disappearing, and we are better off without them. Should the institution of marriage disappear with them? There are signs that it will, as more and more couples live together without getting married.

There are, of course, many ways of making clear the seriousness of a commitment to the other partner, apart from the religious or legal nature of the marriage bond itself. Pooling finances and putting time and energy into the joint home is one; it means that if the relationship breaks up, the mutual investment will be lost. In my own marriage, I felt that it was the decision to conceive a child together, rather than the decision to get married, that created the firmest commitment. I do not mean that my wife-to-be and I conceived, or even sought to conceive, a child before we got married. We were not so unconventional, four years passed between our marriage and the decision to have our first child. Despite the good relationship we had built up during this period and the commitment we had made to each other, before we had a child, staying together seemed optional. Since we did not regard divorce as contrary to any divine or moral law, if our feelings towards each other changed, we could each go our own way. Our decision to have a child closed that option; it could still be opened again, but only with much greater difficulty. (I stress that this is a point about the possibilities of making a binding commitment, rather than about the nature or quality of our relationship.) Our child linked our futures in a much more binding way than any other form of commitment could do, because once a loving bond has developed between parents and child, there is no way of undoing the link between the parents cleanly and completely. No matter how much either or both partners may want to end the relationship and begin afresh, the existence of their mutual child makes it impossible for them to do so.

2. ***Do good to those who do good to you, and harm to those who harm you.*** In following Tit for Tat we must steer a course between two great dangers: the danger of getting into an unending series of mutual—and mutually destructive—paybacks, and the danger of being exploited. We start by being friendly and co-operative. But once it is clear that the other party is not being equally co-operative, it is time to change our own policy. How swiftly should we change? In the tournaments Axelrod ran there was a program called Tit for Two Tats that forgave the first instance of unco-operative behaviour, and only retaliated if the failure to co-operate was repeated. It did very well in the first tournament, but not in the second, where there were more programs able to exploit its forgiving nature.

The most momentous historical example of a failure to abide by this second crucial Tit for Tat principle is the policy of appeasement pursued by Britain and France as Hitler progressively tore up the Treaty of Versailles. He began by rebuilding the German army. If the Allies had been following a Tit for Tat policy they would have retaliated in some way, but they did nothing. In 1936 Hitler marched his soldiers into the Rhineland, which the Treaty had made a demilitarized zone. Here, even an exponent of Tit for Two Tats would have acted, but again the Allies did nothing. A similar lack of response greeted Hitler's annexation of Austria in 1938. Before the year was out, he demanded the Sudetenland, the German-speaking regions of Czechoslovakia. For a time it appeared that the Allies had had enough; but at Munich, they again yielded all that the German dictator had demanded. Giving in to unilateral force in this way simply enhanced Hitler's belief that he could achieve what he wanted; it also contributed to his growing reputation with his own people as a leader of genius. Had the Allies stood firm against the remilitarization of the Rhineland, for instance, they would have had an easy victory against a relatively unprepared enemy. When the Allies finally committed themselves to the defence of Poland, war came on much worse terms for them. By being too forgiving, by following what proved to be a policy of Tit for About Five Tats, the British and French governments ensured only that when war came, it would be a far greater catastrophe than it would have been if it had come earlier. Several factors played a role here, especially the guilt felt by many in Britain and France over the harshness of the Versailles Treaty, and a firm desire, very understandable after the slaughter of World War I, to avoid war at all costs. Nevertheless, with the benefit of hindsight, it is clear how tragic a misjudgment it was to allow someone prepared to use unilateral force to achieve what he wanted at no cost at all.

In other situations it may be difficult to apply Tit for Tat at all. The involvement of America and its Allies in the war in Vietnam was often justified by pointed references to the need to avoid the mistake of appeasing communism, as Nazism had been appeased. Behind this thought lay the idea that international communism was a single entity that had advanced across Asia, conquering China, North Korea, North Vietnam, and was now threatening to spread through South Vietnam to Thailand and Malaysia. But this was wrong, the war in Vietnam was more a local conflict than a testing ground for the forces of international communism, and the communist victory in Vietnam did not lead, as the hawks had said it would, to the 'dominoes' of Thailand, Malaysia and Indonesia also falling to communism.

The example of Vietnam shows that Tit for Tat is no substitute for a detailed and accurate understanding of the particular facts of a situation. Even then, it will not bring about the utopia of a world without the use of force, but it will, if intelligently applied and well understood, make war rare, for it will mean that war does not pay. Thus despite the scepticism that greeted President Bush's hailing of the United Nations stand against Iraqi aggression as inaugurating a 'new world order', it is not absurd to see a collective determination to resist clear cases of aggression as the basis for a new world order, based essentially on the simple but powerful principle of Tit for Tat. There is, however, still one great threat to this prospect. Tit for Tat is a rule that does well in a situation of continuing relationships. If the evil that can be visited on the other party is so great that the other party cannot retaliate at all, Tit for Tat cannot apply. Similarly, if to retaliate would only ensure the destruction of both parties, it will not make sense to retaliate, even if one can do so. The existence of nuclear weapons makes both of these possibilities real. Along with everything else they put in jeopardy, nuclear weapons thus threaten the best basis we have for regulating relationships between nations.

3. *Keep It simple.* Tit for Tat is a very simple rule. There are advantages in keeping one's behaviour simple; it makes it easy for the other party to see what is going on. Game theorists use the term Zero-sum Game to describe a game in which if anyone gains, others must lose the equivalent amount. Playing poker for money is, in financial terms, a Zero-sum Game. At the end of an evening's poker, the sum of the winnings of those who are ahead, less the losses of those who are behind, must equal zero. If life were a Zero-sum Game, playing by a simple rule would be a disadvantage, because one could do better for oneself only by making the other player do worse. (In poker you try to win by misleading the other players about your intentions.) In many real-life situations, however, both parties will gain from co-operation, and they will do better if they understand each other from the start. Then they can know how to achieve co-operation. Each will also do better if the other parties know that he or she is not open to being exploited. To be open and straightforward about your policy can thus be in your own interest, for it makes it easier for others to see what you are doing, and to co-operate with you for mutual benefit.

Should Tit for Tat be applied within closer personal relationships? To suggest that it should seems petty and coldly calculating. Surely lovers don't have to play Prisoner's Dilemma games with each other, nor do close friends. Or consider bringing up children: shouldn't parents respond to their children from love and devotion, rather than in the calculating way suggested by Tit for Tat?

It is true that between lovers, in a family, or with close personal friends, where each genuinely cares for the well-being of the other, the question of reciprocity scarcely arises. To put it more technically, in Prisoner's Dilemma games, caring about the welfare of the other player changes the way in which we assess the outcomes. If each prisoner in the Ruritanian gaol cares as much for the welfare of the other prisoner as he cares for his own, he would make his decision so as to achieve not the shortest time in gaol for himself, but the lowest total number of years to be spent in gaol by both of them. Refusing to confess produces a lower total whatever the other prisoner does (if the other prisoner confesses it produces a total of ten years in gaol, rather than sixteen when both confess; and if the other prisoner does not confess it produces a total of one year, rather than ten when one confesses and the other does not). Therefore the altruistic prisoner would refuse to confess, and if both prisoners were altruistic they would both be better off than they would have been if neither of them had cared about how long the other spent in gaol. So lovers, families and close personal friends who care as much for the welfare of the other lover, family member or friend as they do for their own welfare, do not get into Prisoner's Dilemma-type situations with each other.

Genuine concern for others is, then, the complete solution to the Prisoner's Dilemma; it dissolves the dilemma altogether. Where possible, we do well to try to extend it beyond family and close personal friends. We often invite children to put themselves in the place of another. 'How would you like it if she did that to you?' is a commonly heard explanation of why, for example, your daughter should not take another girl's toy. This teaches an important moral point, that others feel hurt or aggrieved, just as we do. If fellow-feeling is sufficiently strong, then there is no need for Tit for Tat, but when it is not, Tit for Tat has a role, even in close personal or family relationships. Especially with children, it is vital that, as a minimum, they come to understand that reciprocity works for the benefit of both parties to a relationship. So when my teenage daughter slouches off to watch television instead of doing her share of the household chores, loving fatherly forgiveness may not be best for her, or for anyone else in the family. Instead, it might be more in her interests, as well as in mine, to let her know that the next time she wants to be driven to her friend's place, she may find me otherwise occupied. It may make me feel bad to do it, but it helps her to appreciate that other people do not exist only for her own convenience.

In the larger society, outside the family and personal relationships, Tit for Tat plays a central role in regulating the way we interact with others. Modern urban life, however, is a much more difficult environment in which to pursue Tit for Tat than the computerized world of Axelrod's tournaments. We can only apply the strategy if we know who is co-operating with us and who is not. The computers have no problem in figuring out who the other player is, or what the other player is doing, because the program tells them. Nor is this much of a problem for Max and Lyn in their stable relationship, engaged in a task that can hardly be disguised. There is scope for subtle forms of cheating even in a small-scale society. People on a co-operative food gathering trip may quietly gulp down the tastiest berries they find when no-one else looking. Coping with these minor forms of cheating, however, is a trifling problem compared with those we face in everyday life in large cities. The city forces us to interact constantly with people whom we have never seen before, and will probably never see again; it is hardly surprising that it lacks the cosy security of village life in which no-one locks their doors. Nor should we wonder at the fact that when we seat ourselves in protective steel shells and hurtle around the roads in a manner inherently liable to kill or injure others, some people behave in a less co-operative manner than they do when they are relating to people face-to-face.

We can think of a system of taxation as a gigantic, annually repeated Prisoner's Dilemma. We all want (at least some of) the government services financed out of taxation, but each of us would prefer not to pay his or her share. The difficulty in applying Tit for Tat is that those who do not co-operate are not easily detected. Thus not paying your fair share of taxation can be a winning strategy for each individual to pursue. To change the pay-off we must make the penalties for detection so large that (taking into account the odds against detection) tax evasion ceases to be a worthwhile gamble. We can do this either by increasing the penalties, or by improving the rate of detection, or by doing both at the same time. If we can succeed we will eliminate the Prisoner's Dilemma entirely. The change in pay-offs does not have to be strictly financial. Adding public embarrassment to the fines can make not co-operating still less attractive. In other circumstances, the embarrassment itself may be enough. Changing the pay-offs will not eliminate tax evasion altogether: people commit all sorts of crimes, the consequences of which are predictably damaging to their own interests. To reduce tax evaders to those unable to judge where their own interests lie would, however, be a significant advance on the present situation in many countries.

Much of our system of justice can be explained in the same way. Justice is not, as often thought, a sacrosanct moral principle imposed on us by a divine being, nor is it somehow engraved into the bedrock of the universe. Justice is neither more nor less than a set of conceptual tools for making Tit for Tat work in the real world. As such, it needs to be used with discretion. 'Let justice be done, though the heavens fall' is an ancient saying, but one that invests justice with a shade too much significance. How absolute we ought to be about justice will depend on the circumstances. If, as may happen in rare circumstances, justice works to no-one's benefit, both in the short and the long-term, to adhere to it is pointless.

In his compilation of knowledge about the moral codes of different societies, Edward Westermarck concluded: 'To requite a benefit, or to be grateful to him who bestows it, is probably everywhere, at least under certain circumstances, regarded as a duty'.[7] This duty of gratitude leads us to respond in kind to favours done for us; the corresponding ideas of moral resentment, moral indignation, retribution, and revenge suggest how we are to respond when someone harms us. All of these ideas are aspects of reciprocity. Reciprocity is Cicero's 'first demand of duty',[8] the 'single thread' of the Confucian way,[9] and according to the American sociologist Alvin Gouldner, one of the few moral ideas that can claim to have universal acceptance in practically every society known to us.[10] (Obligations to one's kin, especially of parents to their children, are, as we saw in Chapter 5, also endorsed in every known society; kinship and reciprocity are the two strongest, and perhaps the only, claimants to the title of universally accepted moral principle.)

In this respect, the constancy of the human situation is more impressive than the variations often pointed to by ethical relativists. Polybius, a Greek historian, wrote more than 2,000 years ago that:

> ... when a man who has been helped when in danger by another does not show gratitude to his preserver, but even goes to the length of attempting to do him injury, it is clear that those who become aware of it will naturally be displeased and offended by such conduct, sharing the resentment of their injured neighbor and imagining themselves in the same situation. From all this there arises in everyone a notion of the meaning and theory of duty, which is the beginning and end of justice.[11]

In the true spirit of Tit for Tat, the celebrated code of Hammurabi of Babylon proclaimed justice to consist in 'an eye for an eye and a tooth for a tooth'. (The rule held only between members of the aristocracy; for injuries to freemen or slaves, fines were sufficient.)[12] But is taking out the eye of the perpetrator appropriate compensation for the loss of one's own eye? Here we begin to debate what is or is not fair or just. Perhaps I don't want to put your eye out, but would rather have some more useful compensation for the injury you caused me. What if you didn't put out my eye, but started a fire that burnt my crop, and you, being a shiftless person, don't have a crop of your own anyway? Even if we have an agreed concept of fairness, our lack of impartiality compounds the difficulties of applying it. The feeling that we have been short-changed can lead to retaliation that in turn provokes more serious retaliation, until, like the famous Hatfields and McCoys, we have a full-blown feud echoing down the years and even over several generations.[13] To avoid this we need a concept of impartiality, and a system that will deliver impartial decisions about what constitutes fair dealing. From this it is a short step to the society as a whole taking over and enforcing some aspects of justice, including the task of seeing that serious offenders are appropriately punished.

---

[7] E. Westermarck, *The Origin and Development of the Moral Ideas*, vol. 2, Macmillan Publishing Company, London, 1906.

[8] Cicero, *de Officiis*, J. M. Dent, ed., Everyman, London, 1955, vol. 1, par. 47.

[9] See Chad Hansen, 'Classical Chinese Ethics' in Peter Singer, ed., *A Companion to Ethics*, Basil Blackwell Ltd., Oxford, 1991, pp. 72.

[10] Alvin Gouldner, 'The Norm of Reciprocity', *American Sociological Review*, vol. 25, no. 2, 1960, p. 171.

[11] Polybius, *History*, Book VI, sec. 6, quoted by E. Westermarck, *The Origin and Development of the Moral Ideas*, vol. 1, p. 42.

[12] Gerald A. Larue 'Ancient Ethics' in Peter Singer, ed., *A Companion to Ethics*, p. 32.

[13] Such feuds are common in many societies; see Jacob Black-Michaud, *Cohesive Force: Feud in the Mediterranean and Middle East*, Basil Blackwell Ltd., 1975; or Altina L. Waller, *Feud: Hatfields, McCoys and Social Change in Appalachia*, 1860–1900, University of North Carolina Press, Chapel Hill, North Carolina, 1988.

4. *Be forgiving.* Tit for Tat means always being ready to forget and forgive the past. No matter how black a past the other party may have, all that is needed to make Tit for Tat co-operate is a single co-operative act by the other. This makes it easier to break out of patterns of mutually damaging recriminations. It also avoids complications, and makes it easier for the other party to see exactly what the policy is. In real life, we are reluctant to forget the past, because it serves as a guide to the future. If the other party offers to co-operate, we have to judge if the offer is sincere. When past co-operative overtures have turned out to be followed by attempts to exploit us, we may well be more reluctant to commit ourselves than whether past offers have been genuine. With this reservation, though, the success of Tit for Tat shows the value of remaining open to the possibility of beginning or resuming a co-operative and mutually beneficial relationship with those who have, in the past, been unco-operative.

5. *Don't be envious.* The final factor contributing to the success of Tit for Tat is that it does not mind others doing as well or better than it does. Tit for Tat did better overall because it promoted co-operative situations more often than any other strategy. Had it been envious, it would have tried to overcome the gain that the other player may have got on that single occasion when Tit for Tat made a co-operative move but the other player was selfish. But Tit for Tat could have done this only by being selfish, and that would have led to mutual retaliation and fewer co-operative interactions.

In a Zero-sum Game, it makes sense to be envious. But even poker is only a Zero-sum Game in theory, and not always in real life. If we are more interested in having an entertaining evening than in whether we win or lose a few dollars, we may all gain from the game, irrespective of whether we end up ahead or behind. Life is not a Zero-sum Game. We do better if we are not envious. This is true both psychologically and in terms of Tit for Tat strategy. Strategically, the best co-operative partners we can have are ones who will rejoice in our success, as well as in their own. Deeply envious people are therefore likely to miss out on opportunities for mutually beneficial co-operation. They can try to keep their envious nature secret, but this is not easy to do. Even if they do succeed in this, however, they will pay a psychological cost. Envy is not a pleasant emotion to have. It is intrinsically opposed to contentment, essentially a preoccupation with unfulfilled wants, and this is hardly likely to lead to happiness. If we describe a man as deeply envious, we conjure up a picture of someone who is miserable, unable to enjoy what he has, and obsessed rather with what he has not. Sometimes this takes extreme forms, and drives people to ruin themselves. The Wall Street banker Dennis Levine seems to have been driven by envy. According to a former colleague at Drexel Burnham Lambert, Levine 'bitched endlessly that while he was earning in the six figures, his clients were making nine. "Next to them", Dennis used to say, "I feel like a pisher"'. The way Levine found to move his already ample income into the next bracket ended in gaol both for him and for those with whom he exchanged inside information.

There is no doubt that envy can he a strong motivating force. It can make people strive for positions of high status, or for material wealth. No doubt this is why it survives from one generation to the next, despite its obvious disadvantages both for the envious person and for others. Unfortunately, because it is such a strong motivating force, those who want to sell us their products often appeal, subtly or not so subtly, to the element of envy that is in many of us. They foster a climate of envy and a conception of self-interest based on ranking ourselves relative to others. That, in turn, undermines out tendency to co-operate for mutual benefit.

Self-Interest and Ethics: an Interim Conclusion

Societies evolve ethical rules in order to make co-operation more reliable and more durable. The results benefit everyone in the society, both collectively and as individuals. Adopting an initially friendly and co-operative stance, entering into long-term relationships, but not allowing oneself to be exploited, being straightforward and open, avoiding envy—these are not foreign edicts that command us to subdue our own inclinations and turn away from the pursuit of our best interests. They are sound recommendations for anyone making a happy and fulfilling life as a social being.

If we now draw into this picture points made in Chapter 5 about the ethical significance of family and kinship, we can see that a great deal of ethics fits very well with an evolutionary account of our evolved social nature. In some of the most central areas of ethical behaviour, our desires and our ethics are in harmony. In our life with our family and kin, and with our lovers, friends, partners and colleagues, very often self-interest and ethics will point in the same direction. By these means we can eliminate at least a part of the conflict between ethics and self-interest. To that extent, our ultimate choice of how to live is made less difficult. We can choose to live ethically, and at the same time live in a manner that satisfies many of our most important needs as a human being. On the other hand, the areas of ethics we have been discussing in this chapter and in Chapter 5 are by no means the whole of ethics. The remaining chapters of this book turn to a distinct and much more demanding aspect of ethics, and also to some deeper questions about the true nature of self-interest.

Discussion Question(s)

1. What do you make of Singer's steps for "Doing better with Tit for Tat"? Are they compelling? Do they save Tit for Tat from the criticisms listed in the chapter above?
2. Which is the better maxim to live by: 1. Treat others the way they treat you. 2. Treat others the way you would like to be treated. Which does Singer recommend? Why?
3. Is "genuine concern for others" possible, even for strangers? What does Singer think? How does it affect his evaluation of Tit for Tat?

Selection #3: Tim Kurkjian "A Hard Game played by Hard Men," ESPN.com, May 26, 2006.

Please read article here: http://espn.go.com/mlb/columns/story?id=2458700&columnist=kurkjian_tim

Introduction: In this brief piece for ESPN.com, Tim Kurkjian examines how Tit for Tat thinking plays out in the world of Major League Baseball, including how revenge has become part of the unwritten rules of the game. As you read the article, ask yourself whether the real-world evidence contained in it, supports or raises doubts, about Tit for Tat as a practical philosophy.

Discussion Question(s)

1. Should the umpires police baseball, or are the unwritten but strict "Tit for Tat" rules of the players a better system? Which of the two options will keep players safer? Why?
2. Is Kirkjian right that, "revenge has no expiration date"? Should it?

3. This selection recounts how reciprocation can lead to negative spirals of revenge. Are there (or can you think of) any examples of positive spirals of cooperation in MLB?

Selection #4: Grant Brisbee, *SB Nation*, "Why Gambling Used To Scare Baseball and Why it Doesn't Anymore," December 13, 2018.

Introduction: This philosophic selection from baseball writer Grant Brisbee does a great job of showing the practical implications of philosophy in the world of sport. Given an extrinsic theory of justice, ethics is always reducible to a cost-benefit analysis. Alter priorities, values, or environmental conditions enough and the scales will tip radically from one direction to the other. In this instance, Major League Baseball (and its commissioner Rob Manfred) began singing a very different tune regarding gambling in sport as soon as the costs (and benefits) changed. This was the result, primarily, of a Supreme Court ruling in 2018, "Murphy vs. NCAA," which overturned a Federal prohibition on states legalizing sports gambling. They ruled (following the 10th Amendment) that the Federal government had no legal authority to tell state legislatures what they could or could not do. As a result, U.S. states were free to regulate sports gambling for themselves.

Baseball and gambling used to be mortal enemies. Here's how they fell in love.

The mayor of Las Vegas attended the Major League Baseball Winter Meetings in 2004 with a showgirl on each arm and an Elvis impersonator behind him. This is not an exaggeration. Oscar Goodman was a former mob lawyer who represented "Tony the Ant," the inspiration for Joe Pesci's character in *Casino*, but in his second life, from 1999 to 2011, he was a wildly popular mayor of Las Vegas. His mission was to draw attention to the viability of Las Vegas as a home for a future MLB team. The Expos were on their way out of Montreal, and Goodman had designs on them.

It took a corny stunt for Vegas to get baseball's attention back then, in other words. As the Elvis impersonator snarled "Thankyouverruhmuch" three times a minute and took pictures with attendees, Goodman was desperately hoping baseball would notice Las Vegas. Look at my city. Love my city. Consider my city? Please?

Baseball was never going to consider Las Vegas. It was a city that existed only to celebrate the same vice that had almost ruined baseball nearly a century before. Nine years after Goodman's promotional jaunt, Bud Selig, acting in his capacity as the commissioner of Major League Baseball, testified under oath that gambling was an "evil, which creates doubt and destroys your sport." Selig declared then that Las Vegas would never have a baseball team, and responded to New Jersey's ongoing fight to legalize sports betting by saying, "This is corruption, in my opinion."

The showgirls didn't work at the 2004 Winter Meetings. The Elvis impersonator didn't work. Nothing was going to work. Nothing was ever going to get MLB interested in Las Vegas.

Except fresh blood, perhaps. Fresh blood, a Supreme Court decision, and an absolute shit ton of money. Vegas didn't have to show up to the 2018 Winter Meetings and act corny; the Winter Meetings showed up at Vegas. It's no coincidence that the annual meeting of baseball powerbrokers was in Sin City this year. It's a nice place to take someone that you're dating, after all, and baseball and gambling look so cute together now that they're sharing exclusive and proprietary data. There's a nonzero chance that they'll get drunk and marry.

The Supreme Court decision that broke down the final wall was *Murphy v. National Collegiate Athletic Association*. It was a case originally brought by the four major professional sports leagues and the NCAA against the state of New Jersey after the state passed legislation enacting sports betting. New Jersey argued the federal government doesn't have the authority to limit a state's ability to allow legal sports gambling. The Supreme Court agreed and overturned the Professional and Amateur Sports Protection Act from 1992, and now gambling is up to the states.

This doesn't have to mean new commissioner Rob Manfred is much more open to the idea of a team in Vegas (though he is, especially if it helps him get to his dream equilibrium of 32 teams). No, it means that MLB is suddenly into the whole idea of Vegas, and gambling in general. They aren't putting a toe into the water, they're diving in headfirst, signing an exclusive agreement with MGM that includes the limited sharing of proprietary Statcast information. This is data that even the Major League Baseball Players Association doesn't have access to, and it certainly isn't data that the stat nerds have.

After a century of making the sign of the cross and launching an investigation whenever a baseball player knew a guy who knew a guy with a gambling problem, baseball is suddenly very, *very* into the whole gambling thing. Manfred even did that thing where he said the quiet part out loud, suggesting that baseball's stop-and-start pace of play could be perfect for in-game wagers. This is baseball steering into the skid.

In 2013, Selig gave sworn testimony about the Lovecraftian horrors that would emerge from gambling's depths to consume baseball.

In 2018, his replacement waxed poetic about just how snugly the sport and gambling fit together.

This is how baseball stopped worrying and learned to love the casino.

Black Sox, Pete Rose. "Say it ain't so, Joe," and betting on your own team. Signs in the clubhouse and permanent bans. Repeat over and over again. That's the commonly known story about gambling in Major League Baseball. Black Sox, Pete Rose. "Say it ain't so, Joe," and betting on your own team. Signs in the clubhouse and permanent bans. Don't do it, or you'll be shot into the cold vacuum of space.

There are plenty of other baseball gambling stories out there, though. One day I went to sleep, and when I woke up the next day, I read the words "Don Zimmer" and "November issue of *Penthouse*" in the same sentence. I want you to have that same feeling:

> In an article in the November issue of *Penthouse*, writer Jerome Tuccille details the gambling habits of former Chicago Cub manager Don Zimmer. According to Tuccille, Zimmer bet from $3,000 to $5,000 a week on football and basketball games while managing the Cubs.

If you want to find stories about gambling and baseball, you can go down a rabbit hole that's far deeper than Rose or the Black Sox. The early days of baseball were absolutely fraught with it, and it has come up more recently than you think, too.

Not enough time is spent exploring *why* baseball cares so much about gambling, though. Or why it used to. Gambling used to scare the absolute crap out of baseball, and for good reason, so it's worth a primer.

When members of the Chicago White Sox conspired to throw the 1919 World Series, it had been just 18 years since the American League had joined the National League to create what we now know as Major League Baseball. The Federal League, the last established rival to the major leagues, had been a serious threat just 4 years earlier. Baseball was popular, baseball was beloved, but baseball was not yet entrenched. The idea of a professional sports league *at all* was not yet entrenched. Baseball was the first in North

America, after all. The sport wasn't exactly on shaky doe legs, but it was definitely erring on the wrong side of the fad-to-institution spectrum.

A widespread belief that the sport was irreparably illegitimate could have been fatal.

Baseball wasn't just a place to park a butt for 120 minutes and yell things. It was something that emerged from the Progressive Era, a wholly American invention with rules and manners and structure. The players who played the game were unrefined louts, mostly, but the sport was supposed to be a pure representation of the country's potential and inventiveness. The idea of baseball as being something of a national metaphor wasn't invented by Ken Burns; it was a mythology that came *early* in the sport's history.

From Steven A. Riess' *Touching Base: Professional Baseball and American Culture in the Progressive Era*:

> In the Progressive Era, club owners and sympathetic journalists created a self-serving ideology for baseball. They encouraged the public to believe that the game was one of the foremost indigenous American institutions and that it epitomized the finest qualities of a bygone rural age.

Baseball was seen as an American ideal of manners. It was expected to be far more refined than the sports that were historically controlled by gamblers. One of the fathers of professional baseball, Albert Spalding, devoted several passages of his 1911 book *America's National Game* to the specter of gambling, including this one about the formation of the National League:

> The public was interested in the game, but the gamblers would not permit it to be played except under their direction.

This passage didn't age well, considering that 8 years later, gamblers arranged for the World Series to be thrown:

> In all the former battles for the life of our national sport, the men who stood for the preservation of baseball in its integrity had won. Every form of abuse had been so completely eradicated that public confidence had been regained, the press of the country united in its declaration that the game was clean; that gambling had been kicked out.

A widespread belief that the sport was illegitimate maybe *should* have been fatal.

But new commissioner Kenesaw Mountain Landis acted quickly after the eight White Sox conspirators were found not guilty of conspiracy to defraud. He put all eight players on a newly created ineligible list for life, sending a powerful message. The Black Sox story wasn't even ferreted out until the season after it happened, when Hugh S. Fullerton kept picking at a scab that the Chicago newspapers wouldn't touch, but it soon became an existential threat to the game, to the point where there are still signs in every clubhouse in the majors warning players and coaches that the penalty for violating Rule 21 is permanent expulsion.

The fear that baseball players will throw games in exchange for money is just one leg of baseball's distaste for gambling, though. There was also the fear of compromised compulsive gamblers cooperating and affecting on-field results to avoid physical harm. If you think that sounds alarmist or abstract, consider Denny McLain, who had two toes dislocated by a mobster looking to collect on a debt.

Getting sucked into an addiction spiral is always an awful fate, regardless of the addiction, but gambling and athletes make an especially poisonous cocktail. With a gambling addiction, it's far too easy for a debt to be wiped clean by an athlete who gives his debtor an educated guess about a future outcome. MLB investigated Zimmer and suspended

McLain even when their betting had nothing to do with baseball. It's a slippery slope once a person involved with the sport starts losing, and the way out might be a simple *quid pro quo* with someone who isn't above breaking toes.

There's the third leg of the stool to consider, too, and that's the possibility that a gambler can affect baseball games *at all*. Rose was a manager who bet on his own games, sure, but he always bet on his teams to win, so what's the big deal?

The big deal was that it would have been nearly impossible for Rose (or any other gambling manager) to compartmentalize in a situation with money and addiction-fueled endorphins at stake. Every pitcher looks like Nathan Eovaldi in the 2018 World Series when there's $50,000 or more on the line. Even if the wager is less important than the outcome, there's no way for a gambler to separate the two when making decisions that affect the game. Decisions that can affect the health and well-being of other players.

Gambling is baseball poison because players might be tempted to throw games for money. It's poison because baseball players can become vulnerable when the debts pile up. It's poison because gambling players, managers, or executives can affect the game. It's a poison that almost ruined the sport before it really got started.

So you can understand why baseball has traditionally treated gambling like, well, poison.

And here's what all of that has to do with Las Vegas and legalized gambling in the year 2018:

Nothing.

Absolutely nothing.

None of the horrors detailed above relate to the current state of legalized gambling. None of it applies to Las Vegas, certainly. The Vegas-as-Disneyland comparison is overused to the point of cliché, but that's because it still works. The final voiceover from Martin Scorsese's *Casino* includes the line, "After the Tangiers, the big corporations took it all over. Today it looks like Disneyland," and it's only gotten Goofier in the quarter-century since.

On the timeline of vice-to-Disneyland, gambling has been OK for awhile now. Whether it was the proliferation of local casinos, state lotteries, or the bring-the-whole-family vibe that Vegas has been cultivating for decades, we're firmly on the other side of the spectrum now.

Or just take it from Commissioner Manfred himself, who said this to ESPN in 2015:

Gambling, in terms of our society, has changed its presence.

No, baseball doesn't want its players gambling. But the corporations sanitized it a long time ago, just like they do with every vice. Strangling people for sport used to be against the rules, but now it's a multi-billion-dollar industry. Bigger and bigger corporations are already coming for legal weed. And, of course, the most obvious parallel is right in front of our nose. Here's Albert Spalding again:

Baseball is the only game which suits the mighty populace and yet is wholly free from ties to bind it to the gambling and the liquor-selling element, whose aim it is to victimize that populace.

Baseball is, uh, not free from the liquor-selling element these days. There is an entire franchise named after the craft of creating alcoholic beverages, and they play in a park named after alcoholic beverages. In the last century, alcohol went from verboten vice to something that made corporations lots and lots of money. Which means it became something that made baseball lots and lots of money.

That doesn't mean any of it is *good* for you. Oh, heavens no. Alcohol or gambling will ruin your life. But they're gonna make someone lots and lots of money.

If there can be a Milwaukee Brewers, surely there can one day be a Las Vegas Pit Bosses. Baseball will start small with the gambling, partnering with MGM for lots and lots of money, while making sure they're a part of how the whole endeavor works.

Controlling just how legalized gambling is going to work in baseball is probably the most important component of this, too. Here's Manfred again:

> We talked to sports (leagues) in Europe when we realized this was coming. They said the single biggest mistake you can make is not being active in trying to determine what the legal framework's going to look like from an integrity perspective.

Rather than worry about the perils of illicit gambling, it's far more preferable to roll around in the revenues from licit gambling and have a say in how it's operated. It might be the only sensible option.

And forget about all those old objections from the last section. They're all ridiculous in the current context. Take the one with the Black Sox throwing a World Series for money. How much would it cost to bribe a player in a sport where the minimum salary is over a half-million dollars per year? Even if you come up with a figure, how would you turn that into enough betting to make a profit without drawing suspicion? This isn't an age where players are getting flat bottles of champagne as a bonus anymore.

There could be, in a perfect storm, a willing career minor leaguer with no delusions of grandeur, someone for whom a permanent ban wouldn't be an existential crisis. Someone intimately familiar with buses and Tacoma motels who is used to making $75,000 a year, at best, while floating through Triple-A. Let's pretend it's a pitcher who gets called up in a roster emergency and starts a game. That player might be interested in some sort of five-figure payday if he knows that he's not likely to stick around in the majors.

Except with legalized gambling, the casinos and sports books have just as much incentive to prevent this as organized baseball, and they're ready for it. There's no way to drop big money on a Tigers-Twins game with a 30-year-old rookie starting without drawing suspicion. Hell, the casinos already know you by your tattoos. The best part about codifying the whole mess has to do with the safeguards, and an underpaid short-term player futzing around with a single game would be obvious. By partnering with MGM Resorts International, there's roughly a zero-percent chance of shenanigans. It's the shenanigans that used to worry baseball so.

If there's another Pete Rose in baseball's future, someone so consumed by addiction that they're willing to risk a permanent ban, they were going to exist with or without MGM partnering with baseball. Those risks aren't gone; they're exactly the same. And that's what's behind baseball's "Why not?" change of heart.

Vegas has always allowed wagering on baseball, so the biggest difference with the MLB-MGM deal isn't going to be felt at a casino. It's going to appear in the form of an app on your phone that will be available in whichever states decide to take advantage of the Supreme Court decision.

If you want to bet on baseball in Nevada, you can do it from the toilet, just like God intended. Push a couple of buttons on a resort-sponsored app, and you're all set—prop bets, straight wagers, whatever you want. Your payment information is saved, so you don't have to keep re-entering the same account number. It's the kind of post-modern, easily accessible harm that can make for bad speculative fiction.

This will spread to other states eventually. Not at first, but money is a contagion that spreads quickly. People are going to be betting on baseball like never before, and it's going to be accessible in a way that would make Mr. Spalding dizzy. Major League Baseball will be tethered to it every step of the way.

But MGM will have a slight advantage with that Statcast data. Brett Smiley is the editor-in-chief of SportsHandle.com, a site that covers the sports-betting industry and related legislation, and he gave me his best educated guess as to how that black-box data might be used.

It could help inform their bookmakers in setting lines and corresponding prices . . . (a lot of) Statcast data isn't public info beyond what they put out on MLB Network and other broadcasts, so if the MGM bookmakers know that Aaron Judge's launch angle has dipped recently, and he's at a park with a higher wall in right field, I suppose they would have an advantage that even the sophisticated sports bettor wouldn't have, and they might adjust the odds on Judge hitting a home run, knowing that people typically like to bet "overs" and on more scoring.

The demand probably wouldn't be that high in a traditional casino setting for ultra-granular prop bets, but technology is going to make it so damned easy. Now imagine it with the ol' MLB.com referral push. And while this is easy to paint as a huge money-making operation figuring out a way to make more money, there's also a compelling case to make that this is a net positive when it comes to baseball's popularity. Think the sport is too boring, that there's too much time between balls in play? Well, maybe you should spend that time making poor decisions that shoot sweet, sweet chemicals around your cerebral cortex. That'll make the time fly by, and, suddenly, baseball isn't so bad.

Gambling is coming to baseball, and it's an inevitable paring that's been a century in the making. The 1919 White Sox gave the World Series to gamblers because that was the only way they were going to make money, and the 2019 White Sox will be a part of a sport that's actively courting gamblers because that's yet another way to make money.

Riess' book can, yet again, help us make sense of this all.

Despite the rhetoric of professional baseball which claimed the sport was free of that vice, baseball was strongly tainted by gambling . . . in fact, several baseball owners were professional gamblers, horsemen, heavy bettors, or friends of professional gamblers.

What's old is new again. Get ready for a whole new era of baseball and gambling.

Grant Brisbee, Vox.com, and Vox Media, Inc. https://www.sbnation.com/2018/12/13/18116936/mlb-gambling-legal-las-vegas-winter-meetings. www.sbnation.com

Discussion Question(s)

1. Will gambling be good for baseball? Will gambling be good for baseball fans? Why? Why not?
2. Do the details in this article support or undermine the argument for an extrinsic theory of justice? Why?
3. Would an MLB team in Las Vegas be a good idea?

Suggested Readings

Haidt, J. (2012). *The righteous mind: Why good people are divided by politics and religion.* New York, NY: Pantheon Books.

Loland, S. (2009). The ethics of performance-enhancing technology in sport. *Journal of the Philosophy of Sport, 36*(2), 152–161.

Schneider, A. J., & Rupert, J. L. (2009). Constructing winners: The science and ethics of genetically manipulating athletes. *Journal of the Philosophy of Sport, 36*(2), 182–206.

Twietmeyer, G. (2015). Religion, theology and sport. In *Routledge handbook of the philosophy of sport* (pp. 238–254). New York, NY: Routledge.

Bibliography

Allyn, D. (2001). *Make love, not war: The sexual revolution: An unfettered history.* New York, NY: Routledge.

Aquinas, St. T. (n.d.). *Commentary on the First Epistle to the Corintians.* (F. Larcher, Ed.) Retrieved July 18, 2008, from Ave Maria University: http://www.aquinas.avemaria.edu/Aquinas-Corinthians.pdf

Aristotle. (2002a). *Nicomachean ethics.* (J. Sachs, Trans.) Newburyport, MA: Focus Publishing.

Aristotle. (2002b). *Metaphysics.* (J. Sachs, Trans.) Santa Fe, NM: Green Lion Press.

Aristotle. (2004). *On the soul.* (J. Sachs, Trans.) Santa Fe, NM: Green Lion Press.

Berger, P. (1969). *A rumor of angels: Modern society and the rediscovery of the supernatural.* Garden City, NY: Doubleday Anchor Books.

Berlin, I. (2002). Two concepts of liberty. In I. Berlin, & H. Hardy (Ed.), *Liberty* (pp. 166–217). Oxford, UK: Oxford University Press.

Brown, W. M. (2009). The case for perfection. *Journal of the Philosophy of Sport, 36*(2), 127–139.

Caplan-Bricker, N. (2016, May 23). *Brazil says its record-breaking condom provision has nothing to do With Zika.* Retrieved July 1, 2016, from www.slate.com: http://www.slate.com/blogs/xx_factor/2016/05/23/brazil_will_provide_450_000_free_condoms_for_rio_de_janeiro_olympics_breaking.html

Chesterfield, P. D. (1998). *Lord Chesterfield's letters.* (D. Roberts, Ed.) New York, NY: Oxford University Press.

Columbia Daily Tribune. (2105, October 25). *TAKE TWO: Tolerating turpitude is OK, but just be honest about it.* Retrieved August 15, 2019, from columbiatribune.com: https://www.columbiatribune.com/article/20151025/Sports/310259958

Copleston S.J., F. (1946/1993). *A history of philosophy volume I: Greece and Rome.* New York, NY: Bantam Doubleday Dell Publishing.

Dewey, J. (1958). *Experience and nature* (2nd ed.). Mineola, NY: Dover Publications.

Eberstadt, M. (2012). *Adam and Eve after the pill: Paradoxes of the sexual revolution.* San Francisco, CA: Ignatius Press.

Ellul, J. (1997). *Perspectives on our age: Jacques Ellul speak on his life and work* (Rev. ed.). (W. H. Venderburg, Ed.) Toronto, Canada: House of Anansi Press.

Fort, T. (2001). *Ethics and governance: Business as mediating institution.* New York, NY: Oxford University Press.

Ganguli, T. (2018, May 14). *NBA has been preparing to embrace legalized sports betting for years.* Retrieved August 15, 2019, from latimes.com: https://www.latimes.com/sports/nba/la-sp-sports-betting-basketball-20180514-story.html

Green, R. M. (2007). *Babies by design: The ethics of genetic choice.* New Haven, CT: Yale University Press.

James, W. (1896/1956). The will to believe. In W. James, *The will to believe and other essays in popular philosophy; human immortality* (pp. 1–32). New York, NY: Dover Publications.

Jimison, R. (2018, February 2). *Olympic Village stocked with 110,000 condoms.* Retrieved February 5, 2018, from https://www.cnn.com/2018/02/01/health/olympic-village-condoms/index.html

Lefton, T. (2019, July 15). *Patches in progress for MLB.* Retrieved August 15, 2019, from sportsbusinessdaily.com: https://www.sportsbusinessdaily.com/Journal/Issues/2019/07/15/Leagues-and-Governing-Bodies/MLB-patches.aspx

Lefton, T., & Lombardo, J. (2019, February 25). *NBA: Big payoff for a little patch.* Retrieved August 15, 2019, from sportbusinessdaily.com: https://www.sportsbusinessdaily.com/Journal/Issues/2019/02/25/Leagues-and-Governing-Bodies/NBA-patches.aspx

Lewis, C. S. (1944, 2001). *The abolition of man.* New York, NY: Harper Collins.

Munthe, C. (2007). Selected champions: Making winners in the age of genetic technology. In W. J. Morgan (Ed.), *Ethics in sport* (pp. 273-284). Champaign, IL: Human Kinetics.

Nagel, T. (2012). *Mind and cosmos: Why the materialist neo-Darwinian conception of nature is almost certainly false.* New York, NY: Oxford University Press.

O'Conner, I. (2016, March 1). *Are these the final days of Rick Pitino at Louisville?* Retrieved July 1, 2016, from espn.com: http://espn.go.com/mens-college-basketball/story/_/id/14873300/rick-pitino-needs-some-decide-run-louisville-over

Ogus, S. (2019, August 13). *NFL expands data partnership with Sportradar, taking first major step toward legalized gambling.* Retrieved August 15, 2019, from forbes.com: https://www.forbes.com/sites/simonogus/2019/08/13/nfl-expands-data-partnership-with-sportradar-taking-first-major-step-towards-legalize-gambling/#3ec175131f58

Plato. (2000). *The republic.* (B. Jowett, Trans.) Mineola, NY: Dover.

Pojman, L. P., & Vaughn, L. (2011). *The moral life: An introductory reading in ethics and literature* (4th ed.). New York, NY: Oxford University Press.

Polanyi, M., & Prosch, H. (1975). *Meaning.* Chicago, IL: The University of Chicago Press.

Rosen, D. (2018, October 29). *NHL, MGM Resorts form sports betting partnership.* Retrieved August 15, 2019, from nhl.com: https://www.nhl.com/news/nhl-mgm-resorts-sports-betting-partnership/c-301392322

Ross, W. D. (1930, 2002). *The right and the good.* New York, NY: Oxford University Press.

Rovell, D. (2016, April 15). *NBA approves on-jersey advertising program.* Retrieved from espn.com: http://espn.go.com/nba/story/_/id/15210151/nba-jerseys-carry-advertisements-beginning-2017-18

Schlabach, M. (2017, September 27). *The step-by-step process of how the words 'corruption' and 'fraud' came to college basketball.* Retrieved August 15, 2019, from espn.com: https://www.espn.com/mens-college-basketball/story/_/id/20834050/the-story-how-fbi-brought-words-corruption

Singer, P. (1995). *How are we to live? Ethics in an age of self-interest.* Amherst, NY: Prometheus Books.

Skaikin, B. (2018, November 27). *MLB becomes third major sports league to form partnership with MGM.* Retrieved August 15, 2019, from LAtimes.com: https://www.latimes.com/sports/mlb/la-sp-mlb-mgm-partnership-20181127-story.html

Chapter 8

How Do We Promote Ethical Behavior?

"To be attached to the subdivision, to love the little platoon we belong to in society, is the first principle (the germ as it were) of public affections. It is the first link in the series by which we proceed towards a love to our country and to mankind"

—Edmund Burke[1]

Students will be able to:

1. Distinguish the difference between mediating and quarantining institutions.
2. Explain how mediating institutions promote ethical behavior.
3. Define solidarity and subsidiarity and articulate how these ideas support the claim that mediating institutions are necessary to the promotion of ethical behavior.
4. Articulate the strengths and weaknesses of mediating institutions.
5. Evaluate how sport, as well as philosophic reflection on sport, can be used to live a good (rather than a merely successful) life.

We have endeavored through the course of this text to examine the basic roots of ethics and philosophy. In Chapter 6, while examining virtue ethics we encountered Aristotle's (2002) admonition that we do not pursue ethical knowledge "in order to know what virtue is, but in order to become good" (1103b27). Studying ethics for the mere sake of understanding is never sufficient. We study, we reflect, we learn, not just to know what is good, but to lead better lives. Therefore we will close this book by examining one final question: How can we make this happen? How do we promote ethical behavior? What is the best way to encourage people to do the right thing?

In pursuit of that goal we will focus on the work of ethicist Timothy Fort. Fort (2001) argues in favor of the idea of mediating institutions, an idea he inherited from the work of sociologist Peter Berger and theologian Richard John Neuhaus (1996). A **mediating institution** is "A small institution where individuals within the organization [are] confronted with the consequences of their actions" (Fort, 2001, p. 8). What this means, Fort argues, is that mediating institutions allow human beings to see, in a concrete way, that "treating others well is important and desirable" (p. 24).

Mediating Institutions: Small structures such as family, church, neighborhood, and team which anchor an individual in society. They *mediate* between the impersonal structures of the state and the isolated individual by rooting them in a community.

---

[1] (Burke, 1790/2009, pp. 46–47).

In contrast to Singer, Fort is also very comfortable with spiritual and religious ideas. This is because within the transcendent understanding of good and evil, which religious commitment provides, we are ultimately accountable to something besides ourselves. Therefore, Fort argues that spiritual or religious motivation gives an imperative to act ethically within a mediating institution framework. As such, religion—within the bounds of a mediating institution structure—should be admissible to public life including our work life.

The format of this chapter will again follow our well-worn pattern. After reviewing Fort, we will examine his work for strengths and weaknesses. After doing so we will turn our attention to the impact an embrace of mediating institutions might have on sport. The book will then conclude with some final thoughts on the place of ethics in sport and the proper place of sport in life.

Mediating Institutions

Fort is interested in the idea of mediating institutions because he is convinced that they are vital to developing the human bonds necessary for community to develop. This is important because he thinks that relationships not rules, threats, or reason are the key to promoting ethical behavior. To be sure, community does not guarantee ethical behavior. Nor is the point that rules and reason have no role to play in ethics. Mediating institutions are simply the best way to *encourage* ethical behavior.

Why is this the case? To answer this question it is important to further unpack the idea of mediating institutions. As Berger and Neuhaus (1996) point out, mediating institutions are "those institutions standing between the individual in his private life and the large institutions of public life" (p. 158). These small structures such as family, church, neighborhood and team anchor the individual in society. They help individuals avoid the anomie (the rootlessness) of being an isolated individual as well as avoid the alienation of belonging only to bureaucratic mega-structures such as the State.

Human beings need community. This is why rules, although necessary, are insufficient. Rules can become separated from real standards and experience. When this happens rules will not effectively deter bad behavior, for they will be seen as merely bureaucratic realities divorced from everyday life. Moreover, even threats of punishment, as we saw in Chapter 7, can be reduced to being mere parameters of an ethical cost benefit analysis. What then is a better way? Fort argues that the "skeleton" of rules needs the "warm flesh" of relationships to function properly. It is important to have a legal framework (rules) but the best way to promote ethical behavior is through the relationships built in mediating institutions. Rules need to be embodied in practice, not merely rationally understood. Just as a home is more than the mere superstructure of the house (foundation, walls, etc.) promoting ethical behavior is more than merely identifying and "enforcing" the rules. We need the house (rules), to be sure, but the goal is a home (community).

Yet, why is this more likely to encourage ethical behavior than rationalistic systems such as deontology or utilitarianism? The reason is simple. Mediating institutions are more likely than bare reason to encourage relationships because I will feel a personal responsibility to you and you will feel a personal responsibility to me, rather than a contractual (or rational) obligation, where our only responsibility is to the rules or to utility.[2] Fort's point is that, "Names and faces make all the difference" (Twietmeyer, 2007, p. 205).

---

[2] "Liberalism's blindness to mediating structures can be traced to its Enlightenment roots. Enlightenment thought is abstract, universalistic, addicted to what Burke called 'geometry' in social policy. The concrete particularities of mediating structures find an inhospitable soil in the liberal garden. There the great concern is for the individual (the 'rights of man') and for a just public order, but anything 'in between' is viewed as irrelevant, or even an obstacle, to the rational ordering of society. What lies in between is dismissed, to the extent that it can be, as superstition, bigotry or (more recently) cultural lag." (Berger & Neuhaus, 1996, p. 161).

Just as a healthy family cannot be reduced to purely rational or utilitarian motives, so too ethics cannot be reduced to mere duty or calculation. Bloodless rationalism, whether based in duty or utility, is too abstract to motivate human beings as well as relationships and community can.[3] A functioning family is one of the best examples (though not the only example) of how mediating institutions are superior to any form of rationalism for promoting ethical behavior. In the family there is a balance between the well-being of the whole and the well-being of the individual. Moreover concern for the whole is not merely instrumental. We do not hold the family together simply as an "economy of scale" but rather out of real love and concern for each other. The bonds that hold a family together are larger than utilitarian concerns such as profit or winning. Fort argues that the same is true of the healthy corporation or team. They should not be understood as purely economic or competitive associations. Since they are human rather than mere economic or competitive institutions, moral, emotional, spiritual needs should also receive consideration. Profit, winning and efficiency are vital goods, but not the only vital goods.

If Fort (2001) is right, then ethics do not primarily come from ethics courses but from, "bonds developed in family, church, schools, neighborhoods, and self-help groups; in other words, from mediating institutions" (p. 12).[4] After making this point, Fort then draws a normative/descriptive distinction between mediating institutions and small communities as such. Small communities are not inherently healthy and good. Unhealthy

Ethics do not primarily come from ethics courses but from, "bonds developed in family, church, schools, neighborhoods . . ."
©red mango/Shutterstock.com

---

[3] It is worth noting one of sociologist Robert Nisbet's (1993) comments on the work of Emile Durkheim here: "Far from being social morality that is the abstraction, it is individual morality, he emphasizes, that is the abstraction, for where other than within the community can the moral life be seen" (p. 89)?

[4] Moreover, if Fort is right, and moral, emotional and spiritual needs allow us to function with larger goals than material gain in mind, then Singer may be shooting himself in the foot when he insists on secular ethics. Why? Because every motivation but materialism is out of bounds in secular ethics. When religious and spiritual motivations are privatized, cold, nothing but the bottom line capitalism, is the practical result. It is the only thing we are allowed to talk about. "Profit and winning are good" is one thing we can all agree on. As a result, perhaps Singer is actually promoting what he decries!?

Quarantining Institutions: Small structures, such as a gang, which although they give an individual a sense of belonging, isolate them (via alienation, fear, and superiority) from the outside world.

small communities, which Fort calls **quarantining institutions**, turn in on themselves and see the larger world and other out groups as the enemy. In contrast, mediating institutions root the individual in the larger society and thereby help them see that their behavior, whether good or bad, impacts other flesh and blood people. As Fort puts it:

> "A mediating institution integrates an individual's good into the common good of others and their associations. It neither quarantines its members, nor does it organize itself on the basis of alienation, fear, or superiority. It socializes its members to see the connection between individual self-interest and the good of others through the means of ethical behavior" (p. 14).

Hence a gang, while a close-knit relational community is a quarantining institution rather than a mediating institution, for it is built on alienation, fear, superiority, etc.

In terms of sport this distinction between mediating and quarantining institutions leads to a very important question: Do leagues, teams, and athletics departments tend to be mediating or quarantining institutions? In American college sport, at least, this is a live question. The first and most obvious reason is the time commitment involved in participating in intercollegiate athletics, which leaves little time for the typical experiences of the life of a college student.[5] Here are two other issues which raise questions regarding whether big-time intercollegiate athletics departments often function as quarantining institutions and thereby see the larger campus as a threat: (1) Advising toward eligibility, (2) Athlete-only or athlete specific facilities.

Advising toward eligibility is a serious problem. In such instances, athletics departments, via their advisors in the athletics academic support program (ASP), encourage athletes to take courses that fit their practice and competitive schedules rather than their educational goals. This is done because the potential ineligibility of players is a threat to wins and revenue.[6] One former NCAA Division I football player described his experience this way: "Now I look back and say, 'Well, what did I really go to college for? Crap classes you won't use the rest of your life?' Social science is really nothing specific. . . I was majoring in football" (Liber Steeg, Upton, Bohn, & Berkowitz, 2008, para. 21).

Athlete tailored or athlete exclusive facilities are another significant problem. They occur in primarily two forms, lavish housing meant for athletes as well as extravagant facilities for their ASPs. Each of these types of facilities isolate and alienate student athletes from getting involved in campus life, which in turn can have a quarantining effect. As former Ohio State quarterback Cardale Jones infamously tweeted "Why should we have to go to class if we came here to play FOOTBALL, we ain't [sic] come to play SCHOOL classes are POINTLESS" (ESPN.com news services, 2012).

An example of this sort of extravagance is Texas A&M University, which recently spent $27 million dollars on an academic support building to serve approximately 600 athletes

---

[5] If the athletic demands on students are so great at to necessitate academic support, then those athletic demands should be curtailed. The solution to the conflict between the demands placed on athletes and their school work is simple. *Lessen those demands.* I have no doubt that the time demands are real. I felt them myself as an NAIA level soccer player in the mid-1990s. I am sure that Division I athletes are under far greater stress in this regard than was I. But again the solution to this imbalance is not to lighten the academic load through specialized advisement, tutoring or fraud. The solution is to free up more time to focus on studying and going to class, by reducing athletic demands. The fact that the opposite road was taken, is itself, a damning indictment of both the ASP model and American higher education.

[6] Unfortunately, in the world of "big-time" sport, running the risk of ineligibility is far too high of a price to pay for personal maturity. Hand holding is therefore necessary. As one academic advisor put it, "you have to monitor everything, there's so much at stake" (Wolverton, 2008). Should one doubt this claim, consider the fact that Ohio State University is now even monitoring the spending and finances of their athletes (Wolverton, 2012).

Are big time athletics departments quarantining institutions? Was Cardale Jones simply speaking an uncomfortable truth when he tweeted "Why should we have to go to class if we came here to play FOOTBALL?"
G Fiume/Getty Images Sport/Getty Images

Solidarity: The claim that human beings are by nature bound to the common good. All human beings share—despite difference in race, culture, religion, etc.—a common humanity. We are, despite our differences, "all in this together."

(Wolverton, 2008). This means that the twenty four thousand square foot building is, according to fall 2017 enrollment numbers, designed to primarily serve slightly more than one percent of the campus.[7] Similarly, in the fall of 2015 The University of Kansas opened an $11.2 million dollar apartment complex for basketball players, which includes a movie theater, a half-court gym, and a barbershop (Shepherd, 2015). Segregating athletes in terms of time, coursework and physical location cannot help but further encourage athletics departments, as well as the athletes themselves, to see the rest of the university as a threat.[8] When this happens athletics departments become quarantining institutions.

Solidarity & Subsidiarity

After laying out the basic concept of mediating and quarantining institutions, Fort then turns his attention to two aspects of Catholic social teaching which he believes support his claims regarding the central importance of mediating institutions. They are, as the title to this section suggests, **solidarity** and **subsidiarity**. He endorses these concepts not to prose-lytize for Roman Catholicism. Fort himself is not Catholic. He is interested in these two

Subsidiarity: The claim that authority should always be passed down to the most local level possible, where individuals close to the problem will know the problem intimately and actually care about solving it. (E.g., the Federal government should never try to solve a problem that a state or local community can. The NCAA should not try to solve problems that an individual school can). Authority should only be passed up to a higher level, when it is clear that the lower, more local, more intimate level, has shown that it cannot solve the problem itself.

---

[7] According to The U.S. Department of Education's EADA data (2017), Texas A&M's fall enrollment in 2017 on the main campus was 46,592. If one takes the total number of varsity athletes reported in the same data and divides that by the enrollment one gets 1.2%.

[8] Another example of this problem is the University of Wisconsin's $77 million dollar "Athletic Village" which was completed in 2014. The "The 38,000-square-foot academic and strength training center" includes "(among other things) offices, study rooms, an auditorium, a library and a computer lab" (Steinbach, 2012, para. 1). This is inherently quarantining and contrary to the NCAA stated goals. Kutztown University professor and Drake Group member (a college athletics reform group) Jason Lanter incisively points out the contradiction and it implications. The NCAA claims in NCAA Bylaw 1.3.1 that "A basic purpose of this Association is to maintain intercollegiate athletics as an integral part of the educational program and the athlete as an integral part of the student body" (NCAA, 2019, p.1). Yet, as Lanter insists, "how can athletes be an integral part of the educational opportunities and the student body when they are geographically isolated from the rest of campus" (Steinbach, 2012, para. 2)?

ideas because he thinks they are catholic "small-c" claims. That is, he is convinced that they are *universally true*, independent of one's confessional or theological commitments. The root meaning of "catholic" is "universal." What then are these two allegedly universal ideas and why are they so important? Solidarity and subsidiarity are important because they make the development of mediating institutions possible. Let us look at each one in more detail.

Solidarity is a commitment to the common good. A firm sense that each human life (despite differences in language, culture, and values) matters. It is a sense of empathy and compassion for one's fellow human beings. Moreover, as Fort points out, solidarity allows one to empathize from within one's own commitments. The example Fort (2001) uses to explain this point is that Gandhi "a devout Hindu" was willing to say he "was a Muslim and a Christian and a Jew" (p. 21).

What is Fort's point? Is he using Gandhi to argue in favor of the modern cliché "That all religions are the same"? No. Our differences are real and should not be simply papered over with cant. Nevertheless, all people, religious or otherwise, deserve our respect as fellow human beings. In fact, the Golden Rule or something like it is found in various religious and philosophical traditions around the globe. Again, Gandhi is useful for exemplifying what this concern for fellow human beings looks like (even for those with whom one has profound disagreements). How far did Gandhi take this concept of solidarity? Even the British were not his enemies. They were wrong. He actively supported Indian independence. But that did not mean the British were sub-human or worthy of ill-treatment.

Solidarity is vitally important for two reasons. First, a sense of solidarity ensures that our mediating institutions (even when centered on parochial concerns) will not have a parochial outlook. Instead those with a sense of solidarity will remain committed to their own values and concerns without shutting out the larger world. Second, solidarity cultivates the sense that human life and human relationships are more important than victory, profit, or pleasure. Obviously solidarity and "winning" are not necessarily in conflict. Nevertheless, when they do conflict, a sense of solidarity means that community always trumps utility.

If this is right, then developing a sense of solidarity is extremely important. This is where subsidiarity comes in. Subsidiarity is the principle that whenever possible, decisions should be made locally by those who intimately know the situation and who will be directly affected by the outcome. That is, by those who have an actual stake in the particular community that will be affected by the decision(s). William J. Byron S.J. (1998), describes the idea this way.

> "no higher level of organization should perform any function that can be handled efficiently and effectively at a lower level of organization by human persons who, individually or in groups, are closer to the problem, and closer to the ground" (para. 24).

Put bluntly, subsidiarity is an argument against bureaucracy and the totalitarian impulse to control free association. Relationships matter. They lead to real concern, real knowledge, and real commitment. As such, mediating institutions should not be undermined, abolished, or micromanaged.

To buttress the idea of subsidiarity, Fort makes one final key claim: Anthropology suggests that there is a limit to the number of people we can relate to in a group. Churches, aboriginal tribes, etc. seem to split when they get above 150 to 200 people. If they are bigger than that, they have subgroups. Both philosophy and biology support the importance of mediating institutions. Fort (2001) then explains the impact of this insight on promoting ethical behavior.

"If ethics has to do with how we treat others, then this cognitive limitation makes a difference to doing ethics well. Put individuals in large groups, and one loses the sense of community that nurtures ethical behavior" (p. 51).

Solidarity is bred in small groups. Subsidiarity simply ratifies the importance of allowing such groups to flourish.

What then are the implications of Fort's argument for subsidiarity? If solidarity is bred in real relationships, and subsidiarity says that a "town" or a "school" can usually handle its problems better than the "State" or "bureaucrats" can, then massive governmental or administrative action will often be problematic. Furthermore, legislation is inherently of limited value, at least in terms of actually inculcating moral behavior. What is generally needed is not more rules, but healthier communities.

When this idea is applied to sport we should understand the impotence of, for example, NCAA reform. Reliance on massive NCAA action is problematic. As Fort insists the frequency of NCAA scandals "indicates the failure of bureaucratic rules to be able to adequately govern moral behavior" (p. 34). First, the NCAA, being remote, will never have the proper pulse of the problem. Second, new rules will always be reactive. Finally, rules and threats, as we have seen, are impotent to inspire virtue. In fact, divorced from the particular, rules can instead inspire jaded, cynical reactions.[9] Nevertheless, it is upon the character of players, coaches and administrators that sports ethics relies. Yet, character is cultivated locally via relationships and good examples, not by diktat or regulation.

This insight brings a general philosophical principle to the fore. *Divorcing yourself from the particular is unrealistic and unwise.* Abstract utilitarian platitudes about "each counting for one" and "no one counting for more than one," which allegedly prove a disinterested concern for all, actually turn out be "elitist and self-absorbed." This is "because the demands of the philosophy (which are fundamentally impossible) seem to be more about proving and congratulating one's own moral standing relative to others, than about really making the world a better place" (Twietmeyer, 2007, p. 211).

In contrast, the *particular* is what breeds compassion. The *particular* is how we know what people really need. The *particular* is the reason human beings care about each other. We always reach out to the wider world from the *particular*. Therefore, true reform is hard, slow work, which will always need to take mediating institutions into account to be fully effective. Legislation, absent such insight, is impotent. Moralizing, absent such insight, is hollow.

The Strengths of Mediating Institutions

There are two strengths of mediating institutions worth emphasizing. The first is that such a philosophy recognizes the importance of nurturing a sense of belonging and, in turn, ownership in the moral life. The point is to place the individual in a set of personal relationships which root him in the larger society. Abstract moral theory (no matter how careful) cannot cultivate moral behavior by itself. Second, Fort's account takes religious and spiritual values seriously. Not so as to impose any set of beliefs upon others, but rather because a "recognition of a spiritual transcendent reality is a meaningful

---

[9] "One of the most debilitating results of modernization is a feeling of powerlessness in the face of institutions controlled by those whom we do not know and whose values we often do not share" (Berger & Neuhaus, 1996, p. 164). "When abstract principles are anachronistically applied, one loses the sense of participation in the law's meaning, purpose and content. Indeed, when anachronistic legalisms are applied, the law ceases to be a constitutive part of the lived life of members of a community, and instead becomes an object. Because it is then an object, it becomes easier to manipulate, and popular confidence in it then decreases" (Fort, 2001, p. 11).

motivation for many to be ethical in business [and in sport]" (Fort, 2001, p. 183). If we are *serious* about improving ethical behavior, we will take this reality into account.

You may recall that in Chapter 1, we spent some time examining Aristotle's claim that human beings are "political animals." There we pointed out that Aristotle was making a specific claim about human nature. What Aristotle meant was that:

> "human beings are *by nature* communal and deliberative. That is, we are social and rational creatures. As social creatures we live in communities and rely on each other to achieve a full human existence. As rational creatures, unlike other animals, we debate the form, content and justice of our social organizations" (Chapter 1, p. 6).

Fort's emphasis on small communities is not based in nostalgia or a trite longing for "mom and pop" ethics, but rather a claim about human nature. Human beings, by nature, need community to thrive.

If you have any doubts about this, consider the following. We are all dependent upon others. Newborns, for example, are helpless. The only reason any of us are here to discuss sports ethics is because someone else (most likely our parents) took care of us before we could take care of ourselves. Moreover, such dependence, in one degree or another, follows us through all the stages of our lives (MacIntyre, 1999). Similarly, you were *given* your name. You inherit language, ideas, values and even facts about the world. As the philosopher Michael Polanyi (1962) compellingly argues, belief not doubt is fundamental to all of our learning. For at root, all learning relies upon an "exceptional degree of confidence in another, the apprentice in the master, the student in the teacher, and popular audiences in distinguished speakers or famous writers" (p. 207). Reliance on, that is, *faith in*, authority is inescapable.[10]

At root, all learning relies upon an "exceptional degree of confidence in another". Authority is inescapable.
©ChameleonsEye/Shutterstock.com

---

[10] "We must now recognize belief once more as the source of all knowledge. Tacit assent and intellectual passions, the sharing of an idiom and of a cultural heritage, affiliation to a like-minded community: such are the impulses which shape our vision of the nature of things on which we rely for our mastery of things. No intelligence, however critical or original, can operate outside such a fiduciary framework" (Polanyi, 1962, p. 266).

All human beings need community. In turn, a sense of belonging allows for a sense of ownership and responsibility which promotes ethical behavior by making plain how our "actions affect others" (Fort, 2001, p. 32). Radical egalitarianism, based in a disembodied rationalism, which seeks to abolish loyalties to family, or team, or creed, is dislocated from the realities of human life.[11] Therefore, it will never work. "Equality," in this sense of eliminating distinctions, leads to universal indifference rather than universal care. Aristotle (1981) makes the point succinctly when describing how such a philosophy would impact families. "Each citizen acquires a thousand sons, but these are not one man's sons; any one of them is equally the son of any person, and as a result will be equally neglected by everyone" (1261b40). Similarly, Fort (2001) draws out the implications for professional practice. "Who will really notice [and who will be harmed] if I embezzle a bit of money from this huge employer" (p. 51)? If you want to promote ethical behavior, ownership, belonging and proximity always trump "equality."

Religious and spiritual concerns are also a powerful spur to ethical action. Again, if we are really *serious* about improving ethical behavior, we will take this reality into account. In fact, the source of hesitance in this regard, the privatization of religion, is a recent and uniquely modern phenomenon.[12] As the anthropologist Talal Asad (2003) reminds us, "The supposedly universal opposition between 'sacred' and 'profane' finds no place in premodern writing" (pp. 31–32). That we are encouraged to hide our religious convictions "at work" is not a self-evident truth but simply one more manifestation of the modern ideological tendency to compartmentalize our lives.[13]

Moreover, the "naked public square" (Neuhaus, 1984) is not neutral. Public life whitewashed of religious expression and ideas is an instance of partisanship, because the practical consequence is to "give the state a monopoly on public space and on the values to be advanced in that space" (Berger & Neuhaus, 1996, p. 192). If churches, synagogues and other houses of worship are mediating institutions and if religious conviction grounds one's actions in a transcendent reality to which one is beholden, then admitting religious and spiritual ideas into the discussion of how to promote ethical behavior is doubly important. For religious faiths can build community, as well as ground one's convictions in a truth deeper than pleasure, will, or desire.[14]

The fact that public religious expression remains taboo, shows how deeply modern we are. Yet, modernity, right or wrong, is *a set of philosophical, not self-evident, commitments*. Which means not only that those commitments can change, but that some of our modern convictions may be mistaken. Fort sets out a compelling case that our fear of the public expression of religious ideas, is one such case worthy of reassessment.

---

[11] "Because we love our fathers, mothers, neighbors, and friends, we comprehend the value of human lives, no matter how distant, or how local. The opposite is just as true; delinquent fathers (or mothers), spousal abuse, and other myriad forms of human callousness create suffering directly in their very action and indirectly in the consequences of those actions. A broken family, for instance, or a broken school is unlikely to nurture the very kind of compassion needed to make the world a better place. In this sense then, local suffering can have near universal consequences. Relationship patterns spread whether healthy or unhealthy" (Twietmeyer, 2007, p. 206).

[12] "Religion", understood as a genus describing the *private, individual* and *spiritual* sphere of belief in "God" or the "transcendent" is itself a modern idea. See: (Nongbri, 2013).

[13] As theologian William Cavanaugh (2009) points out, "What counts as religion and what does not in any given context is contestable and depends on who has the power and authority to define religion at any given time and place . . . The concept of religion as used by theorists . . . is a development of the modern liberal state; the religious-secular distinction accompanies the invention of private-public, religion-politics and church-state dichotomies" (p. 59).

[14] This is by no means a trivial point. As Fort (2001) declares, "no utilitarian, Kantian, nor contractarian position can identify goods more valuable than others for an individual to prefer" (p. 45).

The Weaknesses of Mediating Institutions

Fort's ideas will no doubt be controversial for many readers. I would like to review two criticisms here.[15] The first and most common criticism is that the particularity engendered by a philosophy of mediating institutions will encourage myopic self-concern, tribalism and prejudice. The second criticism simply holds that religion will only add fuel to this already raging fire. As such, mediating institutions, and public religious expression are best kept at arm's length. For they are just as likely, if not more likely, to create problems as they are to solve them. They are just as likely to encourage immoral action as to encourage moral action.

A succinct but hardly unique expression of this concern for tribalism can be found in the work of Peter Singer. In *How are We to Live?* Singer (1995) warns that "If parental love, taken to an extreme, has its dangers in rare cases, these feelings of group devotion are much more deadly, and their consequences are of global significance" (p. 101). This, Singer argues, has manifested itself throughout history, most notoriously in the racist ideology of the Nazis. In contrast to "group devotion" Singer (1993) believes in the "principle of equality" which he defines as being committed to an "equal consideration of interests" (p. 21).[16]

Singer's point is that we ought to consider the interests of strangers of equal value to those of our neighbors, friends and family. "For the principle takes, firstly, no account of proximity or distance. It makes no moral difference whether the person I help is a neighbor's child ten yards from me or a Bengali whose name I shall never know, ten thousand miles away" (Singer, 1972, pp. 231–232). One is no more important than another. "An interest is an interest," Singer (1993) insists, "whoever's interest it may be" (p. 21). Therefore, there is no "sound moral justification for the view that distance, or community membership, makes a crucial difference to our moral obligations" (p. 232).[17]

Religion, in turn, is just one more manifestation (and a particularly volatile one) of "group devotion." It is quite dangerous in this regard and therefore is rightly

---

[15] A third criticism is more subtle. According to this counter argument Fort (2001) is being a utilitarian when he pins his argument on ethical actors realizing what the good is by seeing the "consequences of their actions" (p. 8). As such, "mandating" the importance of mediating institutions is merely a form of rule utilitarianism whereby "seeing the consequences" generally allows for the greatest good for the greatest number. It doesn't seem to me that this criticism holds water. Fort is not answering the question "What is good?" or "Why be good?" but rather "How do we promote ethical behavior?" To acknowledge that seeing and caring about the impact of one's behavior on others is important for encouraging good behavior, in no way requires Fort to commit himself to the idea that the good is reducible to the consequences. Put another way, non-utilitarians are not required to deny any consideration of consequences or pleasure when evaluating ethical ideas, actions or theories. They simply need to deny that ethics is reducible to such things.

[16] Singer (1995) takes this point so far as to apologize for rooting for a particular football team. "Almost every Australian child grows up supporting a football team. It is an affliction to which I am not immune, and which I have been unable to shake off, even as I grow older and presumably wiser" (p. 100).

[17] Singer (1993) attempts to moderate the obvious implications of his principle later in *Practical Ethics* when he states "When families and local communities look after their own poorer members, ties of affection and personal relationships achieve ends that would otherwise require a large, impersonal bureaucracy. Hence it would be absurd to propose that from now on we all regard ourselves as equally responsible for the welfare of everyone in the world; but the argument for an obligation to assist does not propose that" (p. 233). Of course, as we have seen, the "principle of equality" does propose just that "absurd" conclusion. That even Singer cannot fully commit to his own logic, indicates how absurd it is. Nevertheless, all Singer can muster is a "small degree of preference for family and community" which is "decisively outweighed by existing discrepancies in wealth and property" (p. 234).

consigned to the sphere of private life. Theologian Martin Marty (2000) makes the point this way:

> "Those called to be religious naturally form separate groups, movements, tribes or nations. Responding in good faith to a divine call, believers feel themselves endowed with sacred privilege, a sense of chosenness that elevates them above all others. This self-perception then leads groups to draw lines around themselves and to speak negatively of 'the others'" (pp. 25–26).

Given the historical and contemporary record of violence done in the name of God or religion, is it not simple common sense to significantly limit the public expression of religious faith and doctrine? Given that religious violence is just one type of the myriad problems created by "group devotion," how can promoting mediating institutions be a good idea? If each of these criticisms is on target, how can Fort possibly be right?

Responses in Defense of Mediating Institutions

What can be said in reply to these weighty criticisms? Several things. In response to the first criticism two things must be emphasized. First, although it is true on an abstract and rational level that my interests are no more important than any others, it does not follow that I should not prioritize some interests over others. Nor does it follow that because each interest is conceptually of *equal importance*, that I have an *equal responsibility* to the interests of all. Even Singer, the great champion of ethical egalitarianism, showed special care for his mother when she became sick with Alzheimer's disease (Specter, 1999). That is, he put, contrary to his stated philosophy, her interests above the interests of others. Second, Fort is making a normative claim. His point is not that group devotion is inevitably healthy. Rather he argues that group devotion is necessary despite its dangers and that group devotion can be healthy in the context of mediating institutions, because such institutions will root individuals in the larger community.

Intimacy matters.
©XiXinXing/Shutterstock.com

Human nature limits our ability to help others in terms of time, space and cognitive power. We cannot be responsible for everyone (there is not enough time). Nor can we reach everyone (we only have two hands and cannot be in two places at once). Finally, we cannot comprehend intellectually or emotionally the needs, concerns, personality or suffering of all the human beings in the world. Like it or not, intimacy matters. As St. Augustine (1958) insists:

> "Right order here means, first, that he harms no one, and, second, the he helps whomever he can. His fundamental duty is to look out for his own home, for both by natural and human law he has easier and readier access to their requirements" (p. 460).

The point, then, is that a philosophy of mediating institutions takes this reality into account. Genuine concern for others, even strangers, is best cultivated not by abstract principle, but by human intimacy. Not only are those closest to us within reach, we also know their situation and needs better than anyone else. Therefore we have a greater responsibility for their welfare. Moreover, it is loving particular human beings, our mothers and fathers, our friends, spouses, children, co-workers and teammates, that allows one to cultivate a general concern for humanity. By loving our "mother" or "father" we are reminded that even a stranger is someone's "son," or someone's "mother." Finally, as Fort insists, it is by seeing how our actions affect others we learn that our own behavior matters.

It is concrete experience not abstract theory which best promotes ethical behavior. This does not mean that sound theory is useless, it simply means that is should be nested within the mediating structures of human life and experience. Doing so can bring the importance and truth (or falsity) of such a theory to life. It is the family, the team, and the neighborhood, not the textbook which best nurtures (or harms) our moral lives.

This is why the normative distinction between *mediating* and *quarantining* institutions is so important. As sport philosopher Nicholas Dixon (2016) points out, "When a practice is so beneficial, the mere possibility that it could sometimes be abused should not lead us to reject it. Instead, we should criticize the abuse" (p. 247). In the same way, Fort is not defending all small institutions, but only those which cultivate, via intimacy, a sense of the common good. That is, a sense of solidarity. This is why Fort insists that:

> "a mediating institution both promotes internal goods such as participation, solidarity, and loyalty while also 'mediating'; that is, interacting (not quarantining) with the outside world. As such, a mediating institution is an adaptive mechanism for living in the world at large, not a survival mechanism in which the world at large is an enemy" (p. 38).

Can small institutions go bad? Can they turn in on themselves and see the larger world and other "outside groups" as enemies? Of course. This is exactly what quarantining institutions are. Fort's point is not that all small institutions should be lauded simply because they are small. His point is that human beings *need* small institutions to have any real hope of cultivating ethical behavior. This is a fact to be recognized and nurtured rather than lamented.[18]

---

[18] Singer's (1995) half-hearted endorsement of the family is a good example of this. After reviewing ancient and modern radicals' failed attempts to "socialize" the family, he insists "That the family always survives does not itself prove that the family is an ethically desirable institution, but it does call into question the wisdom of any plans for social reform that do not take the strength of the family into account" (p. 96). The more obvious conclusion, that the family is a normative good, because it is the natural foundation of human life and society, escapes Singer. Instead, the most he can muster is this faint praise. "*In the absence of any alternative likely to work better*, there is a lot to be said for encouraging parents to take responsibility for the welfare of their own children"[Emphasis Added] (p. 96).

Mediating institutions are at the root of moral behavior. If so, then we need to take small institutions seriously and seek to cultivate those that mediate between the individual and the larger society. *Cultivating virtue is a social rather than merely individual task.*

What then of the sticky problem of religion? Can its public expression really be defended? Here again the distinction between normative and descriptive is vitally important. Has religion been used in an "us versus them" way? Again, the answer is yes, just as Fort admits. But what follows? The nation, politics, sex, race, ideology, age, language, even the principle of "equality" itself have been used in the same manner. This includes promoting "equality" through violence, as the French Terror and the Communist phrase "enemy of the proletariat" make clear (Burleigh, 2005, 2007). Does the existence of such horrible behavior inherently illegitimate politics or the nation or language or ideology? Of course not.

Why then should public religious expression be treated with inherent suspicion? After all, the negative consequences of bad theology or corrupt religious expression are not the whole story when examining the impact of religious faiths on human life and society. Nor are all religious faiths, ideas, or expression the same. As with "politics" or "ideology," one must avoid criticizing "religion" with too broad a brush. After all, "religion" is an abstraction. No one is "religious" per se. They are Christian, or Muslim, or Taoist, or Buddhist, or Jewish. Within each tradition there is also a variety of interpretations, creeds and denominations.[19] Furthermore, religious passion, conviction and doctrine, can and have spurred great goods. To list just two of the innumerable examples, consider the religious foundations of Gandhi's and the Rev. Martin Luther King Jr.'s commitment to nonviolence and racial equality.

The point of this argument is not to whitewash religious violence. Nor is it to try and win a war of "moral equivalence." Immoral behavior is deplorable whatever its motivation. The point is simple. Violence is not unique to religion. It is a human problem, not a religious problem. The presence of both good and bad ideas or good and bad behaviors are not unique to religious faiths. Checkered histories are not unique to religions. Therefore, examples of violence, foolishness or oppression should not delegitimize the public expression of religion.

Instead, religion should be taken seriously, on its own terms. Religious communities can be mediating or quarantining institutions. Religious influence is real and enduring. These influences can be good, they can be bad, but they are never insignificant. Finally, most human beings, throughout history and throughout the world have religious convictions. It makes sense then to take this into account when analyzing how to encourage ethical behavior. "It is spiritually eviscerating," Richard John Neuhaus (1992) argues, "that what millions of men and women do fifty or seventy hours of most every week is bracketed off from their understanding of their faith" (p. 62). The "naked public square" is a philosophic commitment, not a self-evident fact. As such, it can be argued for or against, but it should not merely be assumed as a given. Fort offers a persuasive case for the admission of religious convictions to public life. His ideas on religion, though controversial, deserve thoughtful consideration.

---

[19] Nor is one ever exclusively their "religion". Instead one's religious convictions are entangled in a nexus of other aspects of one's identity and culture, as this joke from Peter Berger (1999) makes clear: "The same skepticism about the religious nature of an allegedly religious conflict is expressed in the following joke from Northern Ireland: As a man walks down a dark street in Belfast, a gunman jumps out of a doorway, holds a gun to his head, and asks, 'Are you Protestant or Catholic?' The man stutters, 'Well, actually, I'm an atheist.' 'Ah yes,' says the gunman, 'but are you a Protestant or Catholic atheist'" (p. 15)?

Solidarity, Subsidiarity, Mediating Institutions, Sport?

What are the implications of these ideas for sport? Solidarity, subsidiarity and mediating institutions each suggest important lessons for the practice of sport. Here is a brief reflection on each. I will not fully draw out the implications for each idea but simply point in directions that could bear fruit with further reflection, development and application.

Solidarity is a concrete commitment to the common good. A belief that "all human beings are—despite our differences—in this together" would significantly alter our conception of competition. Not in the sense of embracing pacifism but in moderating our conception of what it means to compete well. From within a philosophical commitment to solidarity, our opponents will be understood as just that, "opponents" rather than "enemies." A commitment to solidarity would remind us that at its deepest level competition is co-operative. It is as a form of "mutualism" where "athletic competition is best conceived of [as] (and often is) a significantly cooperative activity in which the parties freely engage in order to meet the challenge framed by the constitutive rules of the sport" (Simon, Torres, & Hager, 2015, p. 51). This is because competitors need each other. Their cooperation make the game possible. Competitors test and challenge each other. Competitors are part of the same community and the same practice. They are fellow lovers of "soccer" or "baseball" or "field hockey."

As a result, solidarity encourages a real concern for the health of the institution(s) of sport, for we have inherited the games we play and we will leave them behind. It is never "my game" but always "our game." A true commitment to solidarity also respects tradition. *For the human community is a historical reality built on the*

Our opponents are just that, "opponents," not "enemies".
©Gertan/Shutterstock.com

foundations of the past and extending into the future.[20] "Here and now" is only a part of the story. Therefore, defending and promoting the health and goodness of "soccer" is always more important than increased profits, individual glory, or a momentary victory.

Subsidiarity is a claim that the particular and local matter. It is "at home" and "in the huddle" and at "the coach's knee" that ethics are truly formed, either for good or for ill. Should anyone doubt this, consider how games are taught and learned. Virtually no one consults the rule book when passing on a game to the future generation. *Instead, games are learned organically.* The student relies on the authority, expertise and experience of the teacher to relay the rules of the game as they are instructed in *the skills* of the game. The rule book is always there for consultation, of course, but it is, by itself, essentially powerless to cultivate a love of the sport and is therefore impotent to create new players, fans, and connoisseurs of the game. This is because no one is likely to consult it for details or clarification until they *already care for the institution of which it is only a part.* Practice trumps formalism and practice always grows and flowers locally through personal interaction.

Administrative rules, even though necessary, are of limited effectiveness. If you want coaches to do the right thing, if you want sportsmanship to flourish and cheating to wither, then you must emphasize practice and example more so than rules and punishment. The bureaucrats and reformers, even if one assumed that they will be listened to, cannot be at all places at all times. Moreover, rules can often create bureaucratic barriers to the good, which breeds cynicism rather than renewal or virtue. (Consider, for example, the Reilly reading in Chapter 5.) The importance of this insight should be clear. If sport is to be good, we need to do the hard work of cultivating virtue, rather than simply writing more rules. This, in turn, means that philosophy must be understood as a lived reality, rather than a mere academic exercise, because philosophy is at the heart of sport. Only good character will reform sport. Yet, character is deeply shaped by example and example grows out of one's convictions. As William James (1896/1956) maintained, "belief is measured by action" (p. 29).[21] Whether born of reflection or assumption, philosophy is always present, which means philosophy always matters.

A commitment to mediating institutions is meant to take these ideas and run with them. To take truths and put them into practice.[22] The local matters. The personal matters. The good matters. As a result, some paths are more likely than others to promote the good. Sport, when done well, *can be* a mediating institution. It can root players in the community

---

[20] "Tradition means giving a vote to most obscure of all classes, our ancestors. It is the democracy of the dead. Tradition refuses to submit to the small and arrogant oligarchy of those who merely happen to be walking about. All democrats object to men being disqualified by the accident of birth; tradition objects to their being disqualified by the accident of death. Democracy tells us not to neglect a good man's opinion, even if he is our groom; tradition asks us not to neglect a good man's opinion, even if he is our father" (Chesterton, 2007, p. 30).

[21] Similarly, MacIntyre (2009) reminds us that in classical philosophy, "To be a Platonist or an Aristotelian, or a Stoic or an Epicurean was not only to adopt *a theoretical standpoint.* It was also to belong to a community of enquirers who aspired *to live out* the doctrines to which they gave allegiance" [Emphasis Added] (p. 21).

[22] As Aristotle (2002) points out, the goal of ethics is not idle talk, but rather to become better people and lead better lives by putting the virtues into practice. "But most people do not perform them, but believe that by taking refuge in talk they are philosophizing and in that way will be people of serious stature, doing something similar to those sick people who listen to the doctors carefully but do none of the things they order. So just as they will be in no good condition in body if they treat themselves in this way, neither will those who philosophize in this way be in any good condition in soul" (1105b12-17).

and allow them to see that the good is larger than themselves or their own desires. A healthy network of mediating institutions within sport can develop a sporting culture which recognizes a broader definition of success than winning, power, and attention. Religious commitment and institutions must be admissible in this regard.

What, then, given these assertions, does sport look like when it is rooted in the larger community as a mediating institution? What does sport look like when it is done well or poorly in this regard? Poorly conducted sport focuses on winning, statistics, records and performance. Sport is turned in on itself and warped to the point that the guiding ethic is reduced to: "You play to win the game" (Battista, 2002). The outcome is all that matters and thus, joy takes a back seat to results, sober duty, and mercenary resolve. That you won is always more important than how you won.

In contrast, sport as a mediating institution, because it situates sport within a larger context, as well as a nexus of personal relationships, encourages a deeper vision. Instead of mercenary resolve, both human achievement and human weakness are recognized (Skillen, 1998).[23] Community and relationships are understood to be the best way to promote and defend the fragile goods of sport. Although victory is unapologetically pursued, it is done not in the spirit of bloodless drudgery, but rather joy. Winning matters, but only as part of a larger context. Winning may be zero-sum. Virtue is not. Virtue can be found in both victory and defeat. So too with vice. The commitment is, therefore, to human excellence (arête). One common translation of arête, as you will not doubt recall, is virtue. Mediating institutions are understood as a key way to make this happen. As Fort (1990) so wisely counsels, "Our goal must not be to change everyone, but to be an example to the person working [or playing] next to us. Who will clean up the ethical mess? Every one of us" (p. 25).

Sport, Philosophy and the Good Life

The goals of this book have been simple. The first goal was to introduce you to the basic concepts, tools and implications of sports ethics and in doing so shake you from the philosophic slumber which contemporary Western culture so successfully induces.[24] "Compared with what we ought to be," William James (1907) insists, "we are only half awake" (para. 6). Too often we stumble through life guided only by immediate and practical concerns, never considering the deepest questions in life until we have been interrupted by great joy or profound tragedy. By introducing you to arguments over good and evil, realism and relativism, utilitarianism, deontology and virtue ethics, among others, I have attempted to wake you to the perennial importance of the philosophic pursuit of

---

[23] "And at the same time, because we have to be 'given' a game by the person who beats or is beaten by us, sport has the capacity to teach us to live within the limits of a human fellowship informed by awareness of our common frailty" (Skillen, 1998, pp. 180–181). Victory is fleeting. All men are mortal. One of the important lessons of sport is that we lose. Yet, too often, vanity, hubris, and immaturity keep us from acknowledging this truth.

[24] "Modern society has banished the night [the terrifying and mysterious aspects of reality] from consciousness, as far as possible. The treatment of death in modern society, especially in America, is the sharpest manifestation of this. Much more generally, modern society has not only sealed up the old metaphysical questions in practice, but . . . has generated philosophical positions than deny the meaningfulness of these questions. 'What is the purpose of my life?' 'Why must I die?' . . . All such questions are not only suppressed in practice, but are theoretically liquidated by relegating them to meaninglessness. To repeat a simile used before, the reality of a middle-aged businessman drowsily digesting his lunch is elevated to the status of final philosophical authority. All questions that do not correspond to this reality are inadmissible. The denial of metaphysics may here be identified with the triumph of triviality" (Berger, 1969, p. 75).

truth. Philosophy matters! It is as the heart of not only our beliefs, but also our actions! It affects our entire lives, even the world of sport! It should not be ignored!

The second goal has been to secure a firm foundation of philosophic skill. It is upon such a foundation that you can build a sound and confident understanding of sports ethics. If you love sport, then ethics should be a chief concern. For if sport is important, it is important to engage in it well, to do things right, to serve and promote the good! There is a mountain of literature in sport philosophy and sports ethics that can help in this regard. Yet it will remain inaccessible and uninteresting to anyone who lacks basic philosophic literacy and to anyone who is indifferent to the philosophic endeavor.

As we have seen there is more than one set of plausible philosophic convictions. MacIntyre (2009) reminds us that, "there are rival and incompatible answers" to philosophic questions and therefore "philosophic enquiry is a source of conflict" (p. 11). Given this reality, philosophic enquiry is often hard work and depends upon careful consideration. Of course, our philosophy is also born of our experiences as well as from the values, commitments, and traditions we inherit from the communities in which we are raised. Sometimes philosophic enquiry will raise doubts about those inherited values, at other times philosophic enquiry will inspire confidence in our inheritance by providing us a deeper and more articulate faith in what we've inherited.

Rightly understood, there is nothing inherently sophisticated about doubt.[25] A philosopher, a lover of wisdom, recognizes the importance of tradition while remaining open to the possibility that in any given instance one's inheritance may be wrong. Many things we have inherited are good, but they are not good simply because we have inherited them.

How then should one proceed? We must take ownership for the truth. Not because truth is relative, but because we are responsible for our own convictions and our own lives. If truth exists, then these rival answers are worth our effort and attention. If there is more than one plausible answer, then we must decide for ourselves what ideas are most worthy of our assent and conviction, in pursuit of living well. Which means our actions should not be guided merely by desire, popularity or convenience, but by what we are convinced is *really true*.

The goal of philosophic enquiry should be articulation rather than consensus (Twietmeyer, 2015). Although all want to live well, we often disagree on what it means to live well. Again, this should not trouble us to the point that we embrace relativism. Consider, for example, that we cannot even agree on whether things as relatively trivial as the designated hitter (DH) in baseball or the Video Assistant Referee (VAR) in soccer are good things. Why then would we expect or insist on such consensus in the much weightier issues of ethics, such as genetic engineering or Title IX enforcement in sport? Again, disagreement does not mean that objective truth does not exist. The truth may be missed or denied for many reasons. Free will means, that even if the truth exists, we may ignore it as an inconvenience. Cognitive limitations and cultural influence mean, that even it if the truth exists, we may not see it because it is hidden behind cultural sediment or our own lack of understanding. In either case, the truth abides.

Similarly, a lack of consensus on this or that issue does not imply that attempts at persuasion are futile or that consensus is impossible. Consensus is in fact common

---

[25] "The skeptic's claim is that our beliefs and judgments are open to doubt, because it is always possible that we may be mistaken in believing as we do and in judging as we do, because there is always the possibility of error. But to point out—quite correctly—that it is possible that we are in error gives us no reason whatsoever to believe that we are in fact in error. And, until we are given such a reason, we have no reason whatsoever to doubt what we otherwise have good reason to believe and to judge" (MacIntyre, 2009, p. 117).

(Finnis, 1980; Kretchmar, 2005). Therefore, neither the existence of consensus nor the lack of consensus on any given issue, should paralyze us. This is the case for two reasons; first, a falsehood can have popular support, and second, the truth can be controversial. Therefore, although one should not court controversy, one should not be afraid to swim against the tide if necessary. For the truth is logically independent of both controversy and popular assent. The bottom line is this: *Find your convictions and stand by them, for as long as you are convinced they are grounded in the truth.*

In closing, I would like to consider one final point: The difference between a good and a "successful" life. This is especially important given how much of the contemporary sports world is dominated by superficiality.[26] I would like to make this distinction by asking you to consider the life of a giant of 20th Century sport; Olympic founder Pierre de Coubertin. According to biographer, John MacAloon (1980), Coubertin was driven by the desire for achievement, by the need to make a name for himself. Given his triumph in reestablishing the Olympic Games and considering his enduring fame, it would seem that Coubertin's life was a success and was therefore good.

The reality, however, is more complicated. In fact, Coubertin died a poor man, living off the charity of others. His marriage and family never recovered from the tragic heat stroke suffered by his infant son, who was accidentally left outside in the sun. The accident left Coubertin's son Jacques mentally disabled and Coubertin's personal life in ruins.

Obviously, the point is not that Coubertin's professional success came as the cost of his personal life. Fate, providence, dumb-luck, call it what you will, influences all of our lives. The point is more sober. It is a case study on why we should avoid centering our lives on shallow concerns. What such a case ought to teach is this: *Given the vagaries of time and space, not everything is worthy of our attention and concern.* What does a good life *really* consist of? How much does adulation count for? Is it a concern in any way worth pursuing? To what should we dedicate our lives?

Coubertin's life clearly shows that fame is noise and by itself amounts to nothing. Moreover, reputation only matters if we have actually done good things. Which means *being* good should be one's focus. Yet, being good will rarely garner attention. A good life consists of far more than that which will win us renown. In fact, many good things will be seen by others as insignificant, pedestrian or even threatening. The point is simply this: *a good life is far more than professional success.* Absent virtue, trophies, paychecks, titles, records, and fame will not make you happy.[27]

This is an important reminder for an achievement based culture such as our own. Baron de Coubertin's insecurity, his hunt for validation, and his belief that recognition (as

---

[26] Nor is the rampant superficiality in Western sporting culture without its victims. One poignant example is former NFL quarterback Todd Marinovich who was "groomed from infancy to be a top-notch quaterback" (Rosenberg, 2019, p. 66). During his youth Todd was often unhappy, but felt compelled to keep up appearances. "He repeated the lie [that he was doing what he wanted] so often that it came more easily than telling the truth. It made sense to him until he joined the [NFL's Oakland] Raiders, with a $2.25 million contract, the culmination of his precise and carefully planned athletic career, and he felt empty. 'They say in our society, if you reach this, you'll be happy,' Todd says. 'I was miserable, but couldn't tell you why. Everything around me is falling apart. I have a bank account, millions of dollars, and that's not making it better. What the f--k is wrong with me" (p. 70)?

[27] Moreover, life itself is fleeting, which means one must wrestle with spiritual questions as well. For, a life, no matter how well lived, ends in death. The question of God, transcendence and the supernatural is of no small importance in ethics. Here again we see the intimate relationship between metaphysics and ethics for living well. Being a *good* human being requires first knowing what a human being *is*. Josef Pieper (2011) makes the point simply: "Ethics is about a right conception of man" (p. 4).

the originator of the Olympic movement) would settle his soul, are all too human traits. Human traits that twenty-first century Americans, in the age of YouTube, Twitter, and Facebook, should be able to relate to and sympathize with. One can only hope that, given such distractions, we are not blind to the overriding lesson.[28]

As MacAloon (1980) points out:

> "Though the idea [of the Olympics] was not his alone and did not originate with him, though his labors were assisted at every step by many others, no modern institution of comparable significance owes so much to a single man. *Yet, in the end, that man could not find in it enough to satisfy his life"* [Emphasis Added] (p. 3).

"Success" is empty if not grounded in a larger vision of the good life. Sport is *only part* of that larger vision. A genuinely good life requires that we treat others as we ought. What does it mean to live well? However you answer that question, it is clear that our choices matter, which means ethics and philosophy are always worthy of your attention.

"Yet, in the end, that man could not find in it enough to satisfy his life."
©rook76/Shutterstock.com

---

[28] "Now if a man rejoiced in receiving glory from an outside source, then some other person or the man who conferred the glory would be able to take it away. But since every virtuous man receives his glory from his own virtue, then he will lose his reward only when he ceases to be virtuous" (Boethius, 2012, p. 119).

PHILOSOPHIC SELECTIONS

Selection #1: Fort, T. L. (2001). *Ethics and governance: Business as mediating institution.* **Chapter 2 "Some Catholic Notions"; Chapter 3 "Natural Law and Laws of Nature". New York, NY: Oxford University Press.**

Introduction: Timothy Fort is an ethicist in the business school at Indiana University. In this selection from his 2001 book "Ethics and Governance," he argues for the reality of catholic "small-c" truths as part of his larger claim that mediating institutions are vital to the promotion of ethical behavior. When catholic is used as an adjective rather than a pronoun (Roman Catholic) it simply means "universal." As such, Fort argues that solidarity and subsidiarity are universal human realities. They are universally true. Human nature requires solidarity (e.g., none of us would be here if we were not raised/cared for by others). Human nature requires subsidiarity (e.g., intimacy, not logic, is the root of our concern for other human beings). Therefore, community, which is best fostered in and through mediating institutions—such as families, churches, teams, and perhaps even businesses—is necessary for the cultivation of moral virtue.

Some Catholic Notions

In Richard Attenborough's film *Gandhi,* the title character is on his way to negotiate with Muslim leaders in conjunction with India's freedom from Great Britain. That freedom lifted the lid off the simmering hatreds between Muslims and Hindus. Gandhi was preparing to negotiate a power-sharing arrangement to prevent Muslim secession (which eventually became Pakistan). As Gandhi began to drive past Hindus protesting these negotiations, he scolded the protesters claiming that he (Gandhi) was a Muslim and a Christian and a Jew: all this from a devout Hindu. His example is a model for a commitment to a particular identity and simultaneously profound openness to others. His commitment is not simply one of tolerance, but of integration and openness. This is the orientation produced by a normative mediating institution.

Perhaps the best word to characterize Gandhi's spirituality is a profound sense of solidarity. Indeed, at the heart of his ethic of nonviolence was a profound commitment of not only respect, for but also empathy with his enemies. Even in the midst of his battles with Great Britain to gain Indian independence, he refused to characterize the British as enemies, but considered them to be friends. In his ashram, he brought together diverse individuals to live together in a community that transcended ethnic and religious identity. Interestingly enough, the population of Gandhi's ashram hovered around 130, a number that will be important later in the book.[1] Bonding with this close association of diverse individuals in the ashram also reinforced Gandhi's embrace of all India as his family[2]. Compare then, Gandhi's spirituality with Pope John Paul's description of solidarity.

---

[1] Infra chapter 4.

[2] See Louis Fischer, *The Life of Mahatma Gandhi* 129 (1950). I make some interpretation to support this claim. In the cited material, Fischer indicates the closeness of Gandhi's ashram and reports that Gandhi said that all India was his family. In the context of Gandhi's decision to live in the ashram as a place of egalitarian simplicity, it seems a fair interpretation to claim that the ashram experience was the daily experience of solidarity that Gandhi also applied to his politics.

This then is not a feeling of vague compassion or shallow distress at the misfortune of so many people, both near and far. On the contrary, it is a firm and persevering determination to commit oneself to the common good; that is to say to the good of all and of each individual, because we are all really responsible for all. This determination is based on the solid conviction that what is hindering full development is that desire for profit and that thirst for power already mentioned. These attitudes and "structures of sin" are only conquered—presupposing the help of divine grace—by a diametrically opposed attitude: a commitment to the good of one's neighbor with the readiness, in the Gospel sense, to "lose oneself," for the sake of the other, instead of exploiting him, and to "serve him" instead of oppressing him for one's own advantage.[3]

One hesitates to think how "at home" Gandhi would be in a multinational corporation. Still, there is a sense in which it is exactly his attitude that would be at the heart of an effective business ethic and which practices the solidarity the pope advocates. In this chapter, I would like to elaborate two notions: solidarity and mediating institutions. To do so, I will rely upon what might be called catholic social thinking. It is *catholic* rather than *Catholic* because I want to emphasize a universality of these ideas. Nevertheless, it is very dependent upon Catholic social thought. To do this, I want to first extend the argument that compassion and empathy are catholic principles. Second, I want to show how Catholic social thought has emphasized the importance of mediating institutions to develop the responsible exercise of these principles, primarily vis-à-vis governmental structures. Third, I want to apply these thoughts to corporate life.

NURTURING EMPATHY, SOLIDARITY, AND COMPASSION

As an example of the catholicity of solidarity, empathy, and compassion, I extend the twin examples of the Hindu Gandhi's essential practice of solidarity and John Paul's articulation of this practice to LaRue Tone Hosmer's summary of world religions. In analyzing world religions, Hosmer offers these summaries from the religions themselves:

Buddhism . . . "Harm not others with that which pains yourself."

Christianity . . . "All things whatsoever you would that others should do unto you, do ye even so unto them, for this is the law and the prophets."

Confucianism . . . "Loving kindness is the one maxim which ought to be acted upon throughout one's life." Hinduism . . . "This is the sum of duty; do naught to others which if done to thee would cause thee pain." Islam . . . "No one of you is a believer until you wish for everyone what you love for yourself."

Jainism . . . "In happiness and suffering, in joy and grief, we should regard all creatures as we regard our own self."

Judaism . . . "What is hurtful to yourself, do not do to others. That is the whole of the Torah, and the remainder is but commentary. Go and learn it."

Sikhism . . . "[A]s thou deemest thyself, so deem others. Then shalt thou become a partner in heaven." Taoism . . . "Regard your neighbor's gain as your gain, and regard your neighbor's loss as your loss."[4]

---

[3] Pope John Paul II, *Sollicitudo Rei Socialis* United States Catholic Conferences, (Washington, D.C.) (1988), para. 38.

[4] LaRue Tone Hosmer, *Moral Leadership in Business* 78 (1994).

One could think of these religious injunctions as variations of the Golden Rule (or the Golden Rule itself) and, of course, one sentence will rarely summarize the richness of any religion. Nevertheless, Hosmer states a fundamental religious perspective, and he notes two interesting aspects of the injunctions. First, they are aimed at creating a sense of community.[5] The second aspect is that although religious beliefs are tied to more specific injunctions for a particular community, at the heart of them is the compassion necessary to form a community. In fact, Hosmer entitles the chart above the quoted summaries "Examples of Compassion in the World's Religions."[6]

There is abundant evidence in human history that religions can be part of an "us versus them" attitude. The religions of Gandhi's own India are proof of this. Yet, the spirituality of Gandhi and John Paul is precisely to foster the compassion that can also be extended to a wider community. One's mediating institution, in this context, becomes the incubator for the compassion, solidarity, and empathy that extends to those outside of one's "in-group." Mediating institutions, in contrast to quarantining institutions, do this.

The contemporary rebirth of mediating institutions as a social means of analysis can be traced in large part to the work of Peter Berger and Richard John Neuhaus, who defined them as "those institutions standing between the individual in his private life and the large institutions of public life."[7] Berger and Neuhaus clearly identified the state as the key "large institution" that could be alienating, but they left open the possibility that other large structures such as multinational corporations and labor unions could also be alienating megastructures.

The important point is that it is within these mediating institutions that solidarity, empathy, and compassion (I do not think it is overly beneficial to separately define each of these terms) are cultivated. At one level, this produces significant problems. One can view militias or gangs as small groups that foster in-group solidarity on the basis of alienation from the rest of the world. These are quarantining institutions, which do not possess the normative *mediating, connective* character of the metaphor I am advocating. The examples of the last chapter provide examples of more ideal mediating institutions. My pension client, for instance, was a mediating institution that fostered solidarity among its various internal constituents, which led to the practicing of positive virtues such as loyalty, truth telling, promise keeping. My consulting client became an institution whose members grew in empathy as they (re)discovered the complexities and humanness of others in the family.

Viewed in this light, what is *catholic* is the importance of nurturing this spirituality of solidarity or, if one prefers, empathy or compassion. Although these notions are not identical, they share a sense of finding one's self interest in the well-being of others. The way this attitude or spirituality is nurtured is through an identification of oneself with others, which might be most deeply understood in the context of relatively small communities. In such communities, one can experience solidarity through a shared commitment to a common good or a common need.

What small communities do that larger structures do not are (1) to provide a more immediate feedback mechanism for how actions affect others; (2) to enhance the relative power of individuals vis-à-vis their community (a) by inculcating a sense of moral identity (which rules out certain choices as unacceptable) and (b) by leaving communal decisions more amenable to individual actions (because the number of individuals are relatively few); and (3) to reinforce a disposition about why treating others well is important and desirable.

---

[5] Id.

[6] Id. at 78–79.

[7] Peter Berger & Richard John Neuhaus, *To Empower People: The Role of Mediating Structures in Public Policy* 2 (1977).

Perhaps more important, small groups provide a greater likelihood of human beings interacting with other multifaceted, complex human beings. Think of the examples from the previous chapter. The family business changed when members saw others as complex persons rather than as unidimensional opponents. It was when they heard the stories important to others that they found the other person was more than a projected Other. Similarly, my pension client was concerned about the fairness of the switch to the new plan because employees were not labor inputs but friends.

To switch to a larger setting, Charles Hampden-Turner found that when Annheuser-Busch made its culture more "high context" (meaning that feelings, beliefs, and ideas of members were woven into the fabric of the corporate culture), its productivity, product quality, and plant safety all improved, resulting in decreases in absenteeism and grievances.[8] From this, it is at least plausible to suggest that solidarity, empathy, and compassion may be heightened when fuller selves are engaged at work. And in small institutions, the chance for seeing fuller selves may be increased. With that engagement comes the possibility of treating others as human beings whose interests transcend economic efficiency.

This emphasis on small institutions relates, but is not identical to another Catholic notion called subsidiarity, which has to do with the specification of authority. Indeed, one of the tasks of Chapters 4 and 5 is to apply subsidiarity to corporations (as opposed to governments) and to suggest that corporations ought to rely upon subsidiarity. That is, it should devolve some kinds of decisions to smaller groups within the corporation in order to nurture the compassion that would encourage a person to want to treat others in an ethical manner.

As is clear from the terminology I am using, this chapter will draw heavily upon Catholic social thought, primarily because that tradition has done excellent work in developing the concepts. Moreover, the Catholic tradition's reliance on natural law, a methodology I will draw upon in the following chapter, contemplates the possibility of all human beings acquiring moral knowledge. It then is inherently catholic, as is reinforced by the opening paragraph, which focused on a Hindu. Hosmer's survey of world religions suggests that concepts such as compassion, empathy, and solidarity have a universality to them. Thus, while giving full credit to Catholic social thought for developing the categories I use in this book, and in particularly in this chapter, I, as a non-Catholic, want also to emphasize their *catholic* potential.

In this chapter, then, I want to begin to connect solidarity and mediating institutions in an effort to show why business organizations should be constructed as mediating institutions and not just collections of individuals contracting in a self-interested way. These concepts are cornerstones upon which one can build a new model of corporate governance.

CORE PRINCIPLES OF CATHOLIC SOCIAL THOUGHT

William Byron, a Jesuit priest and former president of Catholic University, recently distilled from various Roman Catholic ecclesial documents, 10 core principles of Catholic social thought. They are human dignity, respect for human life, right of association, participation, preferential option for the poor and vulnerable, solidarity, stewardship, subsidiarity, human equality, and the common good.[9] I do not wish to argue against these principles. In looking at them, however, it would seem that one could group seven

[8] Charles Hampden-Turner, *Creating Corporate Culture: From Discord to Harmony* 58–59 (1990).

[9] William Byron, "Core Principles of Catholic Social Thought," *America*, October 31, 1998, at www.americapress.org/articles/Byron.htm.

of these principles (human dignity, respect for human life, association, participation, preferential option for the poor and vulnerable, stewardship, and human equality) as practical principles and practices that lead to the creation of a common good.

Moreover, they relate to not just any common good, but to a particular kind of common good. That is, the principles Byron articulates relate to a common good of caring for others. I emphasize this because the attitude or spirituality of solidarity can be linked to a common good in relation to a quest for an important objective, such as a World Series crown, an election to the Senate, or a 30% return on equity. In such quests, people can *minimize* their complex selves in order to reach the particular goal. While at certain times and places these kinds of quests can be good, the common good of which Byron writes and about which I write, is a common good of mutual respect of the dignity of all people. The principles I have noted in Byron's list are those that lead to this kind of common good. Byron's other two principles, solidarity and subsidiarity, seem to have, or at least may have, a different orientation.

Solidarity conveys an attitude or spiritual orientation. A person practicing "a firm and persevering determination to commit oneself to the common good; that is, to the good of all and of each individual"[10] would likely be a person who also respects human dignity, the right to associate, and the other principles summarized by Byron. Thus, in addition and perhaps prior to the implementation of these principles is this attitude or spirituality of solidarity we have already seen. To put it another way, these other principles are actualized by individuals with an orientation manifesting solidarity.

The question is how one cultivates such an orientation. In Chapters 3 and 4, I will present evidence from anthropology and biology that suggest cognitive, neural reasons for why such groups are the place where empathy develops. Before getting to these sources, one can look to more traditional ways in which one cultivates solidarity. Acceptance of a religious faith calling for compassion may be one valid way of doing this. The principle of subsidiarity also suggests a particular structure that also cultivates such an orientation via the government. Subsidiarity, as Byron describes it, relates to the proper role of government. More specifically, it states that "no higher level of organization should perform any function that can be handled efficiently and effectively at a lower level of organization by human persons who, individually or in groups, are closer to the problem and closer to the ground."[11] In such instances, those closer to the ground are more likely to *care* about resolving the problem.

This notion of subsidiarity is also a Jeffersonian notion and one often neglected in critiques of government. Governmental bodies are not monolithic, but themselves must be broken down in smaller segments in order to effectively respond to needs.[12] The Postal Service comes to mind. Although a massive bureaucracy, it must also have a local office. The primary question for Chapter 5 is how a large corporate bureaucracy, like the U.S. Postal Service, integrates *meaningful* suboffices (mediating institutions) that reduce the alienation that large bureaucracies (like the Postal Service and also like a multinational corporation) can produce of those working for them. The simple point, to be more fully developed, is that the principle of subsidiarity may describe a moral preference for noncentralized decision making that may be applicable to corporate life as well as governmental.

---

[10] John Paul, supra note 3.

[11] Byron, supra note 9.

[12] Meir Dan Cohen, "Between Selves and Collectivities: Toward a Jurisprudence of Identity," 61 *U. Chi. L. Rev.* 1213 (1994).

Preliminarily, how might Catholic social thought be applied to business? Robert Kennedy provides the acronym PARTNERS:

Participation (of all employees);

Access (to work for as many people as possible);

Respect (of the dignity of the worker in taking into account the gifts and vocations of individuals);

Trust (as a duty to be developed by making employment stable and permanent as possible and not to view employees as variable expenses);

Needs (in matching work to the human need for meaningful work);

Expression (of employees to express their freedom through work and to make it part of their identities);

Rewards (of a wage for a decent life and that rewards individuals for the contributions they make to the organization); and

Success (in terms of a duty, within moral bounds, toward efficiency and productivity and by eliminating laziness and waste).[13]

It seems again that at the heart of Kennedy's directives is a spirituality of solidarity as applied to work. The identification of one's self-interest with another's well-being would be an experience that would also lead a person to implement PARTNERS. It is exactly when corporate life is linked to a meaningful, spiritual commitment to the dignity of those with whom one works that Kennedy is at his most persuasive, as he writes:

> Most authors tend to agree that the overriding purpose of business is to create a profit and that, at the end of the day, this is the unavoidable measure of business success. The result, of course, is to turn things upside down. Instead of subordinating business activities to genuine human goods (as an Aristotle or Aquinas might say), we instrumentalize ethics (the study of genuine human goods) and make it serve as a tool for the acquisition of money, the instrumental good *par excellence*. This is rather like saying that the ultimate purpose of building a house is to give the carpenter practice in using his hammer.[14]

Of course, such hammering in terms of providing meaningful work for the carpenter is important. Kennedy's point, however, is that the criterion for measuring moral worth is human goods, not simply facilitated choices for later decisions. Instead, the purpose of building a house is not even the completion of the structure, but the creation of a structure that can become a home. Within the context of this book, the idea is to propose a legal architecture in which residents are more likely to develop the bonds and affections that inspire them to practice principles such as those Byron and Kennedy champion and as exemplified by the stories of Chapter 1. That corporate structure is one of creating workplace-mediating institutions in which individuals bond and connect with one another so as to inspire an attitude of solidarity. In short, among the applicable principles of Catholic social thought are the importance of nurturing empathy (or solidarity) in the workplace. In order to cultivate this attitude, mediating institutions become a

---

[13] Robert G. Kennedy, "God's Project: A Catholic Vision of Business," Presentation at 3d Annual John F. Henning Conference (March 5, 1999) (manuscript, at 7–8, on file with author).

[14] Id. at 3.

practical embodiment of subsidiarity that provides a structure to nourish all the principles of Catholic social thought.

THE IMPORTANCE OF MEDIATING INSTITUTIONS

American culture has long been noted for the degree to which individuals voluntarily form associations in order to solve social problems. Alexis de Tocqueville noted this habit and credited it (along with religion) for preventing the individualism inevitable in a non-aristocratic culture from becoming excessively self-centered. The dependence upon others to achieve one's own goals resulted in what Tocqueville described as "self-interest rightly understood," a concept of virtue Tocqueville saw not as noble, but as a trait that on the whole raised the morality of all.[15]

Generally speaking, mediating institutions (leaving aside business communities for now) provide a socialization process whereby identity is developed. Years ago, sociologist Robert Nisbet argued that human beings have a set of very fundamental social needs, usually met by family, local community, and church. These institutions engender notions of affection, friendship, prestige, and recognition and have also engendered or intensified notions of work, love, prayer, and devotion to freedom and order.[16] Mediating institutions, of course, do not meet these needs, but they provide a context in which one deals with other human beings in a way that socializes all the participants. In such contexts, one learns interdependence. Mediating institutions break down an individual's interaction with the rest of the world into more manageable personal interactions with other human beings.

One aspect of this social importance lies in the continuing activation of individual moral concern and contribution to solving social problems. For instance, John Haughey has written that the spiritual weakness of Solomonic Israel occurred with the establishment of the monarchy. Rather than each person being responsible for the welfare of others, such responsibility was transferred to the king and his bureaucracy.[17] Similarly, James Burtchaell writes:

> Somehow we have managed to shift all responsibility for need beyond our immediate reach to officials and organizations. And thus we are morally dwarfed. It is surely ironic that in the very age when citizens have insisted that their governments be more active in socially constructed activity, individuals have been encouraged to transfer any long-distance moral responsibility to appropriate agencies, and to turn into their social torpor, caring not for those who never come into personal touch with them.[18]

Unless one is able to see tangible results of one's efforts (something that is difficult on the level of national politics or in the large global corporation), the incentive to sustain social responsibility can be diminished. Nisbet warns that the most powerful resources of democracy lie not in state protections, but

> in the cultural allegiances of citizens, and that these allegiances of citizens are nourished psychologically in the small, internal areas of family, local community, and association . . . [I]t is the liberal concentration of interest upon the individual, rather than upon the associations in which the individual exists, that serves, paradoxical as it may seem, to intensify the processes that lead straight to increased governmental power.[19]

---

[15] Alexis De Tocqueville, *Democracy in America* 131 (Phillips Bradley ed., 1945).

[16] Robert A. Nisbet, *The Quest for Community: A Study in the Ethics of Order and Freedom* 50 (1990).

[17] John Haughey, S.J., *The Holy Use of Money: Personal Finance in Light of the Christian Faith* 3–6 (1986).

[18] James T. Burtchaell, c.s.c., *Philemon's Problem: The Daily Dilemma of the Christian* 101 (1973).

[19] Nisbet, supra note 16, at 255–56.

Here again, it is important to at least raise the question of the extent to which this is a peculiarly American phenomenon. In fact, the experience of learning empathic responsibilities to others is broader. For instance, in writing about Japanese ethics, Iwao Taka has written about the notion of concentric circles. In this understanding, one has the most intense responsibilities to those with whom one is close, such as family, with decreasing responsibilities as one extends further out into the world.[20] Certainly there is a danger in this creation of an "us versus them" attitude. An emphasis on the importance of "us" can threaten to dehumanize a "them." At the same time, at what point will persons learn that people are affected by their actions and take those consequences into account in places other than small groups? The danger is not that these affections are fostered in the small group, which they practically will have to be, but in whether one also learns a way to further extend them toward others as well. As a corollary, however, if one does not participate in a structure where normative lessons are learned in small groups but are emphasized vis-à-vis a large megastructure (governmental or corporate), then a person may see no reason to think that her vote, her embezzlement, or her voice makes a difference. If this is true, how does one go about proposing a structure for a multinational corporation to attend to the importance of these small groups while maintaining the efficiencies of the large megastructure (which, for better or worse, is probably with us to stay)?

One response is to follow a structure similar to the constitutional system of checks and balances as well as federalism, diffusion of power among groups, which also fosters a social defense against the acquisition of power by any narrow person or faction. This reason not only acts as a rationale against state power, but as normative constraint within the corporation, because it too can be organized with a centralization of power that prevents the meeting of individual social needs.

In addition to these character-forming aspects, corporations, in fact, are dependent upon mediating institutions in important ways. For instance, economic benefits flow to a society in which mediating structures flourish. Economic freedom relies upon institutions that temper self-interest. Robert Bellah and his coauthors write that Adam Smith situated his free market only within the context of a larger public sphere with a "myriad of voluntary associations."[21] Patricia Werhane has made a similar analysis of Smith and free market capitalism, noting that "Smith presupposes a foundation of government, law, and social and religious institutions in which he locates his political economy. Smith does not imagine that a political economy could function without such support, and this crucial point is often neglected by commentators on the Wealth of Nations."[22]

Even free market proponent F. A. Hayek has argued that family and religious institutions efficiently inculcate the morality needed by capitalism.[23] Of course, it is one thing to say that capitalism flourishes in a society populated by mediating institutions. It is another thing to suggest that businesses ought to be mediating institutions. Such institutions may be necessary for capitalism to flourish, but should businesses be places where moral values are inculcated?

---

[20] Iwao Taka, "Business Ethics: A Japanese View," 4 *Bus. Ethics Q.* 53 (1994).

[21] Robert N. Bellah, Richard Madsen, William M. Sullivan, Ann Swidler, & Steven M. Tipton, *The Good Society* 92 (1991).

[22] Patricia H. Werhane, *Adam Smith and His Legacy for Modern Capitalism* 113 (1991).

[23] F. A. Hayek, *The Fatal Conceit* 136–37 (1988).

BUSINESS AS MEDIATING INSTITUTION

Much of a person's conscious life will be involved with work, in addition to traditional forms of mediating institutions. Because so much time is spent working, perhaps more so than has been spent in previous eras of human history, there is also a need to consider the extent to which businesses should also be mediating institutions.

Harvard economist Juliet Schor has argued that prior to capitalism, people did not work long hours and they enjoyed significant leisure time. She calculates that an adult male peasant living in England in 1200 A.D. worked 1,620 hours annually. By the year 1840, the average U.K. laborer worked 3,688 hours, a figure similar to her 3,650-hour estimate for Americans working in the year 1850. While those numbers had declined to 1,949 hours in the United States and 1,856 hours in the United Kingdom by the late 1980s, she argues that work itself was a far more casual affair in the early part of the millennium than that of the industrialized capitalist countries today.[24]

The time available for family, guilds, and associations may be simply less than it once was. Of course, one can argue about the extent to which Schor has fully captured all the work that may have been engaged in throughout history. Nevertheless, if mediating institutions are important, formative moral institutions, it may be better to create more time for traditional mediating institutions rather than to argue that businesses should become mediating institutions regardless of the precise arithmetic. There is little reason, however, to believe that businesses' influence will lessen in the near future. The question then becomes whether businesses can be made into organizations in which, like traditional mediating institutions, each participant gains some of the moral knowledge typically provided by family, church, or voluntary organizations.

Neoconservatives' Classical Understanding of the Corporation

Berger and Neuhaus propose their notion of mediating structures in order to address a "double crisis" in meaning. That is, they see that "megastructures" of society are alienating in that they do not provide "meaning and identity for individual existence."[25] Those individuals who handle this crisis of meaning, they argue, have access to institutions that mediate between individual private life and public life in megastructures.[26] Mediating structures such as neighborhood, family, church, and voluntary associations have a private face in which individuals obtain identity, and a public face where the megastructures gain their meaning and value. The central theme of such structures, according to Berger and Neuhaus, is the empowerment of individuals to have an impact on the actions that affect them. Such empowerment entails responsibility as well as individuals directly witnessing the consequences of their actions on others.

Are business corporations already mediating institutions? Except in family businesses, corporations are not family. They typically are neither neighborhoods nor religious institutions. They might be voluntary associations, but Berger and Neuhaus write: "For our present purposes, a voluntary association is a body of people who have voluntarily organized themselves in pursuit of particular goals. (Following common usage, we exclude business corporations and other primarily economic associations.)"[27]

---

[24] Juliet B. Schor, The Overworked American: The Unexpected Decline of Leisure 27–48 (1992).

[25] Berger & Neuhaus, supra note 7, at 2.

[26] Id. at 3.

[27] Id. at 34.

At least two others, however, extend the notion of mediating institutions to corporations. The difficulty is that in doing so, the normative content of mediating institutions is emptied. Richard Madden provides a classic description of corporation and weds that description to the mediating analogy when he writes that a large corporation diminishes risks for individuals and allows opportunities for "group insurance, pensions, credit unions, and even more unusual benefits—day nurseries, for example. In addition, the corporation provides alternatives for suppliers, customers, and investors in the communities in which it operates. Finally, the resources of a corporation can be used to support other mediating structures that improve the social climate."[28]

In this notion, what the corporation mediates is the relationship between the individual and an amorphous ambiguity of life by providing the monetary return so that individuals can have financial security, so owners can realize profit, and so charities can be funded. Virtually nothing is said about obtaining identity except as that identity is characterized by the ability of the individual to choose what he or she can do with this monetary return.

There is nothing necessarily objectionable when the corporation creates wealth for its constituents, but it does stretch the notion of mediating institution beyond any recognizable form. Like Michael Novak, who also calls the corporation a mediating institution, Madden is clear that ethical virtues are necessary for the proper functioning of business, but he also argues that size "has relatively little to do with whether or not an organization can serve as a mediating structure."[29] If, however, Berger and Neuhaus are correct in describing these structures as "the face-to-face institutions, the people-sized institutions, the mediating institutions where people act as neighbors,"[30] then the large corporation is not necessarily, if it can be at all called, a mediating institution. A small business, like those of my two clients in Chapter 1, may more easily fit Berger and Neuhaus's description of a mediating institution, but a large multinational corporation, if not carefully structured, can be an alienating megastructure. The reason size has everything to do with the analysis is that the large bureaucratic corporation hides the consequences of individual action, so that a person acts without knowledge or concern of how actions affect others.

What is missing from the classical description of the corporation (which is the description offered by Madden) is the communal element necessary to provide meaning and identity. Of course, the corporation, even as a megastructure, can very well foster the common good by satisfying customers, making a return for investors, creating new wealth and jobs, generating upward mobility, promoting invention and ingenuity, promoting progress in arts and sciences, and diversifying the interests of the republic.[31] But such goods are not goods of creating meaning and identity. Nor are such institutions necessarily communities that foster virtue and solidarity. Thus, although there is a sense in which some may wish to characterize businesses as mediating institutions, they do not necessarily nourish solidarity, compassion, empathy, and respect for others. Saying that they are not necessarily mediating institutions does not mean, however, that they cannot become so.

---

[28] Richard B. Madden, "The Larger Business Organization as Mediating Structure," in *Democracy and Mediating Structures: A Theological Inquiry* (Michael Novak ed., 1980).

[29] Id. at 110–11.

[30] Richard John Neuhaus, *Doing Well and Doing Good: The Challenge to the Christian Capitalist* 269 (1992).

[31] Michael Novak, *Business as a Calling: Work and the Examined Life* 139–45 (1996).

Business as Community and Business Virtues

The compelling critique of the capitalist corporation comes from the (religious) neo-conservatives' guide: Pope John Paul II. In his 1991 encyclical, *Centesimus Annus*, John Paul dwelled on the importance of work to human identity. Like the notion of mediating structures, John Paul noted the personal dimension of meaning and the connection of that dimension to the common good in another encyclical: "Work thus belongs to the vocation of every person; indeed, man expresses and fulfills himself by working. At the same time work has a 'social' dimension through its intimate relationship not only to the family, but also to the common good."[32]

Of course, human beings work for their own material needs too, but in doing so they are involved in a "progressively expanding chain of solidarity."[33] Novak, however, had previously warned that solidarity was a "more proper term for the hive, the herd, or for the flock, than for the democratic community," concepts that were more Marxian than American.[34] Nevertheless, the pope had also endorsed a "market economy" that did embrace solidarity with the poor and within the workplace, and each required a wider conception of business than the classical notion.

The difference between these two capitalisms—and they are both versions of the free market—is that the classical version views identity as that which takes place separately from the material production of goods, whereas the spiritual alternative recognizes the doing of work as inherently moral, educational, and social. It is the worker's identification with the product of her work and with those with whom she has collaborated in producing something that teaches her responsibilities to those around her. I will elaborate upon this version at length in Chapters 3 and 4. The spiritual version recognizes our "self" in others, so that moral obligations are not "choices" but our interconnected nature.

Novak addresses the moral, social dimension in part by concentrating on the notion of business as a vocation. But he also rightly understood that to be a vocation in which an individual practiced certain virtues required business to also be a community. For Novak, businesspeople are always building community, because business success depends upon high levels of creativity, teamwork, and morale. Apart from ethical requirements imposed on business from those outside the corporation, business requires internal moral integrity. An important element of community is a relative closeness of managers to the actions of employees. Without that, quality controls can suffer.[35]

Business can be the kind of community Novak describes. It can be an organization in which cooperation, trust, honesty, and commitment flourish. It can also be the kind of place in which bureaucracy overwhelms individual identity and responsibility, just as it can when the bureaucracy is political. In his arresting book, *Moral Mazes*, Robert Jackall describes interviews he conducted with managers in which success was determined by luck, fealty to "the king," milking a division and leaving before long-term realities caught up, and such factors as appearance, self-control, perception as a team player, style, and patron power.[36] Very important to success, he found, was adeptness at inconsistency. Thus, "what matters in the bureaucratic world is not what a person is but how closely his

---

[32] John Paul, supra note 3, at para. 6.

[33] Id., at para. 43.

[34] Gary Dorrien, *The Neoconservative Mind: Politics, Culture and Ideology* 252 (1993).

[35] Novak, supra note 31.

[36] Robert Jackall, *Moral Mazes, The World of Corporate Managers* (1988).

many personae mesh the organizational ideal; not his willingness to stand by his actions but his agility in avoiding blame."[37]

This is not to say that all people in an organization behave this way or even that those who do behave this way do so at all times. It would be difficult for an organization to survive if everyone always acted in this fashion. Nevertheless, the large bureaucratic organization does provide the opportunity to act in this manner before consequences catch up. A simple, quasi-business example may help to demonstrate this point. If a college football coach violates National Collegiate Athletic Association (NCAA) regulations by improperly recruiting star athletes, the coach and the athletes could easily be starring in the National Football League before the NCAA can discover and punish the transgression. The coaches and players of the university who do pay the price in the form of probation and lost scholarships quite likely have had nothing to do with the transgressions. Such events do not happen in all places at all times, and even those coaches who do violate NCAA rules do not do so all the time. But the repetition of such incidents indicates the failure of bureaucratic rules to be able to adequately govern moral behavior. (It also demonstrates how subgroups—here a college—also cannot rely on overarching laws, but must preemptively inculcate moral behavior even if they are simply to stay out of trouble.)

Decentralization is thus necessary so that decisions are made as close to the problem as possible. In theological terms, this is known as the principle of subsidiarity, which neoconservatives have used to critique the federal government. In business terms, Novak correctly writes that "[a] successful corporation is frequently based on the principle of subsidiarity. According to this principle, concrete decisions must be made on the level closest to the concrete reality. Managers and workers need to trust the skills of their colleagues. A corporate strategy which overlooks this principle—and many do—falls prey to all the vices of a command economy, in which all orders come from above.[38]

It is important to note, as Berger and Neuhaus have, that "the management mindset of the megastructure—whether of the U.S. Department of Health, Education, and Welfare, Sears Roebuck, or the AFLCIO—is biased toward the unitary solution."[39] In political terms, the danger of this absence of mediation is that "the political order becomes detached from the values and realities of individual life. Deprived of its moral foundation, the political order is 'delegitimated.' When that happens, the political order must be secured by coercion rather than by consent. And when that happens, democracy disappears."[40]

This is not to argue that corporations ought to become economic democracies, but, as Neuhaus argues, it is "to make democratic capitalism more genuinely democratic . . . A person deprived of freedom cannot do work that is truly his, nor can he enjoy the benefits of that work."[41] Just as political megastructures undermine meaning, identity, and responsibility, so can economic ones. If we learn at work that our self-interest is best enhanced by intrigue, deception, and more self-interest, rather than by virtues of cooperation, honesty, and solidarity, then we have created a bigger hurdle, one that prevents individuals from being citizens interested in republican well-being in any public setting. Using these ideas, one can summarize six reasons why businesses should be mediating institutions.

---

[37] Id. at 193.

[38] Michael Novak, *The Spirit of Democratic Capitalism* 132 (1991).

[39] Berger & Neuhaus, supra note 7, at 41.

[40] Id., at 3.

[41] Richard John Neuhaus, *Doing Well and Doing Good: The Challenge to the Christian Capitalist* 150–51 (1992).

First, meeting human needs is a good thing for individuals and society. As a good, meeting these needs should be done, whether profitable or not. Robert Greenleaf aptly describes the priority of the motivations for pursuing such a good:

> When George Fox gave the seventeenth-century English Quaker businessmen a new business ethic (truthfulness, dependability, fixed prices—no haggling) he did it because his view of right conduct demanded it, not because it would be more profitable. It did, in fact, become more profitable because those early Quaker businessmen quickly emerged out of the seamy morass of that day as people who could be trusted. But the new ethic was a radical demand on those people and they must have had apprehensions about it when it was urged upon them.[42]

Second, since business is the place where people spend a great deal of their waking hours, there is the opportunity to satisfy human needs and socialize workers and managers in interpersonal responsibility. A great deal of learning (of some kind) will inevitably occur on the job. If the lessons of the workplace are different from lessons of solidarity, responsibility, and fairness, workers and managers will rarely see practiced the idea that self-interest is nourished in terms of fulfilling the needs of others in any public economic or even political context.

The third reason is that business has annexed the time previously utilized for meeting associational needs. Just as an acquiring company is liable for the obligations of an acquired company, business should be liable for the needs met in previously nonbusiness time.

Fourth, if one assumes that the legal system will (rightly) insist upon nondiscrimination in the workplace, businesses have the unique opportunity (and concomitant responsibility) to develop a language of common good within the context of multiculturalism. In his book *A Different Mirror*, Ronald Takaki writes that "on their voyage through history, Americans have found themselves bound to each other as workers."[43] It is by our labor that we come to our identity and to understand others who may not be like us. Businesses can be public grounds where people of different faiths, nationalities, races, and genders can work out commonality among diversity. Nondiscriminatory businesses provide a public forum for diversity. This kind of dialogue is likely to produce social models and languages for multiculturalism on a larger political context.

A fifth reason is that the mediating institution concept is particularly well suited for the limitation of business responsibility. The business as mediating institution view is a limited view of corporate action, because a traditional mediating institution such as family, church, or voluntary organization has primary loyalty to its own members. Those members are quite often devoted to a particular external cause, but the organization exists by virtue of a commitment to one another that may lead to addressing that external cause. Similarly, people work in businesses to achieve many external goals other than profitability, satisfying a customer, or feeding one's family. But, in order for them to do so, the organization must have community of people working together.

A chief duty of an organization then is to its members. In a corporation, that would include shareholders and managers, as has often been noted. Without arguing whether a corporation may have duties to the community at large and that meeting those duties may have positive economic consequences in the form of goodwill and reputation, a

---

[42] Robert K. Greenleaf, *Servant Leadership: A Journey Into the Nature of Legitimate Power and Greatness* 143 (1977).

[43] Ronald Takaki, *A Different Mirror: A History of Multicultural America* 426 (1993).

corporation first has a duty to its other internal members: its employees. In fact, as I will argue in this book, a mediating institutions approach primarily demands heightened duties to all internal members, while duties to external constituents ought to take the form of corporate obedience to legal and economically sustainable concerns.

Sixth, there are contemporary management strategies that argue that profitability can be maintained or increased if business does attempt to meet the moral needs of its members. If business does have a duty of wealth creation, then it is morally compelled to create profitable organizational structures. Thus, business does have a moral duty to reinvent itself along the lines of a mediating structure because it has the (perhaps only broad-based) opportunity to address a significant number of people in a way that provides meaning to them while confronting the critical social issues of our days with tools that can make businesses themselves more profitable.

RED AND YELLOW LIGHTS

As I indicated earlier in this chapter, I do not want to be Polyannaish about mediating institutions. They carry with them dangers as well. For instance, does the fact that a gang in an inner city provides identity to its members mean that its actions of drug dealing and murdering are ethical? Does the fact that militias form in small rural areas in reaction to the federal government mean that we should champion the Michigan Militia? The answer is too obvious to require an answer. Yet there is a dangerous potential for clannishness in my proposal that flashes a red light. Berger and Neuhaus, in fact, recognize that "[o]f course, some critics will decry our proposal as 'balkanization,' 'retribalizaton,' 'parochialization,' and such."[44] Still, there are times when clannishness is more problematic than at other times. In Madisonian terms, the multiplicity of organizations itself can be a corrective for those who would otherwise be trapped in organizations from which there is not escape. Berger and Neuhaus again write: "The relevance of the Balkan areas aside, we want frankly to assert that tribe and parochial are not terms of derision. . . . *Liberation is not escape from particularity but discovery of the particularity that fits.*"[45] In other words, the diversity of business-mediating institutions enhances the individual's ability to find the community in which she is most at home.

Moreover, our shrinking world intrudes on the kinds of borders that oppressive institutions erect to maintain their evil. With cameras, televisions, fax machines, telephones, and the Internet lurking around every corner, exposure of wrongdoing is not too difficult. Thus, the possibility of oppressive communities is not as significant as it might have been in an earlier time. Nevertheless, minimizing the problems that mediating institutions may possess is something I will expand upon in subsequent chapters.

One can distinguish between different kinds of groups. To avoid the trap of an ambiguous metaphor and my normative mediating institutions model, I would like to elaborate on an earlier differentiation I made between a quarantining institution and a mediating institution, with some help from another business ethicist who draws upon naturalist categories.

In an extraordinarily challenging integration of complexity theory and morality, Bill Frederick argues that a corporation, like any other living organism, from plant life to the

---

[44] Berger & Neuhaus, supra note 7, at 43.

[45] Berger & Neuhaus, supra note 7, at 43.

nation-state, is a "complex adaptive system."[46] That is, a corporation is an organization of separate parts that mutually support one another within the context of their life as an organization.[47] Putting to the side a remarkable array of other terms, Frederick poses the question of how to relate the corporation to the community at large. He responds that "*[a] community is an ecological system—an ecosystem—consisting of interlinked organisms living within an abiotic (nonliving) setting.*"[48] But such a community is open also because no community can escape basic natural processes whether those be thermodynamics or El Niño.[49] The corporation, he concludes, is itself a community, but it is a community that has no choice but to be open to the realities of natural forces.[50] One could say, although Frederick himself does not, that a community that attempts to insulate itself acts contrary to nature.

Thus, business organizations are communities, but they cannot avoid interacting with the outside world. Communities require attention to the lives of individual members that comprise it in order to provide individuals with the context for meaning-making. Communities must also, however, "flirt" with the outside world lest they become anachronistic. If they do not flirt, their inevitable interaction with the outside world could become oppressive or violent or at the very least, create insularity. While such insularity may work within the context of a particular community, such as the Amish, it is not likely to have much utility in a global business environment.

To the extent a community focuses on itself only and does not remain open to the larger community, it acts as a quarantining institution. In a quarantine, the outside world is closed off (or more accurately, the local world is prevented from going out). Regardless of who is supposed to be going in and out, the important point is that there is a separation of the local community and the outside world. Interactions between the two are dangerous and should be avoided. When there is interaction, it could result in violence.

This is an imperfect, but helpful way to look at the difference between a mediating institution and a quarantining institution. A quarantining institution is closed off. Groups may close themselves off for a variety of reasons, including being alienated from a society in which they have no meaningful ability to participate. While the participation that could occur within the institution may be admirable and while the solidarity and loyalty within the organizational structure may be profound, it is insufficient. Instead, a mediating institution both promotes internal goods such as participation, solidarity, and loyalty while also "mediating"; that is, interacting (not quarantining) with the outside world. As such, a mediating institution is an adaptive mechanism for living in the world at large, not a survival mechanism in which the world at large is an enemy.

There is also a yellow light. This chapter is obviously assuming that religious belief is admissible to corporate life. This is an assumption many will not be willing to accept. As Neuhaus writes, however, "It is spiritually eviscerating that what millions of men and women do 50 or 70 hours of most every week is bracketed off from their understanding of their faith."[51] In part III of this book, I will address the question of the

---

[46] William C. Frederick, "Complexity, Corporation, Community: How Nature Shapes Business's Civic Role," Address to the Midwest Division of the Academy of Management 12 (April 18, 1998) (manuscript on file with author).

[47] Cf. Errol E. Harris, *Formal, Transcendental & Dialectical Logic: Logic and Reality* (1987).

[48] Frederick, supra note 46, at 21.

[49] Id., at 21.

[50] Id., at 21–22.

[51] Neuhaus, supra note 41, at 62.

reasonableness of allowing such spiritual language to intrude into the workplace (and will not surprisingly conclude that I think this is a good thing). For now, however, I simply want to turn on the warning light myself to the concern that the resolution of the appropriateness of this spiritual sense raises significant, secular workplace issues to which I will attend.

In the meantime, having presented notions of solidarity and subsidiarity and their relationship to business ethics, I want to go further down this path to sketch a natural law view of corporate life that extends these thoughts and that also provides a platform from which one can develop a legal architecture to institutionally take advantage of the strengths of this approach.

Laws of Nature

. . . The point to be made is that human beings, while having a good deal of plasticity in the development of their culture, do not have infinite flexibility. Much as we would like, we cannot make our arms into wings so that we can fly. We must build things like airplanes, which take into account our inability to fly by our own physical means. Similarly, while we may want to think that we have a Lockean plasticity in the development of our moral sentiments and our rational achievements, biology suggests that there are limitations. Those limitations impact how we relate to other individuals. If ethics is about how we relate to other individuals, these biological limitations make a significant difference as to how we go about proposing ethics in corporate life or anywhere else.

First, anthropologists have found consistent group sizes among aboriginal populations. These tend to cluster between twenty-five and thirty five (the band) and 400 to 600 (the macroband), which is the largest community that interacts regularly.[52] One of the difficulties in larger groupings is that scalar stress—increasing numbers of disputes within the group—increases exponentially rather than arithmetically when membership in the group exceeds these "magic numbers."[53] All of these relatively small numbers suggest a simple numerical empowerment of individuals. In such groups, morality may be communal, but the individual's influence on her relevant community is arithmetically more powerful. The relationship between the empowering efficacy of these small groups and the large megastructures, such as the multinational corporation, will be explored more fully throughout this book. For present purposes, it is sufficient to see that studies of human behavior indicate ways to blend individual power and communal good.

In his study on the development of human language, psychologist Robin Dunbar reported accounts for the genesis of its development. He noted that a typical explanation for the difference between humans and other animals is the large size of the human brain.[54] But whales and elephants have larger brains than humans, so he instead examined the ratio of the neocortex—that part of the brain responsible for cognition as opposed to the controller of bodily functions and movement—to body mass.[55] In doing this, he found general groupings of neocortex ratios; that is, reptiles were in a certain range, fish in another, primates in another, with human brains having, by far, the highest ratio.[56]

---

[52] Joseph Birdsell, "On Population Structure in Generalized Hunting and Gathering Populations," in 12 *Evolution* no. 2, at 196–99 (1958).

[53] Gregory Johnson, "Organizational Structure and Scalar Stress" in *Theory and Explanation in Archaeology* (C. Renfrew, M. J. Rowlands, & B. A. Segraves eds., 1982).

[54] Robin Dunbar, *Grooming, Gossip, and the Evolution of Language* 56 (1996).

[55] Id. at 56–57.

[56] Id. at 57–63.

Dunbar also noticed that primates tend to limit the size of their group. Above a certain number, the group fissions.[57] He then plotted a graph with coordinates of primate neocortex ratios and group size.[58] Extending the results, he predicted the maximum size of a human group to be 150.[59] This is in the range of the hunter-gatherer numbers we just saw, but does it have any contemporary ratification? In fact, in looking at other studies Dunbar noted that religious groups, such as the Hutterites, have pursued their life in communal farms for nearly four centuries in Europe and in North America. According to Dunbar, the mean size of their communities is 100 and the communities split if they reach a size of 150. Above this number, the Hutterites believe that it is hard to control membership by peer pressure alone.[60] Why is this? Dunbar writes:

> Indeed, there is a well-established principle in sociology suggesting that social groupings larger than 150–200 become increasingly hierarchical in structure. Small social groups tend to lack structure of any kind, relying instead on personal contacts to oil the wheels of social intercourse. But with more people to coordinate, hierarchical structures are required. There must be chiefs to direct, and a police force to ensure that social rules are adhered to. And this turns out to be an unwritten rule in modern business organizations too. Businesses with fewer than 150–200 people can be organized on entirely informal lines relying on personal contacts between employees to ensure the proper exchange of information. But larger businesses require formal management structure to channel contacts and ensure that each employee knows what he or she is responsible for and whom they should report to.[61]

Dunbar has other examples as well. He goes on to note that the Mormons followed a pattern similar to the Hutterites. He writes that when Brigham Young led the Mormons to Utah, he divided his flock of 5,000 into groups of 150.[62] Dunbar also reports that a study conducted by the Church of England found that the ideal congregation size is less than 200, and he also found that over the past 100 years, the military company unit has ranged from 130 (the number in Gandhi's ashram) to 170.[63] These anthropological realities suggest that certain capacities are universal among human beings. The findings themselves do not suggest universal norms, but do indicate basic human capacities that may have an impact on how human beings relate to each other.

Such small institutions, of course, are in a sense "mediating institutions." They stand between the individual and society.[64] They socialize and empower the individual and thereby, ideally, make such individuals into citizens who enter society with the tools to negotiate, knowing that they are social creatures depending upon a community.[65] That is the rosy view. The thorn is that these groups can be insular, violent, and reclusive.[66] The difference between the petals and the thorns is the distinction, made in Chapter 2, between a mediating institution and a quarantining institution. A mediating institution

---

[57] Id.

[58] Id. at 63.

[59] Id.

[60] Id at 71–73.

[61] Id at 72.

[62] Id. at 71–73.

[63] Id. at 74–76.

[64] Peter Berger & Richard John Neuhaus, *To Empower People: The Role of Mediating Structure in Public Policy* (1977).

[65] See, e.g., Cass Sunstein, "Beyond the Republican Revival," 97 *Yale L.J.* 1539 (1988).

[66] Id.

provides a community for its members, but it does mediate, so that it is open to the outside world. It therefore is always negotiating and adapting. While a mediating institution must also have a unique identity, it also contains feedback mechanisms—its cybernetics[67]—open to environmental changes.

The point is that biological anthropology (laws of nature) confirms the natural law (as articulated by Catholic social thought) emphasis on the desirability (and necessity) of small groups. Human beings relate to one another in small groups, where they have feedback mechanisms for the consequences of their actions. If ethics has to do with how we treat others, then this cognitive limitation makes a difference to doing ethics well. Put individuals in large groups, and one loses the sense of community that nurtures ethical behavior. Who will really notice if I embezzle a bit of money from this huge employer? At the same time, an attempt to quarantine a company may lead the company to the continued manufacture of buggy whips in an age of automobiles.

From *Ethics and Governance Business as Mediating Institution* by Timothy Fort. Copyright © 2001 by Oxford University Press. Reproduced with permission of the Licensor through PLSclear.

Discussion Question(s)

1. Does Fort's distinction between mediating and quarantining institutions make sense? Are big-time college athletics departments quarantining institutions? Why? Why not?

2. What evidence does Fort garner in favor of his claim that intimacy and relationships (cultivated within a mediating institution structure) are the best way to promote ethical behavior? Is that evidence convincing? Why? Why not?

3. How might Fort's analysis of the NCAA help us understand the practical importance of the idea of subsidiarity?

Selection #2: Eric Neel, Making Time Stand Still, 2008, espn.com.

Please read article here: http://espn.go.com/espn/eticket/story?page=hospice

Introduction: What counts as success? What is *really* worthy of our attention or esteem? Eric Neel's article about terminal cancer patients and a formerly success-oriented MLB baseball coach, who learned from Catholic nuns how to serve them, brings these questions into stark relief. Western culture (at least in its popular commercial forms) tends to send the message that fame, power, and money are the measures of success. In sport, the formula is the same, with winning being seen as the conduit to fame, power, and money. Neel's account of the spiritual transformation of Bobby Dews tells a very different story.

Discussion Question(s)

1. What do you make of this quote? Is it an example of solidarity? "He saw patients being spoon-fed, propped up and cleaned. He saw them struggle to open their eyes and speak. Now he understood: This was dying. He saw the sisters wiping brows, holding hands, whispering prayers. He saw them walk into every room with a smile and provide some measure of comfort to the patients and their families. This was acceptance. This was love. This was good work. This was time well spent."

---

[67] Roy A. Rappaport, *Ecology, Meaning, & Religion* (1979).

2. Is the Our Lady of Perpetual Help hospice evidence to support Fort's claim that religion should be permissible to public life (even work)? Why? Why not?
3. Can something as "trivial" as sport ease suffering? How? Why?

Selection #3: Gary Smith, ALIVE AND KICKING. *Sports Illustrated*; June 23, 2008, Vol. 108 Issue 25, pp. 56–68.

Please read article here: http://www.si.com/vault/2008/06/23/105705012/alive-and-kicking

Introduction: How does true community develop? The late 19th/early 20th century German sociologist Ferdinand Tönnies famously argued for the distinction between *Gemeinschaft* and *Gesellschaft*. That is, between "community" and "association." A community has thick bonds of obligation, of caring and of being cared for. As such, one has a real sense of belonging in a *Gemeinschaft*. Similar to a mediating institution, a *Gemeinschaft* allows one to feel rooted in a specific place among specific people. A *Gesellschaft*, in contrast, is an instrumental association of individuals whose commitment to the group is relatively thin and contingent upon the individual benefit garnered. Should a better, more convenient or more fashionable opportunity come along, one would quickly leave or dissolve a *Gesellschaft*, for the association was primarily one of pragmatic convenience. Tönnies worried that the modern West—due to utilitarianism, individualism, unfettered capitalism, etc.—was losing its ability to develop true community. Could sport, via the application of a mediating institution mindset, such as we see in this reading on the "Fugees," counteract this trend? Or, is the modern push to use sport in service of winning, fame, publicity, accolades, etc., simply impossible to resist?

Discussion Question(s)

1. Are the "Fugees" a mediating institution?
2. What do you make of this quote? Does it support or raise doubts about Fort's philosophy? "She asked them to divide into groups of four for drills. When they split up by nationality or tribes, she shook her head no and reshuffled them. The East and West Africans sniped at one another. The northern Sudanese begrudged the southern. She made them run laps at the first whiff of old animosities. She outlawed all languages except English to smash any cliques."
3. Is it realistic to expect youth sports to function as mediating institutions? Why? Why not?

Selection #4: Kevin D. Williamson, *National Review*, SCHMUCKS LIKE US: BEFORE YOU LAUGH AT TIGER WOODS . . . (MAY 30, 2017).

Introduction: *Schadenfreude*, finding joy in the pain of others, is a dangerous vice. It spurs pride, negates sympathy, and clouds our sense of justice to the point that it will very likely simply devolve into a desire for comeuppance or revenge. But the point of seeing the mistakes of those around us (whether public or private figures) is not to revel in their pain, loss, or foolishness, but rather to learn from them. The pursuit of virtue is a lifelong struggle *for everyone*. When another falls, the point is not to gloat or laugh or smile, but rather to console, correct, if it is our place, and learn from those mistakes, *in hopes of not repeating them ourselves*. If we consider circumstances honestly, we will likely be called to simply admit, "There but for the grace of God go I." If this is true, then the fall of the rich or famous or proud should be a lesson in humility, rather than an opportunity to gloat. As Williamson so perceptively asks, "Would you pass the Iverson test?"

Before you get too distracted mocking Tiger Woods and his problems, ask yourself: Would you pass the Iverson test?

I don't think I would.

I was for some years professionally obliged to follow the career and life of Allen Iverson, a gifted and troubled basketball star who lived in the Philadelphia suburbs where I edited the local newspaper. He led the 76ers to the NBA finals but could not keep himself out of trouble: drugs and casual gunplay at first—he was great for my newspaper—and then, when the show was over, money problems in his retirement.

The financial difficulties later in life subjected Iverson to a great deal of ridicule: You can get busted for weed and an illegal gun and it's no big deal—not in Philly!—but if your money isn't right, then the world will never, ever forgive you. (Ask poor old Stanley Burrell.) During what turned out to be an excruciatingly embarrassing divorce case, Iverson exclaimed to his wife: "I don't even have money for a cheeseburger!" at which point she handed him $61 in cash—the last cash she had. His problems began to become public when he was ordered to pay a debt of nearly $1 million to a jeweler and was forced to plead that he did not have the funds. He had earned more than $150 million in his NBA career.

Some guardian angel at Reebok saved him from the very worst of it, persuading him to take a modest $800,000-a-year stipend and leave $32 million in a trust fund that he cannot access until he is 55 years old. So he just has to eke out a living on the better part of a million bucks per annum until he gets paid for real. Your sympathy, I am sure, is not without limits.

But how his story began is at least as interesting as where it ended up: On June 26, 1996, Iverson signed a $9.4 million contract with the 76ers. One year, ten months, and 23 days before that, he had been in prison, having received a 15-year sentence handed down under a rarely used antilynching law after a brawl at a Virginia bowling alley. Iverson has broken his share of laws, but he was in prison for a crime that he probably did not commit; he was granted clemency by Virginia governor Douglas Wilder, and his conviction eventually was overturned on appeal for lack of evidence. In January 1999, he signed a $70 million contract extension. He was 23 years old.

If you'd have given me that kind of money—and that celebrity—at that age, it would have killed me, and, while my own upbringing wasn't exactly out of *Ozzie and Harriet*, I think I was emotionally a little more squared-away in my twenties than Iverson probably was with his despair-inducing background. Not that it occurred to me at the time: When Iverson was having his problems in Philadelphia, I rolled my eyes and thought the same thing that most everybody thought: "What is the matter with you? You have everything you could possibly want—why be such a jerk? Why mess it all up?" My views have changed over the years. What's most surprising to me about Iverson now is not that he turned out to be kind of sad and feckless but that he didn't turn out a lot worse than he did.

Iverson did not grow up with a great deal of social capital: unmarried mother, 15 years old when he was born; absentee father; charged with a felony at 17 and dispatched shortly thereafter to prison. The knowledge that his life could have been radically different but for one or two very close calls—and his terrific athletic ability—must have weighed on him in some way: It might have produced deep gratitude, or it might have produced deep nihilism. It probably produced a complicated mix of both. Iverson did not grow up in a family or community with a lot of great role models or the kind of social network that can guide an energetic, gifted, and competitive young man such as himself in the right direction. Professional athletes often do not find themselves surrounded by the best people—and shaping all of those conflicting and terrifying forces into a happy, well-adjusted man would have been a challenge even if he had been. Making good men is hard: Neither the Marine Corps nor the Catholic Church nor the Boy Scouts has a perfect record on that front. Neither does any other institution, or any family, for that matter.

Add to all those challenges the fact that the sort of people who develop extraordinarily rare, world-beating talents—in basketball, chess, music, politics—very often do so to the exclusion of almost everything else that we mean by the phrase "having a life." You see this all the time: celebrities going broke because they just don't know what things cost or how much money they really have, rich and powerful people flummoxed by the simplest things in life and unable to adapt to ordinary social norms, famous people who do not have any friends. I suspect that if Hillary Rodham Clinton tried to get from her house to Bill de Blasio's on the Metro North and the subway, she'd end up in the ICU. And whom would they call on her behalf? Her husband? Having a life that is focused on the One Big Thing is fine when you are at the apex of your career, when the money just keeps coming in and the magical bubble of fame protects you from all manner of consequence.

But when the One Big Thing is gone, there is a double loss—the thing that defined your life is now in the past, and, at the very moment when your income and public profile both are likely to be heading south, you face the real crisis: You have done something extraordinary, but it is finished, and now you do not know what to do. The lucky ones have great marriages and happy families, faith, community, and friendship to take the place of being in the movies or playing basketball. The ones who don't have that will try to fill up the great empty hole in the middle of their lives with other things: alcohol, drugs, sexual promiscuity, recklessness in personal and public affairs, including financial ones. Do you know why so many people who ought to be happy but aren't happy develop problems with cocaine? Because cocaine works exactly as advertised. It makes you happy, until it doesn't.

We love a celebrity comeuppance. This is in part an ugly species of envy: Why should Tiger Woods get to live like a Roman emperor just for being really good at a game that is, after all, the very definition of a trivial pursuit? And how good an actor do you really need to be to star in *Pirates of the Caribbean*? How many hundreds of millions of dollars should someone get just for being pretty? There is something in our puritanical national soul that is satisfied by the fact that those who fly higher have farther to fall. These episodes bring out something ignoble in us. But it isn't just celebrities, of course: The high and mighty are just the ones we talk about. An astonishing share of lottery winners go broke, and it isn't because people with low character or weak wills are just lucky with the numbers. People like Tiger Woods and Allen Iverson, who win life's lottery, often have the same bad luck in the end: the bad luck of being human.

Tiger Woods was arrested for driving while intoxicated. This is not the first time Tiger Woods has run into trouble behind the wheel or had embarrassing personal details made public. He, or whoever writes his public statements for him, knows better: "I thought I could get away with whatever I wanted to," he said after the sex scandal that turned him from sports hero to public laughingstock. "I felt that I had worked hard my entire life and deserved to enjoy all the temptations around me. I felt I was entitled. Thanks to money and fame, I didn't have to go far to find them. I was wrong. I was foolish."

Woods apparently drinks too much sometimes, and, if the tabloids are to be believed, he has expansive sexual appetites. I wonder how alien those problems really are to the average American man. But the average American man does not have $600 million, an almost universally known name, and a face recognized by 98% of the people he encounters. Maybe you haven't behaved the way Tiger Woods does—but how many *Playboy* models do you have on speed-dial? How many of them were *calling you* at the peak of your career or slightly thereafter? Maybe you lead a more virtuous life. Maybe you just lead a smaller one. It is difficult to say without being tested.

And that may be why we love the ritual public denunciation of fallen idols. If we convince ourselves that they are monsters and moral outliers, then we do not have to face the much more terrifying possibility that they are schmucks like us—and that we are schmucks like them.

– *Kevin D. Williamson is NR's roving correspondent.*

From National Review by Kevin D. Williamson. Reprinted by permission.

Discussion Question(s)

1. What does Williamson mean by "social capital"? Why does he think it is so important in understanding Iverson's story?

2. What does Williamson mean by the "one big thing"? Why does he think such focus can be dangerous?

3. What does Williamson mean when he says "Maybe you lead a more virtuous life. Maybe you just lead a smaller one. It is difficult to say without being tested"?

Selection #5: Timothy L. Fort, *The Chicago Tribune*, Who will clean up the mess?, (1990, June 15), Sec. 1., 25.

Please read the article here: http://archives.chicagotribune.com/1990/06/15/page/25/article/who-will-clean-up-the-mess

Discussion Question(s)

1. Is Fort's analysis of how best to combat the "ethical plague" convincing? Why? Why not?

Suggested Readings

Berger, P. (1963). *Invitation to sociology.* New York, NY: Anchor Books.

Berkowitz, P. (2000, January 10). Other people's mothers: The utilitarian horrors of Peter Singer. *The New Republic*, 27–37.

Feezell, R. (2013). Sport, religious belief, and religious diversity. *Journal of the Philosophy of Sport*, 40(1), 135–162.

Torres, C. R., & Hager, P. F. (2013). Competition, ethics, and coaching youth. In R. L. Simon (Ed.), *The ethics of coaching sports: Moral, social and legal issues* (pp. 167–184). Boulder, CO: Westview Press.

Bibliography

Aristotle. (1981). *Politics.* (T. Sinclair, & T. J. Saunders, Trans.) New York, NY: Penguin Books.

Aristotle. (2002). *Nicomachean ethics.* (J. Sachs, Trans.) Newburyport, MA: Focus Publishing.

Asad, T. (2003). *Formations of the secular: Christianity, Islam, Modernity.* Stanford, CA: Stanford University Press.

Augustine, St. (1958). *The city of God.* (G. G. Walsh, D. B. Zema, G. Monahan, & D. J. Honan, Trans.) New York, NY: Bantam Doubleday.

Battista, J. (2002, October 31). Edwards's take on Jets: Quitting is never an option. *The New York Times*, p. D5.

Berger, P. (1969). *A rumor of angels: Modern society and the rediscovery of the supernatural.* Garden City, NY: Doubleday Anchor Books.

Berger, P. (Ed.). (1999). *The desecularization of the world: Resurgent religion and world politics.* Grand Rapids, MI: Eerdmans.

Berger, P., & Neuhaus, R. J. (1996). *To empower people: From state to civil society.* (M. Novak, Ed.) Washington DC: The American Enterprise Institute for Public Policy Research.

Boethius. (2012). *The consolation of philosophy* (S. Goins, Ed., & B. H. Wyman, Trans.). San Francisco, CA: Ignatius Press.

Burke, E. (1790/2009). *Reflections on the revolution in France.* New York, NY: Oxford University Press.

Burleigh, M. (2005). *Earthly powers: The clash of religion and politics in Europe, from the French Revolution to the Great War.* New York, NY: Harper Perennial.

Burleigh, M. (2007). *Sacred causes: The clash of religion and politics, from the Great War to the War on Terror.* New York, NY: Harper Perennial.

Byron S.J., W. J. (1998, October 31). *Ten building blocks of Catholic social teaching.* Retrieved July 20, 2016, from americamagazine.org: http://americamagazine.org/issue/100/ten-building-blocks-catholic-social-teaching

Cavanaugh, W. T. (2009). *The myth of religious violence: Secular ideology and the roots of modern conflict.* New York, NY: Oxford University Press.

Chesterton, G. K. (2007). *Orthodoxy.* Radford, VA: Wilder Publications.

Dixon, N. (2016). In praise of partisanship. *Journal of the Philosophy of Sport,* 43(2), 233–249.

ESPN.com news services. (2012, October 5). *Cardale Jones: Classes pointless.* Retrieved October 24, 2013, from www.espn.com: http://espn.go.com/espn/print?id=8466428&type=story

Finnis, J. (1980). *Natural law and natural right.* New York, NY: Oxford University Press.

Fort, T. L. (1990, June 15). Who will clean up the mess? *The Chicago Tribune*, Sec. 1., 25.

Fort, T. L. (2001). *Ethics and governance: Business as mediating institution.* New York, NY: Oxford University Press.

James, W. (1896/1956). The will to believe. In W. James, *The will to believe and other essays in popular philosophy; human immortality* (pp. 1–32). New York, NY: Dover Publications.

James, W. (1907). *The energies of men.* Retrieved February 11, 2008, from Psychology Classics: http://psychclassics.yorku.ca/James/energies.htm

Kretchmar, R. S. (2005). *Practical philosophy of sport and physical activity* (2nd ed.). Champaign, IL: Human Kinetics.

Liber Steeg, J., Upton, J., Bohn, P., & Berkowitz, S. (2008, November 20). *College athletes studies guided toward "major in eligibility".* Retrieved December 27, 2012, from USAToday.com: http://usatoday30.usatoday.com/sports/college/2008-11-18-majors-cover_N.htm

MacAloon, J. J. (1980). *This great symbol: Pierre de Coubertin and the origins of the modern Olympic Games.* Chicago, IL: The University of Chicago Press.

MacIntyre, A. (1999). *Dependent rational animals: Why human beings need the virtues.* Chicago and LaSalle, IL: Open Court.

MacIntyre, A. (2009). *God, philosophy, universities: A selective history of the Catholic philosophical tradition.* Lanham, MD: Rowman & Littlefield Publishers Inc.

Marty, M. (2000). *Politics, religion and the public good: Advancing a distinctly American conversation about religion's role in our shared life.* San Francisco, CA: Jossey-Bass, Inc.

NCAA. (2019). *2019–2020 NCAA Division I manual.* Indianapolis, IN: The National Collegiate Athletic Association.

Neuhaus, R. J. (1984). *The naked public square.* Grand Rapids, MI: W.B. Eerdmans Publishing Company.

Neuhaus, R. J. (1992). *Doing well and doing good: The challenge to the Christian capitalist.* New York, NY: Random House.

Nisbet, R. (1993). *The sociological tradition.* Piscataway, NJ: Transaction Publishers.

Nongbri, B. (2013). *Before religion: A history of a modern concept.* New Haven, CT: Yale University Press.

Pieper, J. (2011). *The Christian idea of man.* South Bend, IN: St. Augustine's Press.

Polanyi, M. (1962). *Personal knowledge: Towards a Post-critical philosophy.* Chicago, IL: The University of Chicago Press.

Rosenberg, M. (2019, January 14). Learning to be human. *Sports Illustrated, 130*(1) 64–74.

Shepherd, S. (2015, October 17). *Inside McCarthy Hall, the KU basketball team's 'insane' new home.* Retrieved July 21, 2016, from http://www2.kusports.com/: http://www2.kusports.com/news/2015/oct/17/inside-mccarthy-hall-ku-basketball-teams-insane-ne/

Simon, R., Torres, C., & Hager, P. (2015). *Fair play: The ethics of sport* (4th ed.). Boulder, CO: Westview Press.

Singer, P. (1972). Famine, affluence, and morality. *Philosophy & Public Affairs, 1*(3), 229–242.

Singer, P. (1993). *Practical ethics* (2nd ed.). New York, NY: Cambridge University Press.

Singer, P. (1995). *How are we to live? Ethics in an age of self-interest.* Amherst, NY: Prometheus Books.

Skillen, A. (1998). Sport is for losers. In M. McNamee, & S. Parry, *Ethics and sport* (pp. 169–181). New York, NY: Routledge.

Specter, M. (1999, September 6). The dangerous philosopher. *The New Yorker, 75*(25), 46–50; 52–55.

Steinbach, P. (2012, February). *Are athletic support centers worth the investment?* Retrieved August 28, 2019, from athleticbusiness.com: https://www.athleticbusiness.com/college/are-academic-support-centers-worth-the-investment.html

Twietmeyer, G. (2007). Suffering play: Can play and games be defended in a suffering world? *Quest, 59*(2), 201–211.

Twietmeyer, G. (2015). God, sport philosophy, kinesiology: A MacIntyrean examination. *Quest, 67*(2), 203–226.

U.S. Department of Education. (2017). *Get data for one school.* Retrieved August 23, 2019, from EADA: Equity in athletics data analysis: https://ope.ed.gov/athletics/#/

Wolverton, B. (2008, September 5). *Rise in fancy academic centers for athletes raises questions of fairness.* Retrieved December 27, 2012, from Chronicle.com: http://chronicle.com/article/Rise-in-Fancy-Academic-Centers/13493

Wolverton, B. (2012, December 10). *Ohio State's sports program aims to play it straight.* Retrieved December 28, 2012, from chronicle.com: http://chronicle.com/article/Ohio-States-Sports-Program/136189/

Writing an Ethical Position Paper

Finding a Question and Developing a Thesis

An ethical position paper is one in which you advocate in favor of a normative claim on some ethical issue or controversy. The first step to writing any ethical position paper is finding a question worthy of your consideration. Here are three examples:

1. **Playing time:** How should playing time be allocated in youth sports? Should talent determine who plays and how much or should the educational mission of youth sport require minimum or even equal playing time?

2. **Mascots:** Are Native American mascot names (such as the Washington Redskins) offensive? If so, should they be banned? If not, why not?

3. **Title IX:** Does equality between the sexes ever justify cutting men's intercollegiate sports in the name of sex equity? If so, under what circumstances can cutting a men's team be justified? If not, what measures should be used to assure women's sport get an equitable share of the athletics department's resources?

Once you have settled on a question then you have to generate a thesis. That is, a normative claim in favor of one side of the issue. Let us use the first, "playing time." In this circumstance it could look something like this: "Youth sports should require minimum playing time." Notice the normative character of this thesis. It is not focused on whether or not youth leagues do require minimum or equal playing time. Nor is it focused on the popular opinion on the issue. In each of those cases the thesis would then become descriptive (see below):

1. Descriptive thesis #1: "Most youth sports leagues do not require equal playing time."

2. Descriptive thesis #2: "Most Americans believe that playing time—even at the youth level—should be earned on merit alone."

As you are aware from reading the text, philosophers are primarily interested in normative claims. As you outline and plan your paper, make sure you settle on a normative thesis that focuses on the rightness or the wrongness of the action, behavior or issue involved.

Moving forward we will use example #1: "playing time" as our question. Our thesis will be that: **"Youth sports should require a minimum amount of playing time for every player."**

Outlining

Once you have settled on a thesis, the second step to writing an ethical position paper is to outline your argument. This involves brainstorming and then organizing your arguments into a basic skeleton or outline of the paper as a whole. Brainstorming and outlining your paper before beginning the writing process will greatly improve the overall quality of the paper you produce.

Brainstorming involves reflecting upon and then writing down every argument you can think of to support your thesis. If a counter argument pops into your head while brainstorming, write that down as well. As you brainstorm avoid the temptation to evaluate the strengths and weaknesses of any given argument. You will do that later. Right now, at the brainstorming stage, you simply want to get all possible arguments on the table. In the included outline template (pp. 303–304) you will see a circle on the front page. Within that circle simply write down everything thing you can think of in support of the claim that: "Youth sports should require a minimum amount of playing time for every player."

Here is one list of example arguments:

"Coaches are supposed to be promoting life-long activity, which is best promoted by active participation."

"Minimum playing time will encourage self-esteem."

"Minimum playing time puts skill development ahead of winning."

"Minimum playing time will keep parents happy."

"Most youth sports coaches are not good enough judges of talent to assign playing time based upon skill."

"Since parents pay equal amounts of money for their children to be on the team, each player should have equal or at least guaranteed access to the playing field."

This list is simply an example. It is by no means exhaustive. Each argument would also be expanded in any paper in which they were used. However, even in embryonic form, this list does get at many of the common concerns in this debate. Given this list, our next step is to prioritize. Which of these arguments is the strongest? After giving this question some thought, try and narrow the list down to the three strongest arguments, ranking them from #1 (the best) to #3 (the weakest). These three arguments, once developed, will constitute the main body of your paper.

For the purposes of our example, here are three we have settled on:

Best argument: "Skill development"

Second best: "Self-esteem"

Third best: "Life-long activity"

Looking at the second page of the outline template (p. 304) you should see that there are spaces for three arguments. In your own words, using the arguments above, write a topic sentence or two introducing each of these arguments in the outline (Roman numerals II, III, and IV). As you do this, put the argument in reverse order of strength. That is, argument #1 on the outline will be your weakest (life-long activity) and argument three will be your strongest (skill). This is done as a matter of both rhetoric and logic. If your reader agrees with your weakest argument, they should be "putty in your hands" by the time you get to the strongest one. In contrast, if they are skeptical about "life-long activity" you still have two more powerful arguments to try and convince them with.

Once you have topic sentences written, it is time to consider counter arguments. Counter arguments are responses to the initial arguments you've put forth (e.g., skill, etc.). Spend some time brainstorming again, but now focus on how a critic might respond to the each of your three arguments. What, for example, might a defender of merit based playing time say in response to the "skill" argument? Obviously there is more than one counter argument that could be made against any given argument. Nevertheless, for the purposes of our example, we will use the following.

Argument #1: "Life-long activity"

Counter #1: "A hand-holding, 'everybody wins' mentality will not spur a love of the game. Lovers of 'soccer' or any other sport are born of challenge and a commitment to excellence, including the challenge of earned playing time."

Argument #2: "Self-esteem"

Counter #2: "We live in a competitive world. Kids need to learn how to deal with the fact that playing time, like everything else in life, is earned. Self-esteem will develop from real accomplishment, which in turn is the result of earned achievements."

Argument #3: "Skill"

Counter #3: "Skill is developed in practice. Therefore, there is no threat to skill development if playing time is allotted to the most-skilled players. Playing time should be earned."

Returning then to the second page of the outline, write a topic sentence for each of the counters at II a, III a, and IV a. Once they are written we should return once again to the brainstorming stage and look to develop rejoinders. Rejoinders are responses to the counters in defense of your original arguments. As before, more than one rejoinder is possible, but we will settle on the following.

Argument #1: "Life-long learning"

Counter #1: "A hand-holding, everybody wins mentality will not spur a love of the game. Lovers of 'soccer' or any other sport are born of challenge and a commitment to excellence, including the challenge of earned playing time."

Rejoinder #1: "Life-long learning and a love of the game is not developed on the bench. It is through 'sliding in safe', or 'making a diving save' or 'breaking a tackle' that children learn to love the games we teach them. If you want to spur life-long activity, the children must first *be active*. This cannot be done on the bench!"

Argument #2: "Self-esteem"

Counter #2: "We live in a competitive world. Kids need to learn how to deal with the fact that playing time, like everything else in life is earned. Self-esteem will develop from real accomplishment, which in turn is the result of earned achievements."

Rejoinder #2: "Children will have plenty of time to learn the harsh realities of life later. Self-esteem must be nurtured before children are exposed to the hypercompetitive world of adult activities."

Argument #3: "Skill"

Counter #3: "Skill is developed in practice. Therefore, there is no threat to skill development if playing time is allotted to the most-skilled players. Playing time should be earned."

Rejoinder #3: "Youth sports is about learning. Learning to play the game is done—and can only be done—on the field. Although skills can be developed in practice, true mastery requires that those skills be tested and executed in the pressure of a real game situation."

More can and should be said about each of these arguments, counters and rejoinders. In fact, a well written paper would likely have 2–3 full paragraphs on an argument followed by 1–2 paragraphs on the counter, followed by 1–2 paragraphs on the rejoinder. This pattern would then be used for each of the arguments (life-long activity, then self-esteem, then skill). At this early stage, however, we have still made significant progress. We have secured a clear outline of what our thesis is and how we are going to approach defending it. The entire body of our paper has been organized. We simply need to use this outline to flesh out the details.

Beginnings and Ends, Introductions, and Conclusions

Introductions

The introduction of your paper has two broad goals. First, to introduce the problem. Second, to propose a solution. To accomplish these goals you will need four elements in your paper; the hook, the template, caveats/definitions and the thesis.

The hook is a way to pull the reader in. The point it to get them interested and engaged in the topic. This can be done several ways. Here are a few examples; (1) You can tell a poignant story, for example, about the hypercompetitive nature of youth sports where, for instance, there is even a golf world championship for six year olds. (2) You could tell a personal story, for example, about riding the bench in Little League. (3) You could cite statistics or quote an expert in the field, for example, on the number of adolescents who drop out of sport due to burn out. There is no single right way to go about this task. The key to a good hook is simply to get the reader's attention regarding the importance of the issue. The test of a good hook is if encourages the reader to keep reading.

The template is a roadmap. It sets the stage for the reader by briefly introducing the arguments you will use in support of your thesis. A good template should spend a sentence or two telling the reader what you're going to argue and how you're going to argue it. There are two strategies for doing this. One option is to introduce the thesis and then follow it with the template in support of that claim. A second option is to set the template first, by introducing the reasons you will examine in the body of the paper (in this case) for why minimum playing time should be required. Closing out the template would then be the thesis statement. Either ordering option is fine as long as your template clearly communicates to the reader where you are headed. To that end you need to specify what the arguments will be as well as keep the order of arguments you will pursue in the body of the paper. This is very important. A confused, frustrated or lost reader is likely to stop reading! Consider the difference between these two templates:

> **Poor Template: "In this paper I will persuade you to believe that youth sports should require minimum playing time by examining several important reasons that show the importance of giving kids an equal chance to play."**

> **Good Template: "There are several important reasons that youth sports coaches should give young athletes minimum playing time. First, coaches are supposed to be promoting life-long activity. It is hard to see how a "love of the game" can develop on the bench. Second, equal playing time will encourage self-esteem. Children will have plenty of time to learn the harsh realities of life later. At this young age coaches should focus on what kids can do, not on what they cannot. Finally, equal playing time puts skill development ahead of winning. Youth sports is about learning. Learning to play the game is done— and can only be done—*on the field.*"**

In the first instance the reader has learned nothing specific about how the paper will proceed. In the second instance the reader has knowledge of the basic argument and a specific understanding of how you plan to proceed. Again, more could be said on each topic, but that will be done in the body of the paper.

Caveats and definitions are important in any instance where ambiguity is present in your thesis. Consider our thesis again: **"Youth sports should require a minimum amount of playing time for every player."** What precisely does this mean? How are we *defining* "minimum?" Five minutes, one quarter, one inning, half the game? How are we defining youth sports? High school? Middle school? Where does youth end and adolescent or adult sport begin? All of these questions should be specifically and clearly answered in the introduction, for instance, by saying something like this: "When I speak of youth sports, I mean children up to 14 years old. Once children enter high school a focus on merit is justifiable." Of course one might also object to the level or type of league or competition. For example, should the same "minimum" requirement apply to a youth gymnast training for the Olympics or even to a travel soccer team? If, for example, you wanted to focus on only recreational sports, you could offer a *caveat* like this: "I realize questions of playing time are complicated by travel and developmental teams. Although those are interesting questions, for the purposes of this paper, I will simply focus on the recreational leagues, such as Little League or YMCA Soccer, which introduce the vast majority of children to sport."

The bottom line is this. Definitions are important for clarifying your thesis. Caveats are important whenever you need to set something aside for the sake of brevity or focus.

Returning then to the second page of the outline. Quickly write out a few sentences in the hook, template and definition/caveat sections of the introduction (Roman numeral I).

Conclusions

The conclusion of your paper should be at least 1–2 paragraphs. It should accomplish two things. It should summarize your case and it should reaffirm your thesis. To achieve the first goal, you need to remind the reader of the one or two salient points regarding each of the arguments you've covered. By the time you get to the conclusion it will have been several pages since the reader last considered your "life-long activity" argument. As such it is important to remind them of a take-home point on each of your arguments. To achieve the second goal you should explicitly connect, one final time, the weight of your arguments to the truth of your thesis. One crude example of this would be: "Given the fact that minimum playing time is the best way to promote life-long activity, spur self-esteem and cultivate skill in young players, it is clear that youth sports **should require a minimum amount of playing time for every player.**"

Closing thoughts: What separates average from excellent ethical position papers?

1. Good writers write. If you want to write well, write often. Even more importantly, good writers re-write. They are not afraid to edit, delete, or revise. This means, of course, that good writing takes time. It takes time to cultivate your writing skill and it takes time to review and edit your work. Last minute work rarely ends in a good grade.

2. Good writers in philosophy engage research. Reading up on a topic and seeing what others have said means you don't have to reinvent the wheel. It means you develop expertise and build knowledge. Most likely, many others have thought about the question you're writing on. See what they have said. Engage it. Evaluate it. Cite it.

3. Write for the general reader. Don't assume knowledge for your audience. Just because we've talked about the "1st Categorical Imperative" in this text/class doesn't mean you can avoid explaining (and citing) what the "Categorical Imperative" is, if you use it in your paper.

4. Proofread, proofread, profread . . . ☺. Typos happen to the best of us. Take the time and polish your work. Philosophers want to communicate because they're convinced ideas are important. Ideas move the world. Yet, even the best idea can get buried under inarticulate, sloppy or confusing language. If you are passionate about an idea, take the time to communicate it clearly!

KIN 401
Fall 2022

Persuasive Paper—Brainstorming & Outlining

Brainstorming

Question: _____

Thesis: _____

Arguments:

Outline:

I. Introduction
   a. Hook: _____

   _____

   b. Thesis: _____

   _____

   i. Definitions/Caveats: _____

   _____

   c. Template: _____

   _____

II. Argument #1: _____

   _____

   a. Counter: _____

   _____

   i. Rejoinder: _____

III. Argument #2: _____

   _____

   a. Counter: _____

   _____

   i. Rejoinder: _____

IV. Argument #3: _____

   _____

   a. Counter: _____

   _____

   i. Rejoinder: _____

V. Conclusion: (Summarize Arguments & Reaffirm Thesis)

   _____

   _____

   _____

   _____

Common Logical Fallacies

Below you will find a list of 10 common logical fallacies. It is by no means an exhaustive list. This list is meant to give you an introduction to the kind of logical mistakes you will want to avoid when making arguments (or when writing an ethical position paper). I have provided sport-related examples for each of the fallacies. This list will also be valuable in helping you recognize fallacious reasoning in arguments that are made to you (in readings, in the sports media, by classmates, coaches, sport administrators, politicians, and so forth). Given its cursory nature, this list of fallacies and examples is brief and incomplete. It is simply meant to pique your interest and hopefully spur further investigation. If you want to know or learn more, see the suggested readings at the end of this appendix.

1. The Fallacy of Bare Assertion

The mistake of believing that the mere assertion of a claim (absent evidence) is sufficient to prove one's case. This fallacy often results from an appeal to what "everybody knows," to clichés that have become "common sense" or to "politically correct" dogma which allegedly no member of polite society would ever doubt or question. Nevertheless, saying it's so, does not make it so. WHENEVER A CLAIM IS CONTROVERSIAL OR DEBATABLE, IT SHOULD BE BACKED WITH EVIDENCE.

Example(s):   "Sport builds character."

"Diversity is our strength."

"The tradition of playing the National Anthem before sporting events is a vital part of our national heritage which builds community and social cohesion."

Three key points:

1. Each of the points above *may* be true, but their mere assertion does not make them so. They each need to be backed with evidence and argumentation to be worthy of support. This is no less true of a popular assertion than it is of an unpopular one.

2. Merely citing a source in support of your claim without an explanation of who the source is or why and how the citation supports the claim being made is not persuasive. It simply moves the "bare assertion" up one level to "because I and my citations say so." But why should I or anyone else believe that you or your source(s) are right? Perhaps you're simply citing another bare assertion. Therefore, to use a source in support of your assertion correctly, explain who the source is (why are they an authority on the topic), and then, when relevant, further explain what arguments they made in support of your claim.

3. Pointing out the fallacy does not prove that the defenders of the arguments presented above are wrong on the larger points. It only proves that they've made a bad (insufficient) argument.

2. The Strawman Fallacy

Rephrasing an opponent's arguments in the weakest and most unpersuasive way possible, so as to make their argument easy to defeat (and thereby avoid addressing the real argument being made).

Example: "Title IX—like any law—is imperfect. Insofar as Title IX compliance can currently be achieved by cutting men's opportunities (without adding women's), the law should be reformed."

Strawman characterization: "My opponent calls for Title IX 'reform' because he wants to eliminate the law, so that he can eliminate women's sport."

Three key points:

1. The recharacterization is not accurate. The initial claim did not advocate for the elimination of women's sport.

2. The recharacterization is far easier to defeat because it mischaracterizes the initial claim in such a way as to unfairly inflame passions against the argument on the grounds that it is misogynistic.

3. Pointing out the fallacy does not prove that the defenders of Title IX are wrong on the larger point. It only proves that they've made a bad argument.

3. *Ad Hominem Fallacy*

Attacking the person making the arguments rather than the arguments that they made.

Example: Former San Francisco 49ers Quarterback Colin Kaepernick claims that "Racism and inequality in the United States are rampant."

Ad Hominem Response: "No one needs to take him seriously, because Colin Kaepernick (like anyone who kneels during the National Anthem) hates his country."

Three key points:

1. The response does not address the claim being made.

2. The response, even if true, is irrelevant. The character of the claimant does not disprove the claim. It could be the case that racism in, for example, law enforcement is a real problem in the United States *and* that Colin Kaepernick hates his country. If he did hate his country, that would have no bearing on his claim. That is, his claim is either true or false independent of his character.

3. Pointing out the fallacy does not prove that the opponents of Colin Kaepernick's position are wrong on the larger point. It only proves that they've made a bad argument.

4. *Moving the Goalposts Fallacy*

This fallacy is the result of repositioning/raising one's demanded level of evidence (after the fact) so that one can avoid conceding a point to the other side. No evidence presented is ever sufficient to score a point against one's position, because the goalposts are always moved, so that the argument never hits its target.

Example: Speaker 1a: "Wrigley Field has always been an irreplaceable and beloved 'modern sporting cathedral'"

Counter 1: "Did you know that in 1918 the Cubs played the World Series at Comiskey Park (home of the Cubs' hated rival the Chicago White Sox) instead of Wrigley Field?"

Speaker 1b: "1918 is too early to count as evidence. I meant that it *became* a cathedral through the course of its storied history."

Counter 2: "Did you know that in the early 1960s Wrigley Field's upper deck was regularly closed due to low attendance?"

Speaker 1c: "Wide recognition of Wrigley's status as an architectural gem wasn't fully realized until the 1980s when games were broadcast around the country on WGN…"

Three key points:

1. Moving the goalposts means that one never has to concede a point to the other side. By constantly changing what counts as legitimate evidence, the speaker is able to deny that any counterevidence has even been produced.

2. Moving the goalposts and clarification of your argument are not the same thing. If you concede the point made and then look to revise your initial argument by taking that point into account, you have not succumbed to the fallacy. If the speaker above abandons his initial claim, he may be able to defend a modified version similar to "1c."

3. Any sincere seeker of truth cannot simply hide behind the clarification caveat listed above. That is, there must eventually be ground on which one stands firm. "Clarification" cannot go on forever. If, for instance, "1c" cannot be defended, then the whole argument should likely be abandoned. At some point the claim either has to be successfully defended or given up.

5. *The Question Begging Fallacy*

This fallacy is a circular form of reasoning which results from assuming a conclusion rather than offering arguments for it.

Example: "College athletes ought to be paid."

Question begging response: "Paying college players a salary is wrong because intercollegiate sports are meant to be amateur."

Three key points:

1. This claim begs the question because it *assumes* as true what is *under dispute* (should college sport be amateur?).

2. If college athletes should be amateur, you have to *offer arguments* in favor of amateurism, not merely assume that amateurism in college sport is good.

3. Pointing out the fallacy does not prove that the college athletes should be paid. It only proves that the defenders of amateurism have made a bad argument.

6. *Red Herring Fallacy*

This fallacy comes about from changing the subject so as not to confront the issue at hand. It is about making an argument which is beside the point, so as to avoid arguing what is actually relevant to the topic.

Example: "Major League Baseball (MLB) has a moral obligation to extend netting from foul pole to foul pole to protect spectators from getting injured by balls hit into the stands."

Red herring response: "Major League Baseball revenue has risen for each of the last 10 years. Clearly the league is doing something right."

Three key points:

1. The fact that MLB is increasing revenue has no bearing on whether or not they have an obligation to extend netting in their stadiums. The response is about avoiding the issue by changing the subject.

2. The second claim may very well be true and thereby show that MLB is doing many things right. However, that was never the issue. The key question is, are they doing right by their fans *on this particular issue.*

3. Pointing out the fallacy does not prove that MLB has failed to meet their moral obligations. It only proves that the defenders of the MLB status quo have made a bad argument.

7. *False Dichotomy Fallacy*

This fallacy is the result of reducing a problem to a set of dichotomous options when a third (or fourth or fifth) option might be available.

Example: "Either you support equal pay for the U.S. Women's National Soccer Team or you're sexist."

Three key points:

1. The claim is a false dichotomy because these are not the only two options available. Why not? Because what—precisely—"equal pay" means is debatable. Would it be equal, for instance, if both teams got an equal share of the gate receipts (and the gate receipts generated were different)? One might love women's sport, support the generic idea that the women deserve higher pay and still reject their specific proposals for equal pay. That would not make one sexist.

2. To point out the reality of any given false dichotomy does not mean that dichotomies are never real or legitimate (e.g., either you use the steroids or you do not, etc.). You cannot sort of or partially use steroids.

3. Pointing out the fallacy does not prove that the proponents of equal pay are wrong on the larger point. It only proves that they've made a bad argument.

8. *Post Hoc Ergo Propter Hoc Fallacy*

The logical mistake of assuming that since event B followed event A, event A must have caused event B. (This logical point in closely related to the statistical idea that correlation is not causation).

Example #1: "Title IX" was passed in 1972. In 1999 the United States won the Women's World Cup with players who grew up in a post Title IX era (they were "Title IX babies"). Therefore, Title IX caused the success of the 1999 Women's World Cup team.

Example #2: I bought new cleats at the beginning of the season. We are undefeated since I bought new cleats. Therefore my new cleats caused our undefeated season.

Three key points:

1. The logic of each of the two examples is exactly the same. The simple fact that one thing precedes another does not (by itself) prove that it was the cause (or one of the causes) of the other. If the *cleats-preceding* victory is dubious as a cause, so is Title IX *preceding* World Cup victory.

2. Many will object that a law ensuring women's equality in education is a plausible cause of World Cup success, while "magic cleats" is not a plausible cause of victory. But this is to miss the point of the fallacy. The fallacy simply points out that the prior occurrence of an event is—by itself—insufficient to prove that the two events have a causal relationship. If Title IX helped cause the 1999 success, then direct evidence would need to be given. This is especially true given that it is not hard to raise doubts about the typical "Title IX babies" account. How so?

   Here are just a few points which complicate the standard narrative. First, if we assume that a typical player in 1999 was between 23 and 30 years old, then the "Title IX babies" would have been born roughly between 1969 and 1976. However, there were no substantive regulations to guide Title IX compliance until 1979 when many players would already have been playing the game for several years. Second, for many players their initial and perhaps formative experience would have come in recreational and club soccer which (since it does not receive Federal funding) is not covered by Title IX. Third, due to the *Grove City vs. Bell* Supreme Court decision, athletics was exempt from Title IX from 1984 to 1987, which would have been key years for the development of these players. Finally, the law has not been (and was not) vigorously enforced in high schools, which means whatever benefit they got from playing high school soccer would have been due to far more than the threat of Title IX violations (because that threat was so miniscule). Moreover, private high schools rarely receive Federal funding and would therefore generally be exempt from Title IX.

3. Pointing out the fallacy does not prove that Title IX is unimportant or that it had no influence on the success of the 1999 World Cup team. It only proves that if one asserts that since Title IX preceded the World Cup team's success, Title IX *must have caused* that success, then one has made a bad argument.

9. *The Fallacy of Special Pleading*

This fallacy results from making a special exemption of yourself or your own interests from the general principles you espouse as applying to all, without sufficient justification.

Example: "All cheating is wrong. It selfishly undermines the integrity of the contest and should be punished accordingly."

Special Pleading Response: "New England Patriots Quarterback Tom Brady's intentional pregame deflation of footballs—while against the rules—did not affect the outcome of the contest and is therefore a trivial violation of the rules."

Three key points:

1. This type of argument is often made if defense of a "my country/my team right or wrong mentality." Here we see that since Tom Brady is a popular Super Bowl winning quarterback, the speaker is tempted to believe that his cheating is somehow different or less worthy of condemnation.

2. What counts as "sufficient justification" is debatable, so claims to special pleading need to be analyzed carefully. In this case, given that the general principle states that "undermining the integrity of the contest" is sufficient to condemn and punish all cheating, it seems clear that "not affecting the outcome" is not a sufficient justification to make an exception. Because this fallacy usually results from wanting to justify one's own interests or position, one should be on guard for this fallacy in their own reasoning, as it will be harder to see.

3. Pointing out the fallacy does not prove that the proponents of nuance in punishment (of cheating or anything else) are wrong. It simply shows that notions such as mercy, forgiveness, circumstance, etc., should be applied blindly. Whether or not one is "Tom Brady" should have no bearing on the justice one receives.

10. *The Appeal to the Crowd Fallacy*

This fallacy results from assuming an argument is true because the argument/belief is popular or commonly held.

Example: "Most Americans believe that team prayer before an interscholastic game is acceptable. Americans are a level-headed people. Therefore, team prayer in school sport must be good."

Three key points:

1. The popularity of a belief or action is independent of its goodness. Slavery was a universal human practice up to the 19th century. There are still millions of slaves today around the world. Those two facts do not make slavery good. Similarly, if prayer should be allowed in school sport, the justification cannot simply rest on the fact that it has popular assent, for popular assent can be wrong.

2. In essence, this fallacy is simply the conflation of normative and descriptive claims. To say that something is done, or that something is popular, does not prove that it ought to be done or is good.

3. Pointing out the fallacy does not prove that pregame team prayer in school is wrong. Perhaps, absent obvious coercion to participate, "free exercise" should trump "establishment." What the fallacy does show is that if one defends prayer merely on the grounds that it has popular support, one has made a bad argument.

Suggested Readings

Arp, R., Barbone, S., & Bruce, M. (Eds.). (2019). *Bad Arguments: 100 of the most important fallacies in Western philosophy.* Hoboken, NJ: John Wiley & Sons.

Bennett, B. (2019). *Logically fallacious: The ultimate collection of over 300 logical fallacies.* Retrieved September 10, 2019, from www.logicallyfallacious.com: https://www.logicallyfallacious.com/tools/lp/Bo/LogicalFallacies

Gensler, H. J. (2010). *Introduction to logic* (2nd ed.). New York, NY: Routledge.

GLOSSARY

Chapter 1

Aesthetics: The branch of philosophy which focuses on the beautiful (e.g., "Is beauty objective or subjective?"; "Can beauty be measured?"; "Is sport a form of art?," etc.).

Descriptive Claim: An ethical claim which focuses on describing rather than evaluating actions or beliefs (e.g., "Many baseball players lie to the referee"; "Most Americans believe lying to the referee is wrong").

Ethics: The branch of philosophy which focuses on the nature of the good life as well as on how we should treat other people.

External Good: Any good or excellence which, though a real good, is not internal to the game or "practice" itself (e.g., "winning," "health," "fame," and "money" are real goods, which often come from sport, but which can also be procured many other ways such as "medicine," "politics," "employment," etc.).

Extrinsic Good: Any good which humans value for the sake of something else (e.g., playing baseball for the money).

Internal Goods: The "central excellences" of the game or "practice" which are made possible by and can only be found in the game or practice itself (e.g., the "stolen base" is an internal good of baseball because it can only be procured in baseball, the "diving header" can only be found in soccer, etc.).

Intrinsic Good: Any good which humans value for its own sake (e.g., playing baseball because we love baseball).

Metaphysics: The branch of philosophy which focuses on the nature of things (e.g., "does God exist?"; "what is a human being?"; "Is chess a sport?," etc.).

Normative Claim: An ethical claim which focuses on the in principle goodness or badness, rightness or wrongness of an action or belief. Normative claims are about "what *ought* to be done" (e.g., "one should never lie to the referee").

Chapter 2

Crude Hedonism: A hedonistic philosophy centered on pursuing immediate sensual pleasure.

Explicit Goods/Evils: Those goods which delight or surprise us (e.g., acts of moral courage). Those evils which shock or abhor us (e.g., the 1972 Olympic massacre).

"God is Dead": Nietzsche's famous claim which is meant to show that the foundations of Christian morality cannot survive the fact that we now know that God is not real, but rather an idea that we created. As a fiction, we can kill him off.

Hedonism: A pleasure-based philosophy which sees the good as pleasure and evil as pain.

Illusion/"Useful Fiction": A philosophy which argues that standards of good and evil are manmade. As such, good and evil either don't really exist or are convenient bureaucratic fictions which have practical value, but which are not actually true.

Philosophical Hedonism: A hedonistic philosophy centered on deeper, more enduring pleasures such as friendship or skilled performance.

Privation: A lack of some good that something ought to have. Evil is often defined as a privation (a lack, misuse, or corruption of some real good).

Subtle Goods/Evils: Those goods we take for granted (e.g., shaking hands) and those evils which we justify and rationalize (e.g., "cheap shots").

Summum Bonum: The highest good, often equated with God or one's right relationship with God.

Supererogatory Act: An action which is above and beyond the call of duty.

"The Will to Power": Nietzsche's account of morality which defines moral excellence as domination (i.e., exercising one's powers, free from the constraints of traditional morality).

Transcendence: A school of thought which argues that good and evil are based in reality. That is, good and evil transcend human will or desire. As such human beings are obligated—by reality—to pursue the good and avoid evil. The source of this transcendent reality is usually understood, but does not have to be, God.

Chapter 3

"Beg the Question" Fallacy: A form of circular reasoning where one assumes a conclusion rather than give arguments for it (e.g., "Paying college players a salary is wrong because intercollegiate sports are meant to be amateur"). This claim begs the question because it assumes as true what is under dispute (should college sport be amateur?).

Deductive Argument: A logic-based argument where, if your reasoning is valid, the conclusion *necessarily* follows from the premises (e.g., if all great basketball players deserve to be in the Hall of Fame, and if LeBron James is a great basketball player, then it follows (necessarily) that LeBron James deserves to be in the Hall of Fame).

Descriptive Relativism: The claim that any careful survey of human customs, cultures, moral codes, and behaviors will reveal that human beings disagree in a multitude of ways regarding what is morally right or wrong.

Epistemology: The branch of philosophy which studies the nature of knowledge. That is, what do we know and how do we know it? What does it mean to know? What forms of knowledge claims deserve intellectual assent? What forms of knowledge claims deserve to be treated with skepticism, etc.?

Inductive Argument: A probabilistic argument based in experience. (e.g., "All NBA basketball players I've ever seen are tall, therefore all NBA basketball players are tall," or "this new NBA basketball player is likely to be tall").

Moral Realism: The claim that *real* and objective answers to moral questions exist and can (at least sometimes) be found.

Moral Relativism: The claim that morality is merely the result of cultural forces. That is, morality is *relative* to race, religion, language, etc.

Title IX: A law passed by the U.S. Congress in 1972 which bars discrimination on the basis of sex in all federally funded educational programs (including athletics).

Chapter 4

Act Utilitarianism: The form of utilitarianism which focuses on evaluating the balance of pleasures or pains produced by any particular action.

Consequentialism: Any moral theory which bases right action not upon the intrinsic nature of the act but rather upon the consequences any action produces or is likely to produce.

Rule Utilitarianism: The form of utilitarianism which focuses on which rules will best promote the greatest good. In contrast to act utilitarians, rule utilitarians are not interested in what should be done in any particular case, but instead are focused on which general rules will—taken in aggregate—lead to the greatest good for the greatest number (e.g., "even if prohibitions against PEDs won't produce maximized pleasure in every specific instance, they will in most cases").

Qualitative Hedonism: The form of hedonism which bases the evaluation of pleasure both in terms of the amount (quantity) and type (quality) of pleasure produced. For the qualitative hedonist, both the amount and type of pleasure produced matter.

Quantitative Hedonism: The form of hedonism which bases the evaluation of pleasure simply in terms of the amount (quantity) of pleasure produced. For the quantitative hedonist, only the amount of pleasure produced matters.

Quid Pro Quo: A Latin phrase meaning "something for something." When used in reference to sexual harassment, it describes actions where some good (such as employment, a raise, etc.) is used as an enticement or threat for the procurement of sexual favors (e.g., "sleep with me or you're fired").

Utilitarianism: The consequentialist moral theory which argues that one should maximize pleasure by pursuing the "greatest good for the greatest number."

Chapter 5

Broad Internalism (Interpretivism): A theory of sport which emphasizes the central excellences (internal goods) of any given sport as the best way to understand sport. This is because the internal goods clarify the "points and purposes that underlie the game." Rules are important, but as means (to further our access to internal goods) not as ends in themselves.

Categorical Duties: Duties which admit of no exceptions (e.g., if we have a duty to be honest, we should *always* tell the truth. Period. Consequences be damned.).

Conventionalism: A theory of sport which argues that in addition to rules one must pay attention to the "ethos" of the practice community. Conventionalists argue that focusing on the norms, habits, "unwritten rules," and customs of any given practice community (e.g., players, coaches, administrators, and fans) is the best way to understand sport.

Deontology: "The study of duty." Any ethical theory which considers duty—as well as the rules which such duties imply—as the proper guide to how we ought to behave.

Formalism: A theory of sport which argues that sport is defined by its constitutive rules.

Internal Goods: The central excellences of any given sport, which cannot be achieved outside the practice of that sport. For an in-depth discussion/review of internal goods see Chapter 1 pp. 13–14.

Intuitionism: A deontological theory of ethics which emphasizes *prima facie* rather than categorical duties.

Kant's First Categorical Imperative: "Act only on that maxim whereby thou canst at the same time will that it should become a universal law." To put it succinctly, if a little too crudely, "don't make an exception of yourself."

Kant's Second Categorical Imperative: "So act as to treat humanity, whether in thine own person or in that of any other, in every case as an end withal, never as means only." Human beings have intrinsic worth and should always be treated as such.

Logical Incompatibility Thesis: A theory based in formalism which says that since games are a product of their rules and since cheaters break rules intentionally, then it follows that cheaters cannot really win, because by breaking the rules, they are not actually playing the game. A game cannot be won by someone who is not playing it. As such, cheating and winning are "logically incompatible."

Prima Facie Duties: A set of objectively valid duties whose specific application depends on the particular circumstances one finds oneself in. When two or more prima facie duties come into conflict (e.g., justice and self-improvement), one must prudentially prioritize one duty over another.

Chapter 6

Arete: The ancient Greek word for the "embodiment of excellence" or "virtue."

"Being vs. Doing": The distinction made between an ethic which focuses on acts (doing the right thing) and an ethic which focuses on character (being the right kind of person).

Courage: Also known as fortitude, this virtue is the willingness to suffer "for the sake of realizing the good."

Eudaimonia: The ancient Greek word for "happiness" or "human flourishing." Aristotle argues that eudaimonia is that good at which "all other goods aim."

Hexis: The ancient Greek word which means "active condition." Just as a tennis player is light on their feet and can react to the course of play because of the habituation and skills they've developed, so too an ethical person can prudentially react with good character because, via habituation, they developed the "active condition" of being "light on their feet" morally.

Justice: The virtue which allows us to give each his due and treat others as we ought.

Prudence: Also known as "practical wisdom," this virtue is the ability to "see reality for what it is and act accordingly." As such, prudence is the chief of the cardinal virtues, because it allows one to do the "right thing at the right time in the right way for the right reason."

Temperance: Also known as moderation, this virtue is the "proper ordering and use of the goods of the world."

The Cardinal Virtues: The hinge or key virtues (prudence, justice, courage, temperance) around which all other good character traits turn.

The Mean: The "just right" condition between two extremes, each of which is a vice. For instance, the virtue of courage is neither foolhardy (excessive) nor cowardly (deficient).

Virtue Ethics: The ethical theory which emphasizes the cultivation of good character traits (i.e., virtues).

Chapter 7

Enlightened Self-Interest: In contrast to 'naked self-interest' which egoistically looks for immediate selfish gain, proponents of enlightened self-interest argue that, even from an egoistic point of view, one's individual good is wrapped up in the good of others.

Extrinsic Theory of Justice: Any answer to the question "Why be good?" which argues that we should treat others as we ought because of the consequences that behavior generates.

Intrinsic Theory of Justice: Any answer to the question "Why be good?" which argues that we should treat others as we ought simply because it is good to do so. Justice is its own reward.

Materialism: The philosophy which argues that only matter (and material things) exist. Nonmaterial entities or realities such as God, ideas, virtues, etc., are either reducible to material causes or do not exist. For instance, it is not uncommon to hear a materialist argue that, "love is just chemicals in your head."

"Ring of Gyges": A short story told by Glaucon in the *The Republic* meant to examine the question: "Should you be good, even in circumstances where you know you will get away with being evil?" That is, are there any good reasons, besides fear of punishment, for being just?

Tit for Tat: An extrinsic theory of justice which argues that we should treat others the way they treat us. More specifically, the basic theory of tit for tat is "cooperate, then reciprocate." That is, start with trust and then respond in kind.

The Myth of Sisyphus: An ancient Greek myth in which Sisyphus is condemned by Zeus to roll a boulder up to the top of hill. Unfortunately the hill's slope and the weight of the boulder are each proportioned in such a way that Sisyphus' muscles always give out as he reaches the top of the hill. As a result, the boulder rolls back down the hill and Sisyphus has to start his toil all over again. The myth is commonly understood to be a metaphor for the human condition, where all of our work and struggles ultimately accomplish nothing and are annihilated by death.

Chapter 8

Mediating Institutions: Small structures such as family, church, neighborhood, and team which anchor an individual in society. They *mediate* between the impersonal structures of the state and the isolated individual by rooting them in a community.

Quarantining Institutions: Small structures, such as a gang, which although they give an individual a sense of belonging, isolate them (via alienation, fear, and superiority) from the outside world.

Solidarity: The claim that human beings are by nature bound to the common good. All human beings share—despite difference in race, culture, religion, etc.—a common humanity. We are, despite our differences, "all in this together."

Subsidiarity: The claim that authority should always be passed down to the most local level possible, where individuals close to the problem will know the problem intimately and actually care about solving it. (E.g., the Federal government should never try to solve a problem that a state or local community can. The NCAA should not try to solve problems that an individual school can). Authority should only be passed up to a higher level, when it is clear that the lower, more local, more intimate level, has shown that it cannot solve the problem itself.

INDEX

A

act-utilitarianism, 80, 86–87
ad hominem fallacy, 306
Aesthetics, 7–8
Agassi, Andre, 23
The Alchemy of Race and Rights (Patricia Williams), 72
Anderson, Doug, 191
appeal to the crowd fallacy, 309
Arete, 145
Aristotle, 6, 113, 153, 255, 263
    conception of ethics, 146
    existence of marriage, family, village, and state, 15–16
    importance of contemplation to happiness, 197
    Nicomachean Ethics, 146–152, 161–174
    soul, 213n15
Asad, Talal, 263
atheism, 25
athlete-only or athlete specific facilities, 258
athletics academic support program (ASP), 258
Augustine, St., 25, 26, 197, 198, 266

B

bad sportsmanship, benefits of, 103–105
bare assertion fallacy, 305
Baron, Marcia, 118
Barzun, Jacques, 195
baseball game, 9, 13, 29
"Beg the question" fallacy, 62, 307
Beijing Olympic Games, 2008, controversy over, 64–67
Being *vs.* Doing, 145
being good, arguments for, 205
    Ring of Gyges, story, 206–207
    Singer *vs* Plato, 210–214
    Socrates' views, 207–208
    sport and, 214–221
    Tit for Tat theory, 209–210
Benedict XVI, Pope, 198
Bentham, Jeremy, 80–85, 86n5, 88–89
    "An Introduction to the Principles of Morals and Legislation," 94–97
    categories of evaluation into account, 82–83
    endorsement of quantitative utilitarianism, 84
    quantitative hedonism, 80–84
Berger, Peter, 119, 220, 255, 256, 263, 267n19, 276, 282–283, 282n25, 285, 285n39, 287, 287nn44–45, 290n64
bounties, 74–75
"bountygate" scandal, 74
Brague, Remi, 190
broad internalism, 13, 121
The Brothers Karamazov (Dostoevsky), 34–41

C

Cadwalader Report, 160
Categorical duties, 122

Catholic social thought, core principles of, 277–280
Callaway World Golf Championships, 194
cardinal virtues, 152–153
    courage, 152, 196–197
    cultivating, 198–200
    historical account of first meeting between Branch Rickey and Jackie Robinson, 174–184
    justice, 152, 194–196
    kinesiology and, 184–189
    prudence, 152, 189–194
    temperance, 153, 197–198
Cavanaugh, William, 263n13
Cheek, Joey, 18
chess, game of, 14
Chesterfield, Lord, 221
China's human rights abuses, 65–67
Christianity
    views of good, 26–28
    virtues of humility, kindness and forgiveness, 30
Consequentialism, 79, 107
conventionalism, 121
cooperative human activity, 13
Coubertin, Pierre de, 272
courage, 152, 196–197
"crude" hedonism, 29

D

Deductive argument, 61
deontological ethics
    deontologist responses, 118–120
    issue of rule enforcement in sport, 122–124
    Kant's strict understanding of duty, 108–112
    moral rules, role of, 107–108
    sport and, 120–121
    strengths of, 115–116
    weaknesses of, 116–118
deontological thinking, 115
Deontology, 107–108
descriptive ethical claims, 2–3
descriptive relativism, 56, 61, 63
    responses to, 59, 61
Dewey, John, 213n13
dualistic conception of good and evil, 26–27

E

Enlightened self-interest, 205, 209
Epistemology, 55
ethical behavior, promoting
    mediating institutions, role of, 256–259, 261–263
    solidarity and subsidiarity concepts, 259–261
ethical issues and controversies in sport, 11
ethics
    defined, 6–7
    other branches of philosophy and, 7–9
Eudaimonia, 148